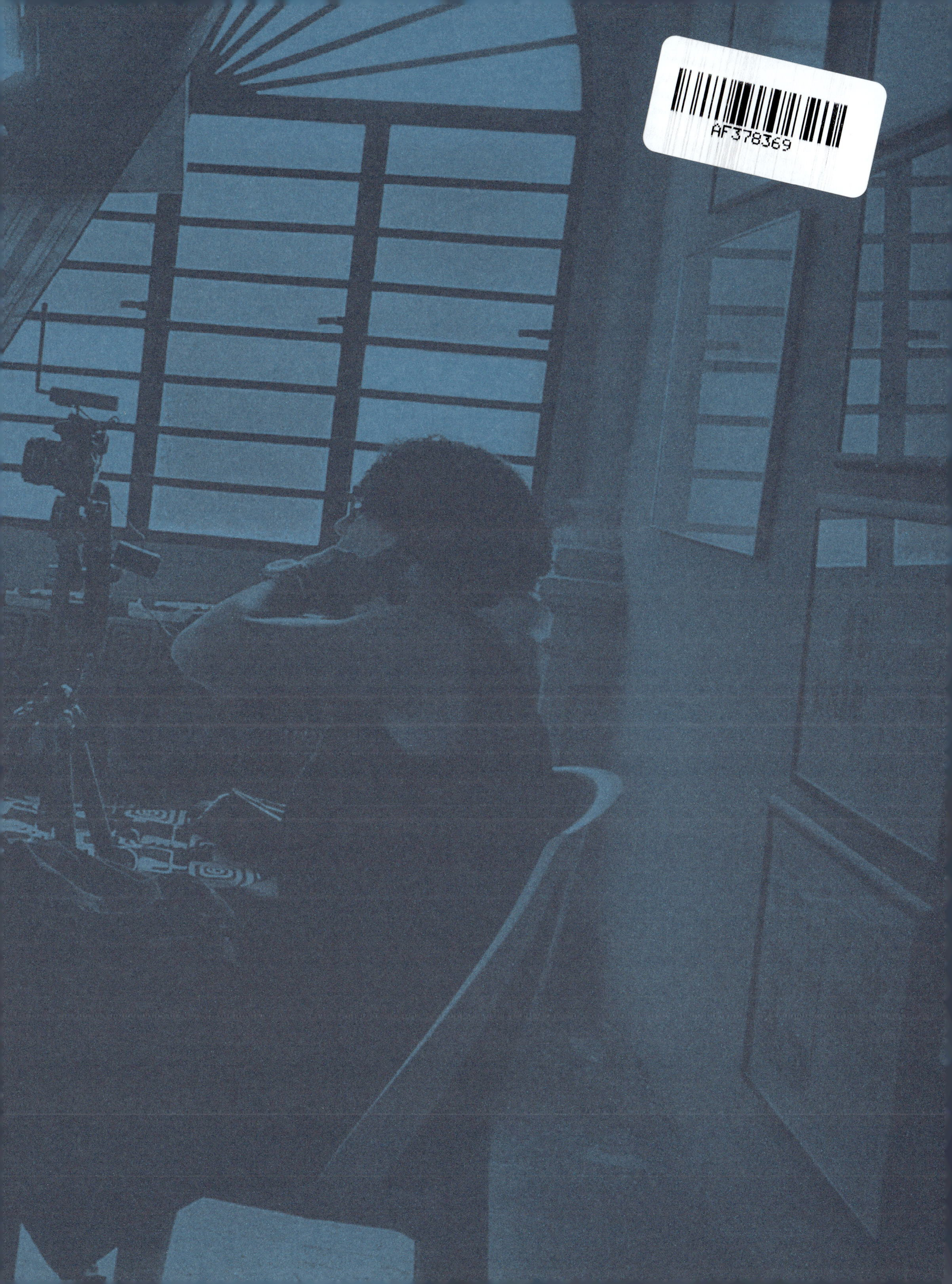

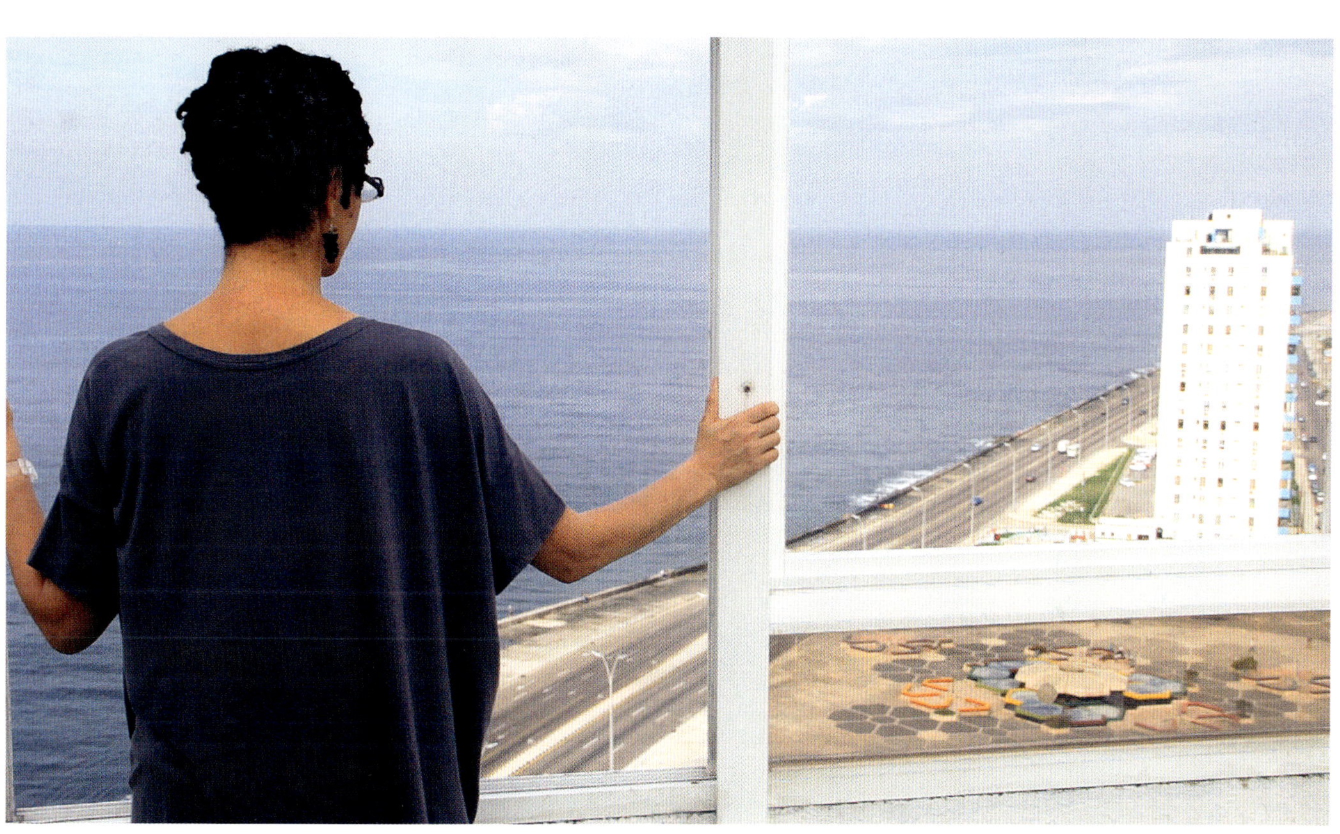

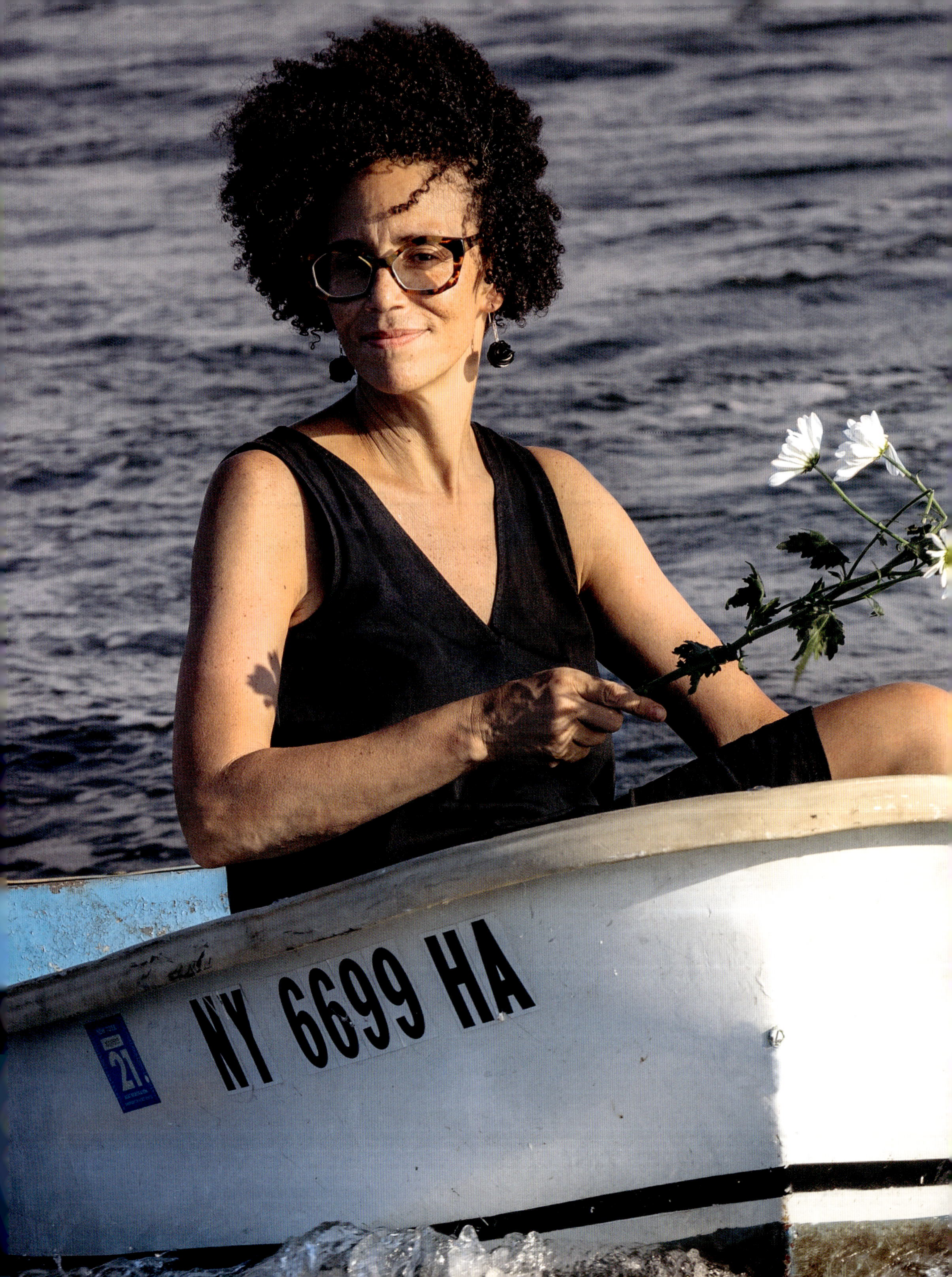
NY 6699 HA

COCO FUSCO

TOMORROW, I WILL BECOME AN ISLAND

Edited by Olga Viso

With 252 illustrations

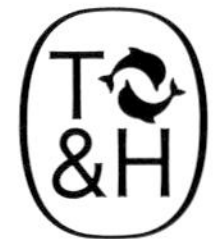

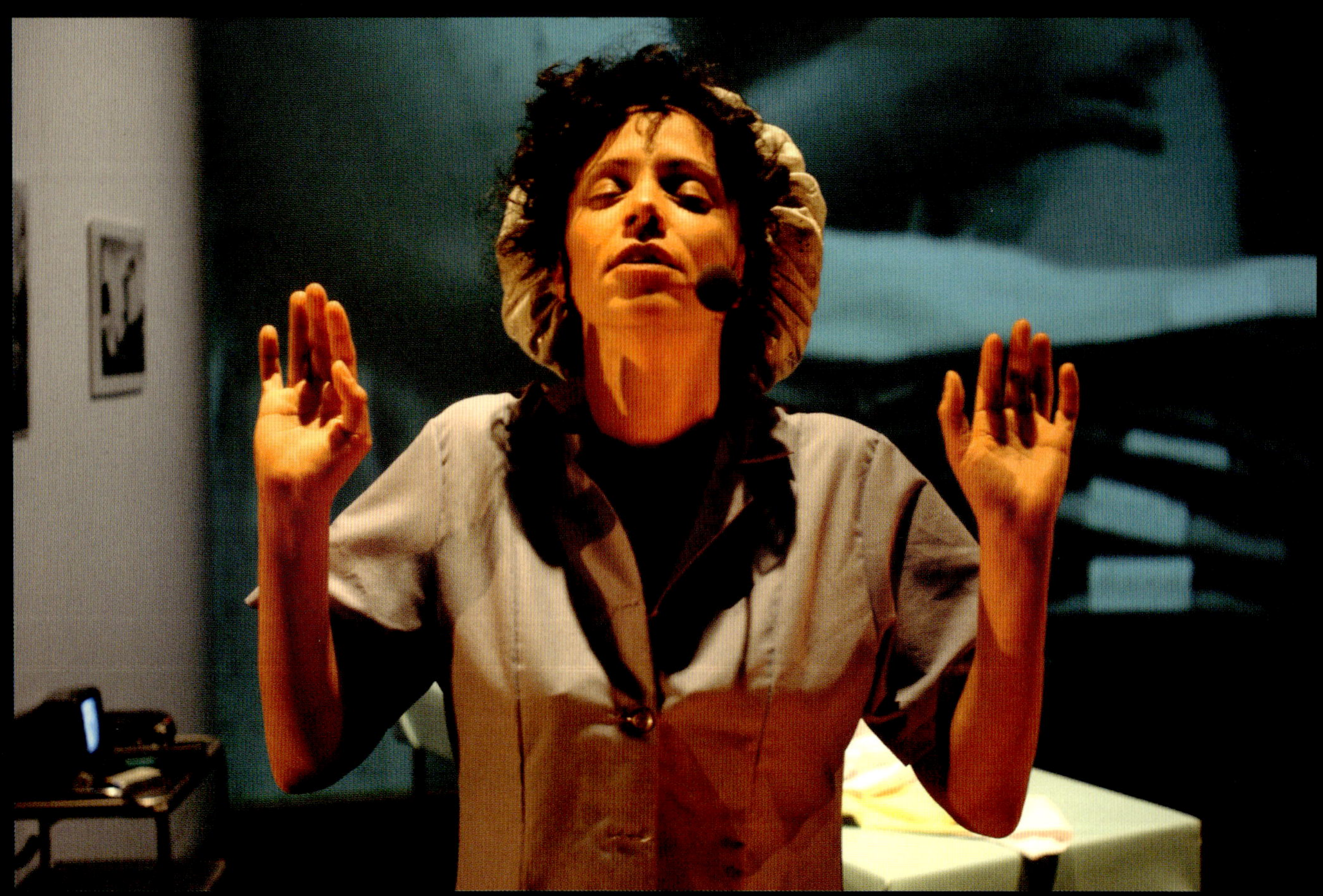

The Incredible Disappearing Woman, 2003, performance

Contents

Foreword

Krist Gruijthuijsen

Director, KW Institute
for Contemporary Art,
Berlin

For the past three decades, Coco Fusco has delved into historical records and colonial archives to create works that underline subtexts and counter-narratives. Back in 2017, she presented a new performance, *Words May Not Be Found*, as part of the event series *The Weekends*, with which I inaugurated my directorship at KW Institute for Contemporary Art. For the performance, she drew parallels between colonial and contemporary perceptions of non-western "others." More than a century after the German military campaign in South West Africa, the conflict that emerged in response to an insurrection by the Nama and Herero peoples of Namibia remains a source of collective trauma for both nations. Fusco's performance focused on the struggle over the words of the native informants.

Now, six years later, KW Institute for Contemporary Art in Berlin presents a retrospective of Coco Fusco in parallel with this monograph published by Thames & Hudson. Eponymously called "Coco Fusco—Tomorrow, I Will Become an Island," the exhibition includes a large selection of Fusco's work from the past three decades, while the publication gives an encompassing overview of her work and includes reflective writings by Julia Bryan-Wilson, Anna Gritz, Jill Lane, Antonio José Ponte, and Coco Fusco herself.

Since the 1990s, Fusco has used performance, video, exhibition practice, archival research, and writing to reflect on how intercultural relationships and colonial history shape the construction of the self and the perception of cultural differences. Her work critically examines society from a postcolonial perspective, touching upon cultural-political debates in the Americas, Europe, and beyond. Concretely, this comprehensive approach is reflected in a wide range of works dealing with themes such as racist stereotypes, feminist politics, animal psychology, ethnographic collection presentations, classified colonial documents, military investigations, sex tourism, and post-revolutionary Cuba. Together, her works create politically relevant spaces for encounters between people and cultures, and repeatedly reflect the entire spectrum of lived socio-political realities.

An iconic example of Fusco's engagement is the performance *Two Undiscovered Amerindians Visit the West*, which Fusco created and staged with Guillermo Gómez-Peña at multiple venues between 1992 and 1994. As the related video *The Couple in the Cage: A Guatinaui Odyssey* (1993) demonstrates, the iterations provoked responses from the audience from the confused to the explicitly critical, but the performance only reflected on exhibition modes underlying the nature of the ethnographic museum, and the museum sphere at large, as we know it today. Within the wide range of her practice, a large number of works dealing with similar problematic, overlooked histories have only resurfaced as part of critical decolonization processes instigated by artists, activists, and scholars like Fusco. This

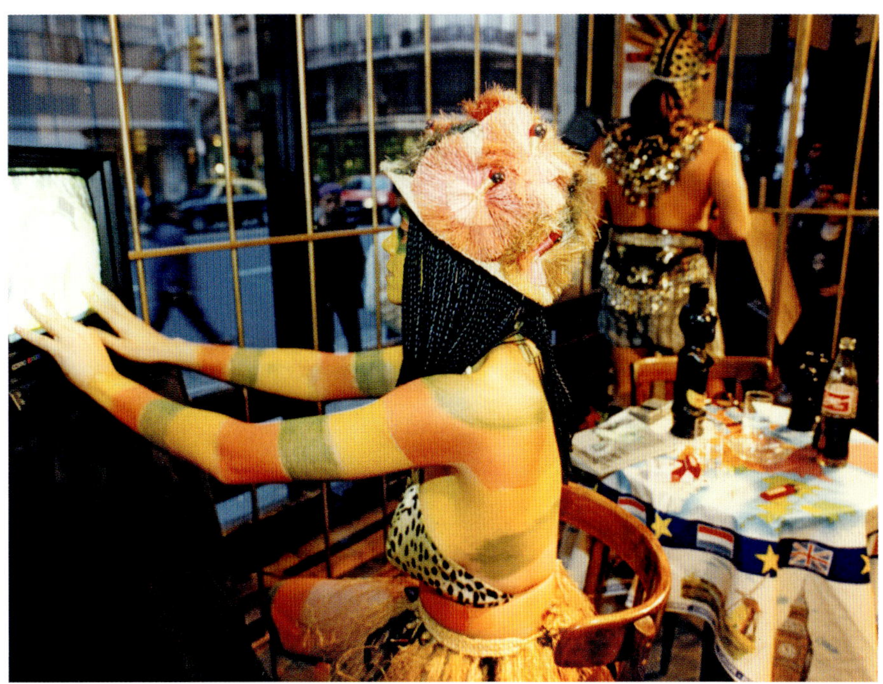

Coco Fusco and Guillermo Gómez-Peña, *Two Undiscovered Amerindians Visit Buenos Aires*, **1994, performance**

publication and exhibition trace the complexities that define Fusco's multifaceted, critical body of work.

Coco Fusco has proven to have a solid sense for pressing issues and an ability to make their complexities palpable through her work. Exhibited at the 2022 Whitney Biennial, the video *Your Eyes Will Be an Empty Word* (2021) reflects on all the lives lost during the COVID-19 pandemic as well as on other pandemics during which mass graves became a terrifying exigency. Being able to create a captivating reflection on something so fresh in the collective memory is rather remarkable.

The relevance of *Tomorrow, I Will Become an Island* does not limit itself to the borders of a specific time frame, nation state, or continent, but shows Coco Fusco's interdisciplinary art practice, her pioneering intellectual contributions, and her intersectional, transnational perspectives on how race, gender, power, and history have constructed the world we live in today. Therefore, I would like to thank Coco for steadfastly standing her ground and for being who she is.

There are so many people who have been instrumental in making this publication and the exhibition come to life. First of all, I would like to thank everybody at Alexander Gray Associates for being involved in every detail of the process, especially Alexander Gray, Ursula Davila-Villa, Laila Pedro, Anna Stothart, and Page Benkowski. My sincere gratitude goes out to Anna Gritz, Léon Kruijswijk, and the KW team for realizing the exhibition. And, last but not least, a huge thank you to all the publication's writers—Julia Bryan-Wilson, Anna Gritz, Jill Lane, Antonio José Ponte, Olga Viso, and Coco Fusco—for taking the time to ponder and reflect on Coco's ever-inspiring practice, as well as to all the other contributors and Thames & Hudson for publishing it. Without the involvement and dedication of everyone mentioned here, none of this would have been possible.

Introduction

Coco Fusco

In a photo taken in November 2021, I am standing in the passageway of an art fair holding a Cuban 20-peso bill out with extended arms. Only the banknote bearing a stamp with the acronym for the San Isidro Movement is in focus—my face is not. My gesture and the bokeh style mirror that of another photograph, one of Hamlet Lavastida, the Cuban artist who designed the stamp that marks the bill I am holding. He sent me his photo to publicize the performance that I would enact in his place in the US while he remained stuck in migratory limbo in Europe. I appear as a surrogate, affirming our alliance by carrying out his wish.

The performance was a way of signaling a political future in which Cubans of all persuasions have a voice in the making of their world. But marking Cuban currency is, according to the Cuban government, a criminal offense. A few months earlier, while conversing with friends in a private chat, Lavastida had proposed to stamp his nation's banknotes with the logos of Cuban opposition groups, invoking a venerable history of symbolic interventions on legal tender by artists and activists seeking to challenge authoritarian regimes. When he returned to Cuba in June 2021 after spending a year in Berlin, Lavastida was arrested and detained for three

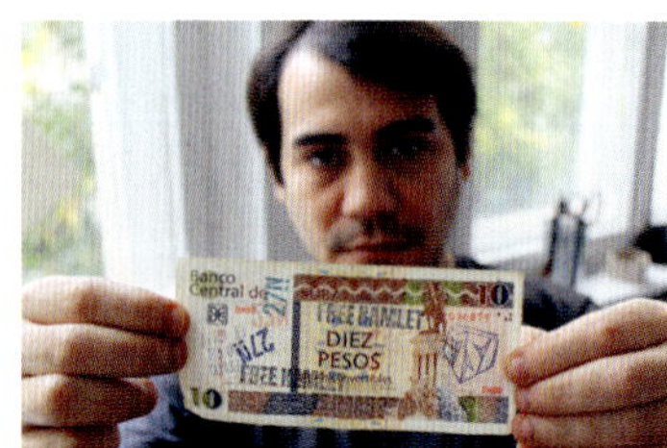

Hamlet Lavastida, *Billetes quemando la calle (Bills Burning the Street)*, 2021, **performance**

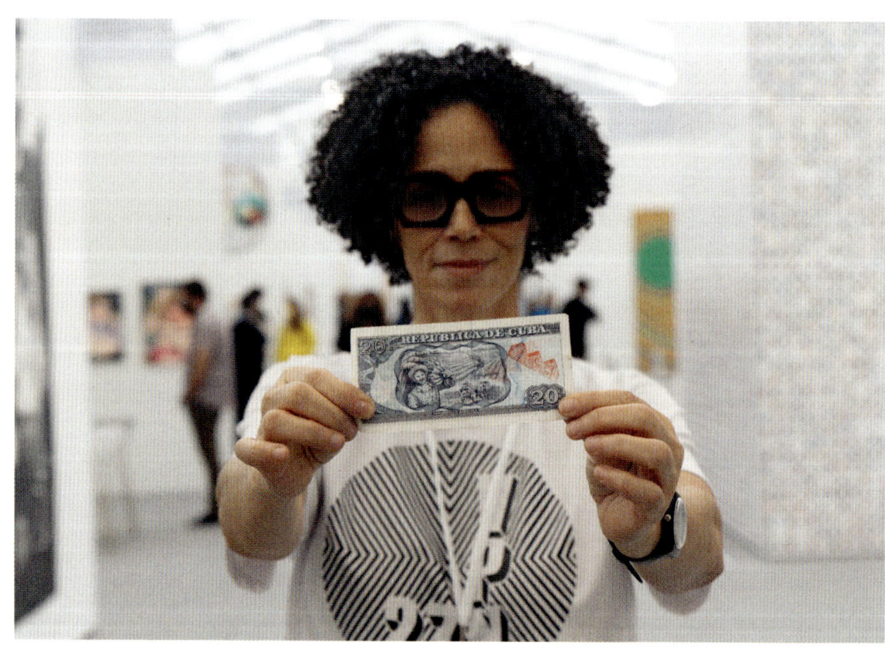

Coco Fusco in Hamlet Lavastida's *Billetes quemando la calle (Bills Burning the Street)*, 2021, **performance**

months at State Security headquarters, accused of "inciting to commit a crime" because of his proposal. In a defiant response to his arrest, his friends in Madrid took up his idea, produced stamps calling for him to be freed, and breathed life into his proposal at the ARCO art fair in July of 2021. I then formed another group to carry on the work during the Untitled Art fair in Miami at the end of the year. Lavastida's release from prison in September and his expulsion from Cuba made it possible for him to create his own stamps for the second iteration of what is now known as *Billetes quemando la calle* (*Bills Burning the Street*). Although Lavastida could not join us in person, he participated virtually, conducting interviews with journalists via Zoom while his proxies stamped bills from a wide range of countries, which curious audience members presented to us.

Why write about a performance to which I do not claim authorship for a book about my work as an artist? Because the work I do is not reducible to the things I make alone—it includes the dreams I share and the cultures I build with others. In recent years, I've immersed myself in collective projects together with Cuban "artivists" who advocate for expanded civil liberties and creative freedoms, but my research in Cuba extends back more than three decades. In the early aughts I engaged in performative protests against George W. Bush with the feminists of the Axis of Eve as well as other protests in support of the mothers of the disappeared in Juarez with Women in Black. In the 1990s, I was involved in daily heated debates with the feminist, net-based Undercurrents group, striving to dismantle utopian fantasies about an internet that ignored the labor conditions in the factories where a largely female workforce assembled new technologies. Prior to that I participated in nationwide art actions in opposition to official celebrations of the Quincentenary and incipient postcolonial debates about structural racism in art institutions and art history. I cut my teeth as a performer by joining peers in a group recitation of Lewis Carroll's *Jabberwocky* to protest the arrival of then CIA director William Casey to our college campus: we believed his presence constituted a greater menace than our impolite interruption of his speech. It's never easy to represent social engagement in an art exhibition, but nothing I have done as an individual artist would have been imaginable were it not for those collective activities.

Although I have labored in the shadow of the flawed multiculturalist discourses that shaped American cultural debates for more than three decades, I have never made my artistic practice into a search for my roots or an exploration of selfhood as distinct from the world. The labels that many insist upon to define themselves interest me much less than the systems of power and knowledge that delimit identity and the relational networks we activate to communicate, resist, and make new meaning. So much of my endeavor over the past three decades has been devoted to relaying, recalling, interpreting, and embodying those who have occupied the place of the other in Western culture. To considering the presence and absence of others. To interrogating otherness, unmasking the practices of subjection that undergird seemingly genteel appreciation of diversity. In the territories where I roam, fictions cannot be disentangled from reality or truth. Fictions that attract us also weigh upon us, and once we invest in them as truths they can never be completely dispelled. I carry their weight when I assume the role of an ethnographic oddity, or a posthuman scientist, or a survivor of colonial massacres, or prisoner of postmodern warfare, or a subaltern service worker peddling fantasies for tourists and assembling trinkets for insatiable consumers. The beings I temporarily inhabit are specters that emerge from unaccounted histories, all bearing inconvenient truths. They haunt me, but in a good way. I haunt you with them.

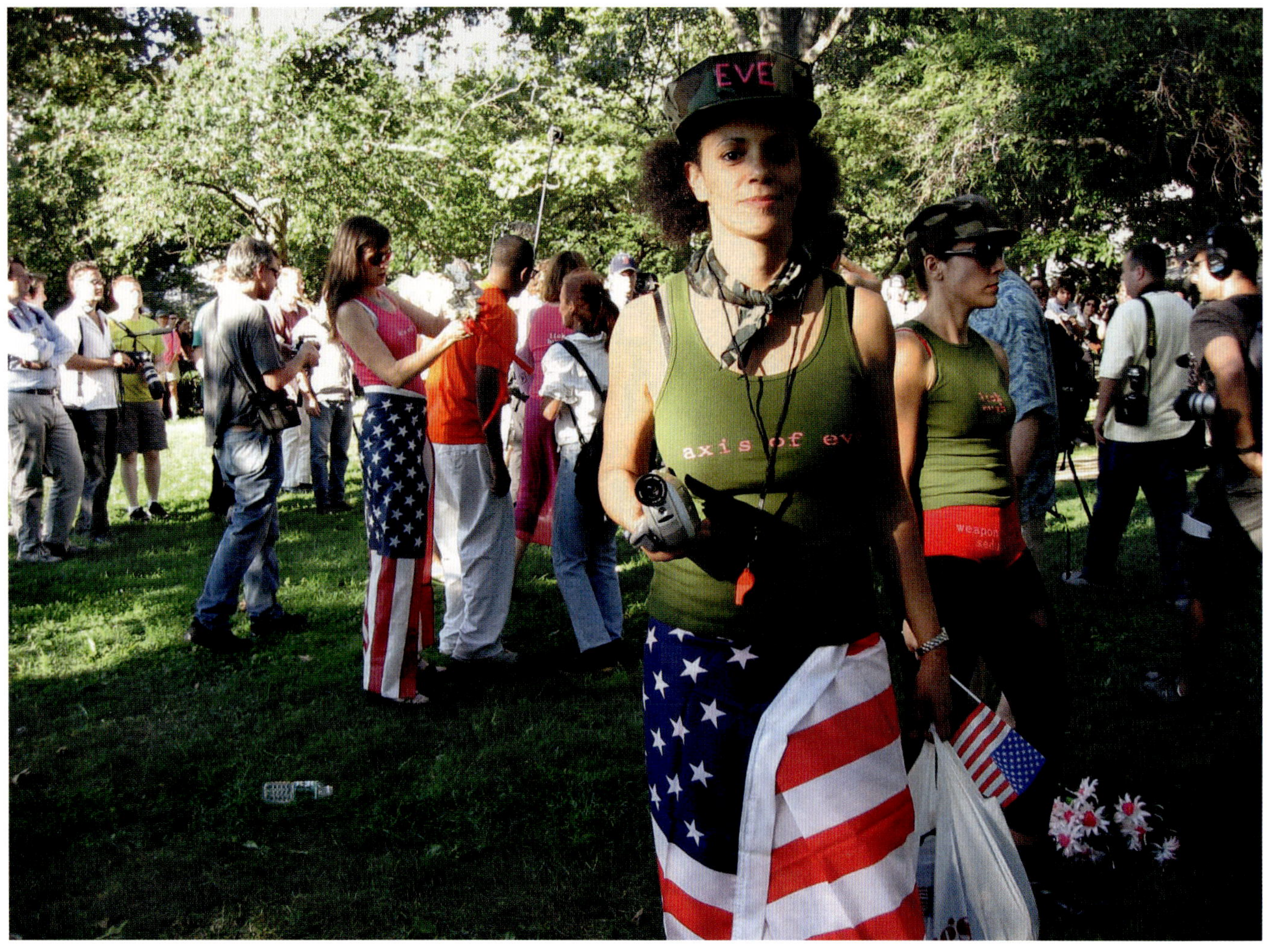

Coco Fusco participating in the Axis of Eve protests against Republican National Convention, 2004

Even though I spend many hours by myself in order to create, my endeavors are never solitary. My work is nourished by conversations with mentors and friends who share their memories and experiences, scholars who share their research, and generous strangers who have taken the time to answer my questions. They all occupy space in my imagination together with the unforgettable stories, films, and artworks that inspire me and the evocative historical documents I've come across, authored by people long gone. I've been fortunate to have enjoyed and wrestled with many artistic collaborators. I am especially grateful to the cinematographers, editors, musicians, actors, poets, sculptors, photographers, graphic designers, and master printers that assisted me, without whom none of my work would be possible. I offer my thanks here to Luis Manuel Álvarez, Arlen Austin, Juan Pablo Ballester, Hima Bee, Raymel Casamayor, Chema Castineyra, Sandra Ceballos, Lynn Cruz, María Cruz Alarco, Enrique Del Risco, Loid Der, Néstor Diaz de Villegas, Ricardo Dominguez, Elvira Dyangani, María Elena Escalona, Enmanuel Galbán, Christy Gast, Juan Si González, David Gray, Clayton Harley, Pauline Kim Harris, Tanwi Nandini Islam, Joel Lara, Fabienne Lasserre, Hamlet Lavastida, David Leitner, Raphael Lyon, Chico MacMurtrie, Trevor Mathison, Trish Maud, Yanelys Núñez Lleyva, Kambui Olujimi, Amaury Pacheco, Sze Lin Pang, Geandy Pavón,

INTRODUCTION

Roberto Poveda, Mike Ritz, Iris Ruiz, Yoani Sánchez, Pamela Snead, Armando Suárez Cobián, Jessie Stead, Dan Turner, Alejandro Yoshi, and Mirelle Zacharis. No doubt this list is incomplete, so I apologize in advance for omissions.

I am also indebted to the people who have been instrumental in making this book and the exhibition it accompanies a reality. Through their extraordinary support and advocacy, Alexander Gray, Laila Pedro, and Page Benkowski have helped me achieve my goals as an artist. I remain humbled by Roger Thorp's support for my writing and my art practice. I am very grateful to Krist Gruijthuijsen for deciding to host a comprehensive exhibition of my work at KW Institute for Contemporary Art, my first major show in Europe after more than three decades of sporadic performing, lecturing, and exhibiting throughout the continent. Curators Ursula Davila-Villa, Anna Stothart, and Anna Gritz have treated this project with exceptional care and professionalism. Olga Viso has shepherded this publication through its many stages with vision and great patience. The magnificent essays penned by Julia Bryan-Wilson, Anna Gritz, Jill Lane, and Antonio Ponte are deeply appreciated—to have my work interpreted so thoughtfully by colleagues that I admire is a precious gift, and I could not have asked for more than what they have so graciously composed.

It is not exactly standard practice to recall unpleasant experiences when one is giving thanks. That said, I would be remiss if I did not admit my encounters with

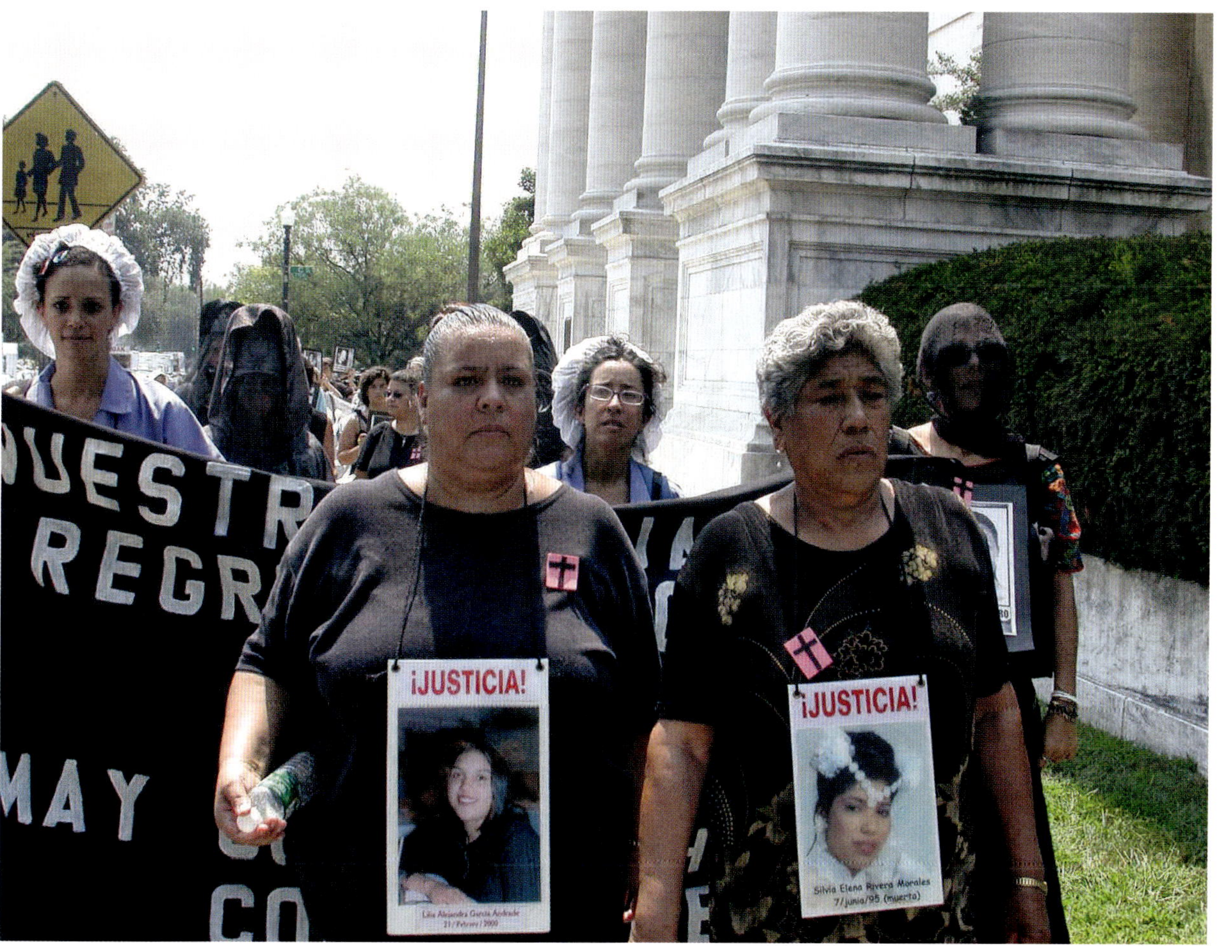

Coco Fusco at march with Nuestras Hijas de Regreso a Casa (Bring Our Daughters Home) from Juarez at OAS, Washington DC, 2002

censure, derision, and exclusion have offered me life lessons that have enlightened me more than any praise could. I started college in 1978, and I remember having to defend the legitimacy of affirmative action as soon as I arrived—the Allan Bakke case had just been decided by the Supreme Court, opening the door to a plethora of tactics aimed at undermining the achievements of the Civil Rights movement. At the same time, throngs of students protested daily in the middle of our campus, demanding that the university divest from South Africa, but the commitment to undoing racial inequality did not at the time extend to reimagining the curriculum. No one challenged the Eurocentric biases of the theories and art practices of the avantgardes that were venerated by my teachers.

When I raised objections to Charles Baudelaire's depictions of his Black lover, Jeanne Duval, in a French literature class, my concerns were rejected by my professor as irrelevant. A few years later, when I sat in an office at Channel Four in London and tried to convince a commissioning editor that he should watch my documentary about postmodern art in Cuba, he replied that Cubans couldn't have postmodernism because he doubted that they had had any kind of modernism. Later, after having published several articles about film in the *Village Voice*, I had the pleasure of listening to my editor tell me that he didn't need my services because he was no longer obliged to hire Latinos. Fifteen years later, during my oral defense of a thesis about postcolonial artists' use of colonial archives, one of my PhD examiners started the session by asking me if postcolonialism actually existed—so instead of simply presenting my arguments, I was tasked with legitimating the existence of my chosen field to secure my degree. The undercurrent of resistance to efforts to democratize culture never disappears, not even when the marketplace appears poised to embrace the new. I've lived long enough to recognize this and not be surprised. I have lost count of how many times I have been told that I am not who I pretend to be, or that I should explain who I really am, that I am not really an artist, that what I do isn't art, or that my research isn't scholarship. All that insistence on the need and the right to impose definitions that either limit or exclude is indicative of how deeply conservative even the most seemingly freewheeling arts professionals can be when their precepts are challenged, regardless of their displays of admiration for iconoclasts of yore.

Navigating the extremes of my professional milieu requires a degree of calculated skepticism. At present, the art world is congratulating itself quite emphatically—once again—for its supposed largesse, while ever larger swathes of the world population endure extreme economic, political, and environmental precarity. The commercial culture of global elites traffics in myriad forms of consumption that masquerade as "self-care" and "clean living" while authoritarian leaders across the globe smash protests, undermine democratic institutions, dismantle public services, cripple labor unions, and collude with corporate superpowers that evade taxation and exploit natural resources with impunity. These dilemmas are not abstract to me—feeling that the world is hurtling toward one disaster after another redoubles my sense of commitment to art-making that disrupts complacency.

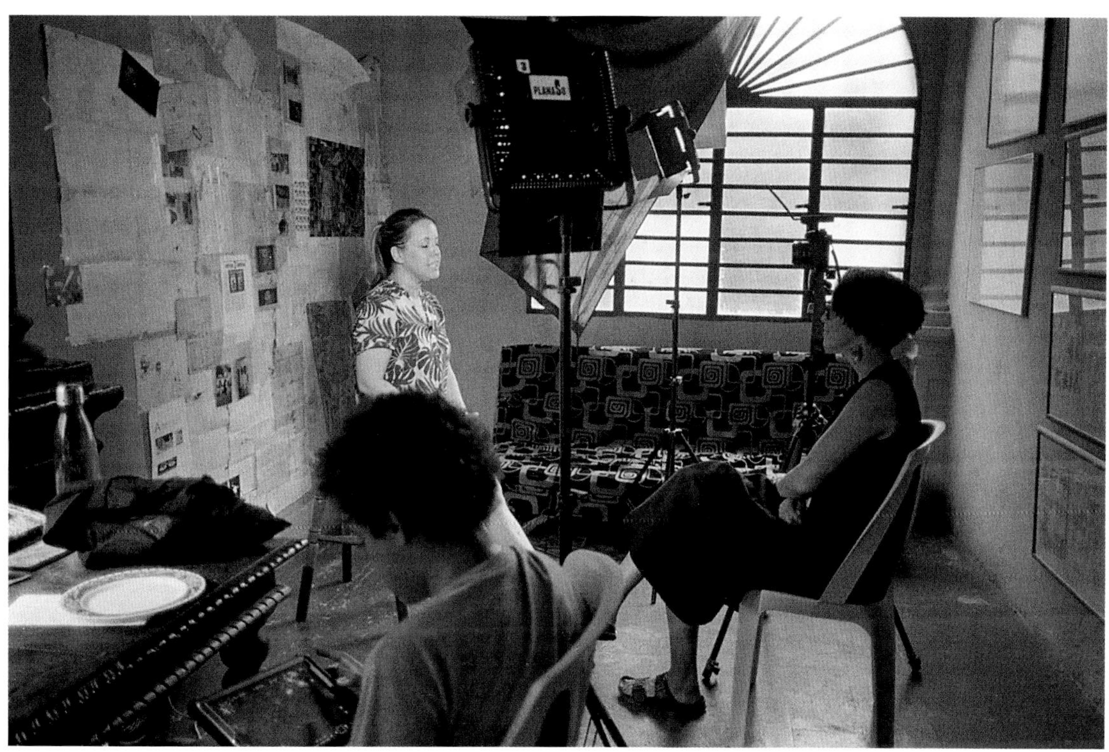

Coco Fusco working in Havana with Grethell Rasúa, 2016

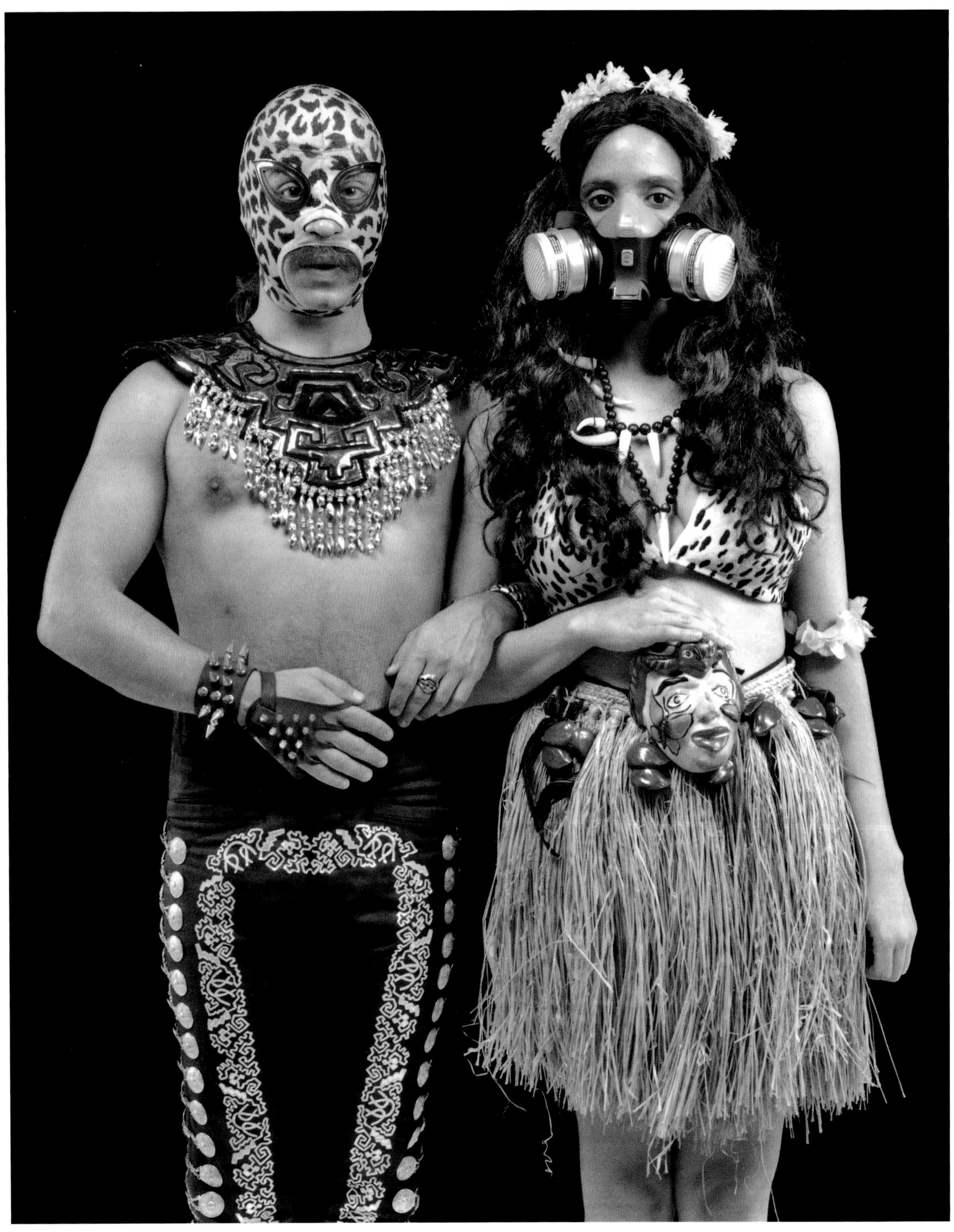

Coco Fusco and Guillermo Gómez-Peña, *The Year of the White Bear*, 1992–94, multi-media exhibition and performances

 TOMORROW, I WILL BECOME AN ISLAND

Tomorrow, I Will Become an Island

Olga Viso

Coco Fusco is a bellwether figure in the realm of performance art and its crossings. Her interdisciplinary artistic practice and scholarly and critical writing are foundational in contemporary performance studies. Throughout her career, Fusco has worked in numerous international contexts and moved fluidly between alternative modes of expression, including sculpture, installation, film, and video art. Over the last three decades, she has made print editions, published artist books and instructional manuals, and produced radio programs and a parody of a *telenovela*. She has staged collective public actions on the internet, performed in public plazas and shopping malls, conceived multimedia projects with others, and curated exhibitions for both mainstream and alternative art venues around the world.

The artist's subject matter has been equally far-ranging. She has explored esoteric subjects such as medieval mysticism. She has examined the plight of *jineteras* (sex workers) in Cuba and *maquiladora* workers (female factory laborers) in Mexico, artistic censorship in post-revolutionary Cuba, the role of women in America's War on Terror, and the construction of national identity in transborder zones. In one of her more poetic recent pieces, *Your Eyes Will Be an Empty Word* (2021), she meditates on themes of isolation and survival and captures the human toll of a global pandemic. The impetus for exploring such a wide span of issues has always been purposeful. Her aim to dislodge hegemonic positions has led her to create a diverse range of expressions that resolutely challenge racial stereotypes, unpack gender politics, expose cultural prejudices, surface decolonial attitudes, and reveal untold histories and previously suppressed narratives.

I first saw Coco Fusco's compelling and incisive art in 1993. I was barely out of graduate school, struggling to make my way as a curator in the nascent Miami art scene. It was the year of the groundbreaking edition of the Whitney Biennial that focused on politics and identity, pushing potent discourses around race, gender, and ideology into the foreground of the mainstream art world. Fusco's contribution to the Biennial publication, "Passionate Irreverence: The Cultural Politics of Identity," remains an essential text that lays out some of the most energetic and defining dialogues of the period. In 1993, Cuba's so-called Special Period—a time of severe economic hardship for citizens on the island following the fall of the Berlin Wall and an end of Soviet protection and subsidy—was already underway. One year later, another wave of Cuban exiles would begin to make their way across the treacherous Florida Straits, just as my own parents had thirty years earlier.

That first encounter with Fusco's work was in the pages of *BOMB* magazine. The January 1993 issue featured an interview with Fusco and her then-collaborator, Guillermo Gómez-Peña, illustrated with two striking images: one a vampy double

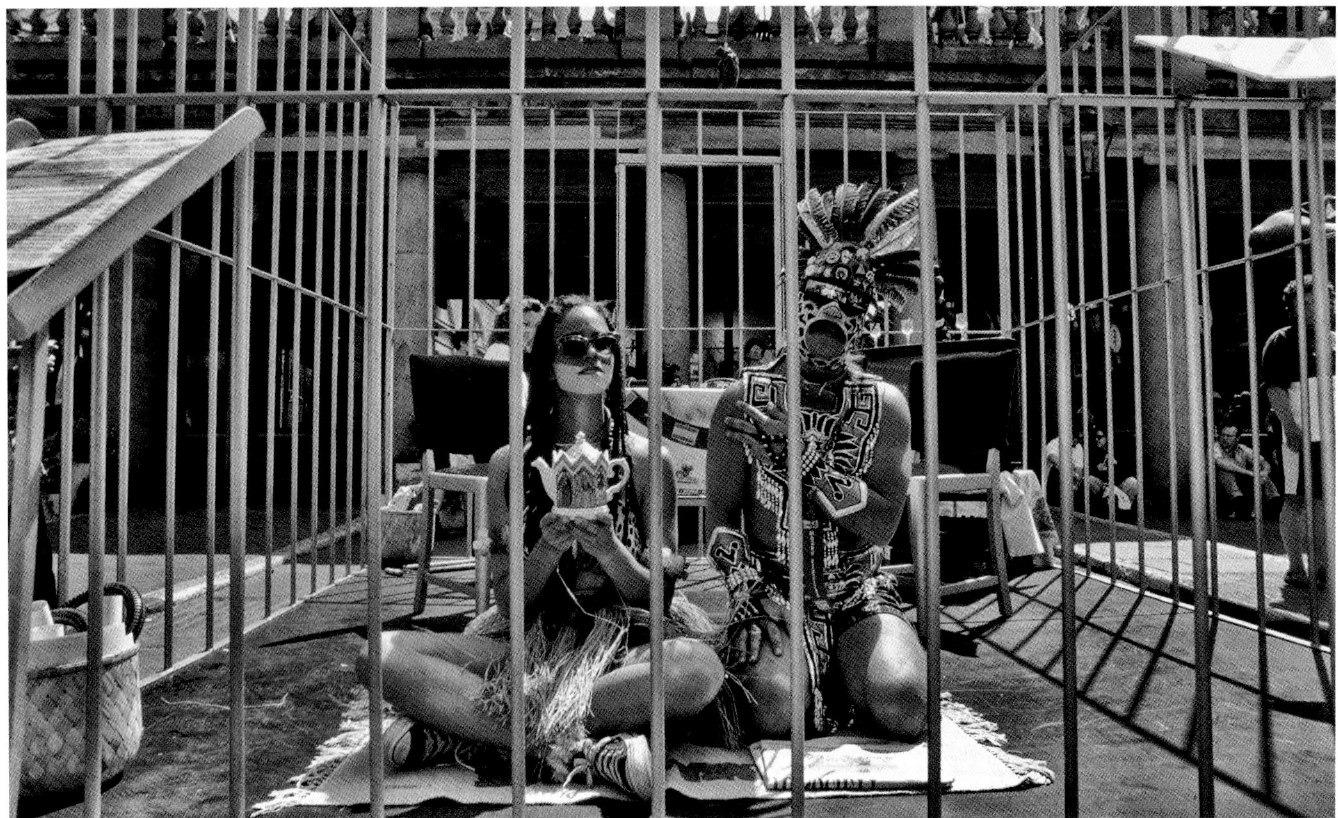

Coco Fusco and Guillermo Gómez-Peña, *Two Undiscovered Amerindians Visit London*, 1992, performance

self-portrait of the two performers in costume, and the other a performance document from the artists' groundbreaking collaboration, *Two Undiscovered Amerindians Visit the West* (1992–94). The spectacle, in which the artists literally put themselves on public display as two "undiscovered" Amerindians from the fictional and uncolonized island named Guatinau, was conceived to upend the global quincentennial celebrations that honored Christopher Columbus's "discovery of the Americas."

Who was this young, Cuban-American woman standing behind bars, posing in a bikini top and grass skirt, wearing Hawaiian *leis*, and irreverently taunting the public? What was her relationship to the gruff Mexican *caballero* dressed in a *conchero* outfit and donning the mask of a Mexican *luchador*? I will admit I found the display perplexing, even unsavory. I was troubled by the liberal appropriation of Indigenous iconography. And I couldn't fathom why Fusco seemed to be consciously playing into such reductive stereotypes of femininity. What would my conservative Cuban mother say? I wondered whether it was not naïve, and in poor taste, for Fusco and Gómez-Peña to engage so directly, and in such sharply satirical terms with these ridiculous western assumptions? Would audiences even understand the artist's gestures as parody, as comical and transgressive forms of critique? Or would the whole thing backfire and reinforce existing cultural biases?

These questions plagued me, particularly in the context of my lived experience at the time as a young, cisgender Latina. They exposed the conservative attitudes of my older parents, immigrants from working-class rural families in Cuba, who urged me to assimilate into American culture. At the same time, the work magnified

TOMORROW, I WILL BECOME AN ISLAND

my frustration at how I myself was often essentialized and misunderstood for my cultural heritage. An infuriating story came to mind that my mother often told about American perceptions about life in Cuba. Shortly upon her arrival to Miami in 1961, she was asked if Cuban islanders still "swung in trees." For a generation of Americans who grew up watching Maureen O'Sullivan and Johnny Weissmuller in the classic Hollywood Tarzan and Jane films of the 1930s and 1940s, this was Cuba.

The encounter with Fusco and Gómez-Peña's art early in my career spurred me to think critically about how I chose to self-identify. As the sole Spanish speaker and one of the few individuals who represented any kind of cultural diversity in my museum workplace in 1993, I was sensitized to how I was being framed by institutions, and, frankly, often used, by white establishment culture to advance the appearance of diversity absent any underlying commitment to effecting change. I recall the attitudes and expectations projected on me and how I would uncomfortably code-switch, as I sought to find my place and position in the contested cultural field of the early 1990s.

Fusco's 1995 publication *English is Broken Here: Notes on Cultural Fusion in the Americas* gave me more expansive and more effective language with which to name these complexities and a critical framework that helped me navigate with greater clarity the politics of my own identity. There were so few writers and role models then, particularly women, who could speak to hybridity and transculturality in the Americas as eloquently, rigorously, and honestly as Fusco did. Her critical writings, and reflections in "The Other History of Intercultural Performance" (1994) about her experience performing *Two Undiscovered Amerindians Visit the West*, offered a sober unpacking of structural racist and colonialist attitudes present in western society. These insights anticipated by decades the decolonial discourses of today.

What impressed me then, and continues to impress me now, thirty years later, is that the force and foresight of Fusco's critical and scholarly interventions is matched by the prescience and sophistication of her art practice. Lauded in the early 1990s for her role in the development of video art, she is also acknowledged as a critical figure in the lineage of groundbreaking female performance artists active since the early 1960s. She is among a group of women whose performance works engage the corporality of their own bodies and involve risk and endurance: Yoko Ono, Carolee Schneemann, Martha Rosler, Adrian Piper, Ana Mendieta, and Marina Abramović.

While the visual arts world and art museums, in particular, have been slow to collect Fusco's art and assess her contributions in their totality, scholars of performance and media, ethnic and cultural studies, art history, anthropology, women's studies, and African diaspora studies have for decades emphasized the magnitude of Fusco's contributions. In recent years, Fusco has been included as a pivotal figure in expansive museum exhibition surveys, including "Arte ≠ Vida: Actions by Artists in the Americas 1960–2000" (2008), a chronicle of performative actions created by Latinos in the US, Puerto Rico, the Dominican Republic, Cuba, Mexico, and Central and South America, and in "Radical Presence: Black Performance in Contemporary Art" (2013), a comprehensive survey of performance art by Black artists working from the perspective of the visual arts.

Throughout her career, Fusco has moved fluidly between many different art worlds in North and South America, Europe, Asia, and the Middle East and has been a critical voice in hemispheric considerations of the arts across the American continent. Within the context of the visual arts, she is squarely situated with the generation of artists who came of age during the infamous 1993 Whitney Biennial. This includes other Black and Brown Biennial artists who addressed the politics of identity and racism, such as Glenn Ligon, Pepón Osorio, Gary Simmons, and Lorna Simpson. Fusco's works also have clear consonance with other participating artists engaged in institutional critique, including Andrea Fraser, James Luna, Daniel J. Martinez, and Fred Wilson. Fusco's installation of historical artifacts, *The Year of the White Bear,* which she conceived in collaboration with Gómez-Peña in 1992 at the Walker Art Center, was among the earliest examples in the 1980s and 1990s of artists using the language of museology and ethnographic display to critique the objectification and exoticization of colonized cultures in western museums.

Outside the US, Fusco was also closely associated in the 1980s with Black filmmakers in London, including Isaac Julien, then a member of the Sankofa Film and Video collective, and John Akomfrah, of the Black Audio Film Collective. She organized the first American tour of the work of these collectives in 1988. The narrative and poetic nature of Fusco's films, and her sharp editing style, deserve closer examination with these and other British artists, including Steve McQueen, an artist who has also moved fluidly between visual art, performance, and film, and Julien, whose films similarly involve narration and engender an experience of catharsis in viewers, often through poetic exegesis.

Fusco is further associated with several generations of Cuban artists whose contributions she has helped give voice to in the US since the mid-1980s. For over twenty years, she has supported the work of Sandra Ceballos and her independent gallery, Espacio Aglutinador. In the 1990s, she helped foster appreciation of other transdisciplinary artists, including Mendieta, whose untimely death and presumed murder in 1985 divided the art world across gender lines. She insisted on Mendieta's legacy as an artist rather than a murder victim and criticized Mendieta's appropriation by other artists and causes as a symbol in feminist struggles. In 1997, she created the performance *Better Yet When Dead*, a series of wakes for Latina women—Frida Kahlo, Evita Perón, Selena, and Mendieta—whose dramatic and untimely deaths led to their fame.

Fusco's admiration for Mendieta extends beyond the impact of her artworks. Like Fusco, Mendieta, a Cuban exile, "delved into issues, scenarios, and situations related to her connection to the island with amazing intensity. She ventured where others didn't dare."[1] Born in New York, and a frequent visitor to Cuba with strong ties to its artistic community, Fusco is a unique voice in the complex discourses around Cuba. As a citizen of the United States, she is not silenced in the same way as artists living on the island (although she has faced her fair share of harassment from the Cuban authorities). Because she is not positioned within Miami's Cuban exile community, where discourse around Cuba frequently coalesces into a monolithic conservative consensus, Fusco provides a rare perspective on Cuban issues that critiques political realities inside the island, with a deep knowledge of its byzantine government and cultural symbols, and how those realities are interpreted and dealt with abroad. She has never hesitated to parse this complex, polarizing terrain and is today a leading voice on Cuban issues, particularly as they relate to art, culture, and freedom of expression.

In the context of Latin American art, Fusco's artistic contributions, and in particular her collaboration with Gómez-Peña, stand among the key figures of the late 1980s and 1990s. *Two Undiscovered Amerindians Visit the West* is iconic among a handful of watershed artworks and installations that came to define this period. These include Juan Francisco Elso's *Por América* (1986), James Luna's *Artifact Piece*

1 Coco Fusco in "Coco Fusco on the Enduring Legacy of Groundbreaking Cuban Artist Ana Mendieta," interview by Jared Quinton, *Artsy* (February 3, 2016).

TOMORROW, I WILL BECOME AN ISLAND

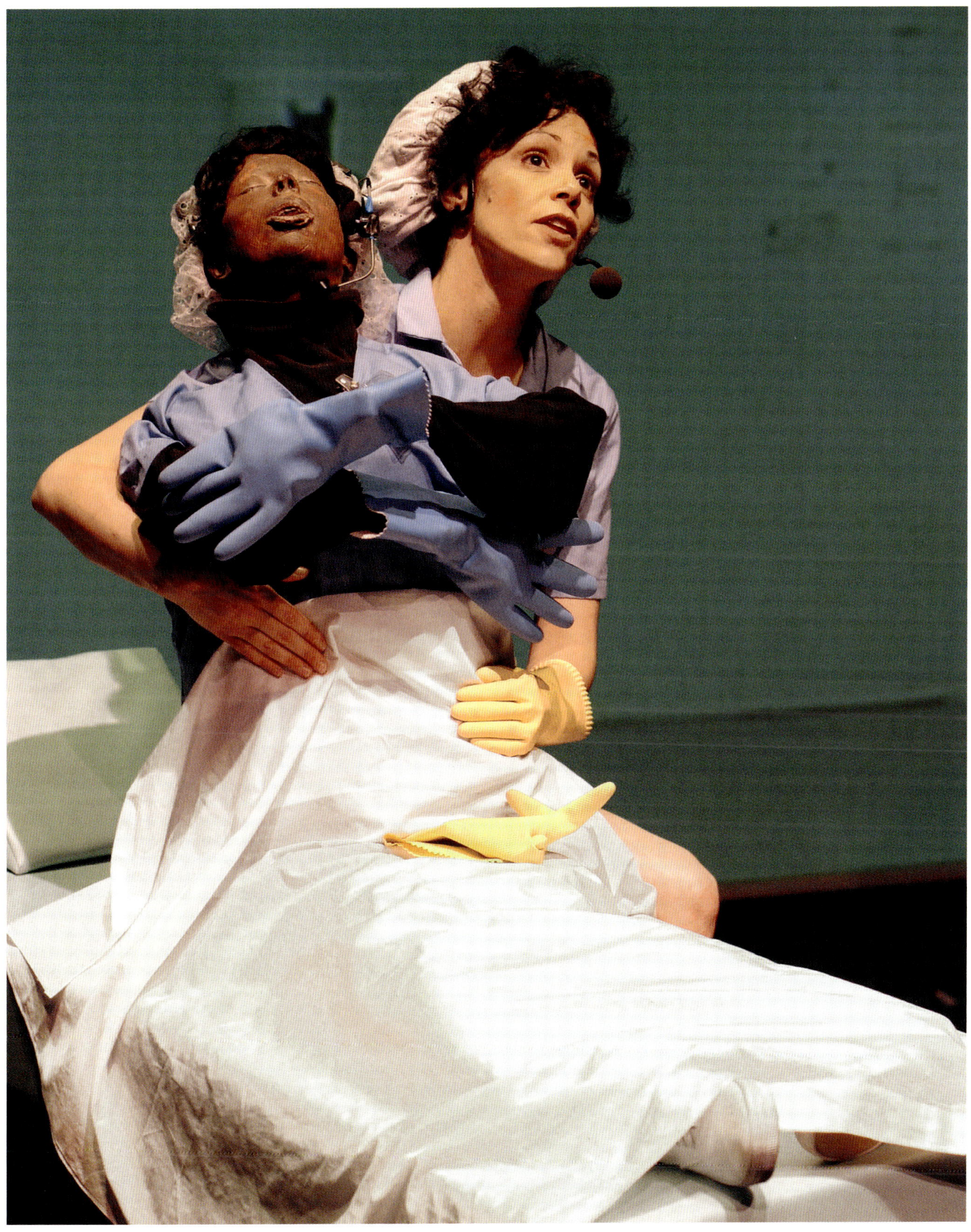

Coco Fusco, *The Incredible Disappearing Woman*, 2003, performance

(1987), Cildo Meireles's *Missão/Missões* [*Mission/Missions*] *(How to Build Cathedrals)* (1987), Jimmie Durham's *Malinche* (1988–92) and *Cortez* (1991–92), and Fred Wilson's *Mining the Museum* (1992–93). While these iconic pieces represent a wide range of expressions, they each staged in public unforgettable humanistic encounters that effectively instantiated the moment of conquest when the colonizer confronts the experience of those colonized.

Fusco's formidable contributions as author and cultural theorist have at times overshadowed recognition of her equally considerable artistic achievements; she has frequently had to create the context for her work to be understood and appreciated. She has accomplished this with her writings and curatorial initiatives, which have also served to expand the field for so many other artists. Since the mid-1980s, she has authoritatively contributed to critical discourses on film, performance, the visual arts, and postcolonial theory. She has been an advocate of Black, Caribbean, and Latin American artists, as well as a commentator on issues of race and gender. She has organized groundbreaking curatorial projects. The exhibition "Only Skin Deep: Changing Visions of the American Self" (2003), for the International Center of Photography in New York, was the first comprehensive survey of racial representation in American photography. The publication *Dangerous Moves: Performance and Politics in Cuba* (2015) offered the first critical survey of the history of political performance on the island. And *English Is Broken Here*, that 1995 treatise on cultural fusion in the Americas, is as fresh to read today as it was thirty years ago. In it she expounds on the varied constructions of race and identity in Latin America and North America that predate current discourses.

Tomorrow, I Will Become an Island, and the concurrent survey exhibition organized by KW Institute for Contemporary Art Berlin, provides a long overdue corrective and comprehensive assessment of the artist's influential thirty-year career. In the pages that follow, Fusco's video, performance, visual art, installations, and book projects are surveyed and considered in tandem. There is no hierarchy around media or insistence on distinctions that prioritize the artist's formal work from related writing projects and ephemera connected to her social practice. The contributors to the publication, who represent different fields of practice, similarly elucidate Fusco's career from their particular disciplinary points of view while recognizing the totality of the artist's resolutely hybrid practice.

Art historian Julia Bryan-Wilson eloquently describes the "politics of discomfort" as the vital medium of Fusco's art. She surveys the full expanse of the artist's interdisciplinary oeuvre and compellingly argues that passive participation is never possible when engaging Fusco's art. Performance scholar Jill Lane examines the artist's trajectory through the lens of corporality and critique and contextualizes the legacy of *Two Undiscovered Amerindians Visit the West* within Fusco's broader oeuvre. Anna Gritz, an art historian specializing in the rich intersections between film, performance, and visual arts, considers Fusco's approach through the prism of institutional and infrastructural critique. She focuses on Fusco's performances from the 1990s and early 2000s and the artist's selection of presentation practices that operate on the boundaries of institutional reach. Cuban poet and essayist Antonio Ponte, who has written extensively about the contemporary politics of Cuba, provides vital context for understanding the artist's important relationship to the island and her career-long commitment to battling artistic censorship there.

In 1996, art critic Jean Fisher recognized Fusco's unprecedented position "among a generation of cultural theorists and practitioners then emerging from an expanded field of postcolonial critique, bringing with them new paradigms

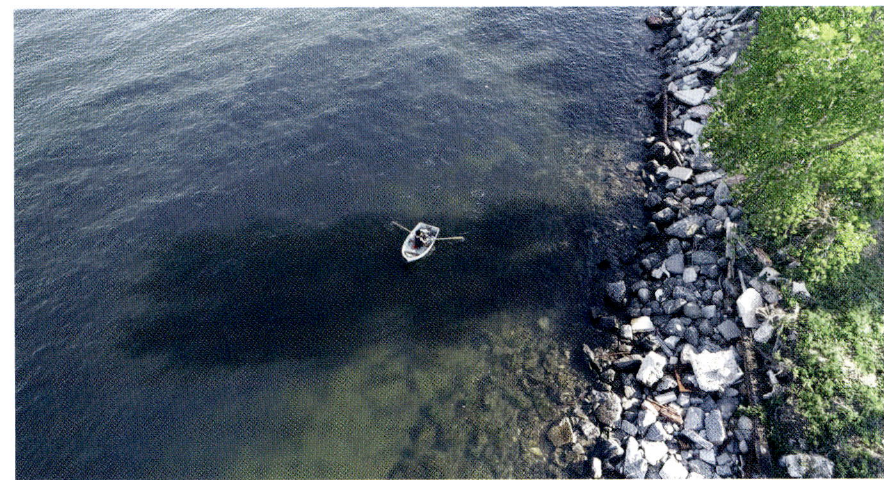

Your Eyes Will Be an Empty Word, 2021, **video**

of cultural politics developing in cross-border zones and post-national global networks." Fusco's response to the critic's framework is telling. She notes: "We didn't theorize post-coloniality after the fact, learn about it from a workshop, or wait for multiculturalism to become foundation lingo for 'appreciating diversity'—we lived it and struggle[d] to make art about it."[2]

Coco Fusco continues to live this struggle every day. For the last thirty years, she has investigated the complexities of race and gender, the legacies of slavery and colonization, and the operations of censorship and the authoritarian state, responding with urgency and clarity to the major political and cultural issues of our time. She has been, as Bryan-Wilson notes, "refining a politics of discomfort" that "pushes against conventions of spectatorship." She also illuminates, as Lane acknowledges, "the body as a site of contestation over knowledge and power and as a source of performative critique." Fusco's interdisciplinary oeuvre, seen here in its totality for the first time, thus offers a potent and instructive primer about what it means to be, and remain, a relevant and engaged artist who is *of*, *for*, and ceaselessly *ahead of* her time.

As I reflect on the artist's practice and revisit my 1993 self, I realize the discomforts I felt in my youth before the undiscovered Amerindian woman are not dissimilar to the feelings of disquiet that the best of Fusco's art still engenders in me, and in viewers, today. Fusco's oeuvre offers the world an archipelago of poetic islands to traverse and ponder. These islands are not autonomous spaces of isolation. Fusco's islands of tomorrow extend bridges and footpaths to the outer reaches of assumed knowledges. They close the gaps between untenable divides, while also revealing their underlying structural weaknesses and failures. The areas she exposes require care, attention, and likely even wholesale reconsideration. Her art reminds us, as do the words of the Nobel Prize-winning Saint Lucian poet Derek Walcott: "Poetry is an island that breaks away from the main."[3]

2   Jean Fisher, "Witness for the Prosecution: The Writings of Coco Fusco," *The Bodies That Were Not Ours: And Other Writings* (London: Routledge/Iniva, 2001): 223.

3   Derek Walcott, "The Antilles: Fragments of Epic Memory," Nobel Lecture, December 7, 1992, https://www.nobelprize.org/prizes/literature/1992/walcott/lecture/.

Coco Fusco and the Politics of Discomfort

Julia Bryan-Wilson

From the moment she emerged in the 1990s as one of the most significant artists of her time, Coco Fusco has been refining a politics of discomfort. Through her incisive live performances, video and photography projects, curatorial initiatives, and critical writing practice, she relentlessly and thrillingly pushes back against conventions of spectatorship that place the viewer in a passive or receptive role. Instead, when witnessing Fusco's work, we are confronted, challenged, and provoked—as when she peddled "ethnic talent" to shopping mall buyers (*Mexarcane International*, 1994–95), set up ersatz passport checks to control audience entry to the Johannesburg Biennale (*Rights of Passage*, 1997), and oversaw the mass cleaning with toothbrushes of the São Paulo street in front of the US consulate by students dressed as prisoners (*Bare Life Study #1*, 2005), to name just a few examples. The generation of unease plays a central role in Fusco's hard-hitting critiques of colonialism, gendered regimes of labor, the consolidation of state power, and racism.

I do not understand this discomfort as either monolithic or as universal, because we as viewers and readers come to her work occupying radically distinct subject-positions; as a result we all hold different tolerances for the calculated and urgent difficulties she offers. In order to think through some of these dynamics with nuance, I speculate about three bodies that Fusco's work makes uncomfortable and puts under pressure: "ours" (that is, the collective body of critics and art historians); "hers" (Fusco's own endurance practice is remarkable); and lastly, "mine" (in which I recount tensions I experienced first-hand while witnessing her performances). Forced migration, torture, sexual violence, the economic exploitations of globalization, censorship: many of the issues that Fusco grapples with are disturbing. But I also want to emphasize the care she takes in all of her projects—her moments of grace or humor, her aesthetic thoughtfulness with well-framed shots, her sentences that land just so. Though she is an artist who probes politics with necessary gravitas, she is also above all just that: an artist, one who endeavors to bring a measure of poetry to her working process.

OURS

To take Fusco's discomforting work seriously is to raise troubling questions about the exclusionist assumptions that have structured 20th- and 21st-century art history in the US. Fusco has been central to the intersecting realms of feminist art, Latinx art, Cuban diasporic art, and Black art—to name a few of the by no means discrete arenas in which she has been historicized—with appearances in exhibitions and publications like *Art and Feminism*, "Arte ≠ Vida," "Radical Presence,"

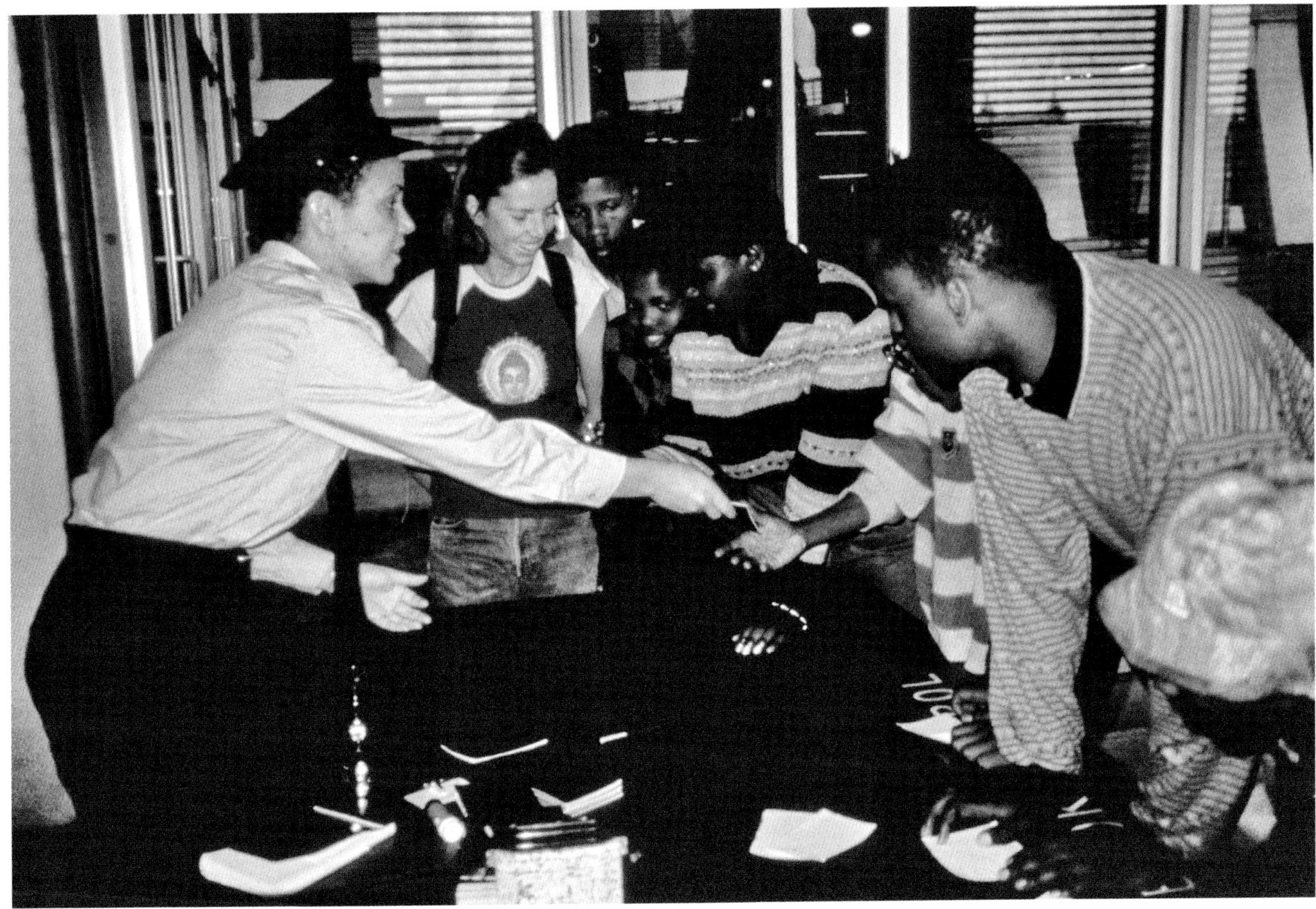

Coco Fusco at a workshop about her 1997 performance, *Rights of Passage*

and her high-profile 2021 Latinx Artists Fellowship.[1] She is also recognized as a crucial figure within hemispheric histories of "performance art in the Americas," a category she helped define with her edited anthology *Corpus Delecti*, a volume that remains the definitive reference on the topic.[2] Her early interventions have been positioned within the rise of, and furious backlash against, the discourse around multiculturalism during the US Culture Wars of the late 1980s and early 1990s, and her texts appeared in influential books that chronicle these debates.[3]

At the same time that her work has undeniably served as a crux, and while she is now hailed as an essential part of feminisms and of live art by artists of color, she experienced years of neglect as market fortunes turned against performance art (a genre that is less easily purchased than, say, painting and in its nascent years was more resistant to capitalist modes of collecting), against explicitly political work, and against work that interrogates racism and sexism. Until somewhat recently, the main critical texts that helped explicate Fusco's art were written by Fusco herself.

I point this out not to diminish the force of her writings—her work is certainly studied within art history, and she is one of the main voices writing more inclusive and plural art history that has prioritized Black and Brown women—but to acknowledge that without advocates, an artist who deals with unpopular subjects or occupies a position seen as less-than-marketable can be further condemned to invisibility. Fusco's edited collections, such as *Only Skin Deep* (2003), and her single-authored books, including *Dangerous Moves: Performance and Politics in*

1   Peggy Phelan and Helena Reckitt, *Art and Feminism* (London: Phaidon); "Arte ≠ Vida: Actions by Artists of the Americas," curated by Deborah Cullen (New York: El Museo del Barrio, 2008), and "Radical Presence: Black Performance in Contemporary Art," curated by Valerie Cassel Oliver (New York: The Studio Museum, 2013).

2   Coco Fusco, ed., *Corpus Delecti: Performance Art of the Americas* (London and New York: Routledge, 2000).

3   See Coco Fusco, "Passionate Irreverence: The Cultural Politics of Identity," in *Art Matters: How the Culture Wars Changed America*, eds., Brian Wallis, Marianne Weems, and Philip Yenawine (New York: New York University Press, 1999).

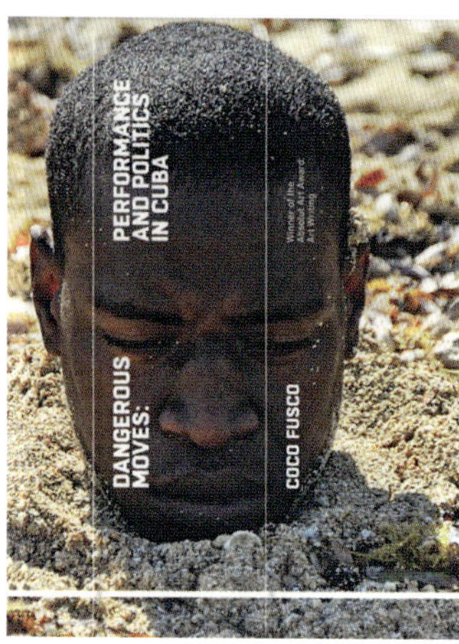

Dangerous Moves: Performance and Politics in Cuba, 2015, publication

4 Coco Fusco and Brian Wallis, eds., *Only Skin Deep: Changing Visions of the American Self* (New York: Harry N. Abrams, 2003); Coco Fusco, *Dangerous Moves: Performance and Politics in Cuba* (London: Tate Publishing, 2015).

5 See Arlene Dávila, *Latinx Art: Artists, Markets, Politics* (Durham, NC: Duke University Press, 2020).

6 Carolina A. Miranda, "How a Project to Honor Artist Felix Gonzalez-Torres Devolved into an Instagram Stunt," *Los Angeles Times* (June 5, 2020); and Joshua Smith, "Why a Felix Gonzalez-Torres Project Was One of 2020's Biggest Flops," *ArtNews* (December 9, 2020).

7 Coco Fusco, "Traces of Ana Mendieta 1988–1993," in *English is Broken Here: Notes on Cultural Fusion in the Americas* (New York: The New Press, 1995), 121; see also Jared Quinton, "Coco Fusco on the Enduring Legacy of Ana Mendieta," artsy.net (Feb. 3, 2016), https://www.artsy.net/article/artsy-editorial-ana-mendieta-s-enduring-legacy-in-the-words-of-coco-fusco.

8 Fusco, "Traces of Ana Mendieta," 125.

9 Coco Fusco, "Preface," *The Bodies That Were Not Ours: And Other Writings* (London: Routledge/Iniva, 2001): xiv.

Cuba (2015), act as a crucial corrective to this; in these projects she has investigated the construction of race in US photography and fiercely championed the work of under-recognized artists.[4] Yet her own art has not fit easily within normative whitewashed timelines of contemporary art that have persistently relegated Latinx art to the sidelines—major but under-studied; vital yet marginalized.[5]

Another sphere in which Fusco might be productively situated is within the distinctly queer and feminist work of Cuban-American artists who preceded her, including that of Ana Mendieta (born twelve years before Fusco) and Felix Gonzalez-Torres (older than Fusco by three years). Unlike Fusco, both Mendieta and Gonzalez-Torres were born in Cuba, and both have achieved canonical, even near-mythical status, owing in part to their premature deaths at the ages of thirty-six and thirty-eight and also owing to the more allusive nature of their art. At times this allusiveness has rendered Mendieta's and Gonzalez-Torres's work vulnerable to be hijacked and redirected away from its politically rooted origins. For instance, though indelibly shaped by queer desires and the devastating losses wrought by HIV/AIDS, Gonzalez-Torres's elliptical works have proven open-ended enough to be appropriated for decidedly less political ends, such as the 2020 crowdsourced social-media recreation of his 1990 *Untitled (Fortune Cookie Corner)* that many found hit a dissonant note of lavish excess during a summer ravaged by pandemic-related food shortages and militant street uprisings around racist policing.[6]

Similar to the dilution of Gonzalez-Torres's strident legacy, Mendieta has become a literal poster child for causes quite remote from the ones she agitated for during her life. Despite Mendieta's defiant return to Cuba in 1980, her activist work with solidarity networks between leftist US artists and Cuban artists, and her site-specific earth-body works that reference specific Afro-Caribbean and Indigenous spiritual practices, the rigors of her work threaten to be overshadowed by the sensationalized trial for her murder and debates about women's visibility in the art world. Fusco notes that Mendieta—who was an important connector for Fusco's own research-based practice in Cuba—was "one of the first Latin American women artists, and the only Cuban, to achieve indisputable prominence on the art world's terms, without compromising her own."[7] Fusco laments how Mendieta was turned into an instrumentalized icon and symbol in white feminist protests for the Women's Action Coalition after her death, writing that "there are more than a few of Ana's colleagues who, remembering her struggles to gain recognition in that same milieu, find the current appropriation of her image painful and even exploitative."[8] This sharply phrased commentary, one that rubs against the grain of triumphalist narratives of Mendieta's ascension to martyrdom, exemplifies how across her writings and her artworks Fusco does not shy away from taking oppositional stances.

The continued broad uptake of Mendieta and Gonzalez-Torres within institutionalized art history acts as a decisive contrast to Fusco's work, which in the late 1990s during a return to formalism and the regressive rush to champion straight white male artists in the aftermath of the Culture Wars was more stutteringly received in the US. In 2001, Fusco wrote: "Since the backlash against 1980s' identity-based art exploded in the early 1990s, the artworld has grown increasingly hostile to the deployment of personal experience as [an] aesthetic or political gesture. And in the 1980s, when multiculturalism enjoyed a brief period of positive attention and autobiographical confessions were the order of the day, I remember voicing a good deal of skepticism about 'the emotional striptease' that white audiences so often demanded."[9] Refusing to conform to expectations,

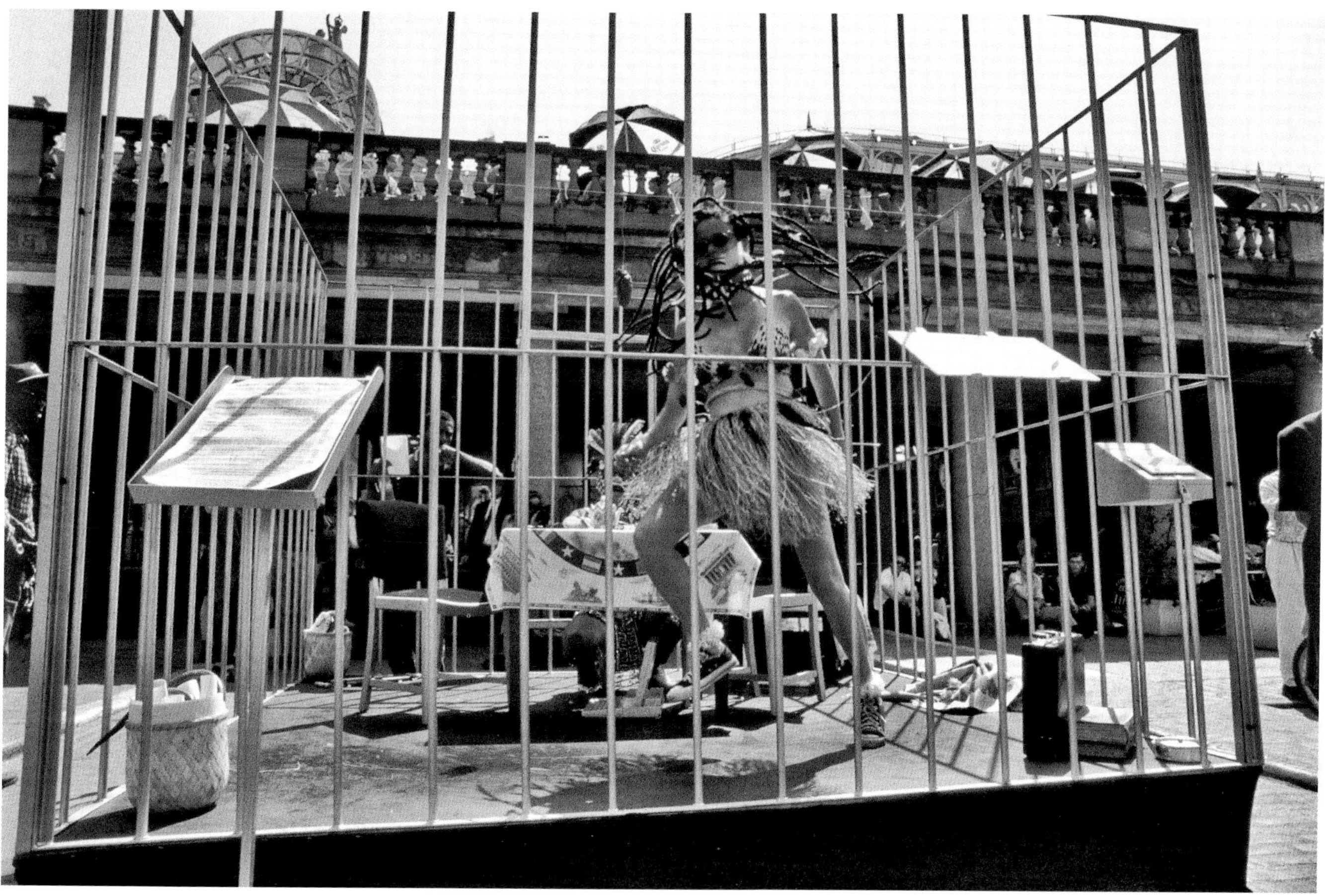

Coco Fusco and Guillermo Gómez-Peña, *Two Undiscovered Amerindians Visit London*, 1992, performance

Fusco articulates her own discomfort with the way her work has been understood and (more often) misunderstood within the confines of the art world's narrow categorizations. Demonized and caricatured as essentialist, "identity politics" was not a transient 1990s art-trend but rather is an entire political philosophy first coined by the Black feminist Combahee River Collective in the late 1970s that has been extended in important and creative ways by Fusco's work.[10]

HERS

Fusco's decades-long solo practice as an interdisciplinary editor, author, and performer is frequently eclipsed by what remains her most famous collaboration, one that pivots on a multi directional exchange of discomfort between audiences and performers, *Two Undiscovered Amerindians Visit the West* (1992–94), first performed with Guillermo Gómez-Peña in 1992. Given that much has been written about this work and its critiques of the colonial logic of museums and histories of ethnographic displays of "primitive" others, I will only briefly touch on the imbalanced, gendered strain sustained by Fusco while touring this piece—she bore much, but not all, of the brunt of lascivious gazes and unwanted touches from viewers.[11] This gendered difference underlines how discomfort is unevenly distributed and contingently experienced depending upon one's positionality.

10 Combahee River Collective, *The Combahee River Collective Statement*, April 1977, retrieved from the Library of Congress, http://www.loc.gov/item/lcwaN0028151/.

11 See Coco Fusco, "The Other History of Intercultural Performance," *TDR: The Drama Review*, vol. 38, no. 1 (Spring 1994): 143–57; Fusco and Paula Heredia, "Couple in a Cage," 30 min. video, 1993. For one widely circulated analysis of this work see Diana Taylor, "A Savage Performance: Guillermo Gómez-Peña and Coco Fusco's 'Couple in a Cage,'" *TDR: The Drama Review*, vol. 42, no. 2 (1998): 160–75. Fusco wrote a response to Taylor with her own reflections in a subsequent issue of *TDR*.

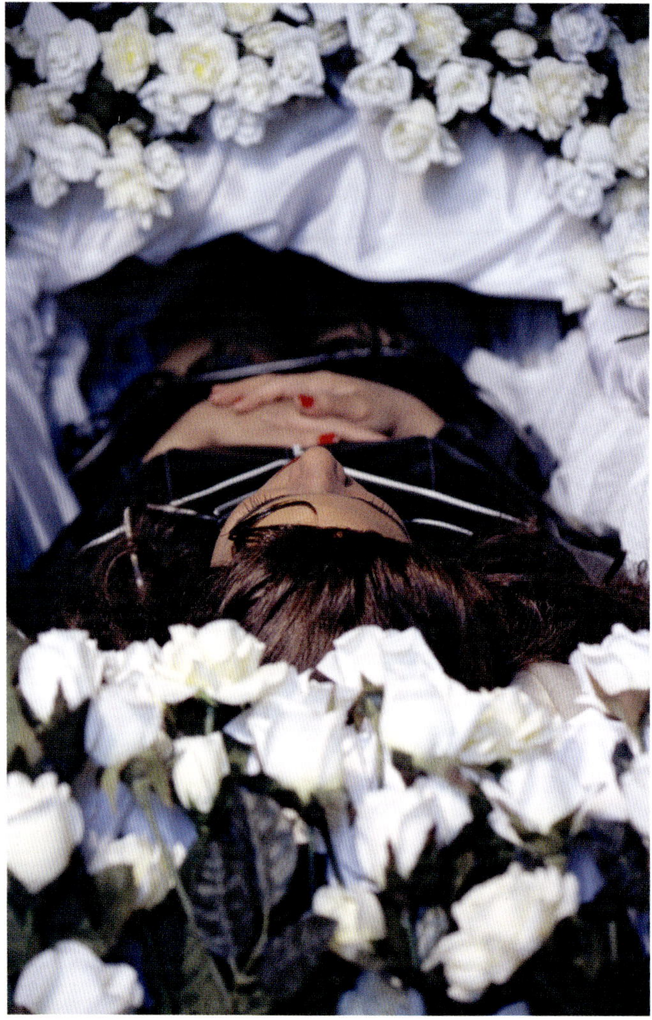

Better Yet When Dead, 1997, **performance installation**

Fusco grasps how discomfort is inherently social; it wells up when thresholds are breached. Another way to conceptualize discomfort is that it is a corporeal reaction to felt frictions. The sound of discomfort is the rasping of boundaries as they are transgressed. Discomfort is a word people sometimes use to describe what transformative growth, or real learning, feels like: the stretch can hurt. In her poignant and biting 1997 piece *Better Yet When Dead*, Fusco lay still in a flower-bedecked coffin dressed as the corpse of four different famous Latinas (Mendieta, Frida Kahlo, Selena, and Eva Perón) as a way to visually intertwine histories of syncretic religious cults in Latin America, with their fixation on "pure" virgins and female saints, and the fetishized necrophilia of celebrity and art-market cultures that value the dead above all. Fusco states, "I was particularly interested in how a Catholic culture negotiates this kind of commercialization of the dead women."[12]

In her account of this work from *The Bodies That Were Not Ours: And Other Writings* (2001), Fusco describes the diverging reactions of the audience when she performed the piece in different locations, in Canada at YYZ Artspace Toronto and in Colombia at the International Arts Festival in Medellín, noting that she trained herself to modulate her breath so it was almost imperceptible, to will away any muscular urge to twitch, and learning how to "withstand having limbs

12 Transcript of lecture by Coco Fusco, Museum of Modern Art, New York, 1999, https://www.moma. org/interactives/projects/1999/ conversations/trans_cfusco.html.

13 Fusco, "Better Yet When Dead," in *The Bodies That Were Not Ours: And Other Writings*, 24.

     COCO FUSCO AND THE POLITICS OF DISCOMFORT

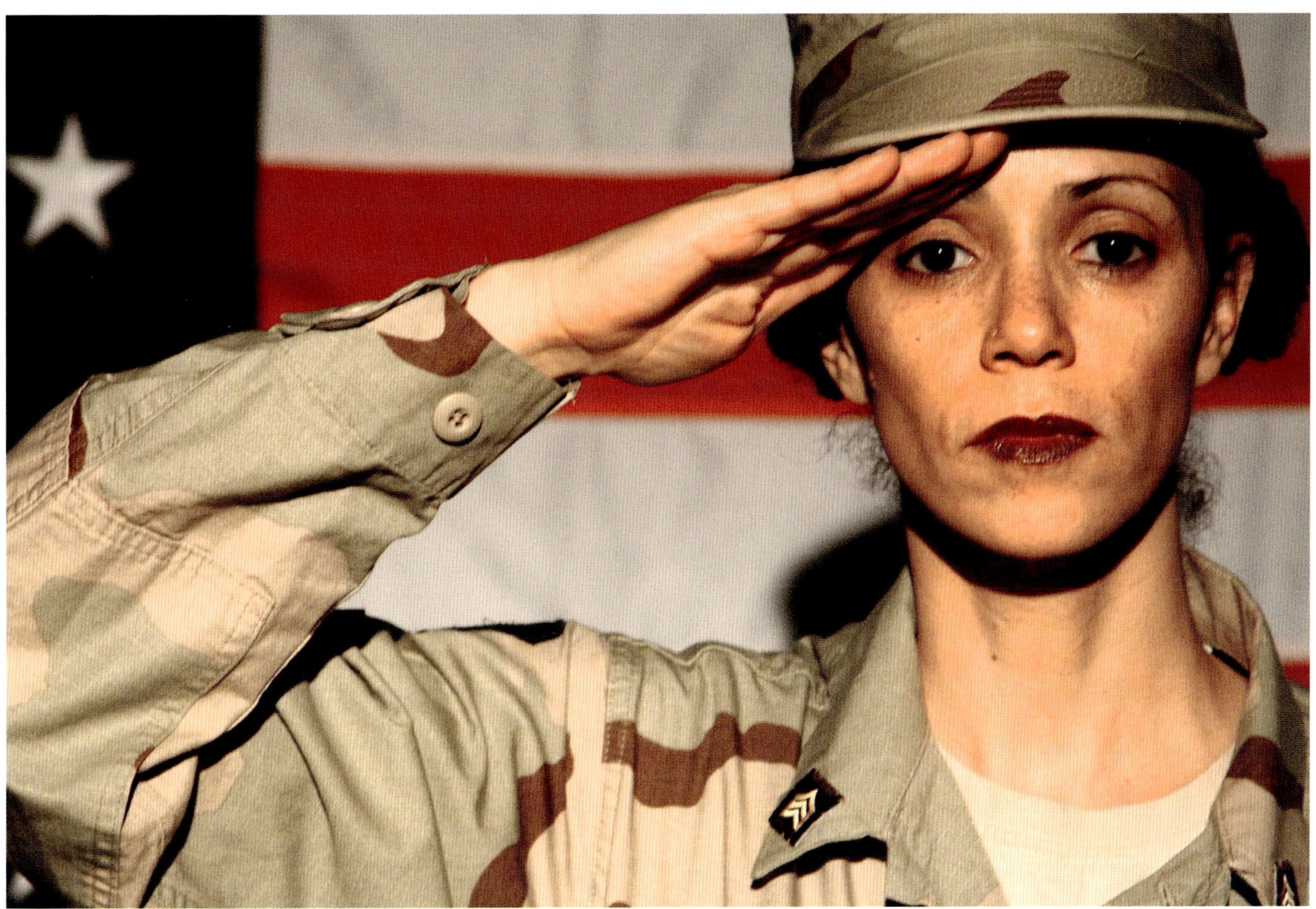

A Room of One's Own: Women and Power in the New America, 2006–08, performance

fall asleep."[13] In Colombia, even as wine was poured on her and reporters yelled at her to comment on the strike she launched in protest of nonpayment for her appearance at the festival, she did not move.

As this illustrates, Fusco has demonstrated her high tolerance for enduring distressing circumstances. While audiences might feel ideologically indicted by the situations she creates, the body placed at most risk is her own; in response to pieces like *Rights of Passage* and *Better Yet When Dead* she recounts being threatened, screamed at, belittled, ignored, non-consensually kissed, and harassed, among other indignities. She has contributed to a lineage of performance work in which the artist's physical limits are tested; for example, in 2000's *El evento suspendido* (*The Postponed Event*), she buried herself up to her chest in the ground in Havana for three hours while typing the same letter continuously—a missive that contains an emphatic declaration of her existence. In *Votos* (*Vows*), also from 2000, the audience was invited to cut off her hair and burn it.

In Fusco's most far-reaching examination of discomfort, from 2004 to 2009 across an interlocking series of performances, publications, and videos, she immersed herself in the role played by US women combatants in the War on Terror. In 2005, Fusco, along with six women collaborators, attended a mini-course set of workshops taught by Team Delta (retired US army personnel) to steep herself in military interrogation and survival techniques. Out of this embodied research were born her resultant projects, including *A Room of One's Own: Women and Power*

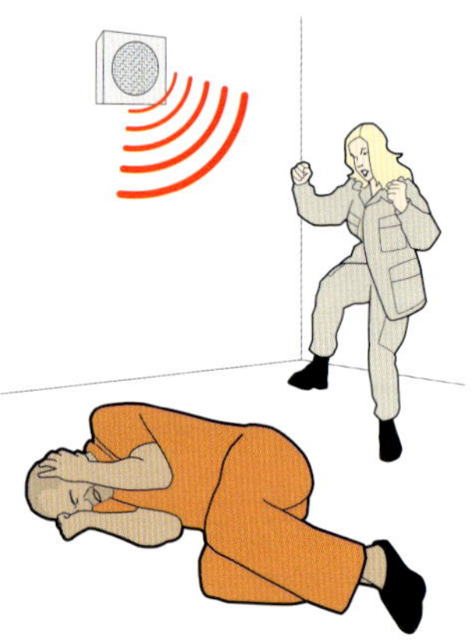

A Field Guide for Female Interrogators, 2008, publication. Illustrations by Daniel Turner

14 Coco Fusco, *A Field Guide for Female Interrogators* (New York: Seven Stories Press, 2008).

15 Coco Fusco and José Esteban Muñoz; "A Room of One's Own: Women and Power in the New America," *TDR/The Drama Review*, vol. 52, no. 1 (2008): 138.

16 Karen Beckman, "Gender, Power, and Pedagogy in Coco Fusco's *Bare Life Study #1* (2005), *A Room of One's Own: Women and Power in the New America* (2006–08), and *Operation Atropos* (2006)," *Framework: The Journal of Cinema and Media*, vol. 50, nos. 1/2 (Spring and Fall 2009): 127.

17 Coco Fusco, "Fusco, Censorship, Not the Painting, Must Go," *Hyperallergic* (March 27, 2017); and Coco Fusco, "The Artist as Hostage: Luis Manuel Otero Alcántara," *e-flux*, #118 (May 2021).

18 Coco Fusco, email regarding *La sombra de Heberto Padilla*, April 2021.

19 A vast literature of competing theories from Aristotle to Émile Durkheim discusses the function of catharsis in drama as well as in social dynamics; recapitulating these theories falls outside of the scope of this essay.

in the New America (2006–08), which concretized the notion of a "theater of operations" by recreating military tactics in a multimedia presentation complete with a monologue and PowerPoint slides. Fusco's cluster of works showcase how the US government weaponizes female sexuality as a tool to coerce confessions at the Abu Ghraib and Guantánamo detention centers. Her 2008 artist's book, *A Field Guide for Female Interrogators*, chillingly catalogues a repertoire of techniques that include humiliation, fear, sexual degradation, and the flouting of Muslim religious and cultural taboos.[14]

José Esteban Muñoz notes that Fusco's work on military tactics is not meant as entertainment but rather is intentionally "harsh," implicating herself and her audience in the brutal realities of post-9/11 gendered geopolitics.[15] Her video documentation in *Operation Atropos* (2006) of the workshops of Team Delta is grueling to watch; here is a strategic wielding of escalating stresses that progress from mild unease to full-blown torture. As Karen Beckman comments, this project "disrupts a version of feminist discourse that has persistently placed women in the role of victim."[16] Instead, Fusco bracingly examines the complicity of women as they enact systemic abuses. Putting her own body on the line, her work regarding military interrogation illuminates how engendering tension subtends much of her work at the levels of content, affect, and form.

One might say that regardless of genre, discomfort is her medium. Not only that, in her critical writing, Fusco is consistently unafraid to take bold and sometimes counter-orthodox stands, such as her assiduously researched piece on the Dana Schutz *Open Casket* controversy from 2016—in which she encourages viewers to question why a work that elicits "strong reactions" should face calls for its destruction—and her more recent work that sheds light on ongoing conflicts in Cuba. In Spring 2021, she published a searing text addressing state violence against Black Cubans and orchestrated a choral reading of poet Heberto Padilla's 1971 forced confession/self-denunciation that resonates with current protesters in Cuba and their calls for freedom of expression.[17] With this performance, Fusco amplifies and also collectivizes Padilla's words, as twenty different voices recite his statement. As the press release states, "Padilla's confession is a study in political abjection that is painful to witness and reproduce. But it is necessary, especially now when a new generation of Cuban artists and intellectuals are challenging the state's authority over them."[18] Painful but necessary: these are the watchwords for Fusco's practice. The footage for *La sombra de Herberto Padilla* (*Padilla's Shadow*, 2021), which Fusco meticulously designed to resemble the original black-and-white archival broadcast, is also moving and poetic (in fact, the poet José Yanes is invoked by name) as a stream of various faces solemnly respeak his words.

MINE

While classical dramatic theater emphasizes a cathartic release of culminated tension, Fusco's work instead cultivates and sustains these pressures.[19] I was in the audience for a 2006 live performance of *A Room of One's Own* at PS 122 and can attest that it was a prickly experience; the ruthlessness of Fusco's exquisitely paced performance, coupled with the fact that I had "excellent" seats front and center in close proximity to the action as it unfolded, fostered a level of immersion into the performance that I can only describe as borderline excruciating. I mean this as a great compliment, for Muñoz is right: the performance is not light entertainment

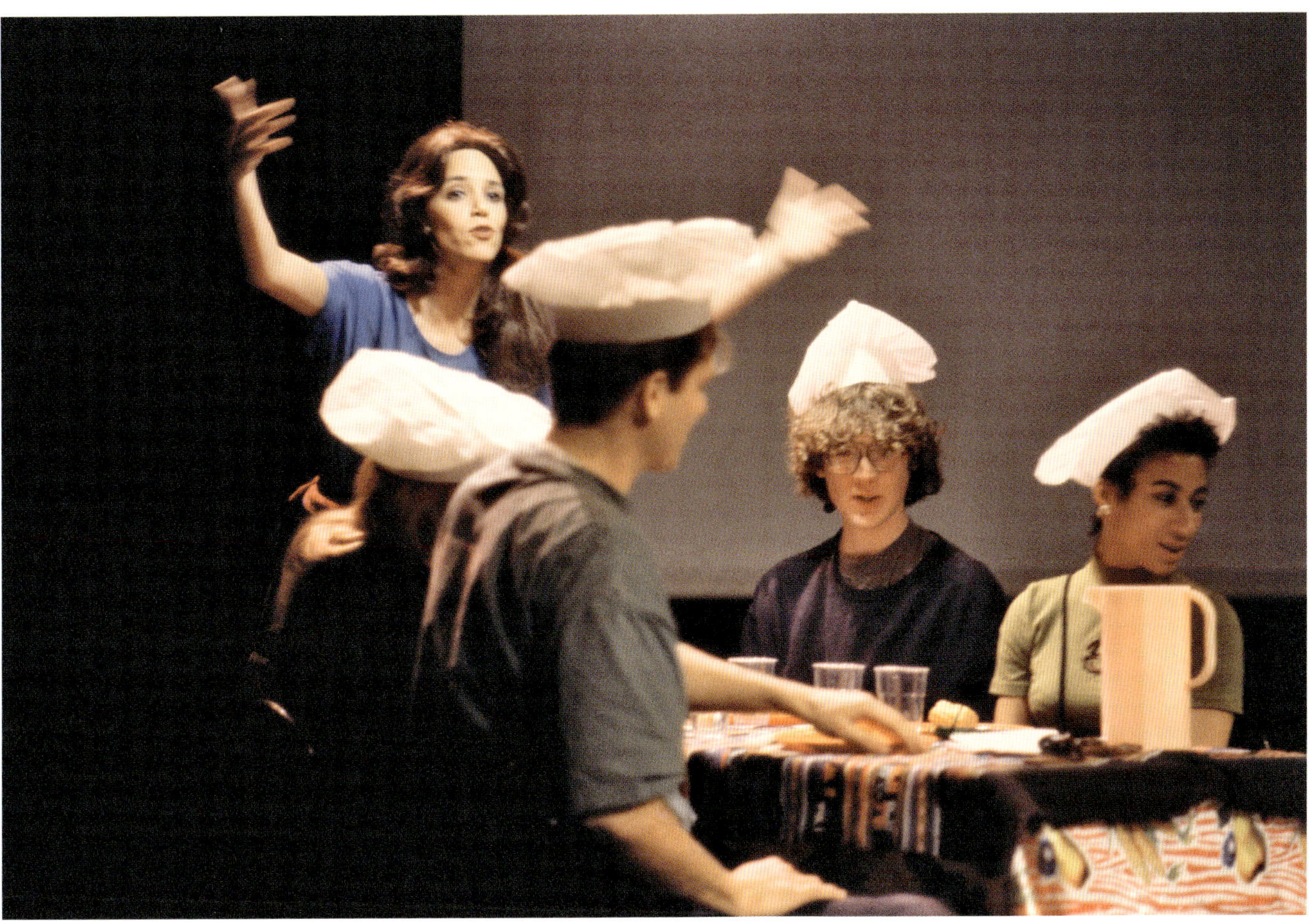

Coco Fusco and Nao Bustamante, *Stuff*, 1996–99, performance

but offers profound insights that have stuck with me about the imbrication of gender, violence, and religion. Staged a short three years after the commencement of the US war against Iraq in 2003, Fusco's performance asked questions about how certain strands of liberal white feminism, ones that entrench the two-gender binary and erase racial difference across national contexts, had become entangled in the US government's amorphous War on Terror. Fusco proffered a transnational anti-war feminist analysis that insisted on delving deep into how women have been conscripted into and are active agents within militarized regimes.[20] Because of the irresolvability of the situation Fusco engineers and the ambiguity of the positions she enacts (oscillating between sympathetic and abhorrent), the performance simmers; and because she withholds any kind of release valve or crescendo, I walked away still holding its lessons.

A different kind of lesson was on offer in 1997 when I attended a performance in Portland, Oregon of *Stuff* (1996–99), a collaboration between Fusco and Nao Bustamante that investigates the metaphoric consumption of exoticized women and the hunger for "authenticity" around Latin American and Latinx food, culture, and sex.[21] *Stuff* is a complex and layered performance; in a series of linked vignettes, Fusco and Bustamante draw on tourist postcards, the rhetoric of New Age spiritual retreats, and the artists' research with sex workers in Mexico and Cuba. About halfway through, Fusco reads a manifesto of sorts connecting

20 I draw on the language articulated by Paola Bacchetta, Tina Campt, Inderpal Grewal, Caren Kaplen, Minoo Moallem, and Jennifer Terry in their October 2001 statement "Transnational Feminist Practices Against War," *Meridians*, vol. 2, no. 2 (2002): 302–8.

21 For the script of this piece, see Nao Bustamante and Coco Fusco, "*STUFF*," *TDR/The Drama Review*, vol. 41, no. 4 (Winter 1997): 63–82.

the Brazilian modernist embrace of anthropophagia (cannibalism) with white culture's rapacious devouring of Brown traditions and bodies. She concludes, "The more visceral your desires, the more physical our labor." The performance is disarming and frank; at another point, a female voiceover rhapsodizes about how oral sex with a woman tastes while Bustamante picks her teeth with a toothpick.

This moment was charged for me at the young age of twenty-three, because I was there on a date with a woman whose name I don't remember. Though I had been out as queer for years, she was "questioning" (it was her first date ever with a woman), and *Stuff*'s moment of lesbian "eating" felt electric between us. In addition, I recognized that as two white women who practice yoga, we were some of the targets of the artists' critiques, adding a more complicated element of anxiety to the jitters of a first date. I should also say that I was still experimenting with my own gendered presentations as I groped my way towards a queer self-fashioning that made sense to me. On that night for that date, I decided, for the first time ever, to bind my breasts, seeking a more tomboyish/androgynous/butch-of-center profile. Back then, there were not precise and detailed YouTube instructional tutorials about how to do such things. Maybe I had seen how to do it in a subcultural Xeroxed zine. More likely, I had never seen how to properly do it, so I clumsily wrapped my torso tightly with a long length of Ace bandage and secured it with one small safety pin.

Three quarters of the way through the hourlong show, Fusco roamed the audience and asked if anyone knew what "Quieres mover tu cintura como una mulata buena?" ("Do you want to move your hips like a good mulatto girl?") meant, and I answered. The perils of raising one's hand! Suddenly I was up on stage, being taught basic dance steps of the rumba that included gyrating hips. At a certain dreadful moment, I felt an unwelcome release across my chest, and the bandage began to unspool, visibly falling out of my shirt as my breasts suddenly popped up. This moment of vulnerability and exposure was embarrassing, yes, and it was also telling, for it flipped the script, voiding the usual comforts provided by watching anonymously while seated in the dark. Having my binding unravel during a date (a date that did not end well) was embarrassing but also humorous. Nearly a decade later, I asked Bustamente if she and Fusco had seen my wardrobe fail during the performance; she responded, "No, we didn't notice. But if we had, we would have laughed."

* * *

This essay began with a comment on how Fusco's discomfort has political effects, but I want to return to the poetry that resides within it. Such poetry is evident throughout her work, and is explicitly present in her video *Your Eyes Will Be an Empty Word* from 2021. This beautifully composed eleven-minute meditation on grief and loss features Fusco rowing a small boat around Hart Island, the largest mass grave in the US where bodies laid to rest still speak quietly about whose lives go uncounted—formerly enslaved people, casualties of HIV/AIDS, unclaimed victims of the COVID-19 pandemic. The voiceover on the soundtrack partly cites a poem by Italian writer and Communist Cesare Pavese (who killed himself shortly after writing it in 1950), read by African American poet Pamela Sneed.

But the text also draws us decidedly into the current moment, describing overflowing hospital beds and the bureaucratization of COVID death tolls. "Breathing means something different now/death is in the air/it invades our lungs and clouds

   COCO FUSCO AND THE POLITICS OF DISCOMFORT

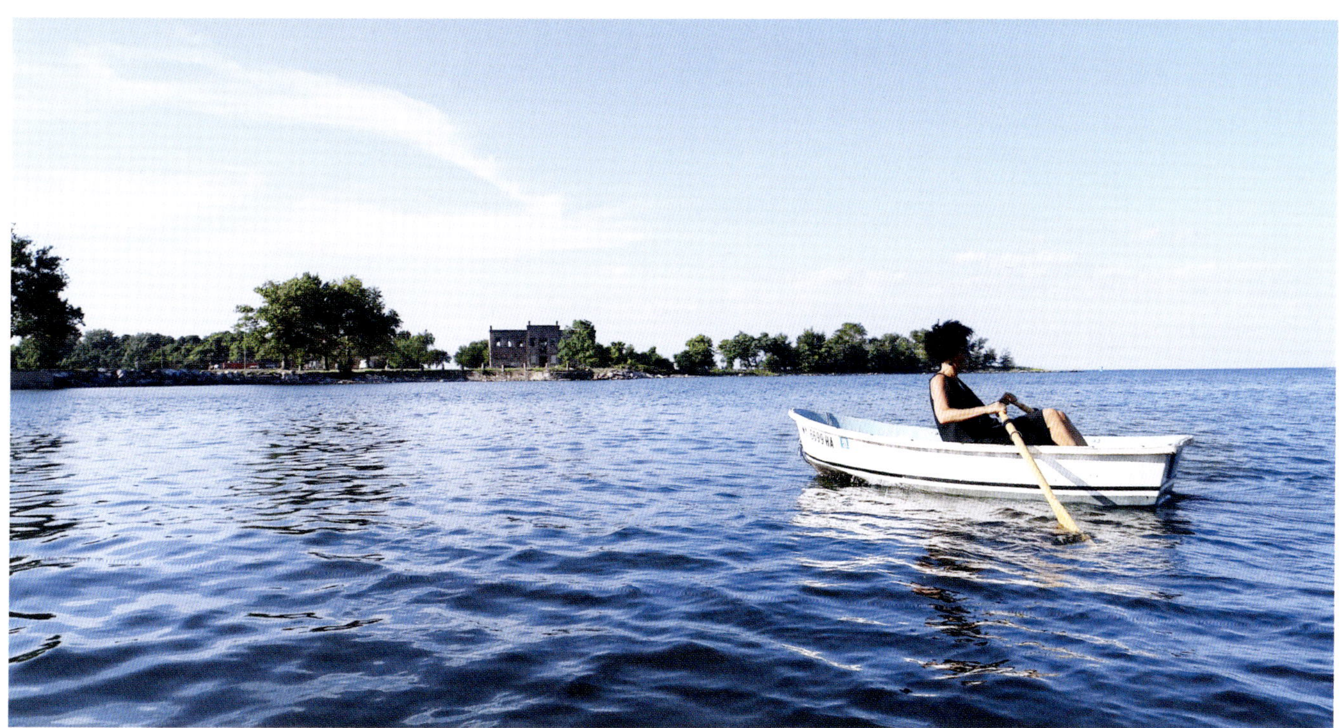

Your Eyes Will Be an Empty Word, 2021, video

our minds/it dictates our moves and our moods./We cannot walk away from the air," reads Sneed. In Fusco's video the words take on multiple meanings in light of the airborne virus and the Black Lives Matter movement catalyzed by George Floyd's inability to breath under the murderous knee of Derek Chauvin. The effect of the lyricism of *Your Eyes Will Be an Empty Word* is not soothing, but deeply sad, as Fusco offers repetitions of historical lines that continue to mournfully echo in our catastrophic present. In this piece, her art of discomfort chimes with the collective rage and exhaustion felt with differing intensities by different populations.

Still in the grip of lockdown, I watched Fusco's video by myself, at my desk, and felt the yawning absence of the live experiences I had with previous works, however unsettling they were at times. The imagery of Fusco alone, rowing herself through the waters around Hart Island speaks to these widespread yet uneven conditions of isolation. The video presents a landscape of grieving and commemoration, and with its footage of gravestones and buildings in ruin, it foregrounds a kind of taking pause. Fusco's act of rowing becomes a ritual of remembrance in the face of overwhelming death and violent inequity. *Your Eyes Will Be an Empty Word*, like so much of Fusco's art, refuses closure, and in so doing opens out to its viewers, exhorting us to continue to do the tough but worthy work of confronting injustice.

Corporeality and Critique

Jill Lane

In 2001, Coco Fusco invited interested participants living in Barcelona to sing the national hymn of Catalonia, "Els Segadors," on camera. Some participants could not quite remember the lyrics of this 19th-century national-romantic musical rendering of the Catalan Revolt of 1640, known as the War of the Reapers or the *Guerra dels Segadors*. Others did not quite remember the tune; some gleefully adapted the song to other musical styles, including rap, salsa, and fado; but all were emphatic in their performance of the climactic chorus: "Bon cop de falç, defensors de la terra!" ("Strike with your sickle, defenders of the land!"). At the time, the anthem anchored competing debates about the appropriate performance of Catalan identity: at the very moment that the government was solidifying efforts to institutionalize Catalan as an official language in the long aftermath of its prohibition under Franco, including teaching this anthem in public schools, Catalonia was experiencing increased migration from Africa, Latin America, and Eastern Europe, a growing population that seemed to threaten the cohesiveness of Catalan identity. Once understood as resistance to the hegemonic Spanish state, strident defenses of the

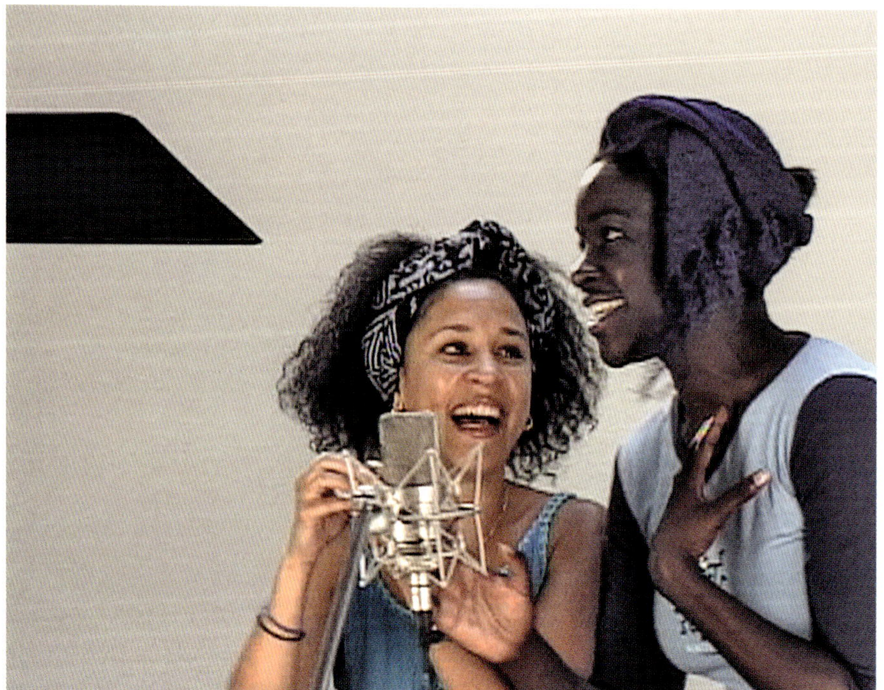

Els Segadors (The Reapers), 2001, video

Catalan language seemed to guard instead against the inevitable diversity produced under the pressure of neoliberal globalization. What does a fulsome performance of "Els Segadors" by the child of a Black migrant from Equatorial Guinea mean in this context? Or by the daughter of those migrants from Andalucía or Galicia who moved to the region in the 1950s with the support of the Franco regime, intent on diluting the pool of Catalan speakers? The resulting video by Fusco captures a range of such performances and the various singers' reflections on whether they are perceived to be authentically Catalan—and most agree they are not. The daughter of the Equatoguinean migrant, born in Catalonia, says she is still congratulated daily for her excellent command of Catalan, a result of "being Black in a world of whites." The daughter of Galician migrants complains that her slightly imperfect Catalan accent has barred her entry to the prestigious theater institute. Another warns that nationalism can quickly turn to racism. Still another, with green hair and earrings, says, "It means nothing to me."

By definition a national anthem is a command performance through which a government or national entity conscripts bodies into a certain behavior, style, and affect. Through these imperfect renderings of the anthem in Fusco's video, we see each performance as a vehicle for a precariously held sense of belonging, shaped by aspiration, obligation, and identification or, in many of these cases, disidentification. Together they conjure the unevenly occupied terrain that is a national community, especially one not fully anchored by the apparatus of a state, as an autonomous region within the larger nation state of Spain. Here the "nation" is no more and no less than the tenuous affect and accent of its citizens' performance. A space—a kind of interval—opens between the imagined song and its embodied rendering; in that interval we glimpse the capillary process by which ideologies of power are mapped onto, enacted, and negotiated by bodies. To the degree that such renderings are always iterations of an absent original, in that interval we also see the theatricality that attends the workings of such power. Fusco's long career as an interdisciplinary and conceptual artist has frequently entered just this space, using performance—often her own body in performance—to explore the complex dynamics through which bodies are marked by power. Grounded most often in the context of the Americas, and in close dialogue with both American and Latin American performance art and cultural theory, her work has long sought to illuminate the workings of colonial and state power, presenting bodies in the crosshairs of colonial and state modalities of knowing, surveilling, categorizing, and seeing "others."

* * *

In 2013, audiences at The Studio Museum in Harlem listened attentively to a formal lecture by a renowned psychologist, introduced by the esteemed technoscience philosopher Donna Haraway, on predatory behavior in humans. Drawing on primatology, neuroscience, and evolutionary biology, the 45-minute lecture analyzed how aggression and predatory behavior inform humans' accumulation of resources, illustrated with slides of exemplary animal and human anatomy and behavior. The psychologist noted, for example, that humans' exceptional capacity for complex thought and language enables them to exercise particularly intricate forms of non-physical aggression, including passive aggression, defamation, and gaslighting. It might have been an unremarkable if interesting lecture were it not for the fact that the speaker was none other than Dr. Zira, the famous chimp psychologist from the 1968 film *Planet of the Apes*, who has, we were told, finally returned after years in hiding to share the results of extended research on human aggression. As Haraway noted, it was only now, in a climate newly open to interspecies relations, that Dr. Zira could share the results of her research.

Unlike recent prequels to the *Planet of the Apes* series, in this performance and in a subsequent TED talk parody entitled *TED Ethology: Primate Visions of the Human Mind* (2015), Fusco made no attempt to update the costume or makeup techniques of the chimpanzee's cinematic representation, instead replicating the late 1960s aesthetic of the films faithfully, thereby playing with the character's anachronism in both the past and the present: she is the ape from the future who traveled back in time (as per the third *Planet of the Apes* film), and a re-enactment of late 1960s sci-fi representation of an "other" people. Made in the hothouse years of 1968 to 1973, the *Apes* films activate a series of cross-racial fantasies and tropes that have historically structured our understandings of race and the limits of the human. This was most salient in the famous kiss between Dr. Zira (actually the white actress, Kim Hunter) and Taylor (Charlton Heston) toward the end of the first film, a kiss that, through the intense racialization of the chimpanzee characters, raised the specter of miscegenation that no doubt rippled through the day's reigning ideology of white supremacy. *Planet of the Apes* offers a world of reversals—the ape is civilized; the white man is savage—that performs the work of speculative fiction: it casts the problems of the present into a future in which alternate outcomes may be rehearsed and analyzed. Fusco, in turn, performs her own act of Afrofuturist appropriation, recoding that speculative past to project a future shaped and defined by Black experience.

The conceptual conceit is thus far more subtle than the fake chimpanzee hair or feet emerging from the *Star Trek*-inspired costume might suggest. Fusco plays against the artificiality and humor of the Zira impersonation as fully as possible; the lecture is as "straight" in its presentation as her costume is artificial, and the pleasure and discomfort of the piece lies precisely in this tension. Dividing *Homo sapiens* into categories humans often used to study other species, Dr. Zira finds that economic disparity is a form of violence, primarily enacted by the dominant "alpha" males and females against the majority "beta" population. She uses exactly and only the language used by the scientific community to study aggression in animals: we never hear the words neoliberalism, capitalism, exploitation, or wealth. "Excessive resource accumulation beyond any conceivable calculus of need"—what we might otherwise call making profit and exploiting others—is analyzed by Zira as a form of human aggression in which alpha humans deprive beta humans of resources needed for sustenance. Her tone is clinical, her interest in the subject scientific. Through an extended comparison between human and baboon aggressive tendencies, she turns evolutionary racism on its head: human social organization turns out to be not so different and certainly not more advanced than our evolutionary relatives. Dr. Zira finally answers the association of Africans to animal primates with evidence that it is in fact the alpha males of the species—typically white male humans—who bear the most resemblance to a certain genus of primates.

Donning the chimpanzee mask, Fusco effectively—and wryly—allows Zira to study the behavior of those who study animals, thereby reversing a relation of optic and epistemological power. This gesture—reversing the gaze in a field of unequal power—has characterized Fusco's trajectory. The most well-known of these pieces was the itinerant performance she created with Guillermo Gómez-Peña, entitled *Two Undiscovered Amerindians Visit the West* (1992–94), which explored

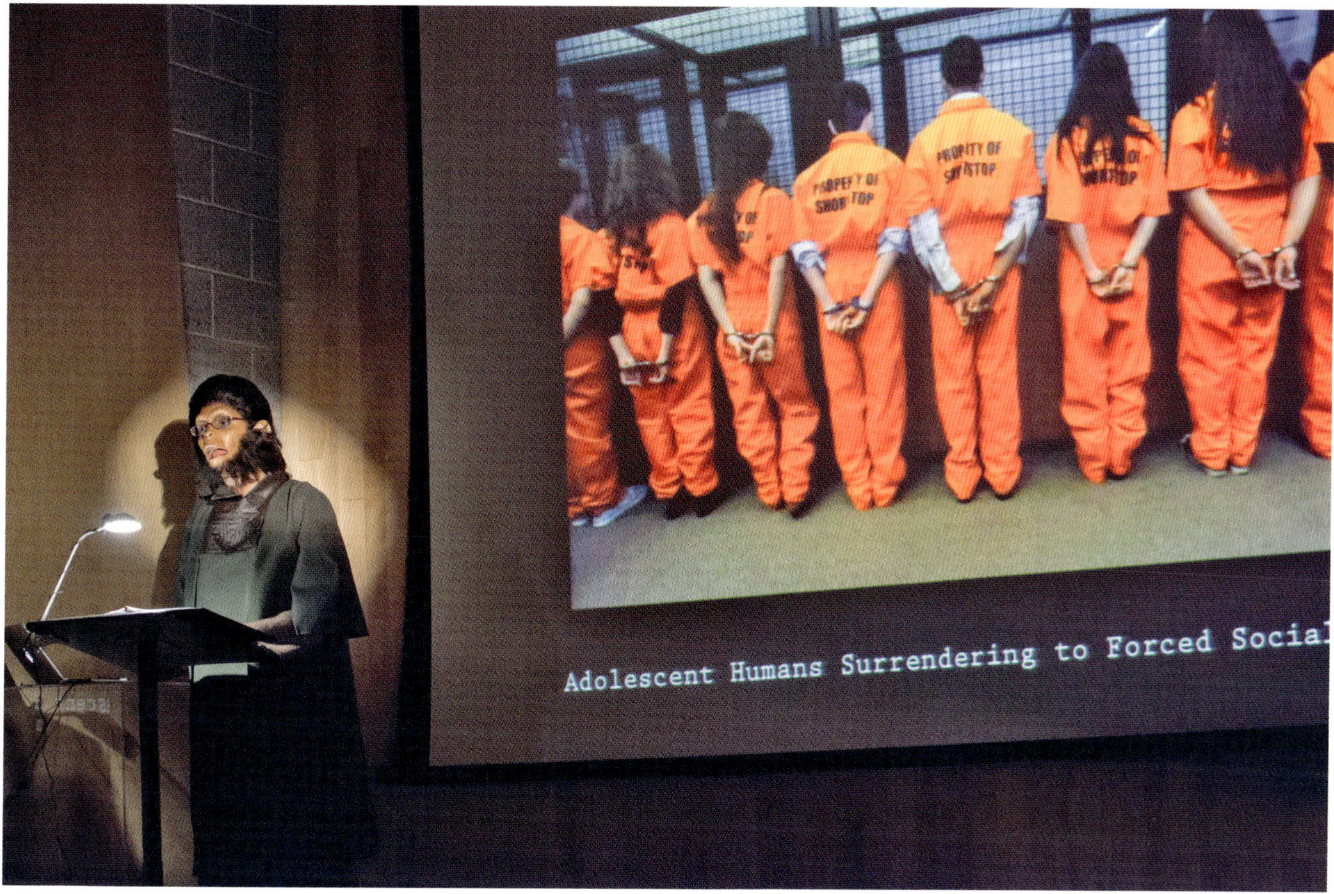

Observations of Predation in Humans: A Lecture by Dr. Zira, Animal Psychologist, 2013–16. Performance in the exhibition
"Radical Presence: Black Performance in Contemporary Art" at The Studio Museum in Harlem, 2013–14

the practice of the ethnographic display of Indigenous people throughout the history of European conquest and colonization. Created in parodic response to multicultural celebrations of the quincentenary of the so-called discovery of the Americas in 1992, Fusco and Gómez-Peña cast themselves as recently "discovered" Indians from an island in the Gulf of Mexico.

Playing with the supposed atemporality ascribed to nonwhite peoples, these anachronistic "Indians" performed in galleries or public spaces in the US and Europe—including Madrid's central plaza, Plaza Colón, named for Christopher Columbus—from inside a large cage. As with historic cases of display of non-western peoples in circuses and world's fairs, the audience was encouraged to interact with the "natives" for a fee—one dollar for a photograph, another to hand feed them, and five dollars for a view of the "male specimen's" genitalia. The unexpected twist was that some members of the audience believed that the performers were, in fact, "real savages," which led the artists to document not only their performance but also the audience's reactions, resulting in Fusco's video documentary, *The Couple in the Cage: A Guatinaui Odyssey* (1993). In this and other works Fusco has explored, in her words, how "the very Western notion of the 'primitive' that emerged during the Enlightenment informs not only anthropology but also Euro-American modernism and postmodernism."[1]

For Nicholas Mirzoeff, "the performative claim of a right to look where none exists" is a practice of counter-visuality that challenges the dominant modality

1   Coco Fusco, "Artist Statement," Associação Cultural Videobrasil, June 2005, http://site.videobrasil.org.br/en/acervo/artistas/textos/212646.

2   Nicholas Mirzoeff, *The Right to Look: A Counterhistory of Visuality* (Durham: Duke University Press, 2011): 24, 3.

3   Coco Fusco, "The Other History of Intercultural Performance," *TDR*, vol. 38, no. 1 (Spring, 1994): 143–67.

4   See Aníbal Quijano, "Coloniality of Power, Eurocentrism, and Latin America," *Nepantla: Views from South*, vol. 1, no. 3 (2000): 533–80. Quijano proposed his notion of "coloniality" in "Colonialidad y modernidad/racionalidad," in *Perú Indígena*, vol. 13, no. 29 (1992), later elaborated into the "coloniality of power" in works such as "Colonialidad del poder, globalización y democracia," *Trayectorias: Revista De Ciencias Sociales De La Universidad Autónoma De Nuevo León* (Mexico), no. 4 (2002). These debates are well captured in the anthology *Coloniality at Large: Latin America and the Postcolonial Debate* (Durham: Duke University Press, 2014).

5   See Joaquín Barriendos, "La Colonialidad Del Ver: Hacia Un Nuevo Diálogo Visual Interepistémico," *Nómadas* (Bogotá: 2011): 13–29. Note that Eduardo Mendieta has used the phrase "coloniality of embodiment" to describe Fusco's work in his excellent essay "The Coloniality of Embodiment: Coco Fusco's Postcolonial Genealogies and Semiotic Agonistics," in *Unmaking Race, Remaking Soul: Transformative Aesthetics and the Practice of Freedom* (Albany: State University of New York Press, 2007), edited by Christa D. Acampora and Angela L. Cotten, 141–58.

THE CAGE - 1994 - BUENOS AIRES
COCO FUSCO & GUILLERMO GÓMEZ PEÑA

Coco Fusco and Guillermo Gómez-Peña, *Two Undiscovered Amerindians Visit Buenos Aires*, 1994, performance. Photograph with Leandro Katz

of visuality that, through practices of naming and categorization, "separates and segregates those it visualizes to prevent them from cohering as political subjects."[2] In her influential essay about the project, "The Other History of Intercultural Performance,"[3] Fusco described this as a process of using performance or media installation to illuminate the "colonial unconscious" that otherwise organizes so much representation and consumption of "other" cultures and peoples. In so doing she anticipated debates among Latin American theorists, notably the Uruguayan theorist Aníbal Quijano, on the "coloniality of power" that marks the inequitable colonial structures of power that characterize social formations long after colonialism as a political structure has ended.[4] Fusco's work has sought to excavate and illuminate the presence and workings of colonial modalities of seeing and consuming others—what we might in turn call, via the art critic Joaquin Barriendos, the "coloniality of seeing."[5]

   CORPOREALITY AND CRITIQUE

6 Coco Fusco, *The Bodies That Were Not Ours: And Other Writings* (London: Routledge/Iniva, 2001): 6.

7 Joseph Roach, *Cities of the Dead: Circum-Atlantic Performance* (New York: Columbia University Press, 1996).

8 Coco Fusco, "Performing the institutionalization of 'Bare Life,'" http://archive.hemisphericinstitute.org/journal/3.1/eng/artist_presentation/cocofusco/index.html.

Undiscovered Amerindians impacted debates in theater and performance studies around performance practice in the late 1980s and 1990s, then called "multicultural," "postcolonial," and, especially, "intercultural." This latter is most associated with the influential theater practice of Eugenio Barba and his International School of Theatre Anthropology, and in the critical writings of Patrice Pavis, whose *Intercultural Performance Reader* (1996) found fast reception in many theater syllabi eager to "update" a curriculum otherwise lacking international dimension beyond Europe. In broad strokes, this theater proposed interculturalism as a modality to bridge a West/East divide, often looking for "universal" performance lexica that precede codification into distinct cultural forms, seeking a mode of "authentic" theatrical presence. For noted directors like Peter Brook or Ariane Mnouchkine, such practice enabled them to draw on "eastern" performance repertoires in their staging of both "western" and "eastern" classics. Looking to the non-West for palliative access to pre-modern expression is, of course, a common Orientalizing gesture of modernism in both art and theater; what is new in this formulation is the collaborative work with international artists and the celebratory insistence that such practice may transcend the "disfiguring" impact of politics and power. Fusco marks "living display" as the first practice of intercultural performance, quite opposed to the self-congratulatory practices of "multicultural exchange" that underline this theater work and that of many celebratory museum exhibitions under the sign of "multiculturalism" in the early 1990s. "Intercultural" practice, she suggests, usually replicates a "West and the rest" binary rather than transcend it.

Further, Fusco suggests that this history of forced exhibition is the relevant historical context in which to understand the development of performance art in particular, especially by artists of color. Through living display, colonized subjects like Saartje Baartman (the so-called "Hottentot Venus") were asked to perform "themselves" and open their bodies to public scrutiny long before such self-referential or explicit performance was the hallmark of body art. In *The Bodies That Were Not Ours: And Other Writings* (2001) she makes a parallel argument about the Black body in performance, arguing that "the interrelationship of nudity, enslavement, and public display of the black body is historically linked to the spectacles of the auction block and of lynching." Contemporary performances by Black artists by necessity iterate and comment upon the "physical, sexual and commercial exploitation of black bodies."[6] We could describe such a performance process as, following Joseph Roach, surrogation; for Roach, surrogation names the imbricated relation of performance, memory, and substitution, whereby postcolonial cultures of the circum-Atlantic index and remake their violent histories of conquest, colonialism, and slavery.[7] When Fusco impersonates Zira or the undiscovered Indian, her body becomes the embodied surrogate for the racialized subjects of a long colonial history that is re-iterated through this very process of impersonation. Through her writing and her performances, then, Fusco suggests that performance art is especially suited both to index and critique the histories of racial and gender violence that have been deeply coded into the ways we both inhabit and interpret the physical body.

Between 2005 and 2008, Fusco appealed to the surveilled body to explore more recent scenarios of intercultural performance: the clandestine military interrogation rooms where US soldiers and officers interacted with predominantly Arab prisoners during the War on Terror. "For many American soldiers," Fusco writes, "these prisons are the only places where they actually confront the enemy face to face. The interrogation room of the American military prison is the main stage."[8] As controversial images of torture and ritualized humiliation emerged from Abu Ghraib prison in 2004, including those of women acting as perpetrators of such torture, Fusco asked, what is the precise dynamic of power, visibility, and subjection on this new stage? What colonial unconscious is visited upon these new inhabitants of America's cage? Fusco explored these questions in several works: *Bare Life Study #1* (2005), which references Giorgio Agamben's provocative notion of the state's ability to reduce at will citizens to their "bare life," was a group street performance in Brazil that used routine methods of humiliation in military prisons as choreography. *Operation Atropos* (2006) is a 59-minute film about the experience she and a group of collaborators had training with retired military interrogators. *A Room of One's Own: Women and Power in the New America* (2006–08) is a theatrical monologue that satirically celebrates the new opportunities afforded to women in these scenes of military encounter: barred from most combat roles, women are nonetheless allowed protagonizing roles as interrogators. Like *Observations of Predation in Humans: A Lecture by Dr. Zira, Animal Psychologist* (2013–16), this piece is staged as a lecture, here given by Fusco in the role of an implacable military officer who offers detailed guidance to female interrogators on how to use gender and sex to their strategic advantage both in the interrogation room and for their career advancement, while the audience watches a detainee in an adjacent interrogation room via CCTV. Based on actual practices authorized by the CIA under the rubric of "invasion of space by a female," these strategies include the women performing unwanted sexual acts or smearing fake menstrual blood on Muslim prisoners

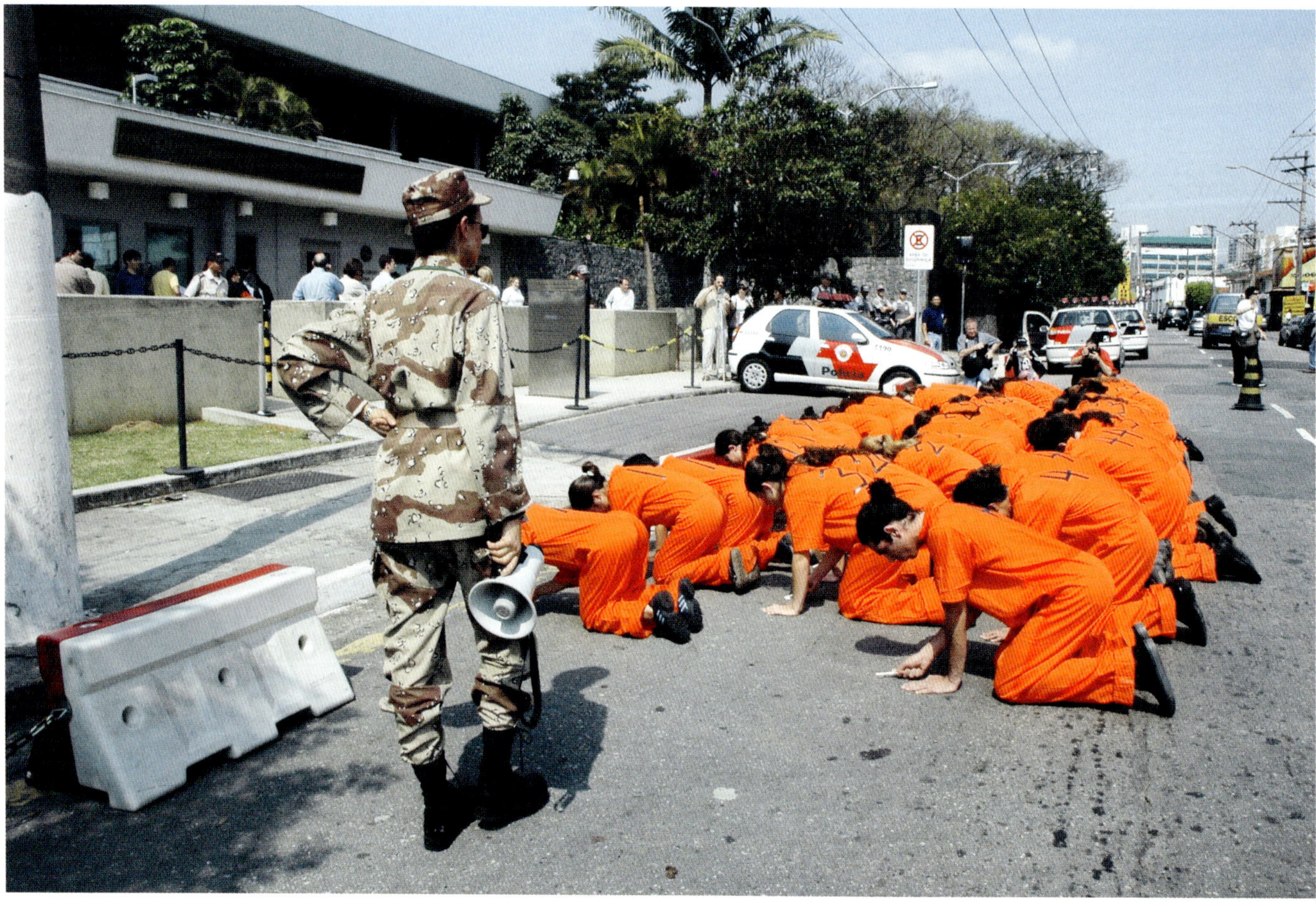

Bare Life Study #1, 2005, **performance**

CORPOREALITY AND CRITIQUE

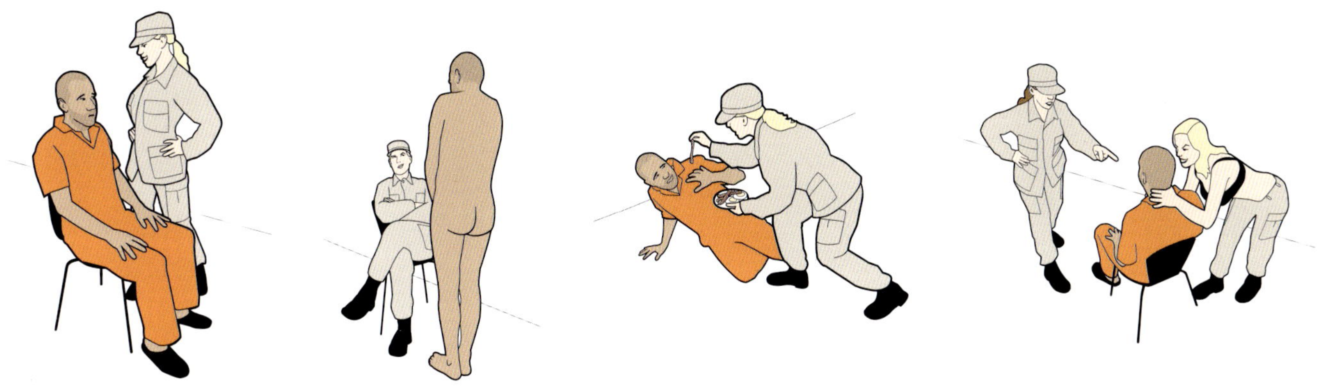

A Field Guide for Female Interrogators, 2008, publication. Illustrations by Daniel Turner

imagined to be specially humiliated by such acts. A critical reflection on these works written as a letter to Virginia Woolf along with a text of this performance were then published as *A Field Guide for Female Interrogators* in 2008. Together these works ask how gathering intelligence about another culture in the interrogation room became "an opportunity for using gender and sex as punishment."[9] Here Fusco switches sides to become the surrogate for military power rather than its victim, challenging the anti-war rhetoric's facile identification with the victim and not the violence enacted in its name.

Fusco has turned to interrogation as a primal scene of contemporary power in several works, notably in her 2001 durational net.art performance with Ricardo Dominguez, *Dolores 10 to 22*, and the related 2002 video, *Dolores from 10 to 10*, which restages the 12-hour punitive confinement of a real world maquila worker and activist by her employer, as well as in the 2004 video *a/k/a Mrs. George Gilbert*, about the surveillance apparatus deployed in the hunt for Angela Davis in 1969 and 1970.

In *Dolores*, audiences only access the performance via an internet broadcast of closed-circuit TV; in *Mrs. George Gilbert*, the camera mimics and multiplies grainy surveillance footage of unnamed Black women in the search for the elusive Angela as we listen to a lead FBI investigator narrate his frustrated attempts to find her. Both implicate the viewer as voyeur: in *Dolores*, internet audiences were invited to propose via chat how the menacing male employer and female worker should interact in subsequent scenes, and some readily suggested that he increase his sexualized aggression. *Mrs. George Gilbert* casts the viewer in part in the position of the FBI investigator; like the investigator, who ultimately confesses his desire for Angela, we too survey the evidence and wonder whether and how the "real" Angela might be revealed to us. Both underscore Fusco's contention that both surveillance and voyeurism inherently theatricalize their subjects,[10] again suggesting the importance of performance as a medium to critique these regimes. Together these two works explore the dynamics of hegemonic surveillance through a strategy that Simone Browne, following Steve Mann, has called "dark sousveillance," where "sousveillance" names "an active inversion of the power relations that surveillance entails." For Browne, "dark sousveillance" is practice informed by "black epistemologies of contending with antiblack surveillance" which create oppositional and, at times, more hopeful imaginaries.[11] *Dolores* uses fictional CCTV to create an archival record that did not exist, thereby allowing the maquila worker's otherwise suppressed resistance to enter

9   Coco Fusco, *A Field Guide for Female Interrogators* (New York: Seven Stories Press, 2008): 47.

10 Coco Fusco, "On-line Simulations/Real-Life Politics: a Discussion with Ricardo Dominguez on Staging Virtual Theatre," *TDR*, vol. 47, no. 2 (Summer 2003): 161. For an excellent analysis of *Dolores*, see Candice Amich, *Precarious Forms: Performing Utopia in the Neoliberal Americas* (Evanston: Northwestern University Press, 2020).

11 Simone Brown, *Dark Matters: On the Surveillance of Blackness* (Durham NC: Duke University Press, 2015): 19, 21.

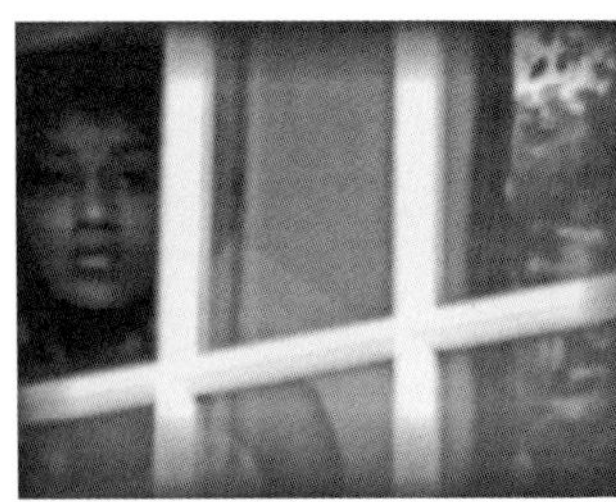
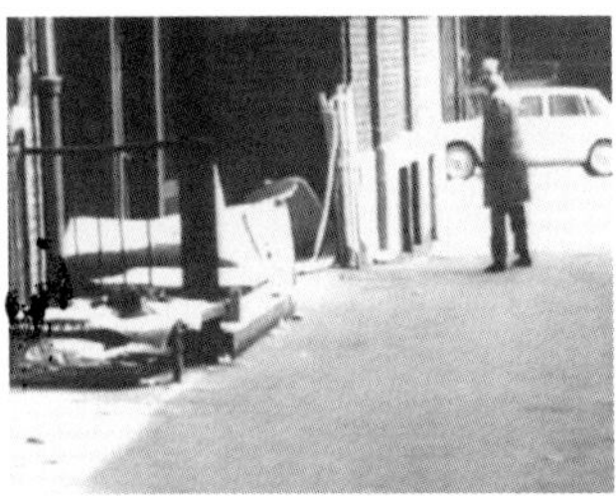

a/k/a Mrs. George Gilbert,
2004, video

into social memory. In *Mrs. George Gilbert*, Fusco deliberately mixes declassified evidence—records and still photos—from the archives with fictional surveillance footage, with the latter serving to defamiliarize and destabilize the supposed objectivity of the former. Both suggest that technology is never disinterested and is itself a site for the articulation of gendered and racialized power.

Throughout her career as an artist and also as a curator and critic, Fusco has explored how performance has offered a special modality of critique in contexts where the State exercises power on and through the bodies of its citizens. In her field-defining work *Corpus Delecti: Performance Art of the Americas* (2000), Fusco illuminates a genealogy of Latin American and Latinx performance art whose animating force is the deployment of the body "in public space as a symbolic confrontation with the state."[12] This text, along with the 1997 ICA exhibition on which it expands, was the first to visualize such a history[13] and effectively articulated the relevant hemispheric referents for her own work. *Corpus Delecti* captures what Mexican performance critic Antonio Prieto Stambaugh would later call the "political corporeality" of Latin American performance art, a corporality that "confronts power through a skin transformed into a parchment disseminating questions," questions that emerge, like scars on skin tissue, when an artist reveals the "traces that the exercise of hegemonic power leaves on his or her body."[14] Fusco has engaged this political corporeality in the context of Cuba where, she argues in her equally field-defining text *Dangerous Moves: Performance and Politics in Cuba* (2015), "proper conduct"—*conducta propia*—has functioned as a privileged currency through which Cubans navigate the exigencies of a surveillance state. She argues that since 1959 the anticapitalist and anti-imperialist ideology of the Cuban state has promised shelter, education, and health care for its citizens, but at same time, "the Cuban state has forged revolutionary conduct by means of restraints upon the bodies of its citizenry, imposing limits on social interaction, behaviour, speech and physical movement on the one hand, and demanding continuous performance of consensus through collective displays of cooperation with state policy and voluntary labour on the other."[15] Proper conduct is an embodied currency wielded in the absence of other commodities, and performance art has become its artistic correlative, an "arena for challenging the ways in which conduct was shaped, valued or condemned."[16]

In recent works Fusco follows in this line of practice, using video and performance both to speak back to the Cuban state, for which she has been censured, and to excavate an archive of dissident performance in Cuba, with a series of works focused on Heberto Padilla (*La confesión*, *The Confession*, 2015; *La sombra de Herberto Padilla*, *Padilla's Shadow*, 2021), María Elena Cruz Varela (*La botella al mar de María*

12 Coco Fusco, *Corpus Delecti: Performance Art of the Americas* (London: Routledge, 2000): 8.

13 It was followed notably in 2008 by the exhibition and catalog "Arte ≠ Vida: Actions by Artists of the Americas 1960–2000," curated and edited by Deborah Cullen at the Museo del Barrio in New York City.

14 Antonio Prieto Stambaugh, "Corporalidades políticas: representación, frontera y sexualidad en el performance mexicano," in Diana Taylor and Marcela Fuentes, eds, *Estudios Avanzados De Performance*, (Mexico City: DF Fondo De Cultura Económica, 2011): 607–28. Author's translation.

15 Coco Fusco, *Dangerous Moves: Performance and Politics in Cuba* (London: Tate Publishing, 2015): 10.

16 Fusco, *Dangerous Moves*, 34.

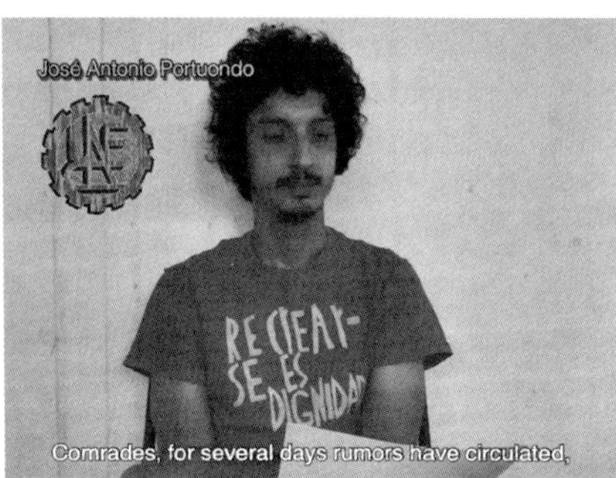

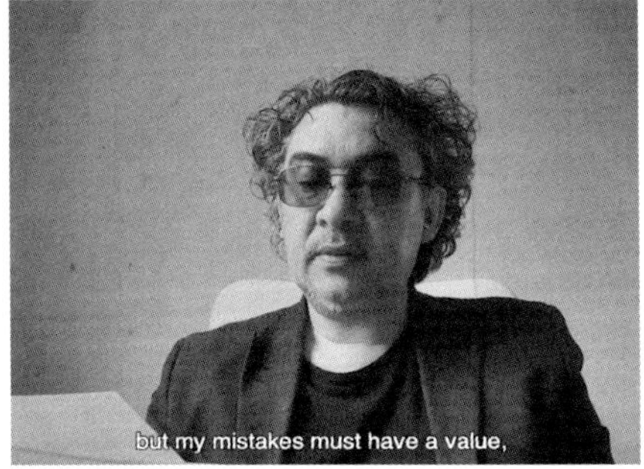

La sombra de Herberto Padilla (Padilla's Shadow), 2021, video

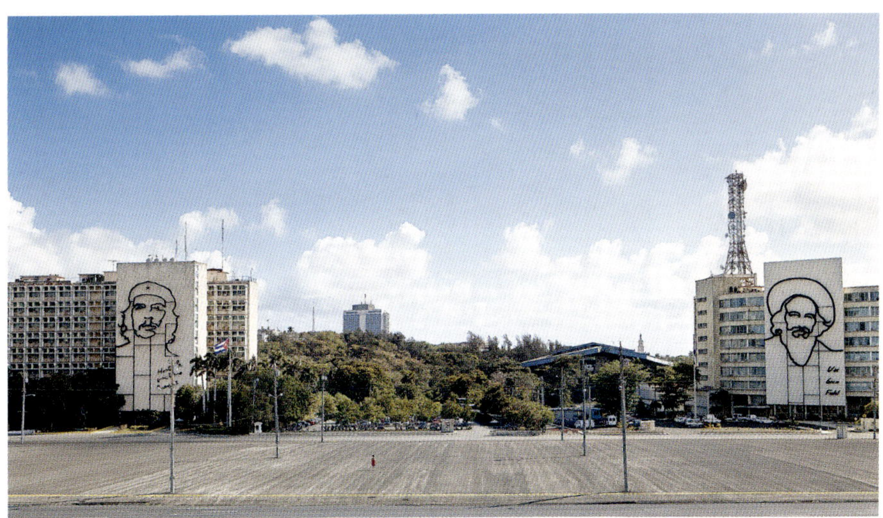

La plaza vacía (The Empty Plaza), 2012, video

Elena, The Message in a Bottle from María Elena, 2015), and Reinaldo Arenas (*Vivir en junio con la lengua afuera, To Live in June with Your Tongue Hanging Out*, 2018).

The limpid *La plaza vacía* (*The Empty Plaza*, 2012) may be imagined as a beginning to this Cuban cycle and a synecdoche for her practice as a whole. This 11-minute video ruminates on the emptiness of Cuba's Plaza de la Revolución, a space expressly maintained by the state for mass political gatherings; through the voiceover text written by well-known Cuban dissident journalist Yoani Sánchez, we learn that such demonstrations of revolutionary fervor are not spontaneous but rather are command performances required of Cubans by the state as part of their daily lives. It is, as it were, the space of proper conduct par excellence. Flanked by giant iron images of the Revolution's martyrs, Camilo Cienfuegos and Che Guevara, and surveyed by a giant central marble statue of the imagined father of the nation, José Martí, the square is home to nesting vultures rather than citizens, who avoid the unbearable heat of its vast asphalt. The camera captures the square as darkness descends, the marble cools, the vultures fold their wings, and low lights gradually illuminate Che and Camilo. A question haunts this empty plaza. Filmed at just the time when the streets and squares of the Global South, Europe, or the US had been occupied with fervent citizen bodies during the Arab Spring, Occupy Wall Street, and other global protests of *indignados*, what do we make of the emptiness of Cuba's plaza? Why, indeed, was there no Cuban Spring? If *Els Segadors* (*The Reapers*, 2001), framed citizenship in that fragile interval between an idealized anthem and its improper performance, *La plaza vacía* looks in vain for such agency in the openness of the empty space, haunted by archival footage of Fidel's May First parades and political marches.

The video includes several frames, shot from varying distances, of Fusco herself standing in the heart of the empty plaza. In most her red dress is a bright but tiny mark against the immensity of the plaza. The image prompts more questions. What can one body do alone in politically haunted space? What can one artist do in a landscape deeply coded by power? What challenges emerge from the parchment that is this artist's skin? Coco Fusco's trajectory has answered just these questions, rendering and illuminating the body as a site of contestation over knowledge and power and as a source of performative critique.

Inverting the Frame

Anna Gritz

Time is an infrastructure because it is a condition of possibility for conscious perception and action; infrastructure is made out of time insofar as infrastructure is that which repeats. The repetition is normalized into everyday routine, and when it stops functioning, an aperture is cut into its artifice—through which history and power relations can be seen.
—Marina Vishmidt [1]

We Need New Institutions, Not New Art
—Coco Fusco [2]

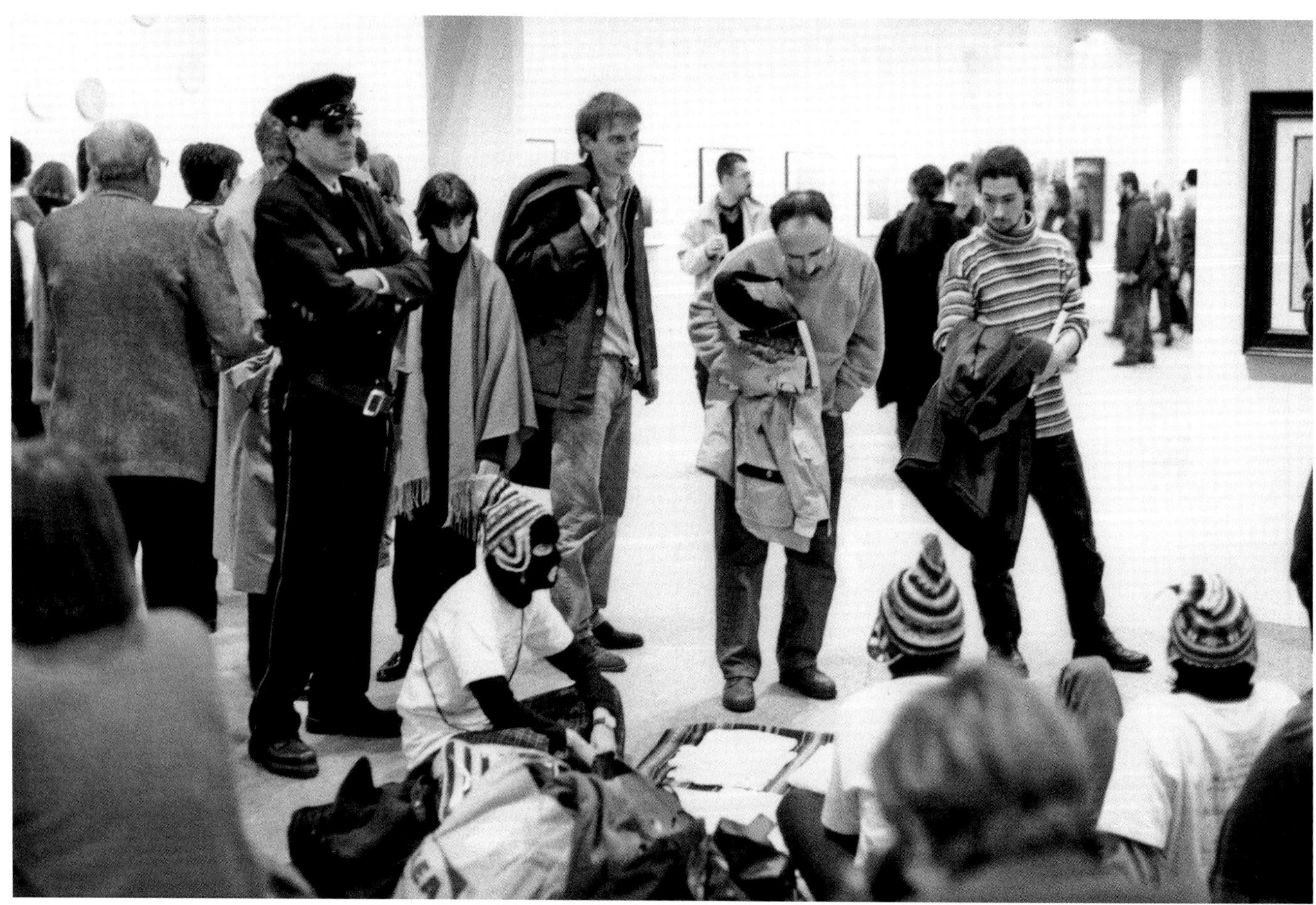

Coco Fusco, María Elena Escalona, Juan Pablo Ballester, and Vladimir Cuenca, *Sudaca Enterprises*, 1997, performance

In 1997 three artists equipped with ski masks and Quechua knit hats, and a fourth dressed as a police officer, entered the ARCO art fair in Madrid and set up an alternative *tianguis*-style market among the neatly arranged grid of booths of the various participating galleries. Arranging blankets directly on the floor of the neon-lit fair, they went about selling a selection of T-shirts in an impromptu, guerrilla-style manner. That year ARCO, in line with a larger awakening of the global art market's interests in production from Latin America, had opened its selection process with the goal of championing art made in the region. Concurrently, however, a change in Spain's immigration policy was implemented that made it exceedingly difficult for immigrants and refugees from Latin America to enter the country and that stifled the support from the Spanish government.[3]

Coco Fusco had been asked to speak at the fair and took the invitation as an opportunity to comment on the apparent dichotomy of these two agendas. The work *Sudaca Enterprises* (1997), conceived by Fusco with Juan Pablo Ballester, María Elena Escalona, and Vladimir Cuenca, ripped a hole in the well-oiled and polished capitalist infrastructure of the art fair. With the help of a human rights lawyer, the group attained information about the legal status of Latin American immigrants in Spain, which became the basis for texts printed on T-shirts offered for sale. Comparing the costs of selling art at ARCO with the living expenses of an undocumented Latin American immigrant in Spain, the shirts stated statistical information,[4] like:

> What you have to have in your bank account to get Spanish citizenship:
> 1,000,000 pesetas
>
> What a fake passport costs:
> 1,000,000 pesetas
>
> What galleries pay per square meter of space at ARCO'97:
> 17,000 pesetas
>
> What a Sudaca is charged as a fee for obtaining a lease:
> 150,000 pesetas

Here, the artists attained the term "sudaca"—or "dirty southerner," an insult customarily used in Spain to refer to Latinos— to emphasize the double standard perpetuated by the fair. The work lays bare both the fair's exclusive selection process, one that privileges galleries that can afford the high fees, and the tendency for art world trends to trail previously underrated markets. In this case the underlying market forces that propelled the increased circulation of Latin American art cynically coincided with policies that limited the movement of people. Over three days of the fair, the group frequently clashed with officials and was repeatedly removed by security personnel. It did however manage to sell all of the T-shirts, some even to museum collections and, by doing so, undermined the regulated acquisition principles at the core of the art fair model.

Since the 1980s, Fusco has immersed her practice in the infrastructures that condition the presentation, circulation, and value production of art (invited and uninvited), and to this day her work continues to present an acute analysis of how colonial histories dictate the frameworks under which conceptions of identity and cultural difference are constructed. This essay seeks to reconsider Fusco's approach through the prism of strategies of institutional and infrastructural critique in light

1   Marina Vishmidt, "Between Not Everything and Not Nothing: Cuts Toward Infrastructural Critique," *Former West: Art and the Contemporary After 1989* (Cambridge: MIT Press, 2017): 265–69.

2   Coco Fusco, "We Need New Institutions, Not New Art," *Hyperallergic*, October 26, 2020, https://hyperallergic.com/596864/ford-foundation-creative-futures-coco-fusco/.

3   Francisco Javier Ullán de la Rosa, *Immigration and Immigration Policies in Spain, in Migration in an Era of Restriction and Recession: Sending and Receiving Nations in a Changing Global Environment* (New York: Springer Publishing, 2015), https://www.researchgate.net/publication/303362376_Immigration_and_Immigration_Policies_in_Spain_in_Migration_in_an_Era_of_Restriction_and_Recession_Sending_and_Receiving_Nations_in_a_Changing_Global_Environment_David_L_Leal_Nestor_P_Rodriguez_eds_Spr.

4   Coco Fusco, *The Bodies That Were Not Ours: And Other Writings* (London: Routledge/Iniva): 177–78.

of her interventions in (art) institutions and in dialogue with a selection of artistic practices operating on the boundaries of the institutional reach. Prompted by Fusco, I want to question the usage of the term "activism" versus "institutional critique," here based on what Fusco calls "a cultural, racial divide." She states that "when the inquiry is perceived as just being about museological language in relation to modernist traditions, then it is institutional critique, but when it is an interrogation of museological language in relation to colonial practices and racism, then it's activism—so what I get is when I do it it's activism, when Andrea Fraser does it it's institutional critique."[5] Resultantly, the question of which direction we operate from is a main focus point here—questioning the biased separation between, on one hand, practices that have been identified as coming from "outside" the system as "activism" and, on the other, those determined as coming from the "inside" as "critique."

Sudaca Enterprises proves characteristic of many of Fusco's works over the years and exemplifies a recurring strategy employed in her practice: that of contrasting two interconnected mechanisms, allowing the intervention of one within the other to reveal the structural inequalities at play. Fusco's unsolicited insertion of *Sudaca Enterprises* into the mechanisms of an art fair highlights the incongruities of its conceptual framework in interplay with larger governmental policies and chimes with the discussion of infrastructural critique by the theorist Marina Vishmidt. Vishmidt constructs her definition of infrastructure based on that which repeats: the mechanisms that sustain the status quo. She draws on the image of the dumbwaiter that architecture theorist Reinhold Martin conjures in his analysis of "infrastructure as a regime of intelligibility."[6] For Martin, the service of the dumbwaiter is illustrative of an infrastructure that only becomes apparent when its inherent repetition comes to an end. "If the wine ceases to appear, at some level and only for an instant, the entire apparatus of slavery comes into view. When you turn on the faucet and water does not flow, the entire water system leaps into the cognitive field."[7] Vishmidt locates the shift from an institutional to an infrastructural critique in the "pervasive tendency to prioritize the 'real' (the irreducible, the traumatic, the chaotic) over the delimited, instrumental impact over symbolic action, agency over indexicality."[8] She calls for an engagement with the real conditions that sustain the institution and its critique, such as "local and global labor markets, corporate power, property development, in as much as they manifest the structural violence of capitalism, racism, and gender, which is so often mediated by the reckless expansionism of art markets and spaces."[9] This text seeks to trace such "real" tactics in Fusco's practice alongside those by other artists in light of their tendency to bridge questions of representation in art institutions with larger governmental metrics and, in doing so, denying the art world its isolated status and revealing its complicity and propensity to reproduce larger structural inequalities.

More than twenty-five years before Fusco's intervention at ARCO, four Chicano artists in East Los Angeles ended up forming the erratic artists collective Asco, derived from "*me da asco*" ("it [your art] disgusts me"). One of the group's most iconic interventions was the tagging of the Los Angeles County Museum of Art (LACMA). One evening in 1972, Harry Gamboa Jr., Gronk (aka Guglio Nicandro), and Willie Herrón III went about spray-painting their names on the front entrance of LACMA, thereby appropriating the institution as a work of their own. *Spray Paint LACMA* (1972), also referred to as *Project Pie in De/Face*, was a direct response to a statement by a LACMA curator who dismissed all Chicano art

5   Coco Fusco, conversation with the author, October 15, 2021.

6   Vishmidt, 266.

7   Isabelle Graw, Reinhold Martin, and André Rottmann, "Do Media Determine Our Situation? Reflections on the Transatlantic Reception of Friedrich Kittler," *Texte zur Kunst*, no. 98, June 2015, 76.

8   Vishmidt, 266.

9   Vishmidt, 267.

   INVERTING THE FRAME

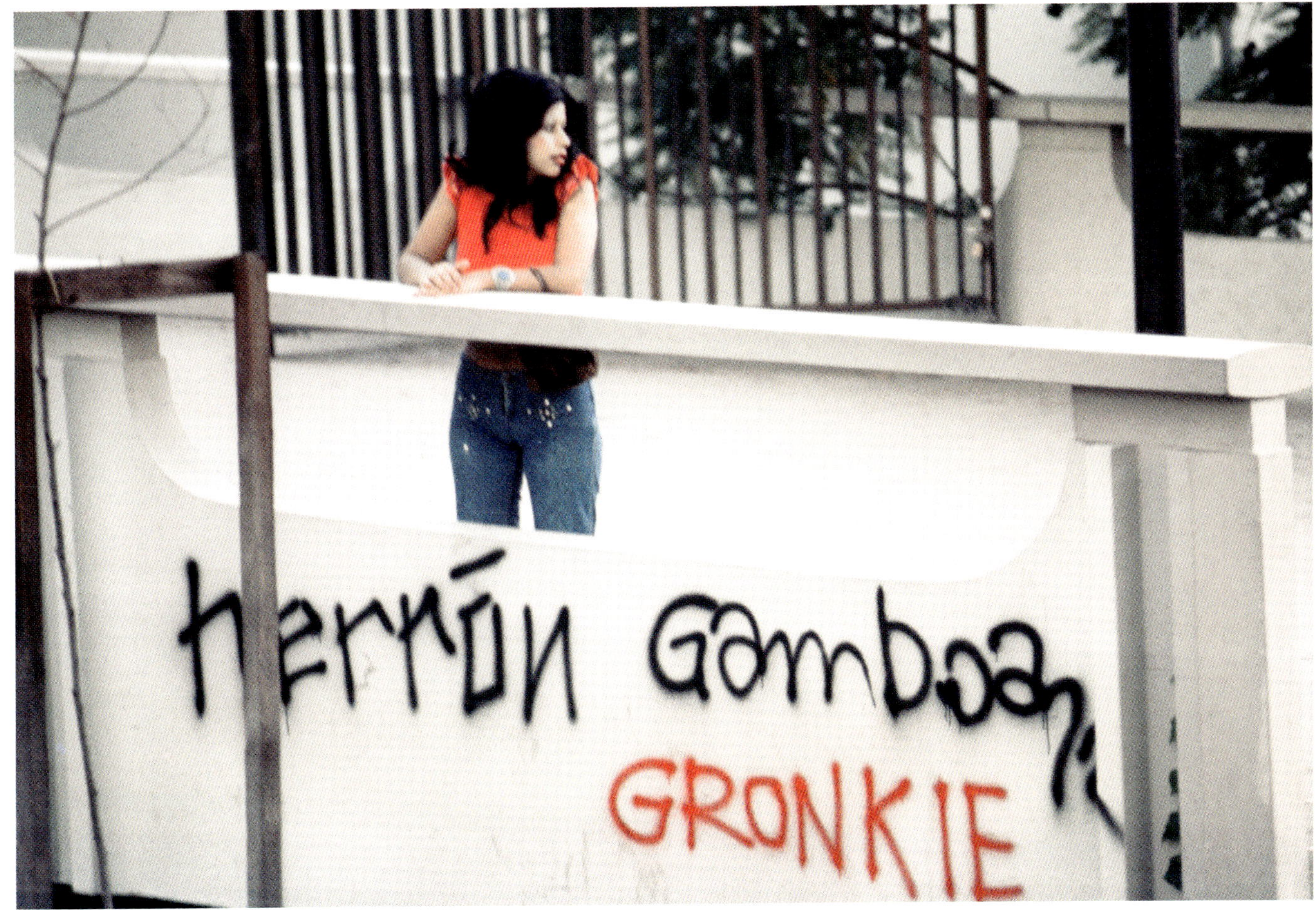

Asco, *Spray Paint LACMA*, 1972

as graffiti, rather than art, when asked to justify the absence of Chicano art in the museum's collection.[10] By signing the institution in spray paint, Asco therefore did not just claim its contents and history as its own, the collective undertook an act of annexation with the means of graffiti, claiming the defiant power of the medium while daring it to be taken seriously as an art form. As with *Sudaca Enterprises*, supposed shortcomings are readdressed as strengths and what is deemed to lie on the outside of the institution is used to question the principles that determine what is invited to be on the inside in the first place.

A few years after Asco's iconic signing, artist Christopher D'Arcangelo staged an unsolicited performance on the doorstep of another major American institution, questioning, again, its very boundaries. For his 1975 action, later titled *The Whitney Museum of American Art*, D'Arcangelo chained himself to the doors of the Whitney, obstructing the main entrance to the museum. A manifesto taped to his back read: "When I state that I am an anarchist, I must also state that I am not an anarchist, to be in keeping with the [....] idea of anarchism. Long live anarchism." The museum's response was to put a swift end to the intervention by rerouting visitors to a separate entrance while installing folding screens around the artist to cut him off from public view, effectively assembling a temporary white cube that extended the museum's footprint. The question of what qualifies as institutional critique lies at the core of this work. According to the reading by

10 The exclusion was therefore twofold, limiting Chicano art to the production of graffiti on one hand while disqualifying graffiti from being a possible medium that would qualify for the collection on the other. (See Chon Noriega, "Your Art Disgusts Me: Early Asco 1971–75," *East of Borneo*, November 18, 2010.

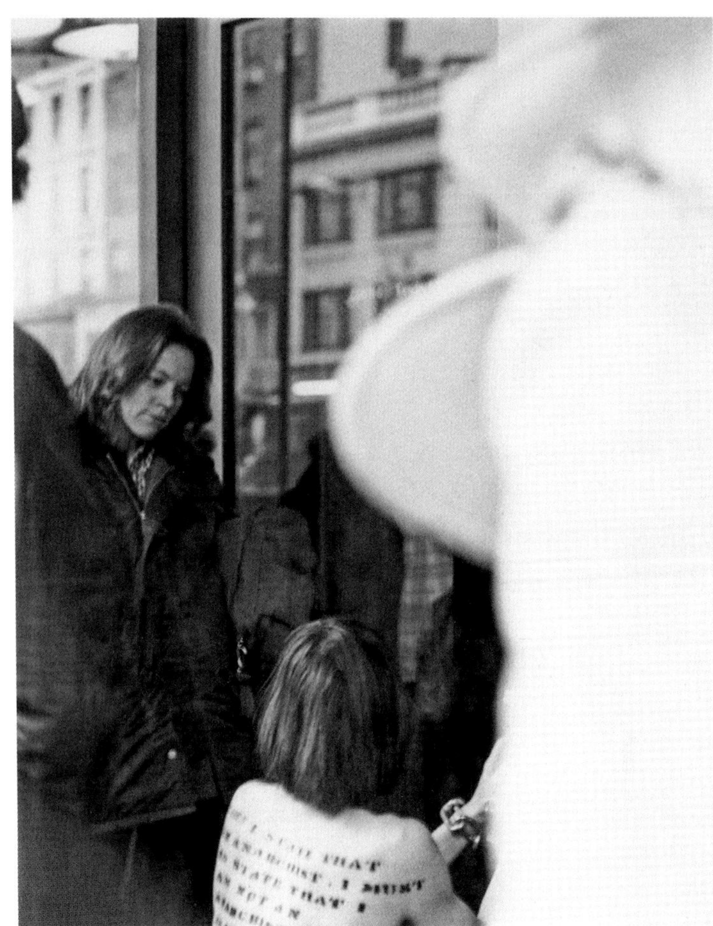

Christopher D'Arcangelo at the Whitney Museum of American Art, 1975

theorist Andreas Petrossiants, in order for the critique of the work to be neutralized, the museum first had to make D'Arcangelo's action a sanctioned "performance" by incorporating it into its "walls," only to then reject it.[11] It appears as if the act of institutional recuperation alone holds some inherent power to soften the critique, as if the change in direction from the outside to the inside inherently fades the potential of real impact.

Another work that took place on the threshold of an art institution is Coco Fusco's *Rights of Passage*, staged in the entrance of the Johannesburg Biennale in 1997. While the work did not redirect public access like D'Arcangelo's intervention, it did tackle questions of access, alongside territory, classification, and identity, in relation to the legacies of apartheid in South Africa, while also reaching beyond the local situation to touch on the art world's commonplace elitist and isolating practices. Invited by the Biennale to present a new commission, Fusco set out to "deal with internal rather than external migration."[12] Fascinated by the passbook, an identity document that regulated the movements of Black and "colored" people during apartheid, Fusco produced a slightly amended facsimile copy of the no-longer-in-use booklets and set up a border crossing station at the Biennale's entrance. Dressed in the uniform of a "glorified traffic cop"[13] and accompanied by two assistants also dressed as South African police officers, Fusco observed a strict protocol that asked every visitor to fill out a passbook with details about their name, nationality, ethnicity, etc. and to have it stamped at the entrance to

11 Andreas Petrossiants, "Inside and Out: The Edges to Critique," *e-flux journal*, no.110, June 2020, https://www.e-flux.com/journal/110/335739/inside-and-out-the-edges-to-critique/.

12 Fusco, *The Bodies That Were Not Ours: And Other Writings*, 106.

13 Fusco, *The Bodies That Were Not Ours*, 107.

   INVERTING THE FRAME

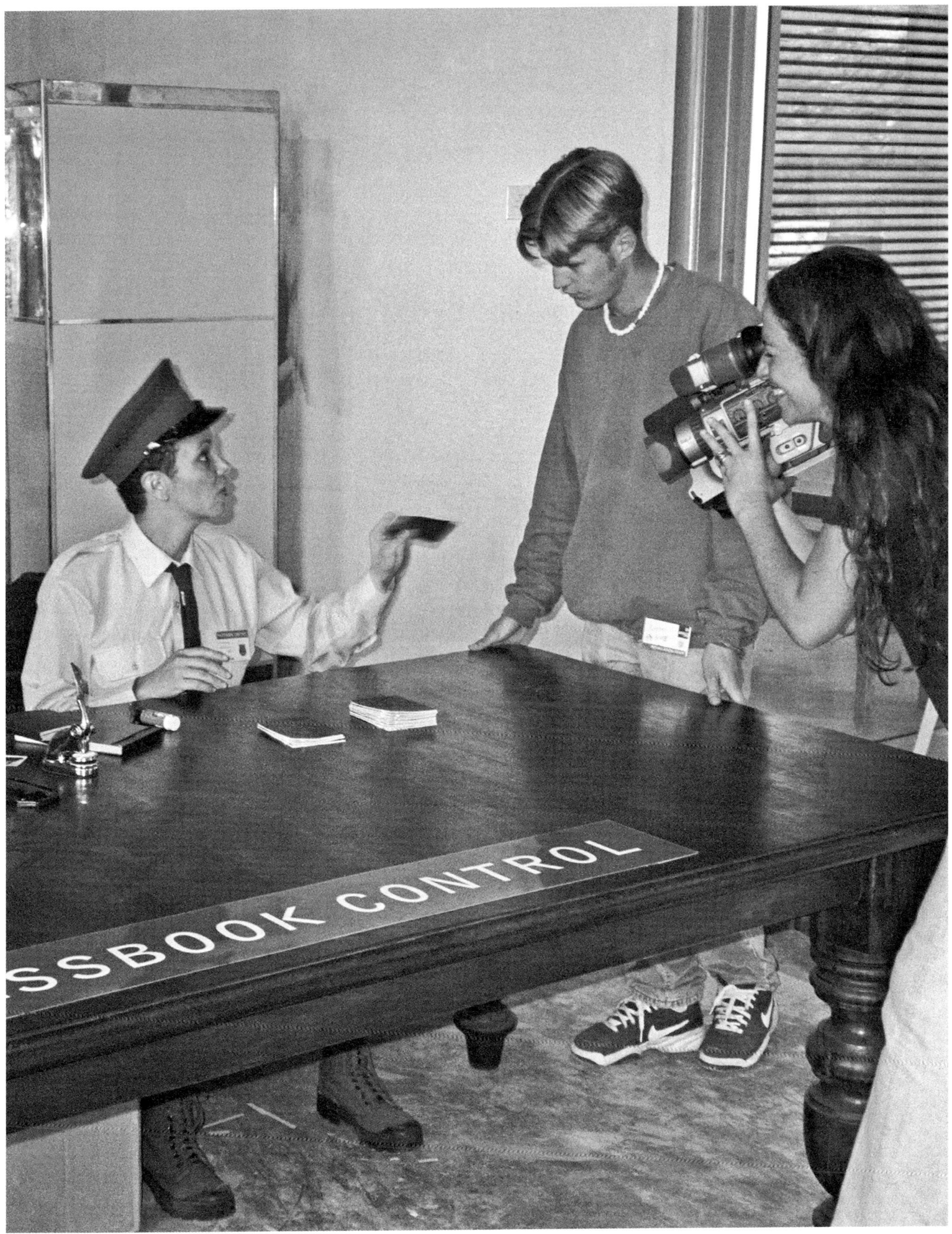

Rights of Passage, 1997, performance

the Biennale exhibits. The sentence "Stop! Do you have identification," voiced in either English by Fusco or Afrikaans by her assistants, will have had a very different ring depending on one's origin and experience with border controls. While Fusco and her team held no official authority to deny access or require people to carry the passbook, staple attributes like the booth, uniforms, and stamps were enough to exude a certain air of authority. As it quickly became apparent among the visitors that the imposed rules were not enforced, the piece eventually took a farcical turn with people coming back repeatedly, filling out multiple passbooks for multiple identities, going so far to fill them out for fictional characters, unknown tribes, Martians, or even their genitals, as Fusco recalls.[14]

The playful attitude towards the identity card revealed the absurdist nature of the classification of people in general and accentuated the dark undertones that the piece carried, evoking both very real circumstances from the past and still very present procedures that force people from certain groups to be classified, regulated, restricted, and forced to carry documentation based on their origin. But in light of the passbook's origin as a document that regulated the movement of certain social groups, *Rights of Passage* also questioned who is customarily granted access to the confines of contemporary art in the first place. Who is invited to take part in art education? Who is able to attain knowledge about art, and has the wealth to afford to make art or work in its institutions? The work highlights invisible lines of demarcation that speak to structural elitism and racism that cannot easily be grasped through more blatant strategies of classification such as the passbooks. Thus, *Rights of Passage* provokes a discussion of belonging that has to consider larger societal inequities in sync with institutional practices. The infrastructures of the art world consequently blend in seamlessly with those outside of it, conditioning the metrics set in place respectively.

The prison, the factory, the museum, the mall—all increasingly made of architectural boxes—all equally represent spaces that have been under extreme scrutiny for ever more streamlined and efficiency-driven procedures and are, as a result, gradually subject to standardization. Fusco has situated her work in various of these institutional bodies—the factory in *Dolores from 10 to 10* (2002), the mall in *Mexarcane International* (1994–95), *Ethnic Talent for Export* (1994–95), the prison in *A Room of One's Own: Women and Power in the New America* (2006–08), and the communication system in *Billetes quemando la calle* (*Bills Burning the Street*), a piece that Fusco initiated with Janet Batet and Marco Castillo after a work by Hamlet Lavastida at the Untitled Art fair in Miami in 2021—probing them for their built and theoretical structural commonalities. In the video installation *Dolores from 10 to 10,* she casts her focus onto the story of a maquiladora worker in a factory at the US–Mexico border. On small CCTV monitors we see five camera perspectives. A man is leading a woman into an office space. Each camera traces a different view of a fictitious assembly plant in an industrial complex on the northern border of Mexico entitled MAXIMEX, S.A: de C.V. Ciudad Industrial Baja California Sur México. The grainy black-and-white security footage offers recorded live feeds from five windowless spaces: a hallway, an office, the women's bathrooms, a staircase, and the office of the plant's foreman. The resolution speaks of the kind of low-quality recording that usually documents for the sole purpose of bureaucracy and record-keeping, witnessing legalities and tracing logistics, like the automated motions of a copy machine. Over the course of the next 12 hours,[15] the cameras depict the extended confinement, deprivation, and increasing intimidation and extortion of a female maquiladora worker (played by Fusco) by her foreman (played

14 Fusco, *The Bodies That Were Not Ours,* 109.

15 Later, Fusco edited the footage down to a one-hour, 39-minute video.

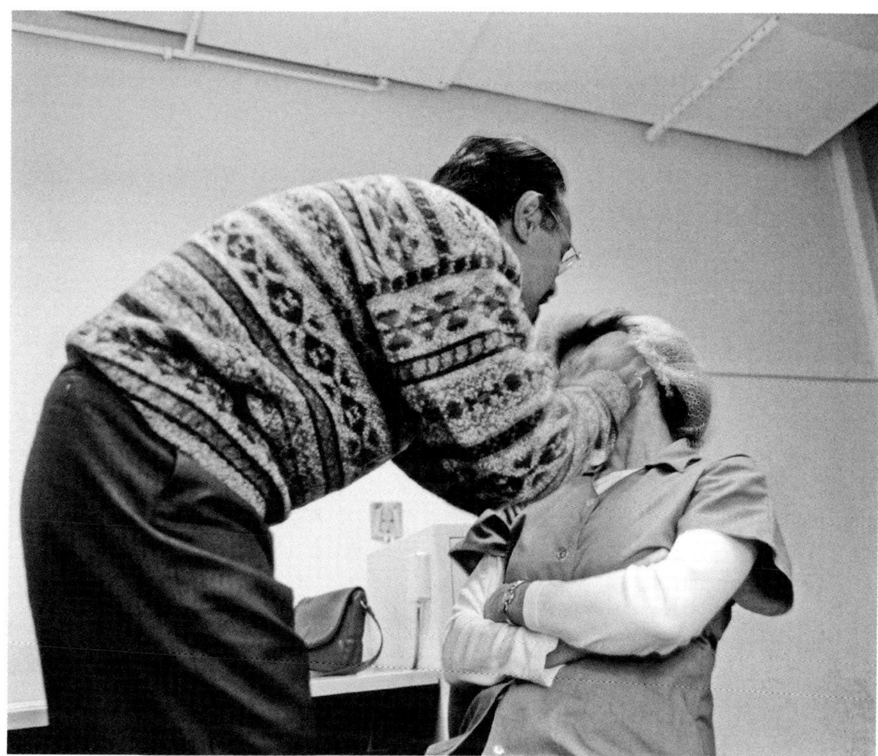

Coco Fusco and Ricardo Dominguez, *Dolores from 10 to 22*, 2001, performance

by Ricardo Dominguez) in the confines of a small white-walled office space. It traces her persistent Bartleby-like acts of refusal that eventually lead to her dismissal.[16]

The performance restaged the story of Delfina Rodriguez, a former maquiladora worker Fusco had met during her research into working conditions of the region.[17] Rodriguez had been accused of attempting to start a union at the plant and was subsequently detained by her employer for twelve hours without access to food, drink, restroom facilities, or a phone to contact her family, in the attempt to force her to sign her resignation letter. Maquiladora plants are the sites where the hardware for large portions of the world's digital infrastructure is being assembled, labor that is outsourced to foreign territories where laws and precarious economic circumstances generate a more economically desperate, and therefore more compliant, work force.

In her essay "At Your Service, Latin Women in the Global Information Network," Fusco critically assesses the field of cyber theory and digital artmaking in the face of its obliviousness to the widespread consequences that the rise of internet culture has had on the exploitation of the global South.[18] Fusco highlights that the "digital disembodiment's fiction of transcendence relies on the expulsion of the abject interrelations between bodies and technologies from the virtual imaginary."[19] The structural exploitation of resources from Latin America in face of the demands of North American consumer culture is also the subject in Fusco's collaborative performance *Mexarcane International*. The work marked the last collaboration with Guillermo Gómez-Peña and was staged in a selection of malls in Toronto, Glasgow, and London in 1994 and 1995.

The work's narrative is based on the promotion and crowdsourcing of a fake multinational corporation that distributes exotic talent for special occasions.

16 *Dolores from 10 to 22* was originally staged on November 22, 2001 by Fusco and Dominguez as an interactive net-performance and live-streamed as CCTV footage on the website of the Finnish Contemporary Art Centre Kiasma for the entire twelve hours that the performance lasted. It was accompanied by a live chat that allowed the virtual audience to comment on the action as it was unfolding on their computer screens, implicating the remote audience in the ongoing abuse on screen.

17 Maquiladoras, also known as "twin plants," refers to a factory or manufacturing plant in Mexico. These corporations, approved for operation by the country's secretariat of Commerce and Industrial Development under a decree established in 1989, are owned by foreign entities, allowing companies to capitalize on cheaper labor.

18 Fusco, *The Bodies That Were Not Ours*, 186–202.

19 Fusco, *The Bodies That Were Not Ours*, 188.

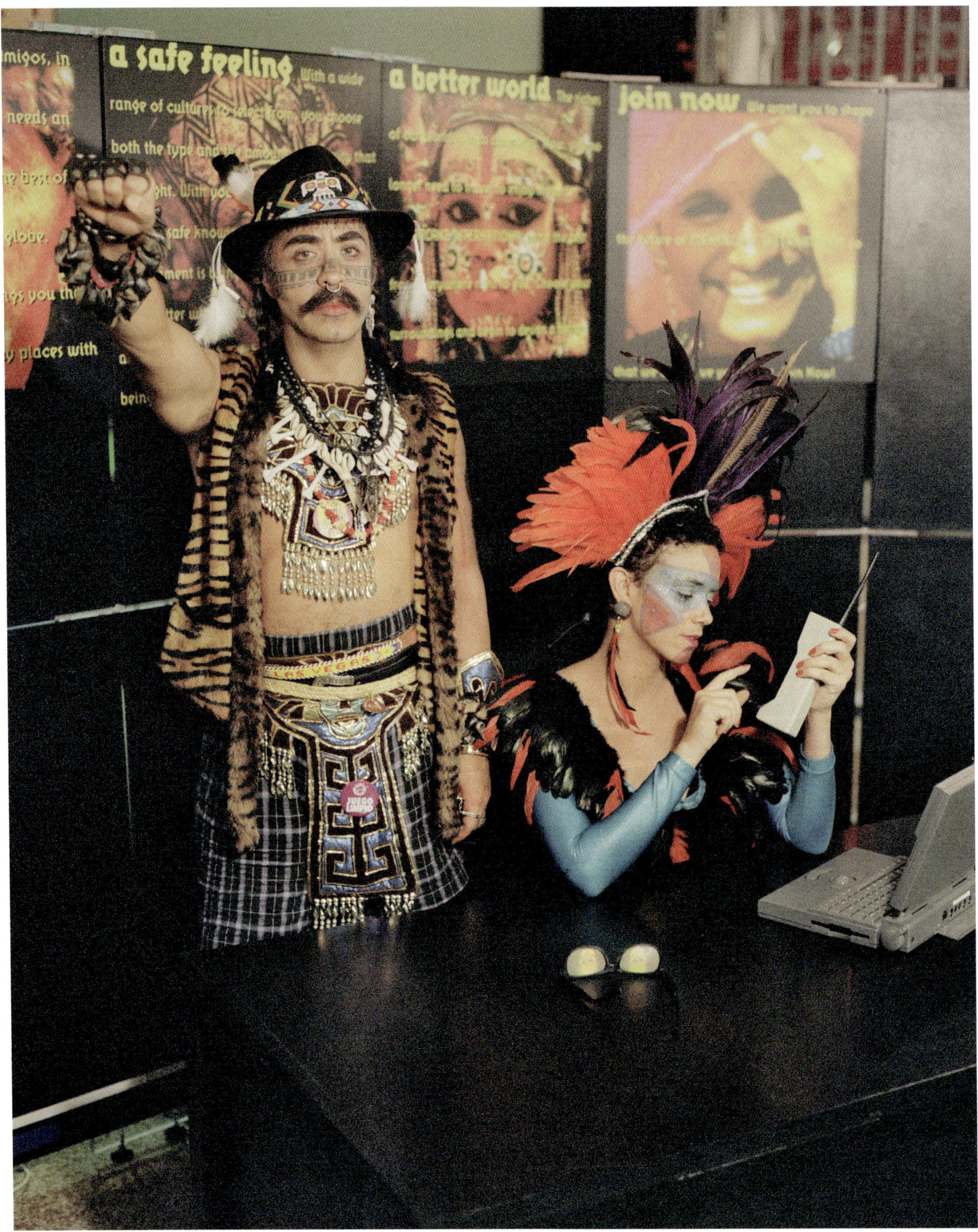

Coco Fusco and Guillermo Gómez-Peña, *Mexarcane International*, 1994–95, performance

    INVERTING THE FRAME

Still imbued by the audience reactions that Fusco and Gómez-Peña had received throughout the tour of *Two Undiscovered Amerindians Visit the West* (1992–94), the work set out to actively include passersby in malls into the structure of the piece. As a micro universe designed to cater to every need via consumption, the mall offered itself as the perfect "safe" backdrop for an interactive performance that plays with the space of no origin that consumer products appear to attain once offered for sale in a mall. Set up in a corner of various malls and wearing corporate attire, Fusco would interact with the flaneuring mall crowd and ask them to fill out a multiple-choice questionnaire that would determine their taste in exotic entertainment. Based on their answers, a code was generated on a small piece of paper that would then initiate a short sneak-preview performance by Gómez-Peña, reflecting their penchants. The overall adjustment of the performance to the language and standards of mall culture and its mode of annexation and classification of things from a wide array of geographies into easily boxed sections highlights the violent consequences of easy consumption. The "exotic" in malls is just a short and controllable *dérive*, a lifestyle choice that comes with no strings attached to the place of its origin or any knowledge of that place, but through Fusco's and Gómez-Peña's blunt and blatant play on the production and management of difference, even the most lulled consumer is forced to come face to face with the abyss of their own stereotype-infused fantasies.

"This space, the box, has been the subject of the tape all along," states the art historian Liz Kotz in a text about the American artist Lutz Bacher's surveillance video piece, *Closed Circuit* (1997–2000). She sees a series of historical spaces being condensed in the shape of the box, the camera, the theater, the industrial warehouse, the white cube, and the prison, the latter both as a real space and as a metaphor, identifying "the structures of psychic and physical confinement which must be reproduced internally to become a coherent modern subject."[20] We are taught a vocabulary that is so all-encompassing that it conditions the preemption of its adaptation without further disciplinary upkeep. Across Fusco's practice, from the early collaborative performances to the recent work about Cuba, we are witnessing her shifting the strategies from institutional critique to infrastructural critique, focusing in on the inbuilt, standardized, and mass-produced logic that conditions the art institution alongside other institutions and that ensures the maintenance of the dominant power equilibrium and the continued exploitation of subaltern communities.

Fusco is inverting the frame, or reversing the gaze, to speak with Stuart Hall, and, in doing so, revealing that there is no outside. Instead, we are looking from one institutionalized box into the other. Nick Axel and Nikolaus Hirsch observe that infrastructure is traditionally associated with "the unthought, the unseen."[21] It is the thing that works best when one does not even notice it working, like an algorithm, once set in motion, running while its course is incessantly reproducing its code. Fusco's work is anchored at exactly this point, but the reversal itself is disrupting the status quo and shedding a light onto inbuilt abusive structures to open up a space that might be able to free itself from the self-perpetuating curse of systemic exploitation.

20 Liz Kotz, "Lutz Bacher," *CTRL [SPACE]: Rhetorics of Surveillance from Bentham to Big Brother* (Cambridge: The MIT Press, 2002): 620–23.

21 Nick Axel and Nikolaus Hirsch, "Editorial," *e-flux Architecture*, August 2020, https://www.e-flux.com/architecture/software/341106/editorial/.

Coco Fusco and the Empty Spaces of Havana

Antonio José Ponte

It is 2015 and Coco Fusco is in Havana. She observes the waxing and waning of the international press's interest in Cuba. An observation that can be understood as a complaint. From time to time, a Cuban news story draws international attention, but once interest wanes, Cuba all but disappears from the newsreel. In the global press, interest in Cuba lasts as long as the strike of a match—a flash of light, then a return to obscurity until another match is lit.

This is what happened when Pope John Paul II visited Havana, and again during the heated custody battle that raged over a child, Elián González, across two shores. Now, as Fusco arrives in Havana, interest in Cuba stirs once again. Diplomatic relations have just recently been restored between Cuba and the United States, and the two embattled nations seem to be progressing towards a normalization of ties. One of the last embers of the Cold War is dying out, and the world's gaze is firmly fixed on Havana.

At times like these, Fusco fields inquiries of a journalistic sort. She is consulted. The questions are about the future of Cuba, and are of an order that only an oracle could answer. Answering would require, on the one hand, the ability to foresee events still to come and, on the other, a gaze capable of penetrating the hazy context in which the Cuban regime makes decisions and operates. A gaze that can pierce the veiled atmosphere this regime creates—an atmosphere as thick and congested as possible, designed to repel any and all influence or interference.

To answer these questions about Cuba, one would need to foresee the future and have knowledge of official state secrets. Thus, such questions cannot be answered categorically, but only with hesitation. Instead, they are answered with approximations, with doubts about what is happening now and what could transpire in the future. Hope is possible at this particular juncture because the restoration of diplomatic relations between Cuba and the United States awakens a sense of hope. Nonetheless, there is the tremendous hopelessness of knowing how things have been, how countless opportunities for change, changes that Cubans desperately need, have been squandered.

We find ourselves at the site of *La confesión* (*The Confession*, 2015), upon Fusco's return to Havana. In 2021, with the benefit of hindsight, we know the hope aroused by the restoration of diplomatic relations would only last as long as the flame of a match. But let's not get ahead of ourselves. We return to *La confesión*. It's still open season for queries on Cuba, and Fusco fields questions she can only answer with hesitation, or with approximations, weighing one option and then, immediately, its alternative. Though she harbors hope that things may change once and for all, she does not ever lose sight of the way things are and the way they have been.

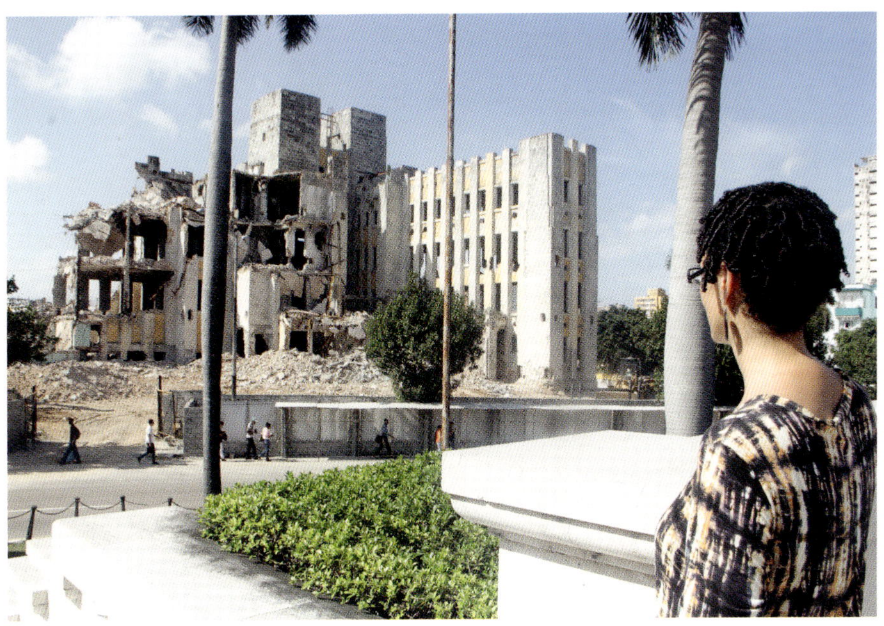

La confesión (The Confession), 2015, video

In Havana, she waits for news, answers to the questions she is asked and the ones she has been asking herself. In her waiting, she turns to the past and total hopelessness, an event that took place forty-some years ago. She revisits an episode that took place in 1970s Havana, at the height of the Cold War. She is staying at the Riviera hotel, on Havana's seaside esplanade, the malecón. The Riviera is the hotel in which key elements of the Padilla case took place.

When it opened to the world, at the end of the 1950s, the Riviera was touted as the greatest hotel-casino in the world, Las Vegas hotels notwithstanding. Meyer Lansky had it built, and his investors were prominent figures of the Las Vegas gambling and mafia worlds. At the time, the Riviera was on a par with the most modern buildings in Las Vegas or Miami Beach, and it would have been the perfect location for the Havana scenes in *The Godfather: Part II.* Since 1960, the year the new revolutionary government banned gambling and nationalized hotels, the Riviera has remained frozen in time. In desperate need of restoration, it was starting to give way to decay when a Spanish company took over its renovation, preserving the hotel's distinctive style, its original murals and decoration. Pierre Golendorf, a photographer who stayed there in the early 1970s, called it a "jail-hotel" for preventative detention. Golendorf's stay at the Riviera coincided with that of the Cuban poet Heberto Padilla, who was provided with a room in which to write. The official pretext was that the hotel would offer better conditions for both men to work. But Padilla's book of poems, *Fuera del Juego,* had already been denounced as counterrevolutionary for its allusions to authoritarianism in the socialist world. Although the book received a Casas de las Americas prize from a majority foreign jury in 1968, it was not published, and Padilla fell from grace as Cuban authorities closed in on him and cut him off from public life. The real objective of allowing him to work in the Riviera was to make it easier for political police forces to follow the photographer and the poet, to ensnare them with their tangle of microphones. The hotel that started out as the ideal stage for a film about the mafia eventually became the prototypical Eastern European hotel of a spy novel.

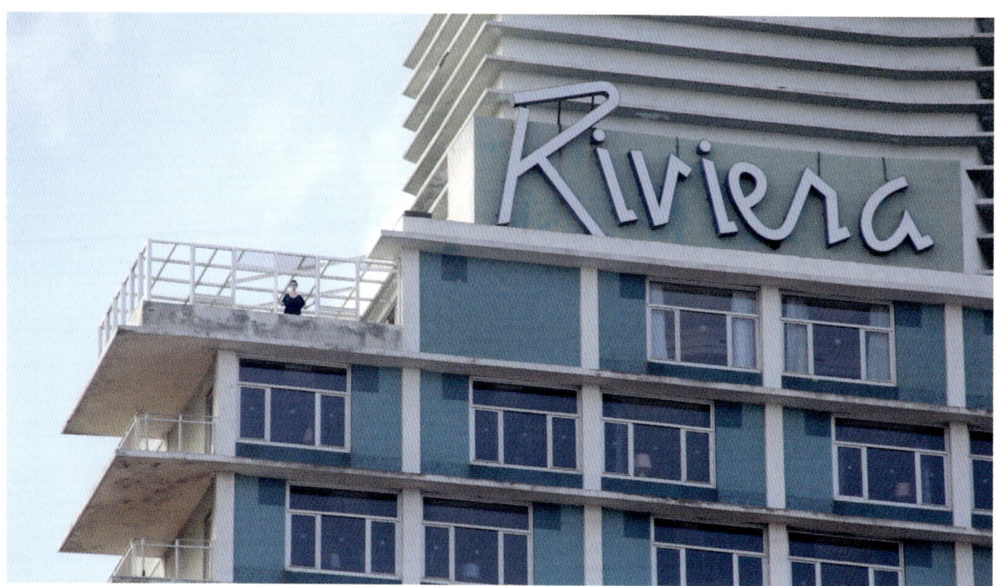

La confesión (The Confession), 2015, video

As Golendorf tells it in his memoirs, everything bore the stamp of the Ministry of the Interior. Microphones, porters, elevator operators, bartenders, waiters—the entire hotel was an instrument of state espionage. Golendorf was forcibly removed from his room, and he spent more than three years in prison. Padilla was interned in the most ominous interrogation center and emerged from there to give a speech in which he accused himself of being a counterrevolutionary and accused his wife and several friends and colleagues of being counterrevolutionaries.

More than four decades later, this is the hotel where Coco Fusco is staying. The hotel of the Padilla Case. The Riviera of *La confesión* is practically empty. At the pool, seen from above, a few guests are sunning themselves. The place has the feeling of a spa in off season, of being closed for repairs.

It is a hotel of memories, and memory's hotels are usually vacant, empty. They have halls that exhaust those who walk them. They stay open for the ones who cannot fall asleep. Hotels for insomniacs and the lone drinker that keeps the bar open late. In this case it is Coco Fusco who is watching the sea from a table.

The poet Heberto Padilla stayed here with his wife, their every movement noted, registered, documented. State Security listened to their phone calls, probed their intimate conversations, even the words they said in their sleep. They gave him the privilege of a hotel room only to further incriminate him. They invited him to live among strangers so he would confess his criticisms about the direction in which the country was heading.

Coco Fusco watches the pool from high in the Riviera. She watches the sea from a table in the utterly empty bar. She walks up and down the stairways with her camera, walks past the mural paintings. All hope raised by the restoration of ties between Cuba and the United States will soon be dashed, supposedly over some business with microphones and surveillance. After all, everything in this country bears the mark of the Ministry of the Interior, and several American and Canadian diplomats based out of Havana will emerge from this incident with inexplicable auditory and neurological damage, as well as memory loss.

La confesión traverses the various spaces of the Padilla case. The Riviera hotel, where Heberto Padilla's intimate conversations were recorded. La Facultad de Artes y Letras de la Universidad de la Habana, where the poet read his poems presaging the Cuban Revolution's shift toward Stalinism. The conference hall of the Unión Nacional de Escritores y Artistas de Cuba (the National Union of Writers and Artists of Cuba), where Padilla made his confession before an audience of friends and colleagues, some of whom he would soon denounce.

Empty spaces all. Spaces of memory, where there is neither person nor witness to be found. Fusco's *La plaza vacía* (*The Empty Plaza*, 2012) features a fixed camera frame of Havana's Revolution Square (La Plaza de la Revolución) as daylight gives way to night. Off camera, a voice names the various neighboring buildings, weaving together a cartography of the square and its surroundings. The camera, however, is unconcerned with showing any of the buildings mentioned. Instead, it remains fixed in one, unchanging direction. When there are no speeches and the authorities have no need of gathered masses, Revolution Square is an enormous and empty sluice. Every now and then a tour bus unloads and a group of tourists walks through this landscape of nothingness. No sign anywhere of the enthusiasm that has filled this place historically. The sluice is empty. The afternoon light falls over a pair of buildings, then night splays over them. A few lights come on. Everything seems reduced to this. Revolution Square is a space for sleepwalking. Any spontaneous gesture by the average person would be suspect here. Only the authorities can open and close the floodgates of this sluice.

La botella al mar de María Elena (*The Message in a Bottle from María Elena*, 2015) features the city of Alamar, which was dubbed the home of the "new man" around the time of the infamous Padilla confession. Alamar was the greatest construction project undertaken by the revolutionary regime. A city of buildings made by those who would soon populate it. Where every construction brigade was made up of the city's future inhabitants. They built the homes where they would live with their families. Nevertheless, they had strict guidelines to follow. These were prefabricated buildings, after all, and none of their future residents were once consulted or asked for input by either the planners or architects.

Such are the limits of existence for this new humanity. Building and living in a prefabricated and predetermined space. No place for change. The common areas that were placed strategically between some of the buildings remained totally empty. As if they had never been imagined in the first place. Alamar, the utopian city born of standardized architecture, looks ruinous in *La botella...*

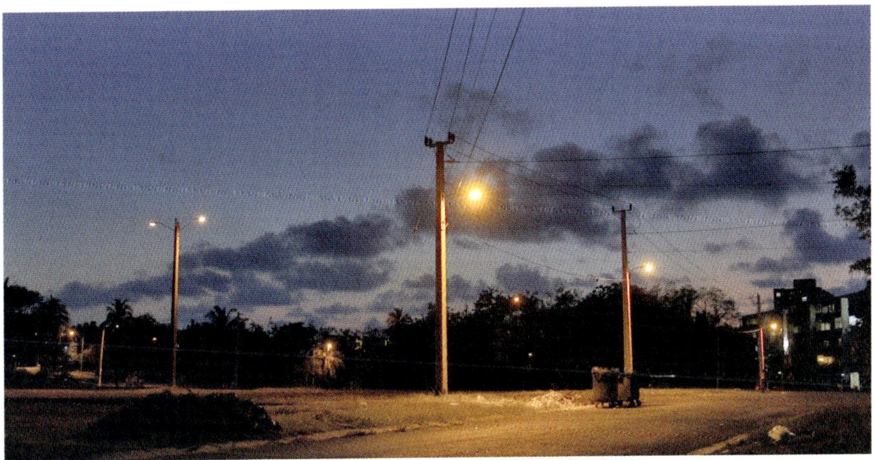

La botella al mar de María Elena (The Message in a Bottle from María Elena), 2015, **video**

The poet María Elena Cruz Varela lived with her family in one of those indistinguishable buildings. One day, a mob of neighbors descended on her apartment, at the behest of the Ministry of the Interior. It was not the content of her literary work that was in question but a public letter she signed demanding the country's democratization, the Letter of the Ten, named after its number of signatories. María Elena Cruz Varela was one of two women who signed it, and the angry mob did not pull any punches. They broke into her house, stuffed her mouth full of pages from her own books, and beat her before finally arresting her. She spent a number of years in prison and ultimately went into forced exile when, returning to Cuba after receiving an award, she was denied entry and her Cuban passport revoked.

Alamar is inhospitable. In the city built by and for the "new man," the common areas are all but deserted. There are scant trees and little shade to sit and chat under. Alamar looks as if it was designed to prevent its denizens from living a city life, to foreclose the life of the *polis*, any semblance of a political life. A group of dilapidated buildings scattered across a landscape as empty as Revolution Square. A prefabricated nothingness. The authorities fill the public space with people at their own whim and leisure—for cheering on official pronouncements or attacking certain pre-specified apartments. The rest of the time, the existence of these places matters none.

In Havana, Coco Fusco films the various spaces repression has emptied such that there can *be* no politics. The sites that lead to the confession of Heberto Padilla. The building where officially sanctioned mobs violently descended upon the home of María Elena Cruz Valera. Revolution Square. When Coco Fusco attempts, five years hence, to return to Havana to film the hideout of another persecuted writer, the novelist Reinaldo Arenas, authorities deny her entry to the country. They give her no reason. They classify her as "inadmissible" and send her back on another plane.

In order to make *Vivir en junio con la lengua afuera* (*To Live in June with Your Tongue Hanging Out*, 2018) Coco Fusco has to have others do the filming and trains American colleagues to go to Cuba on her behalf. The title of the piece is the title

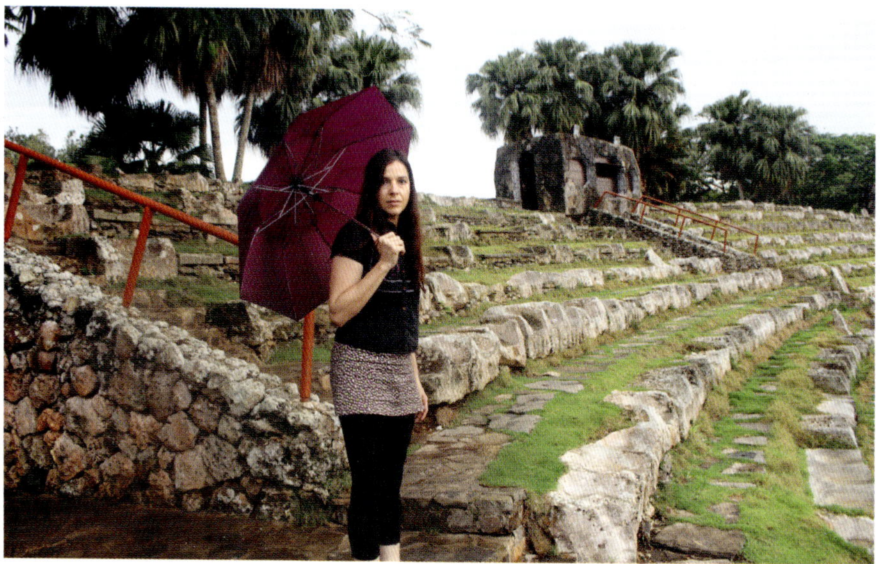

Vivir en junio con la lengua afuera (To Live in June with Your Tongue Hanging Out), 2018, video

    COCO FUSCO AND THE EMPTY SPACES OF HAVANA

of a poem written by Reinaldo Arenas while the police were actively hunting him down. The assistants she sends to Havana visit the José Martí National Library and confirmed that its catalogue does not include Reinaldo Arenas. There is not a single book of his in any Cuban library.

Arenas is one of Cuban literature's greatest writers. In his youth, he worked in this very library. Voracious autodidact that he was, this is where he gorged himself with readings. Here he read and wrote his first texts, shared them with colleagues who were already established writers. The catalogue of this library, which possesses the most resources of any in the country, and where Arenas worked for years, lacks any record of his first book, which was honored with a prestigious award by the Union of Writers and Artists of Cuba. Reinaldo Arenas's memory has been officially condemned to oblivion. Whole generations of Cuban readers do not know his work, have not even heard his name.

Further scrutiny of the National Library catalogue would yield similar results. The names and works of Heberto Padilla and María Elena Cruz Varela are also glaringly absent, along with so many other writers who have suffered persecution, censorship, and exile in the history of Cuban literature since the triumph of the Revolution in 1959.

For a while, Reinaldo Arenas lived in a hideout, in Lenin Park. Located south of Havana and opened around the time of the Padilla affair, this park is also a ruin. Like Alamar. Like most of Havana. Like the Riviera hotel, were it not now run by a Spanish company. And just as the Riviera represents a trace of Americanization because of its architecture and original owners, so too does Lenin Park, with its statue of Vladimir Ilyich Lenin, represent an emblem of the country's Sovietization at the time.

Persecuted by the police, Reinaldo Arenas took refuge in the park's amphitheater in the early 1970s. Heberto Padilla wrote compromising political poems and made critical comments to foreign visitors. María Elena Cruz Varela demanded democracy from the authorities. And Reinaldo Arenas refused to publish a novel under censorship, managed to get it out of the country secretly, and published it abroad. All of this compounded by the issue of his homosexuality.

The Lenin Park amphitheater of *Vivir en junio con la lengua afuera* is an amphitheater worthy of a post-apocalyptic world. Empty, yet surveilled by a security guard. The guard lets Coco Fusco's assistants through. He allows them to film while he continues his rounds. The actresses Lynn Cruz and Iris Ruiz, along with the poet Amaury Pacheco, gather in this amphitheater to recite a poem Reinaldo Arenas wrote in this very place. They receive it via encrypted message and arrive at the park via different routes. Friends who brought Reinaldo Arenas food and news from the outside world while he was hiding here put themselves in great risk. Nearly a half century later, it is still risky to pay homage to the writer. A writer long exiled, censored, and dead.

The actress Lynn Cruz is subject to the violence of political censorship. For Iris Ruiz and Amaury Pacheco, the Interamerican Commission for Human Rights has recommended cautionary protective measures, as they are, in the words of the commission, "in risk due to threats, harassment, surveillance, persecution, detentions, and acts of violence by state agents and third parties." Decades later, the three share with Arenas the burden of censorship and repression under the same regime.

Gathered inside the Lenin Park amphitheater, they recite the poem before the camera, from memory. The poem first reached them via encoded message and they had to learn it by heart. One of them comments that the poem feels immediate and seems to have been written today. All three agree. The poem's presentience astonishes them. Reinaldo Arenas, expelled from libraries, bookstores, and public memory alike, returns now to Lenin Park, his hiding place of yesteryears. In their voices, his poem returns to the place it was written, under the most strenuous of circumstances. Beyond incidents of censorship and repression, historical continuity is found in the connection between the person who wrote the words and the people who now recite them aloud. Historical continuity lives through the transmission of words that political censorship would silence.

Lynn Cruz, Iris Ruiz, and Amaury Pacheco meet in this amphitheater for a rite of memorialization. Recited in two or three voices, the poem hesitantly advances. At times they falter when starting a verse, pausing a moment before restarting. They do this all from memory. For a moment they seem to lose the flow but just as soon recover it and the poem gushes forth. It blooms. The memory of poetry works against the void, from within the void itself.

Coco Fusco completed her research on the Padilla Case with *CONFIDENCIAL, AUTORES FIRMANTES* (2015) and *La sombra de Heberto Padilla* (*Padilla's Shadow*, 2021). Twenty memos and official communications, and a collection of books, comprise the first of these works. The memos and communications focus on the repression and censorship of Heberto Padilla and a group of foreign authors who stood in solidarity with him and condemned the Cuban authorities.

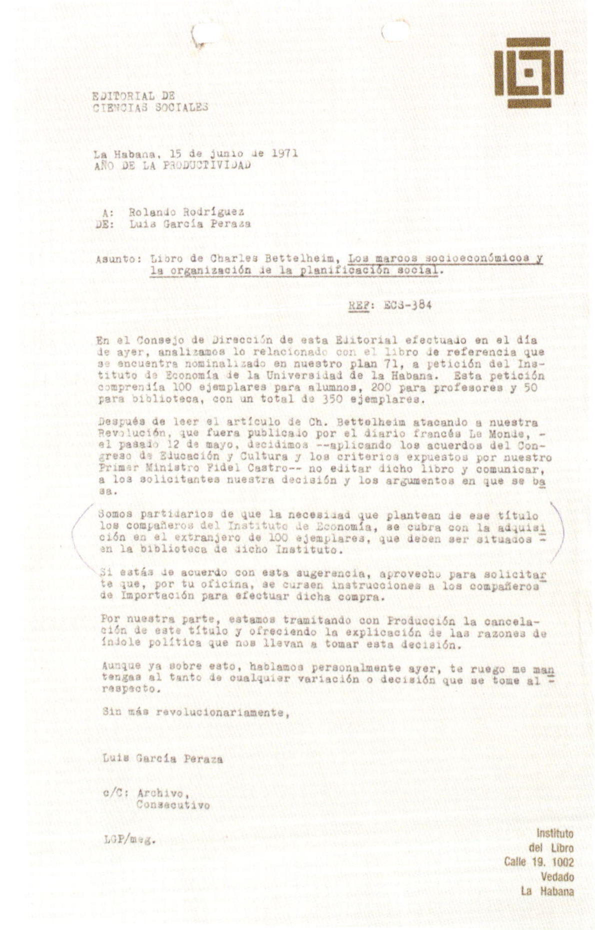

EDITORIAL DE
CIENCIAS SOCIALES

La Habana, 15 de junio de 1971
AÑO DE LA PRODUCTIVIDAD

A: Rolando Rodríguez
DE: Luis García Peraza

Asunto: Libro de Charles Bettelheim, Los marcos socioeconómicos y
la organización de la planificación social.

REF: ECS-384

En el Consejo de Dirección de esta Editorial efectuado en el día de ayer, analizamos lo relacionado con el libro de referencia que se encuentra nominalizado en nuestro plan 71, a petición del Instituto de Economía de la Universidad de la Habana. Esta petición comprendía 100 ejemplares para alumnos, 200 para profesores y 50 para biblioteca, con un total de 350 ejemplares.

Después de leer el artículo de Ch. Bettelheim atacando a nuestra Revolución, que fuera publicado por el diario francés Le Monde, - el pasado 12 de mayo, decidimos --aplicando los acuerdos del Congreso de Educación y Cultura y los criterios expuestos por nuestro Primer Ministro Fidel Castro-- no editar dicho libro y comunicar, a los solicitantes nuestra decisión y los argumentos en que se basa.

Somos partidarios de que la necesidad que plantean de ese título los compañeros del Instituto de Economía, se cubra con la adquisición en el extranjero de 100 ejemplares, que deben ser situados - en la biblioteca de dicho Instituto.

Si estás de acuerdo con esta sugerencia, aprovecho para solicitarte que, por tu oficina, se cursen instrucciones a los compañeros de Importación para efectuar dicha compra.

Por nuestra parte, estamos tramitando con Producción la cancelación de este título y ofreciendo la explicación de las razones de índole política que nos llevan a tomar esta decisión.

Aunque ya sobre esto, hablamos personalmente ayer, te ruego me mantengas al tanto de cualquier variación o decisión que se tome al - respecto.

Sin más revolucionariamente,

Luis García Peraza

c/C: Archivo,
Consecutivo

LGP/mvg.

Instituto
del Libro
Calle 19. 1002
Vedado
La Habana

CONFIDENCIAL, AUTORES FIRMANTES, **2015, installation**

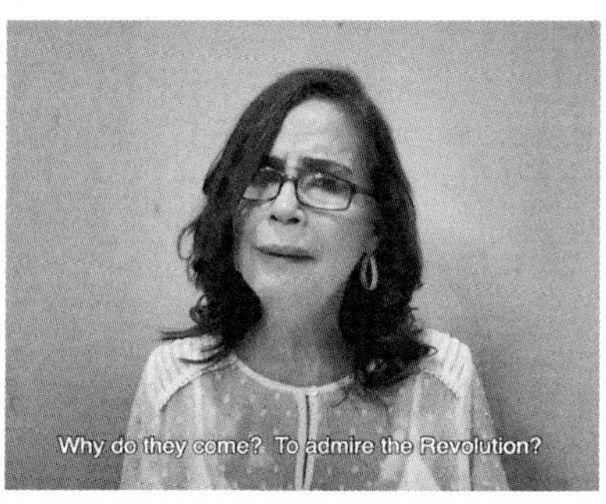

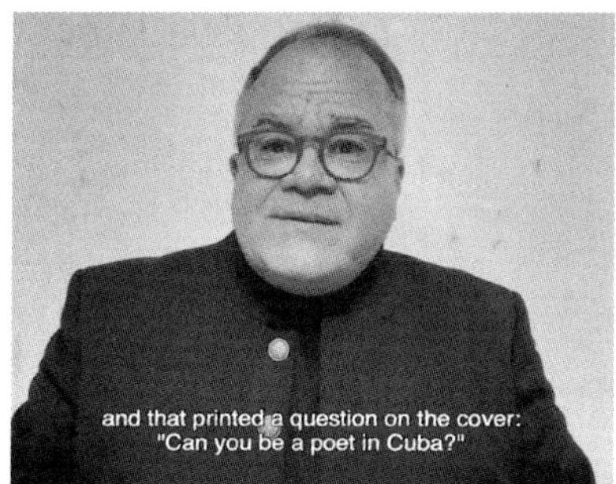

La sombra de Herberto Padilla (Padilla's Shadow), 2021, **video**

Coco Fusco recreates these documents from the archives of the Cuban Ministry of Culture. She not only fabricates them, but fabricates *for* them the patina of age. To these documents she adds Cuban editions of texts written by the censored authors and adds books from other Cuban writers censored by officialdom. *C O N F I D E N C I A L, AUTORES FIRMANTES* features examples of the writers' work and that of government officials who decide whether the books will be published, or silenced.

In *Padilla's Shadow*, a multi-generational cohort of Cuban intellectuals living in Cuba and in exile repeat the words of Padilla's self-incriminating speech before the camera. They film themselves while repeating Padilla's speech with all of its attacks and denunciations. Coco Fusco, able to reproduce the work of censors, has a group of intellectuals relive and embody the forced confession Padilla would make that fateful April night in 1971 in the conference hall of the Union of Writers and Artists of Cuba.

Gathered inside the Lenin Park amphitheater to recite a poem written by Reinaldo Arenas, Lynn Cruz, Iris Ruiz, and Amaury Pacheco see themselves in the poem's words. They are euphoric at discovering that Arenas's poem could have been written today, that it could have been written by any of them at this very moment. They memorize the poem; it is already theirs. But those who read fragments of Padilla's self-denunciation in *Padilla's Shadow* before the camera do not identify at all with the words they say.

Coco Fusco acknowledges that many of the participants in *Padilla's Shadow* suffer anxiety and panic attacks, insomnia and night terrors. This is the price of embodying certain words. Not euphoria but disgust. Coco Fusco defines Padilla's speech as "a study in political abjection, painful to witness, and to bring to life in these times." Nevertheless, painful though it may be, reanimating this speech today may be useful in a way that is different from breathing life into a censored poem. It is useful because the Cuban government is still using the same accusations once hurled against Heberto Padilla against those it perceives as threatening today.

The collective recitation of a deceased author's work still censored today revives his memory. It lifts but for a moment the silence officially imposed on him and against him. It works as a rite of invocation. The collective recitation of a writer's abject and forced confession, on the other hand, reveals the abjection of official policy itself, and its ceaseless operations, both in 1971 and today. And a recitation of this sort works as nothing short of an exorcism.

In *La confesión*, when we find ourselves in the conference hall of the Union of Writers and Artists, where Padilla made his speech, the group of empty chairs, crammed together with hardly a space between them, feels ominous now. Those chairs are waiting, ready to welcome the spectators of whatever farce presents itself next. They are chairs for contemplating destruction. By contrast, the chairs in the Lenin Park amphitheater, on which the camera lingers in *Vivir en junio con la lengua afuera*, evoke another, completely different feeling. They are made of stone. Stone eroded by the ravages of time and elements. They are in ruins now but—as an effect, perhaps, of the poem memorized by these three artists—seem to suggest a future audience for the poem. For all that's been obscured and will return one day. And all that must still emerge. It is about an audience still to come, citizens for the emptied spaces in which Coco Fusco lingers, whether or not the authorities let her into Havana.

Coco Fusco's work exists for the audience still to come.

Translated by José A. Portela

Body of Work
1990–2022

Norte / Sur

**(in collaboration with
Guillermo Gómez-Peña)**

1990

Created in collaboration with Gómez-Peña, *Norte / Sur* was composed of an experimental radio program and a performance that was presented at the Mexican Museum in San Francisco as part of the Festival 2000 (October 3– November 25, 1990). Exploring the cultural, linguistic, political, and demographic presence of Latin America in the United States and vice versa, the radio program engaged with stereotypes associated with Latinos in the United States.

**Coco Fusco and Guillermo Gómez-Peña,
Norte / Sur, 1990, performance**

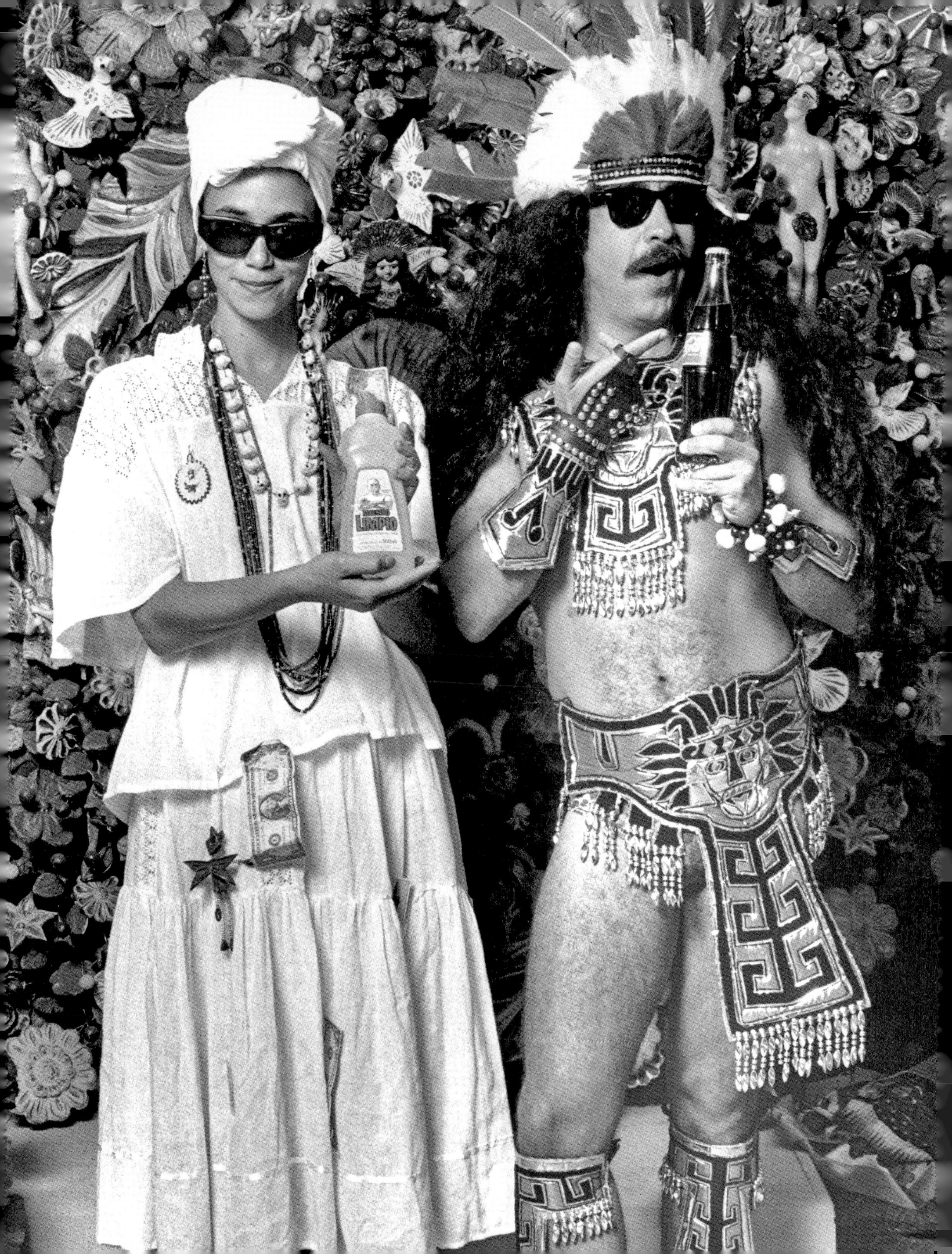
LIMPIO

La Chavela Realty Company

1991

La Chavela Realty Company was a site-specific performance held at the Brooklyn Academy of Music during the 1991 Next Wave Festival. Fusco commissioned artist Pepón Osorio to create a costume of Queen Isabella, a role she created and performed by selling American land deeds to visitors who were treated as though they had just landed in the New World.

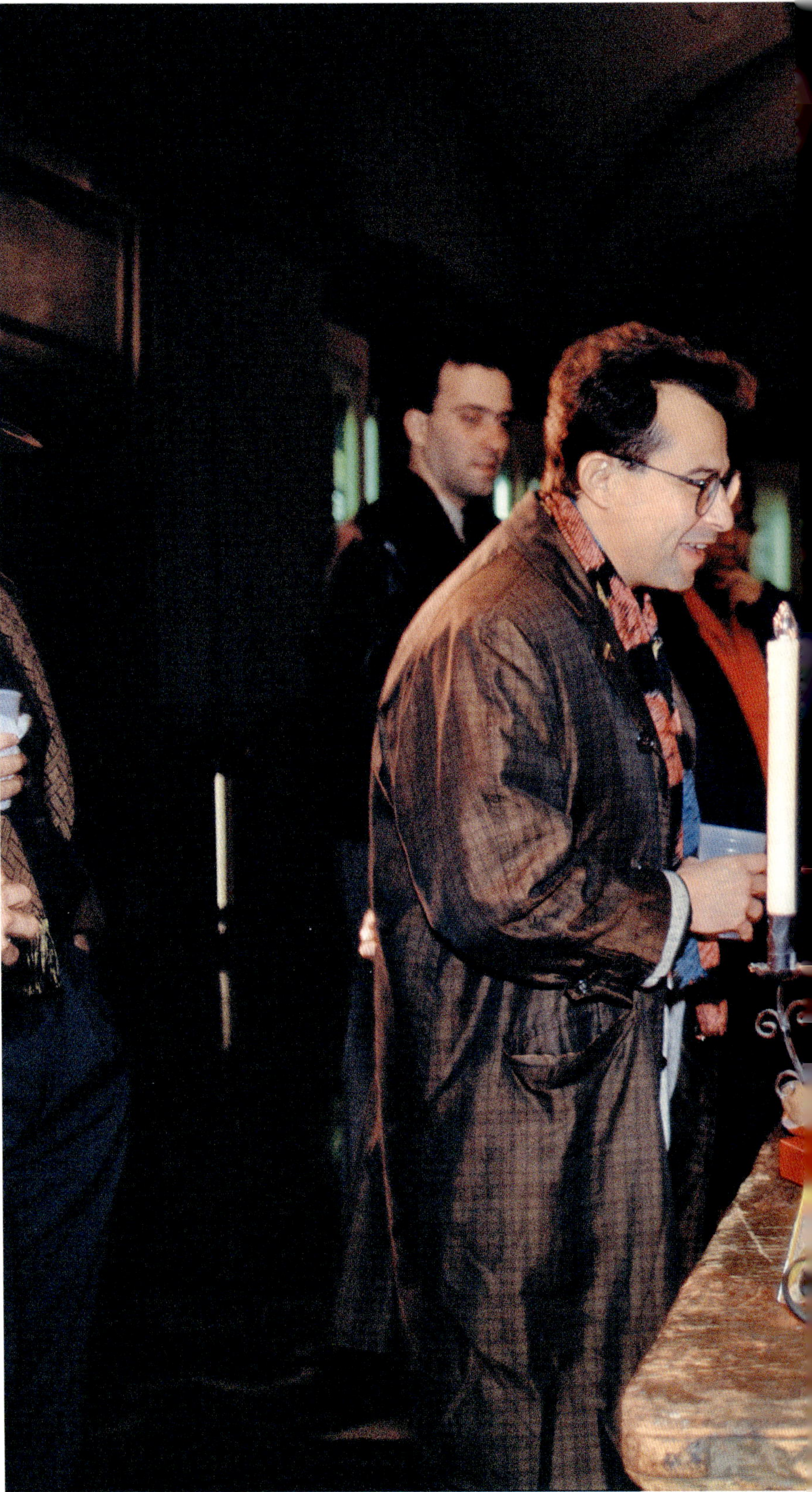

La Chavela Realty Company, 1991, performance

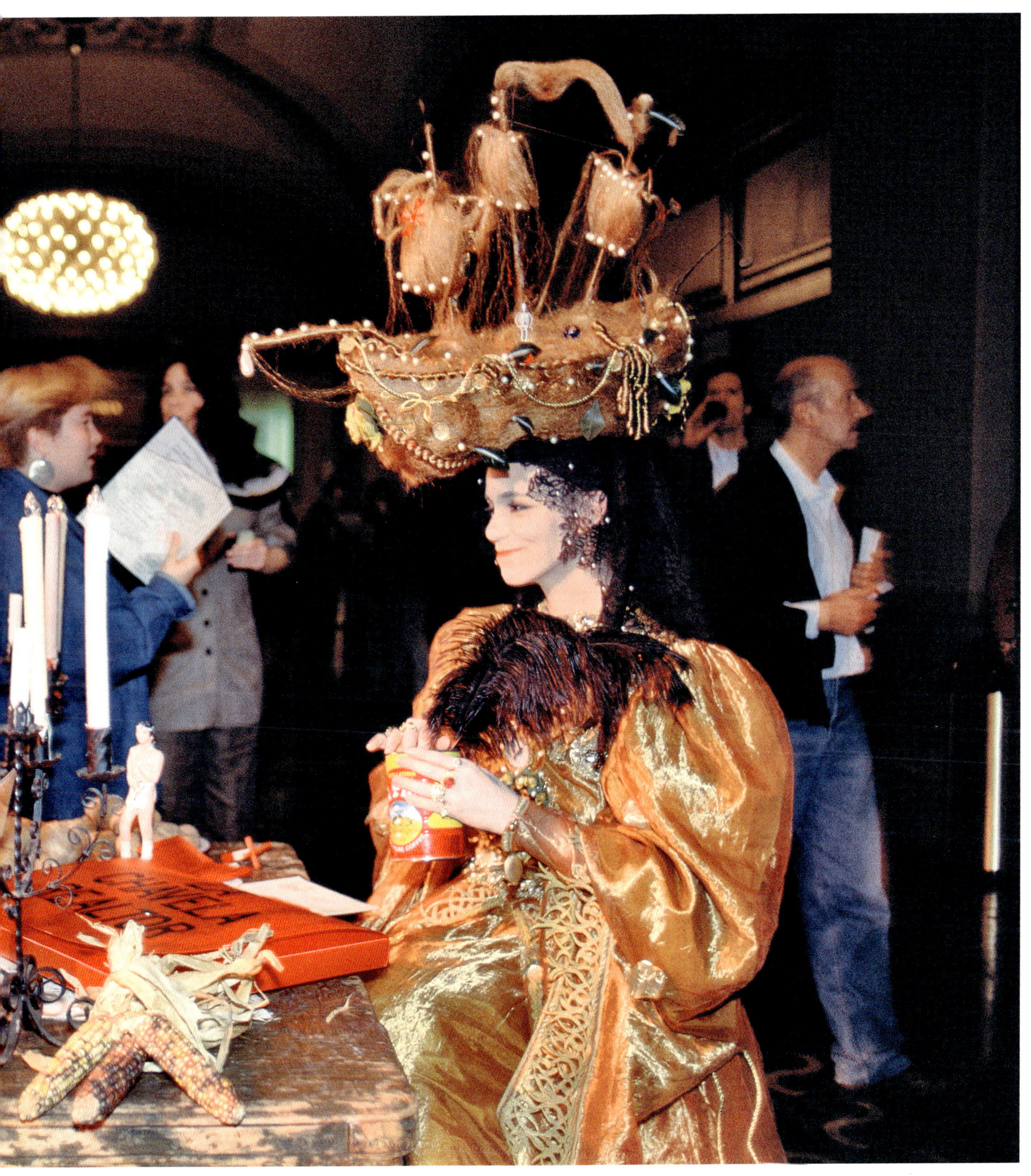

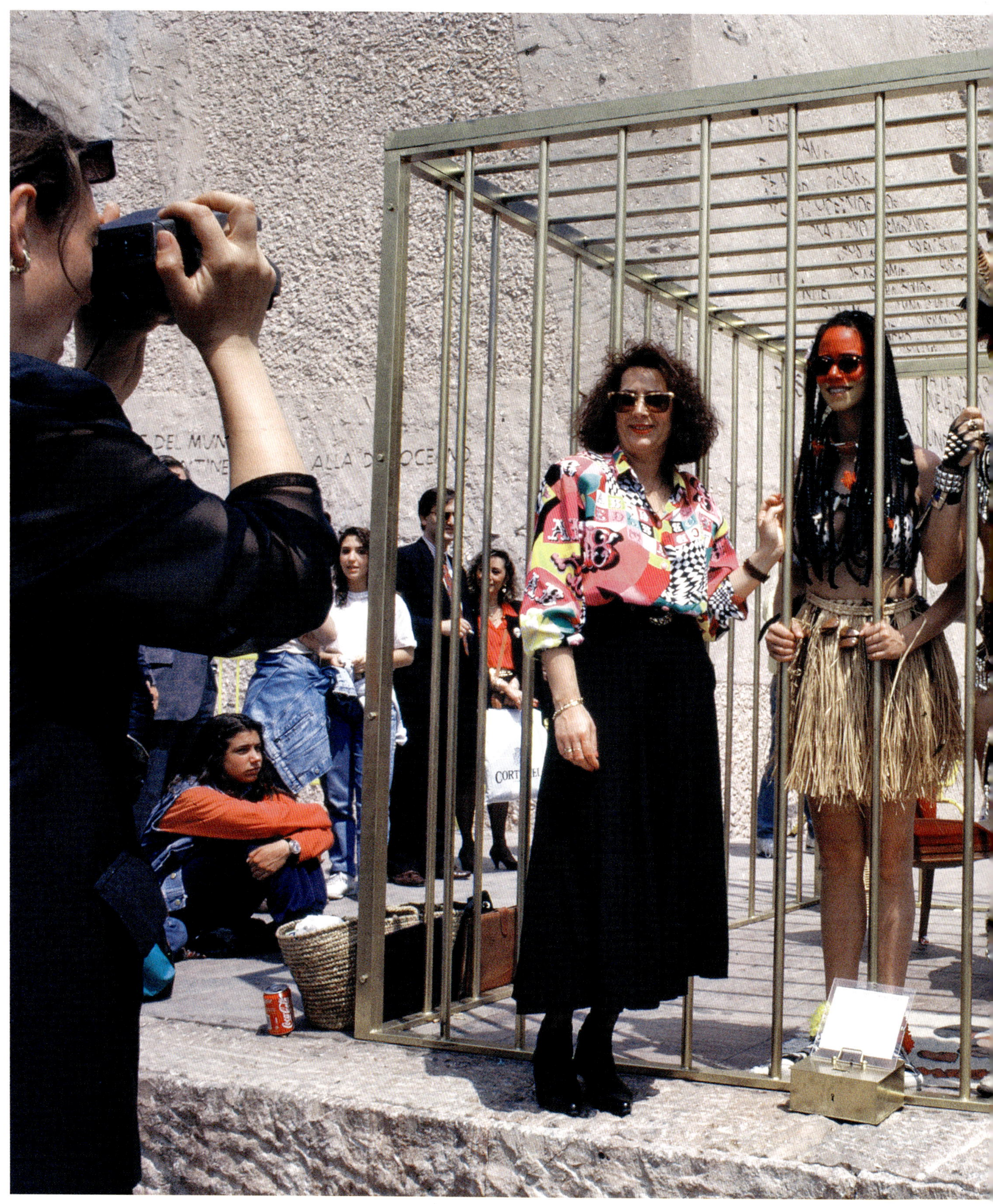

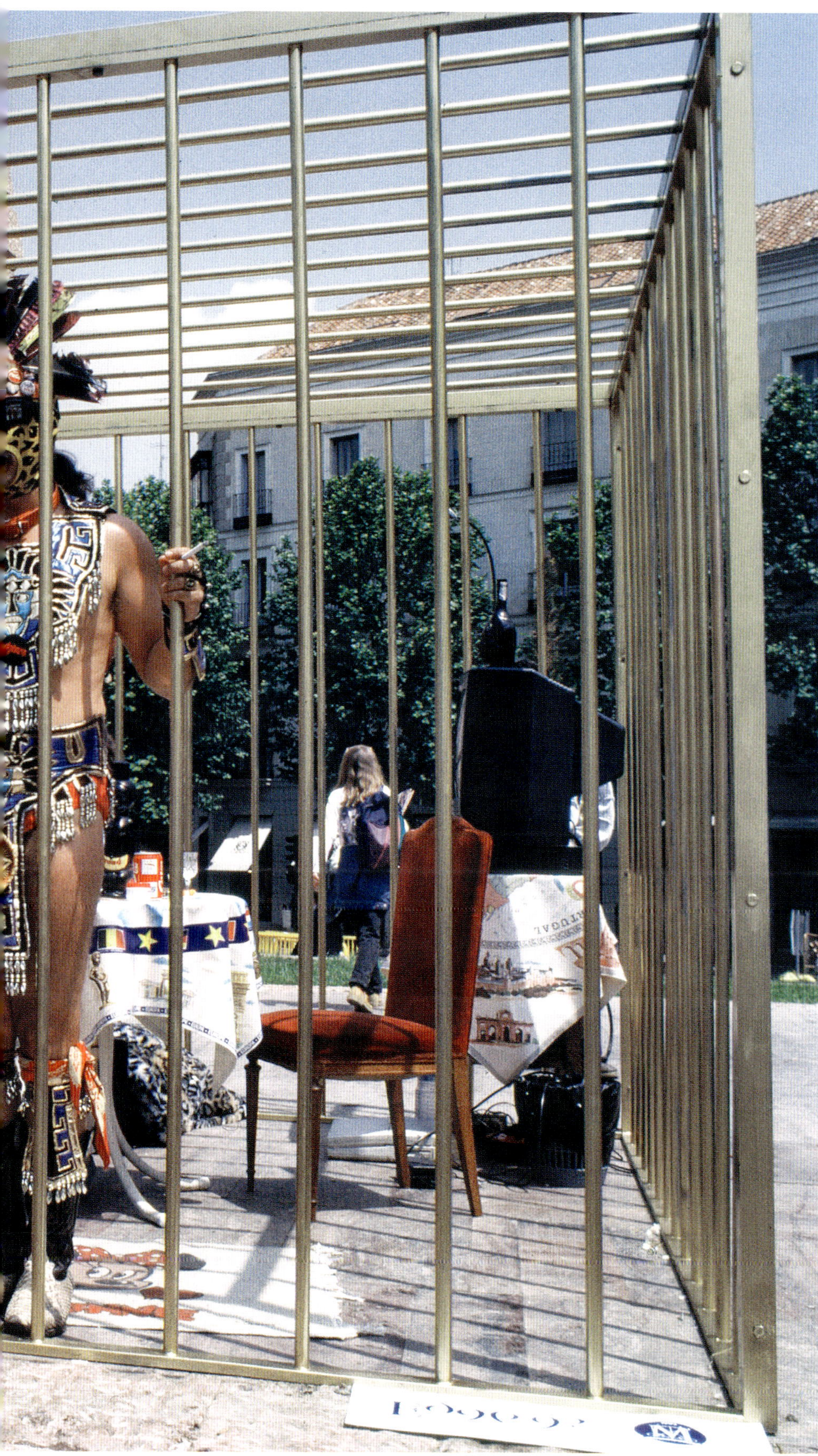

Two Undiscovered Amerindians Visit the West

(in collaboration with Guillermo Gómez-Peña)

1992–94

Created by Fusco and Gómez-Peña, *Two Undiscovered Amerindians Visit the West* offered a creative, satirical investigation/interpretation of the history of representation of the "discovery" of the Americas. The artists, presenting themselves as "undiscovered Amerindians" from an island in the Gulf of Mexico, traveled to Madrid; London; Minneapolis; Washington, DC; Chicago; Buenos Aires; and Irvine, California, and the work was featured in the 1992 Sydney Biennale and the 1993 Whitney Biennial.

Coco Fusco and Guillermo Gómez-Peña,
Two Undiscovered Amerindians Visit the West,
1992–94, performance

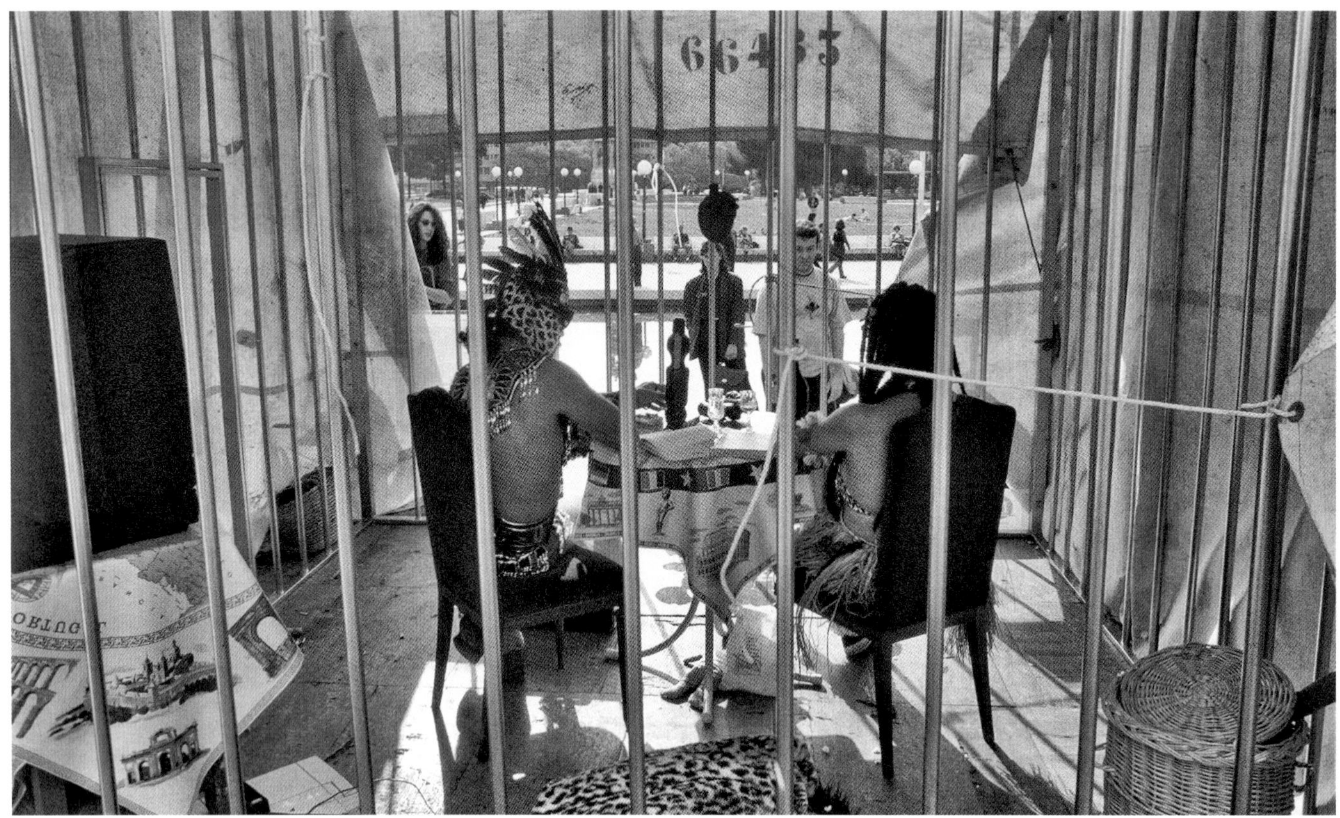

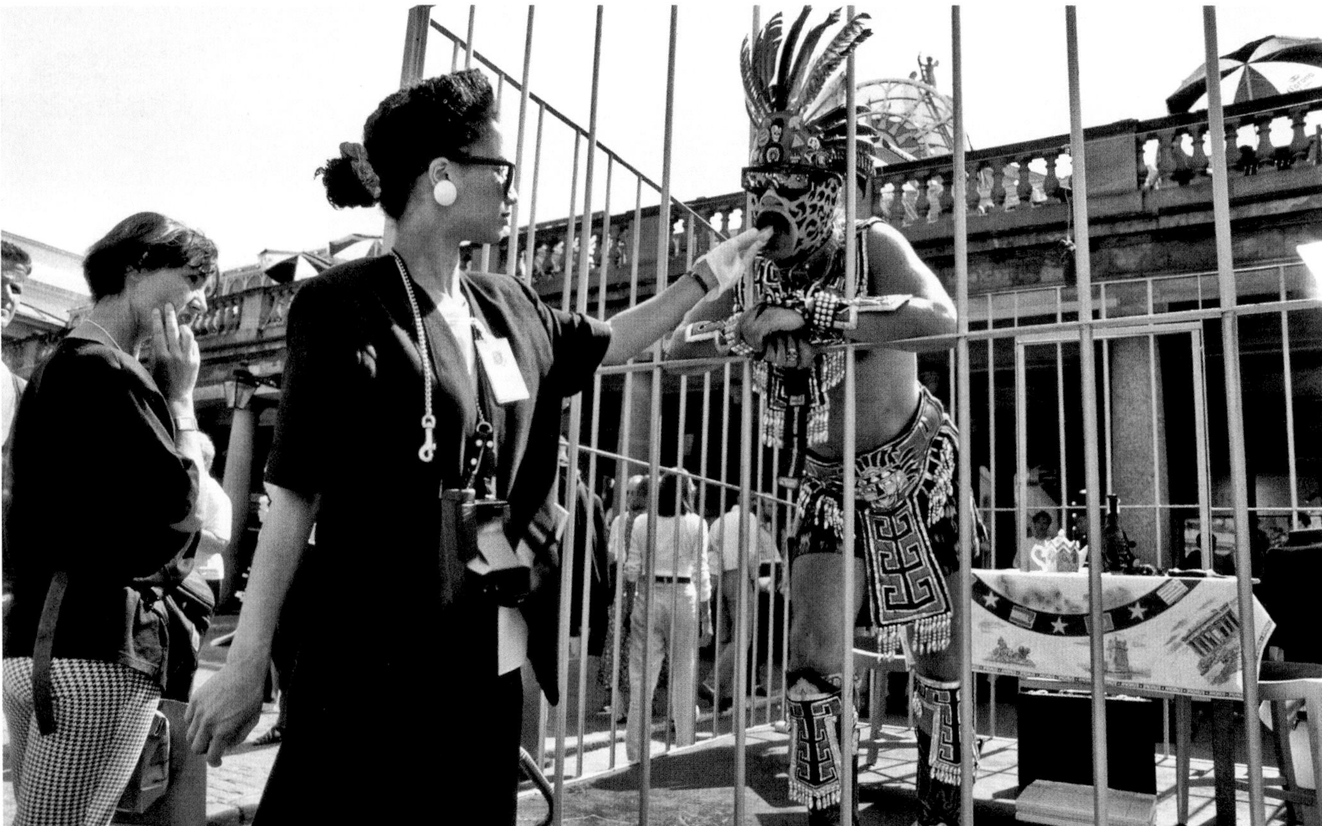

**Coco Fusco and Guillermo Gómez-Peña, *Two Undiscovered Amerindians Visit the West*, 1992–94, performances
(top, opposite above: Madrid; above: London; opposite below: Minneapolis)**

     BODY OF WORK 1990–2022

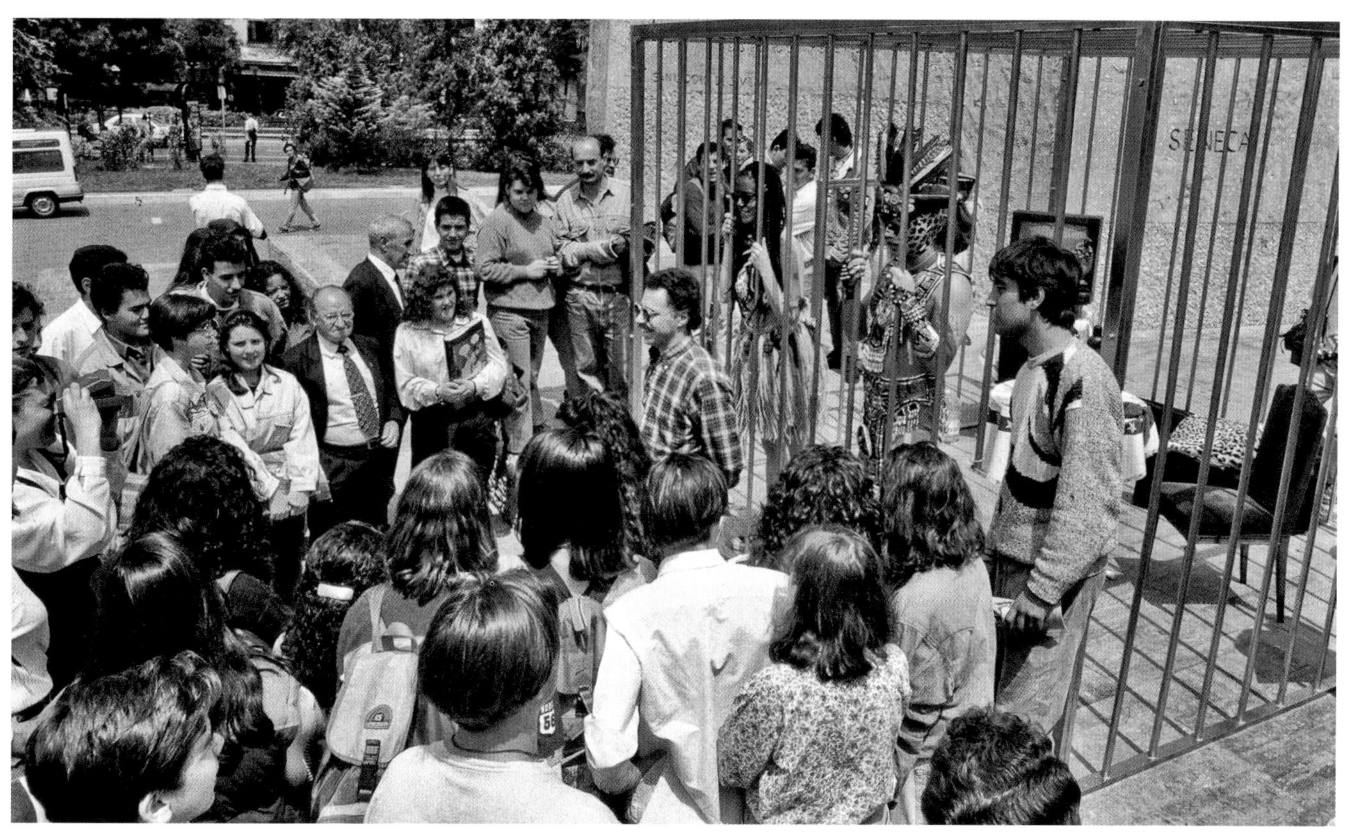

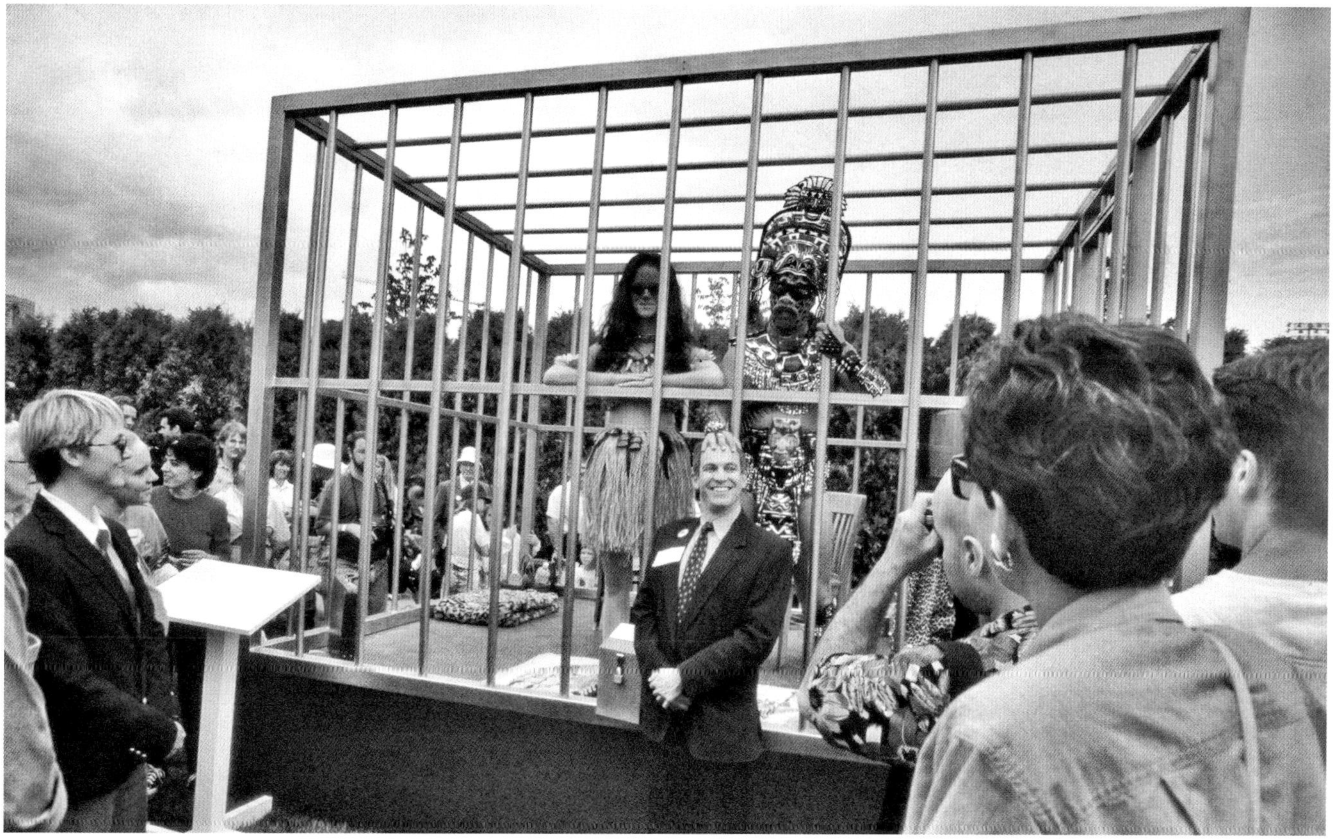

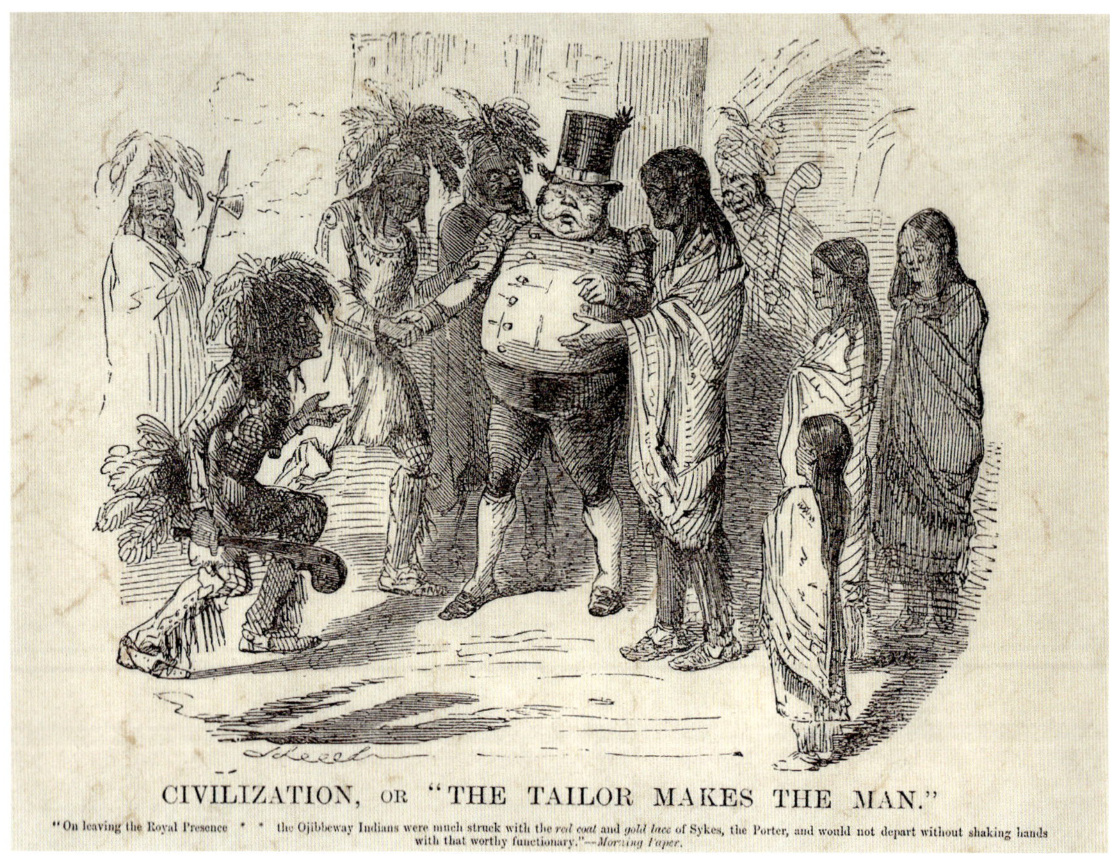

The Couple in the Cage: A Guatinaui Odyssey

(co-produced by Paula Heredia)

1993

The Couple in the Cage: A Guatinaui Odyssey documents the traveling performance of Fusco and Gómez-Peña's *The Year of the White Bear* (1992) and *Two Undiscovered Amerindians Visit the West* (1992–94), in which the pair exhibited themselves as caged Amerindians from the undiscovered, imaginary island of Guatinau. While the performance was intended as a satirical commentary on the notion of discovery, it became clear that regardless of whether the viewer believed the artists were "savages" from a previously unknown tribe, the majority knew how to play along with an established cultural script. *The Couple in the Cage* is a work Fusco created applying the "reverse ethnography" technique in which observers became the subject rather than the "exotics" on display. The different scenes show interactions with audiences in the United States, Australia, Spain, and the United Kingdom that rendered visible the pervasiveness of cultural misinformation and objectification of non-white bodies. Fusco and Gómez-Peña's lived experiences are interwoven with archival footage of ethnographic displays from the past, giving historical dimension to the artists' social experiment. *The Couple in the Cage* is both comic fiction and a poignant reflection on the morality and history of western ethnography and anthropology's tendency to exoticize and objectify human beings as curiosities for public amusement.

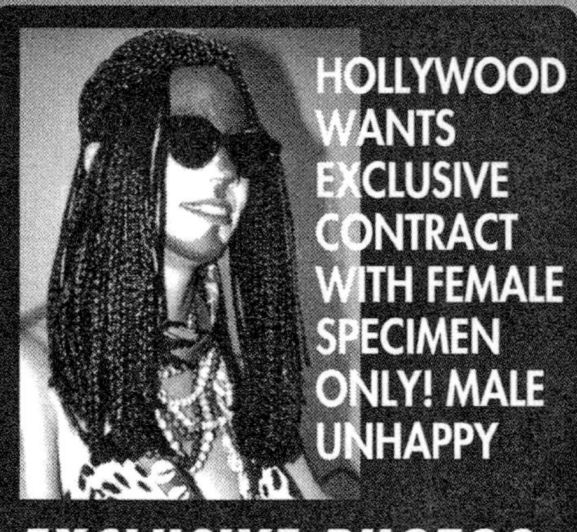

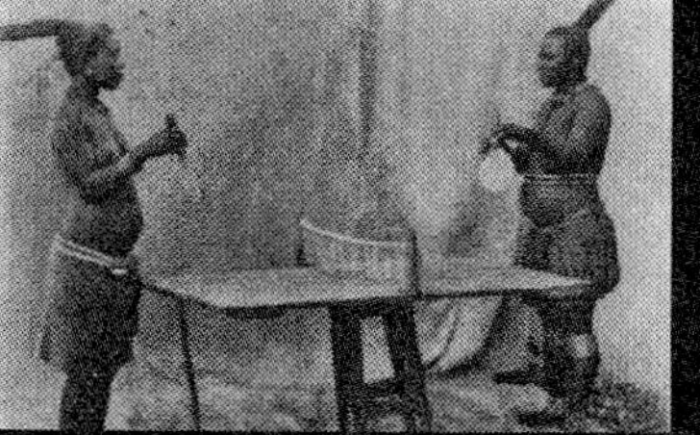

NATURAL ENQUIRER

AUGUST 1993

$1.00/$1.29 OTHER   LARGEST CIRCULATION OF ANY PAPER IN THE AMERICAS

GUATINAUI NEWLYWEDS FROM ISLAND IN GULF OF MEXICO EXHIBITED IN CAGE! MUSEUM VISITORS OUTRAGED!

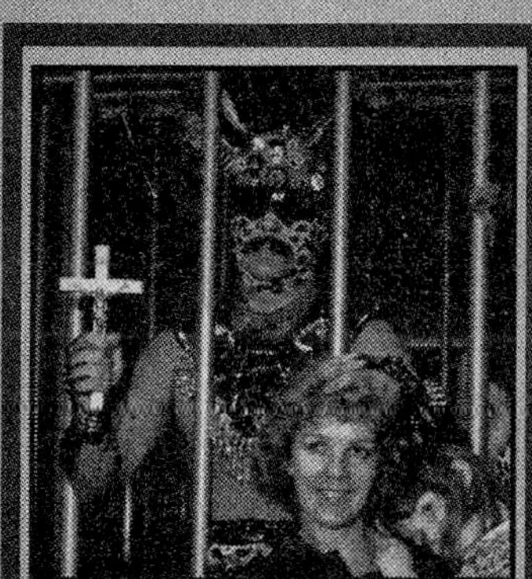

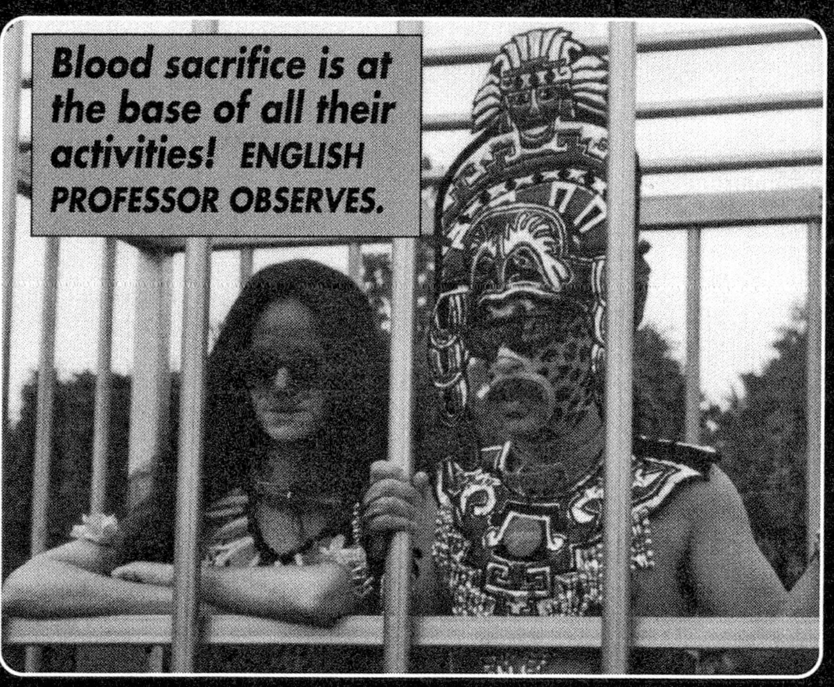

THE COUPLE IN THE CAGE:
A GUATINAUI ODYSSEY

a video by Coco Fusco and Paula Heredia

EDITED BY DAISY WRIGHT, PERFORMANCE BY GUILLERMO GÓMEZ PEÑA AND COCO FUSCO

RUNNING TIME 30 MIN

Performance Art in the West did not begin with Dadist "events". Since the early days of European "conquest," "aboriginal samples" of people from Africa, Asia, and the Americas were brought to Europe for aesthetic contemplation, scientific analysis, and entertainment. Those people from other parts of the world were forced first to take the place that Europeans had already created for the savages of their own Medieval mythology; later with the emergence of scientific rationalism, the "aborigines" on display served as proof of the natural superiority of European civilization, of its ability to exert control over and extract knowledge from the "primitive" world, and ultimately, of the genetic inferiority of non-European races. Over the last 500 years, Australian Aborigines, Tahitians, Aztecs, Iroquois, Cherokee, Ojibways, Iowas, Mohawks, Botocudos, Guianese, Hottentots, Kaffirs, Nubians, Somalians, Singhalese, Patagonians, Tierra del Fuegans, Kahucks, Anapondans, Zulus, Bushmen, Japanese, East Indians, and Laplanders have been exhibited in the taverns, theaters, gardens, museums, zoos, circuses, and world's fairs of Europe, and the freak shows of the United States. Some examples are:

1493 An Arawak brought back from the Caribbean by Columbus is left on display in the Spanish Court for two years until he dies of sadness.

1501 "Eskimos" are exhibited in Bristol, England.

1550s Native Americans are brought to France to build a Brazilian village in Rouen. The King of France orders his soldiers to burn the village as a performance. He likes the spectacle so much that he orders it restaged the next day.

1562 Michel de Montaigne is inspired to write his essay *The Cannibals* after seeing Native Americans brought to France as a gift to the king.

1613 In writing *The Tempest* Shakespeare models his character Caliban on an "Indian" he has seen in an exhibition in London.

1617 Pocahontas, the Indian wife of John Rolfe, arrives in London to advertise Virginia tobacco. She dies of an English disease shortly thereafter.

1676 Wampanoag Chief Metacom is executed for fomenting indigenous rebellion against the Puritans, and his head is publicly displayed for twenty-five years in Massachusetts.

1788 Arabanoo of the Cammeraigal people of North Sydney, Australia, is captured by Governor Phillip. At first Arabanoo was chained and guarded by a convict; later he was shown off to Sydney society. He died a year later from smallpox.

1792 Bennelong and Yarnmerswannie of the Cadigal people of South Sydney travel to England with Govemor Phillip where they are treated as curiosities. Yarnmerawannie dies of pneumonia.

1802 Pemmulway, an Aboriginal resistance fighter from the Bidgegal people, is shot by white settlers in Australia. His head is cut off, preserved, and sent to England to be displayed at the London Museum.

1810–1818 "The Hottentot Venus" (Saartje Benjamin) is exhibited throughout Europe. After her death, her genitals are dissected by French scientists and remain preserved in Paris's Museum of Man to this day.

1822 "Laplander" family is displayed with live reindeer in the Egyptian Hall in London.

1823 Impresario William Bullock stages a Mexican "Peasant" diorama in which a Mexican Indian youth is presented as ethnographic specimen and museum docent.

1829 A "Hotentot" woman exhibited nude is the highlight of a ball given by the Duchess du Barry in Paris.

1834 After General Rivera's cavalry completed the genocide of all the Indians in Uruguay, four surviving Charrúdas are donated to the Natural Sciences Academy in Paris and are displayed to the French public as specimens of a vanished race. Three die within two months, and one escapes and disappears, never to be heard from again.

1844 George Catlin displays "Red Indians" in England.

1847 Four "Bushmen" on exhibit at the Egyptian Hall in London are written about by Charles Dickens.

1853 Thirteen Kaffirs are displayed in the St. George Gallery in Hyde Park, London.

1853 "Pygmies" dressed in European garb are displayed playing the piano in a British drawing room as proof of their potential for "civilization."

1853–1901 Maximo and Bartola, two microcephalic San Salvadorans, tour Europe and the Americas, and eventually join Barnum and Bailey's Circus. They are billed as "the last Aztec survivors of a mysterious jungle city called Ixinaya."

1878 The skeleton of Truganini, a Tasmanian Aborigine, is acquired by the Royal Society of Tasmania. Her remains are displayed in Melbourne in 1888 and 1904 and then renamed to the Hobart's museum where they are displayed from 1904 until the mid-1960s.

1879 P.T. Barnum offers Queen Victoria $100,000 for permission to exhibit captured warrior Zulu Chief Cetewayo, and is refused.

1882 W.C. Coup's circus announces the acquisition of "a troupe of genuine male and female Zulus."

1893 The skeleton of Neddy Larkin, an Aborigine from New South Wales, is sold to the Harvard University Peabody Museum together with a collection of stuffed animals, stones, tools, and artifacts.

1898 At the Trans-Mississippi International Exposition in Omaha, Nebraska, a mock Indian battle is staged, and President William McKinley watches.

1905 The sole surviving member of the Yahi tribe of California, Ishi, is captured and displayed for the last five years of his life at the Museum of the University of California. Presented as a symbol of the U.S.'s defeat of Indian nations, Ishi is labeled the last Stone Age Indian in America.

1906 Ota Benga, the first Pygmy to visit America after the slave trade. is put on display in the primate cage of the Bronx Zoo. A group of Black ministers protest the zoo's display, but local press argue that Ota Benga was probably enjoying himself.

1911 The Kickapoo Indian Medicine Company is sold for $250,000, after thirty days of performances in the United States. 150 shows include one or more Kickapoo Indians as proof that the medicines being hawked were derived from genuine Indian medicine.

1931 The Ringling Circus features fifteen Ubangis, including "the nine largest-lipped women in the Congo."

1992 A Black woman midget is exhibited at the Minnesota State Fair, billed as "Tiny Teesha, the Island Princess."

In most cases, the human beings that were exhibited did not choose to be on display. More benign versions continue to take place these days in festivals and amusement parks with the partial consent of those on exhibit. The contemporary tourist industries and cultural ministries of several countries around the world still perpetrate the illusion of authenticity to cater to the Western fascination with Otherness. So do many artists.

The Year of the White Bear, 1992–94, multi-media exhibition and performances (above: text accompanying performance)

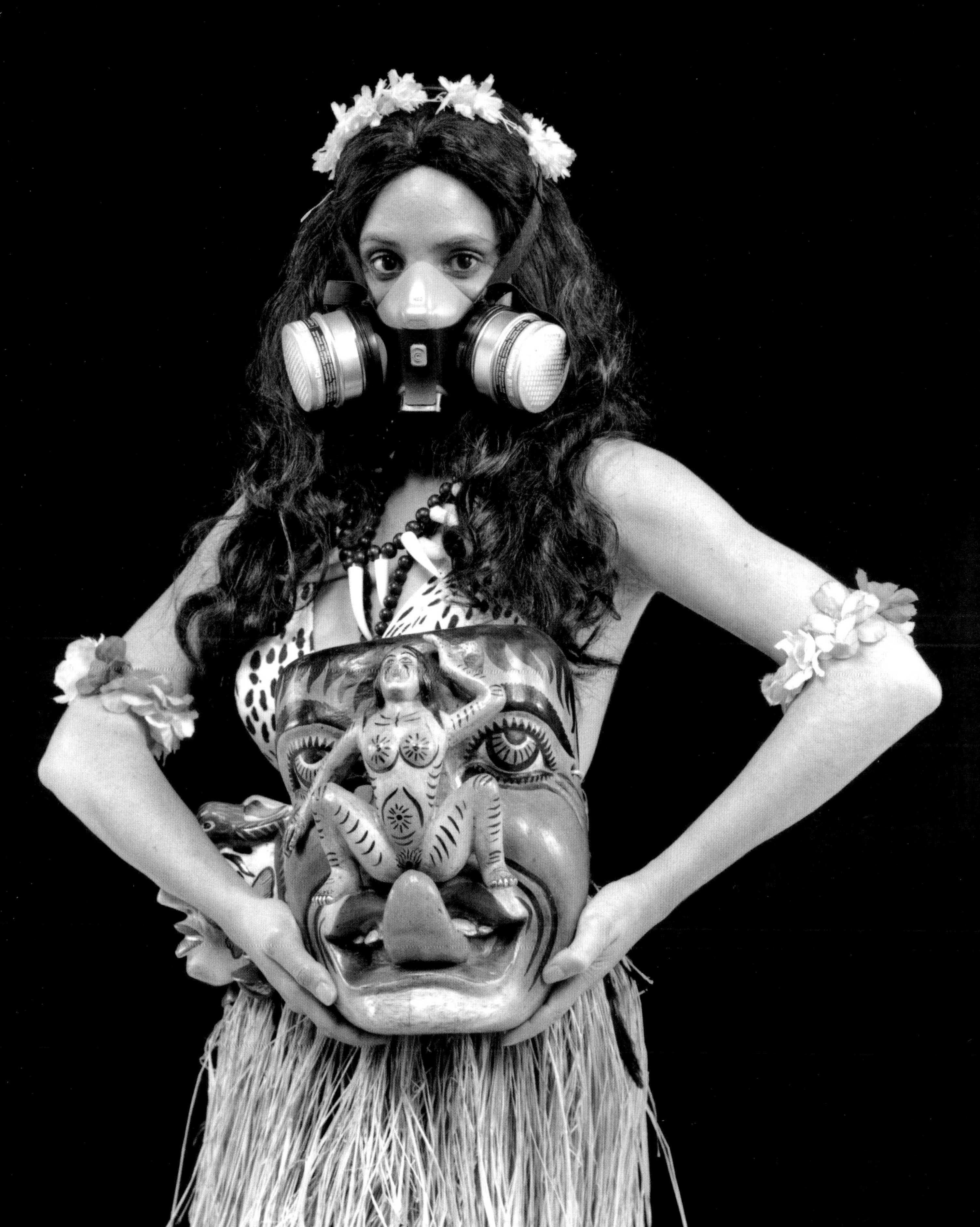

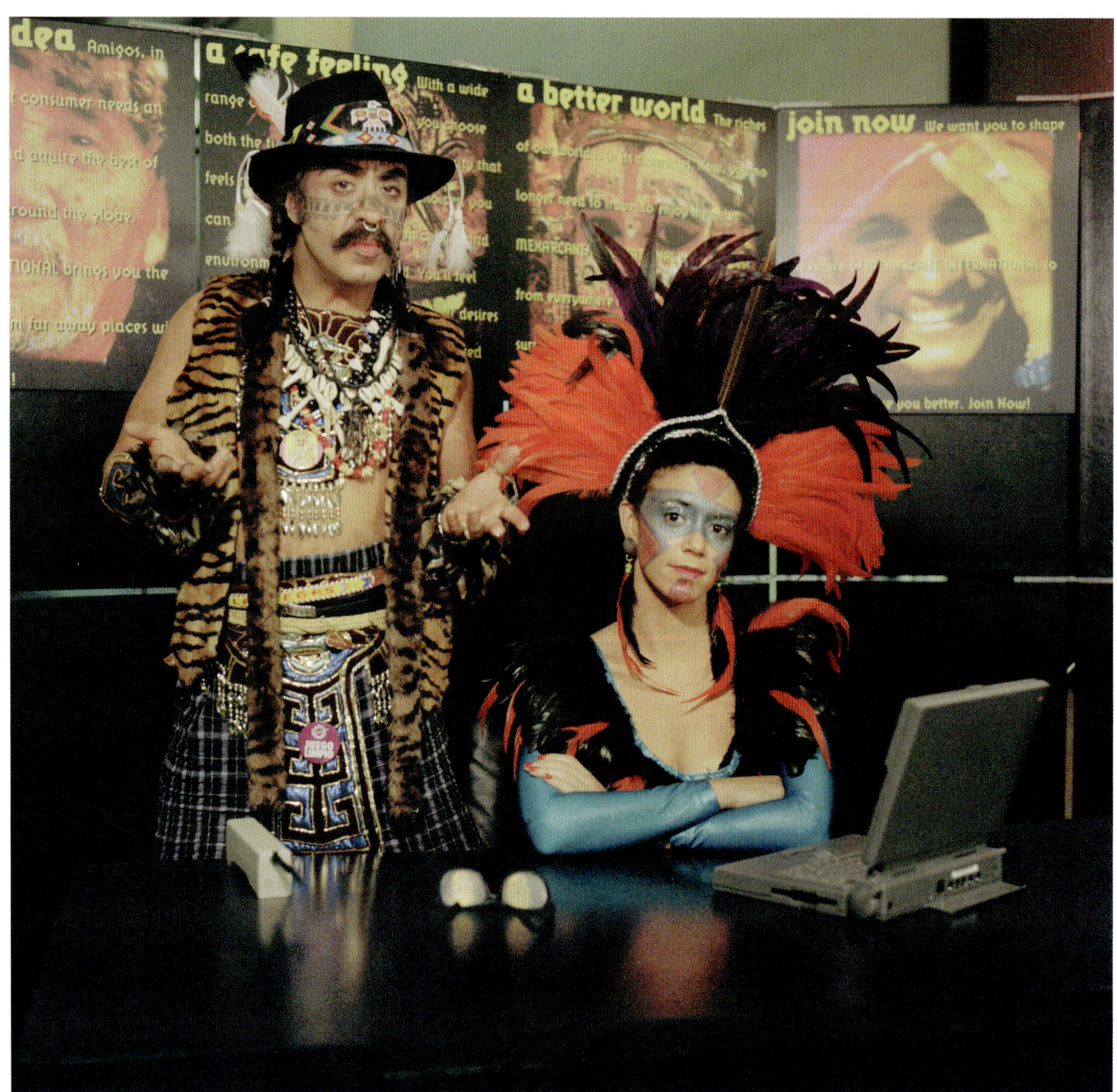

Coco Fusco and Guillermo Gómez-Peña, *Mexarcane International*, 1994–95, performance

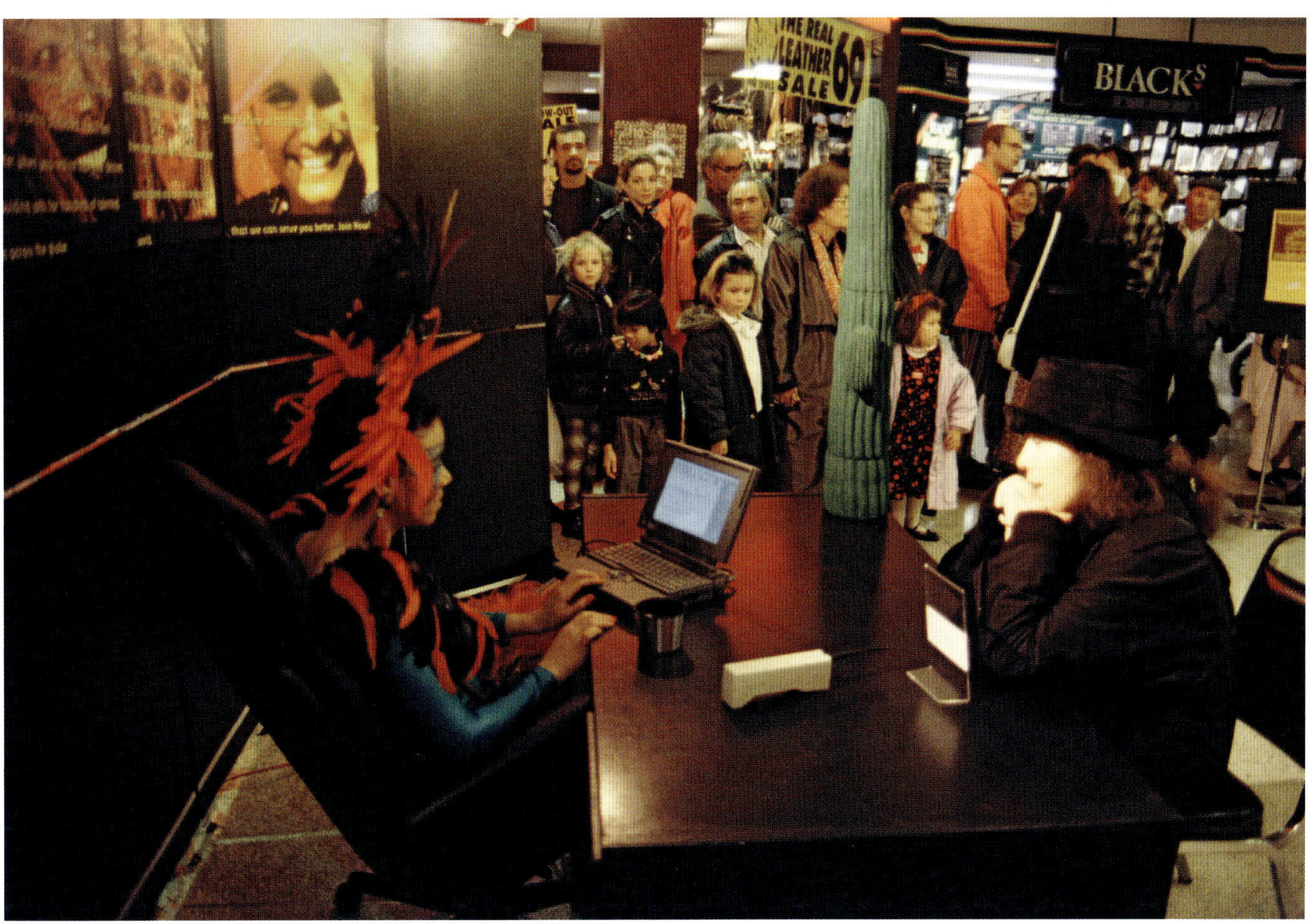

Mexarcane International

(in collaboration with Guillermo Gómez-Peña)

1994–95

Marking the final collaboration between Fusco and Gómez-Peña, this performance centers the shopping mall as the embodiment of global culture in the post-Cold War era, spaces that supposedly deliver complete satisfaction through consumption. For this work, Fusco and Gómez-Peña posed as representatives of a multinational corporation that marketed and distributed exotic talent for special events. Fusco's character was a secretary charged with conducting market research to investigate the popular tastes for exotic cultures. The duo did not present themselves as artists, so passersby would arrive at their own conclusions upon encountering their services. While Fusco and Gómez-Peña were able to present the performance in malls in Canada and the United Kingdom, they were never able to get the necessary permission to present the performance in an American shopping center. *Mexarcane International* premiered in 1994 at the National Review of Live Art in Glasgow and was presented at the Dufferin Mall in Toronto under the auspices of YYZ Artists Outlet and Mercer Union, as well as at the 1995 London International Theatre Festival.

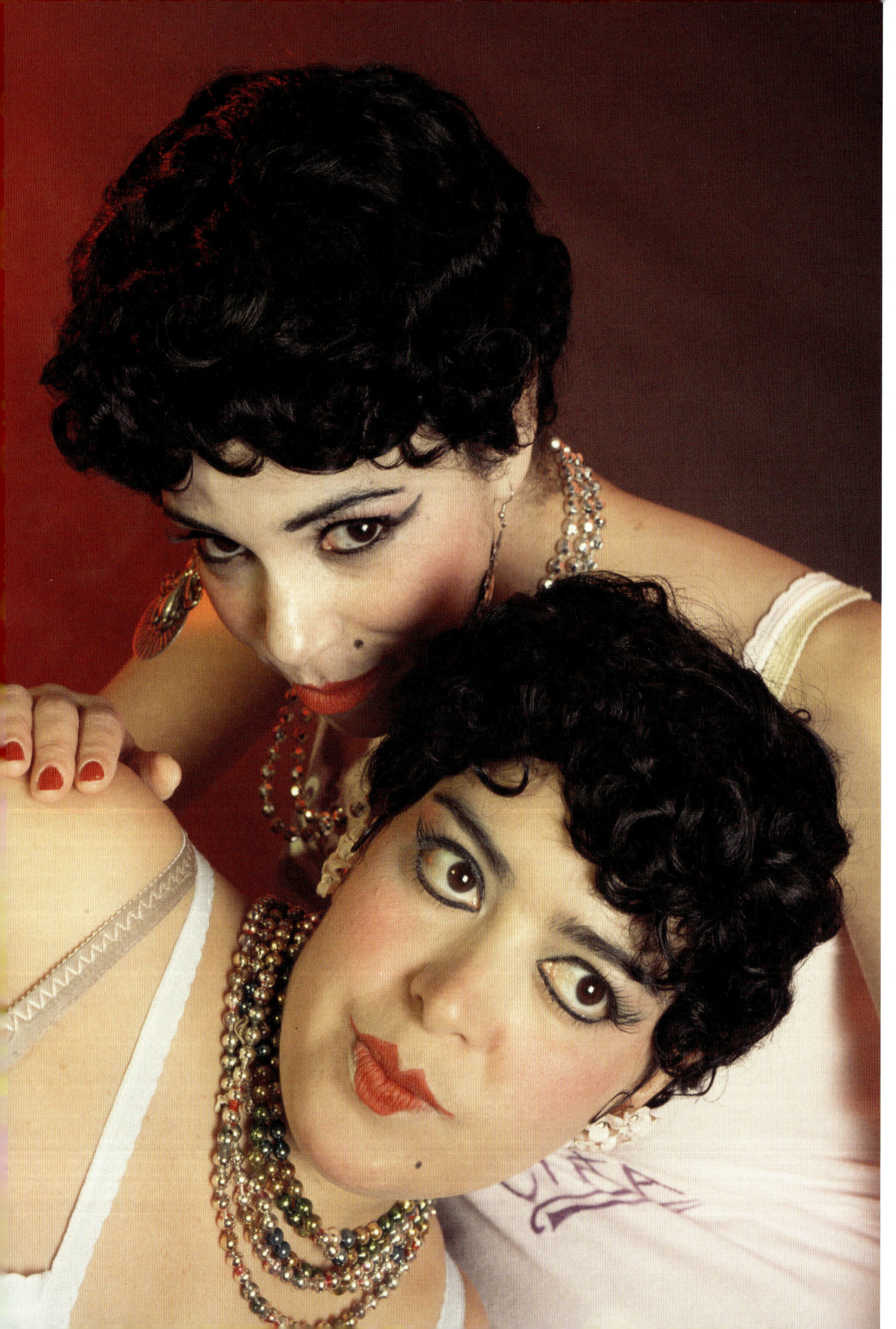

Paquita y Chata

**(in collaboration with
Nao Bustamante)**

1996

Paquita y Chata is a photographic collaboration between Fusco and the renowned Chicana interdisciplinary artist Bustamante that explored the complexities around perceptions of Latin women's sexuality. For *Paquita y Chata,* Fusco and Bustamante dressed up like dolls that are commonly sold in Mexican folk art shops. Often made of paper mache, the dolls are representations of prostitutes from the port city of Veracruz, Mexico—busty, cute Mexicans with dark and curly hair, their names hand-painted across their undershirts. The work takes the form of a fotonovela featuring the characters Paquita and Chata (entitled *Paquita y Chata se Arrebatan—Paquita and Chata Go Over the Top*) through photographs accompanied by suggestive texts written by Fusco and Bustamante.

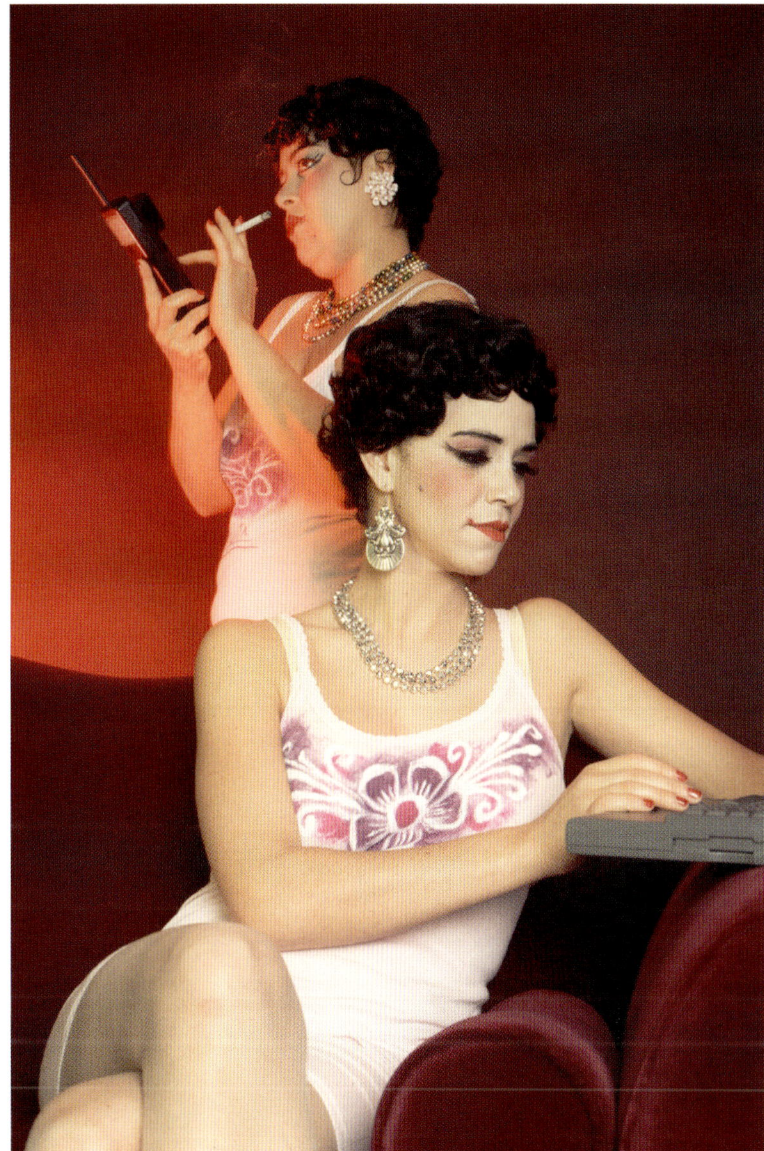

Coco Fusco and Nao Bustamante, *Paquita y Chata*, **1996, photography
(also overleaf and pages 79–81)**

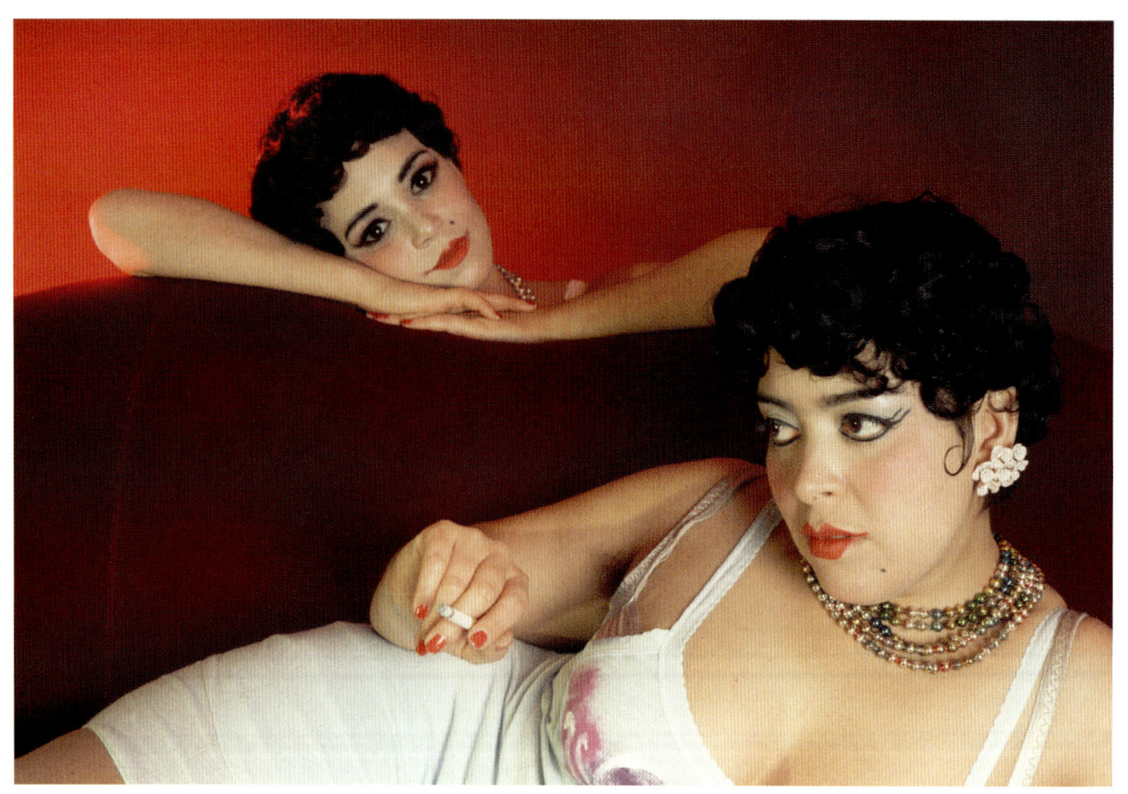

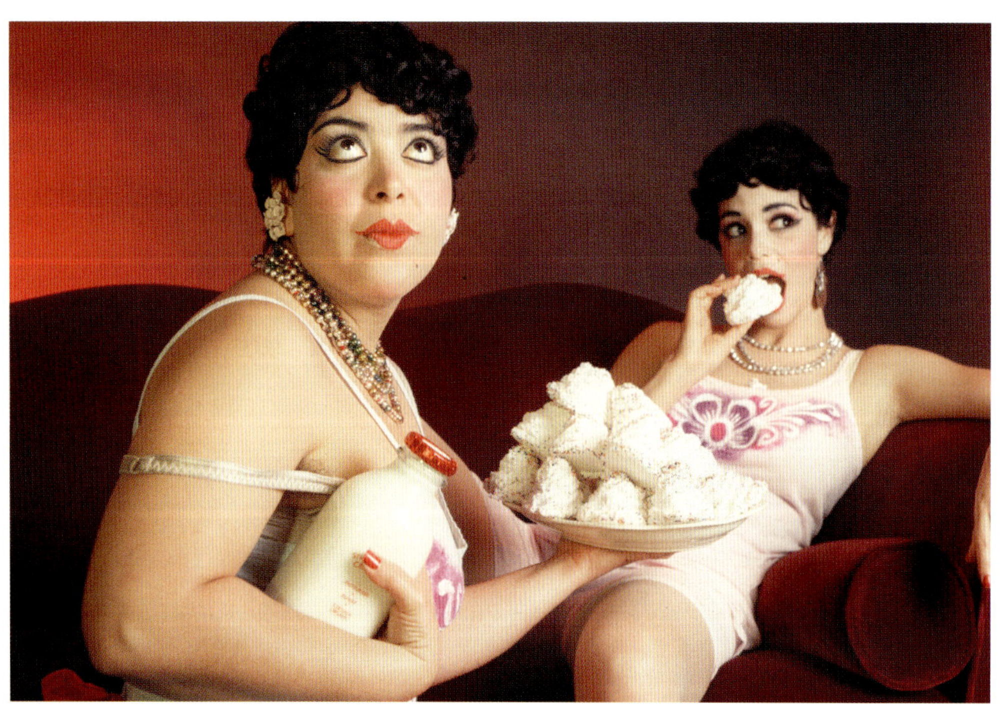

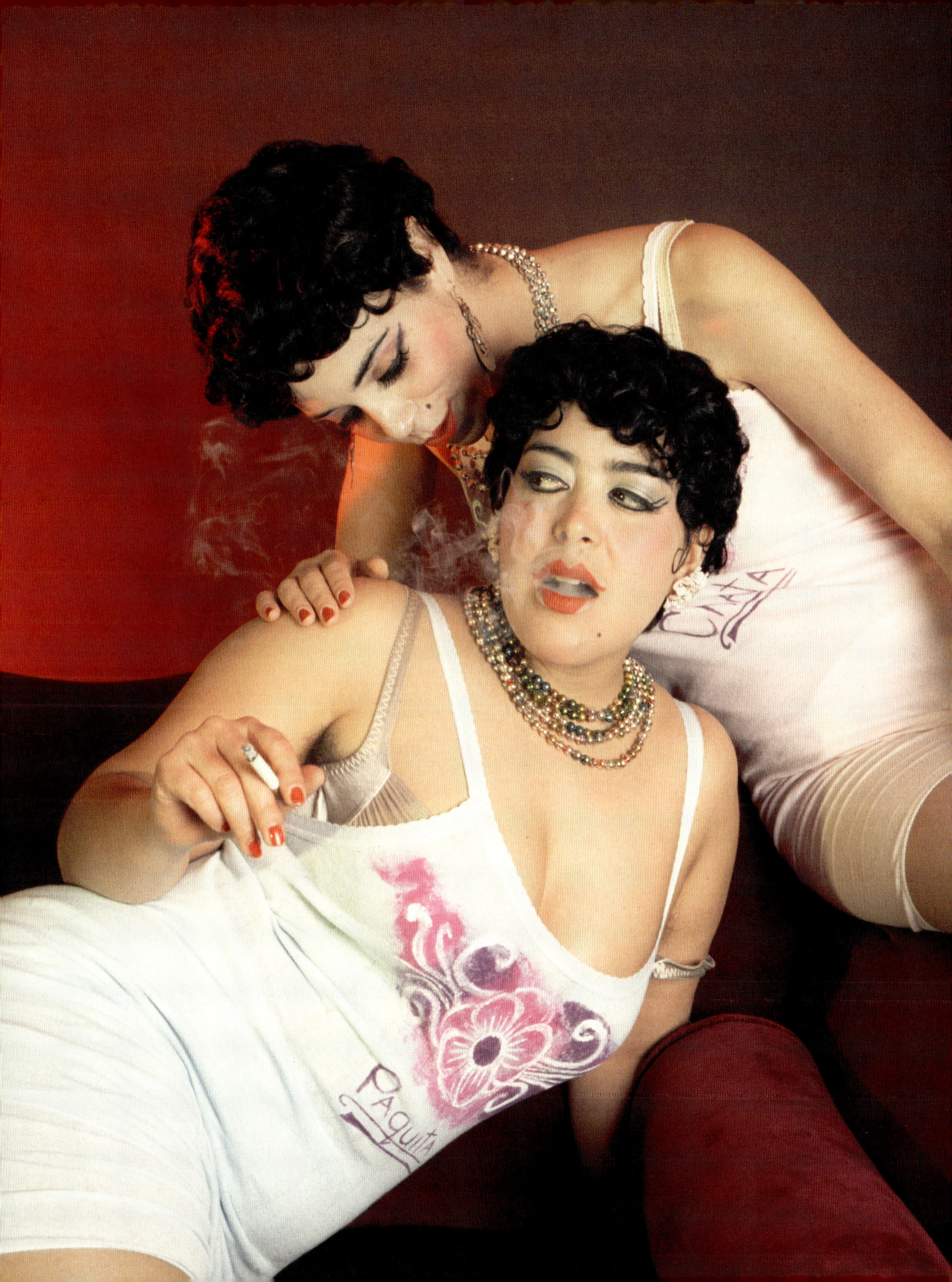
PAQUITA

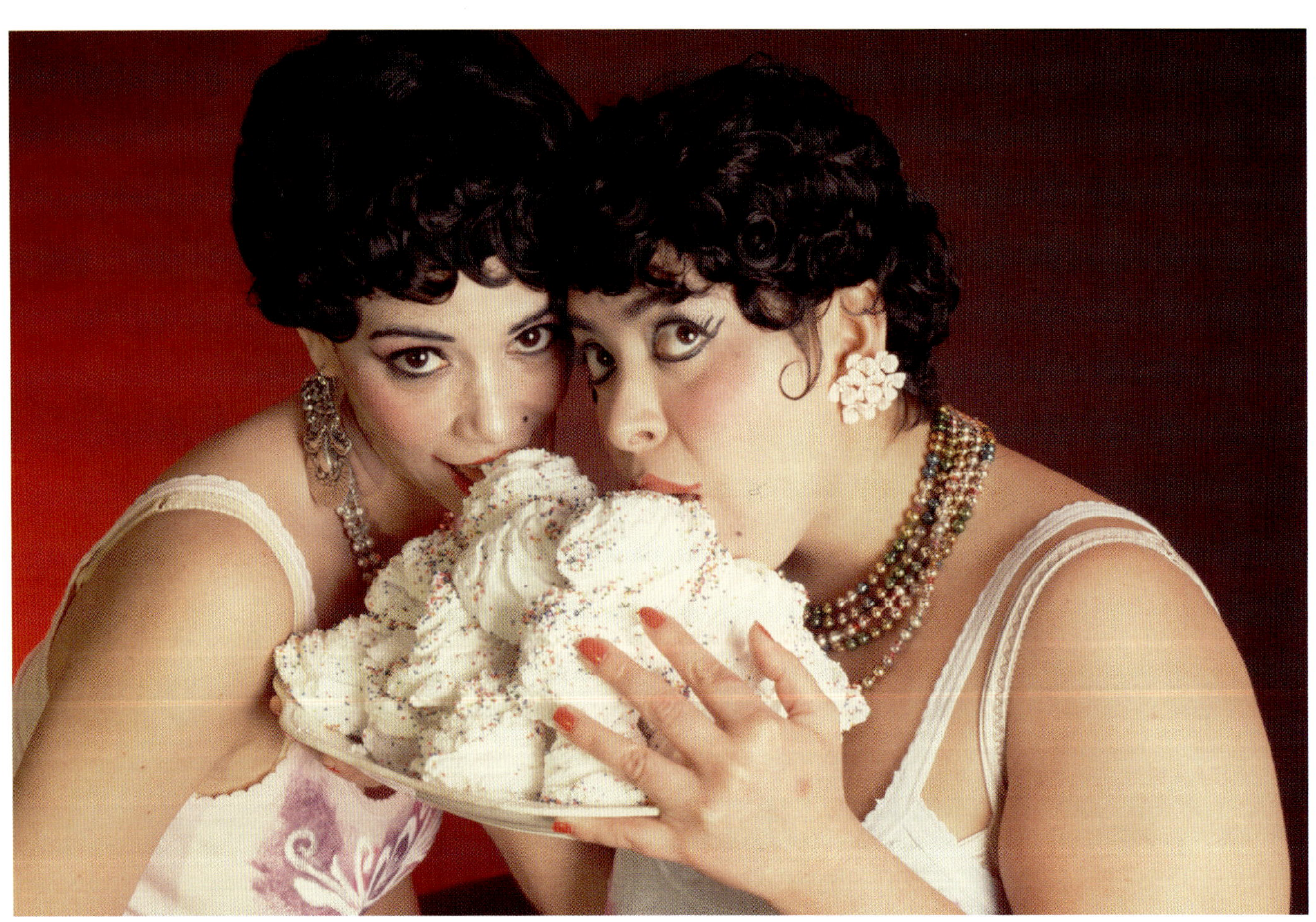

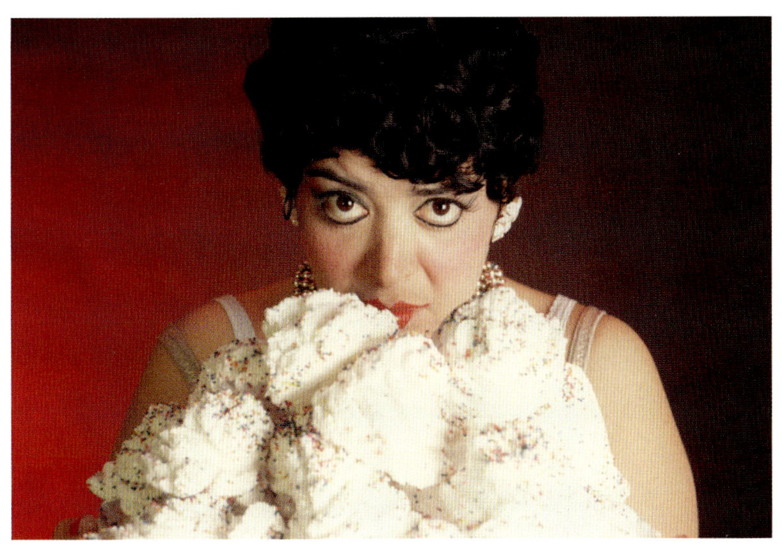

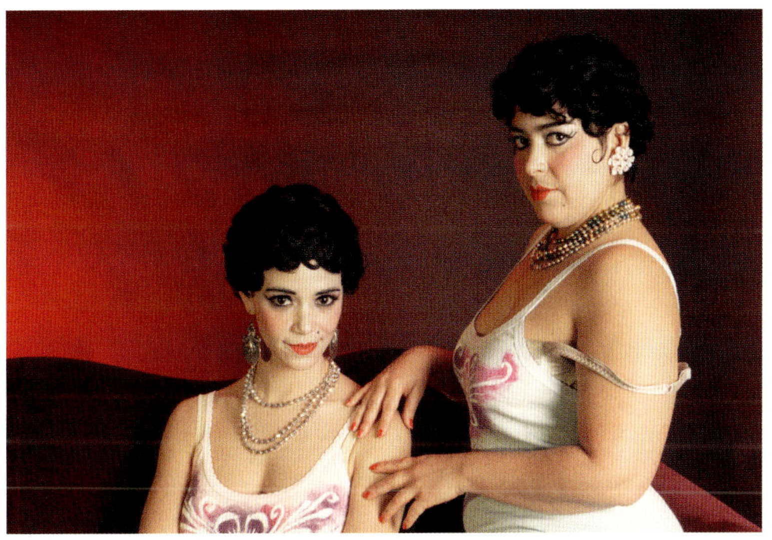

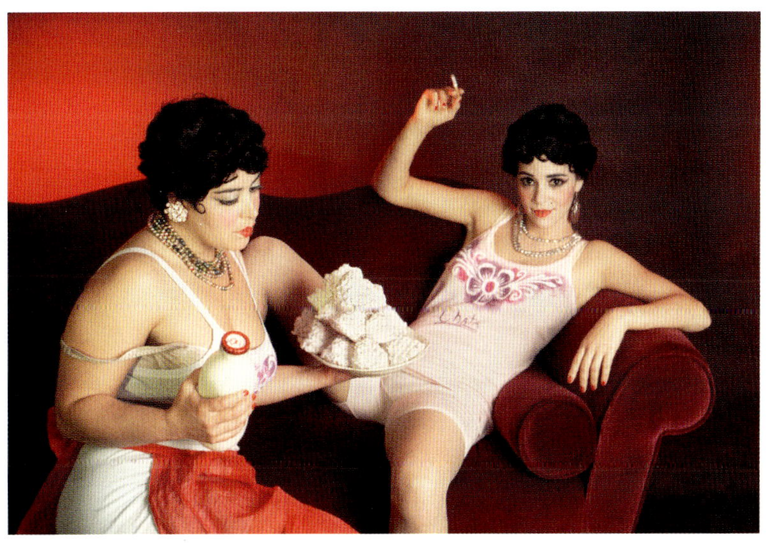

Stuff

**(in collaboration with
Nao Bustamante)**

1996–99

The collaborative, scripted performance *Stuff* explored Latin women, food, and sex through tourism. "Though only five percent of the world's population travels for leisure," writes Fusco, "the international tourist industry is the second largest employer in the global economy, and the most important link to North America for much of South America's population." Commissioned by the Institute of Contemporary Arts, London; Highways Performance Space, Los Angeles; and the Portland Institute of Contemporary Art, the performance was a spoof of sorts, employing multilingual sex guides, fast food menus, and bawdy border humor to expose cultural myths linking Latin women and food to eroticism in Western popular imagination. Fusco and Bustamante also integrated references to cannibalism in the context of Latin American literature—as an Indigenous ritual practice, a trope for European and American ravaging of Latin American resources, and symbolic revenge of the colonized who ingested and reinterpreted cultural influences of the colonizer. For the artists, this type of cultural consumption involves the trafficking of one's identity, cultural myth, and body. *Stuff* is a commentary on how globalization and "cultural tourism" leave Latin women little choice other than to fulfill the consumer's fantasy of an eroticized "other" female body.

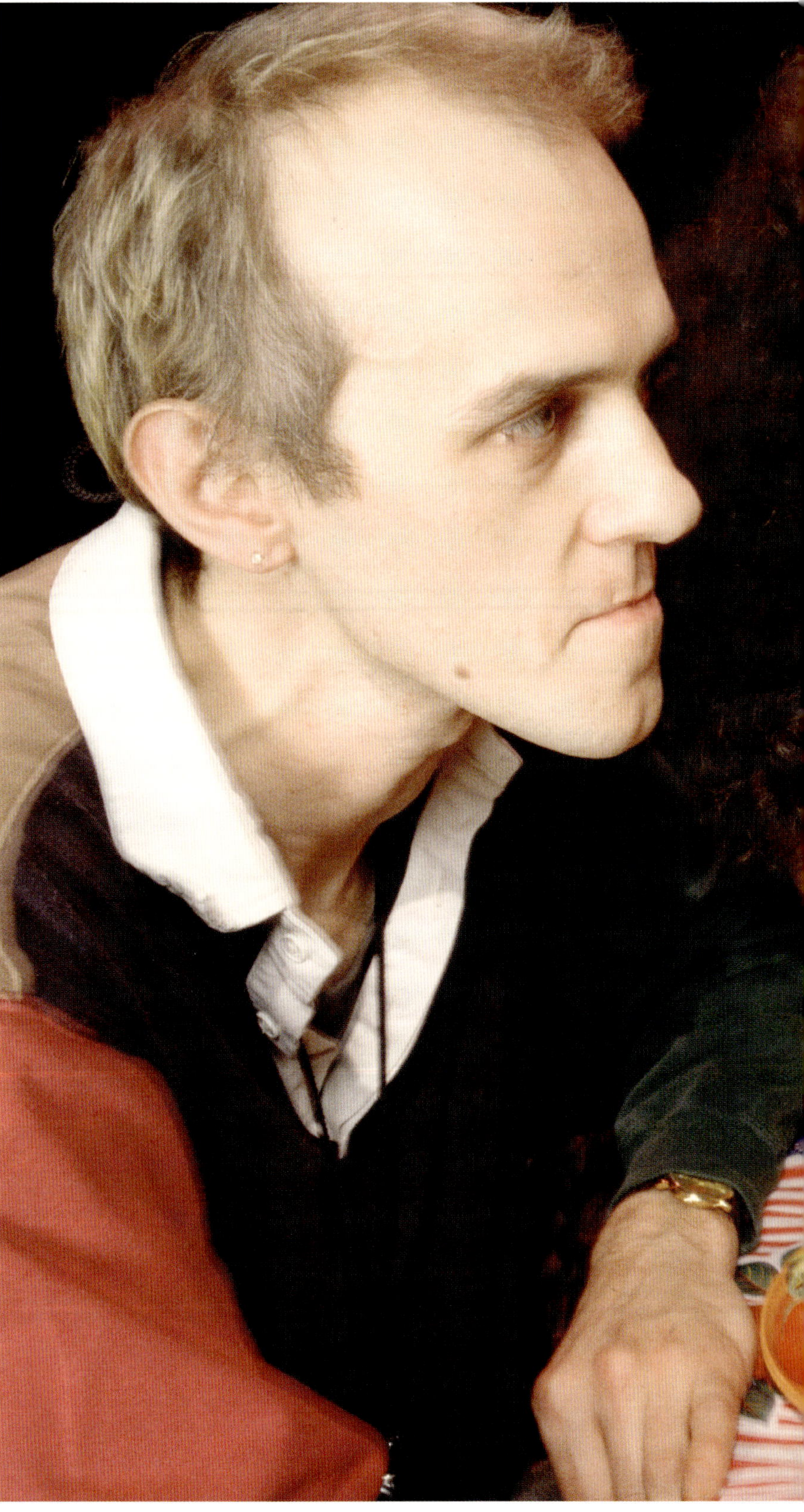

Coco Fusco and Nao Bustamante, *Stuff*, 1996–99, performance (also overleaf and page 85)

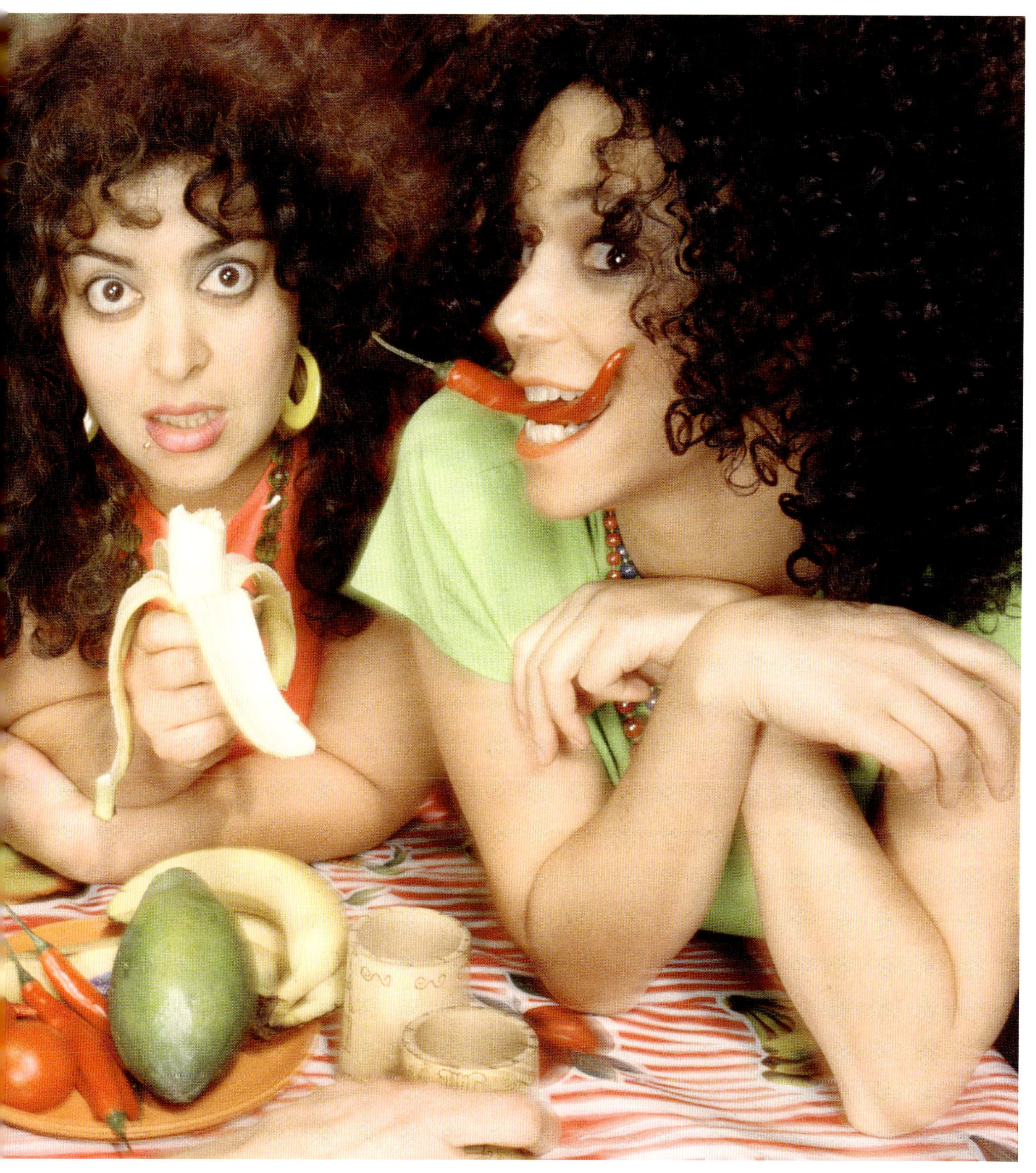

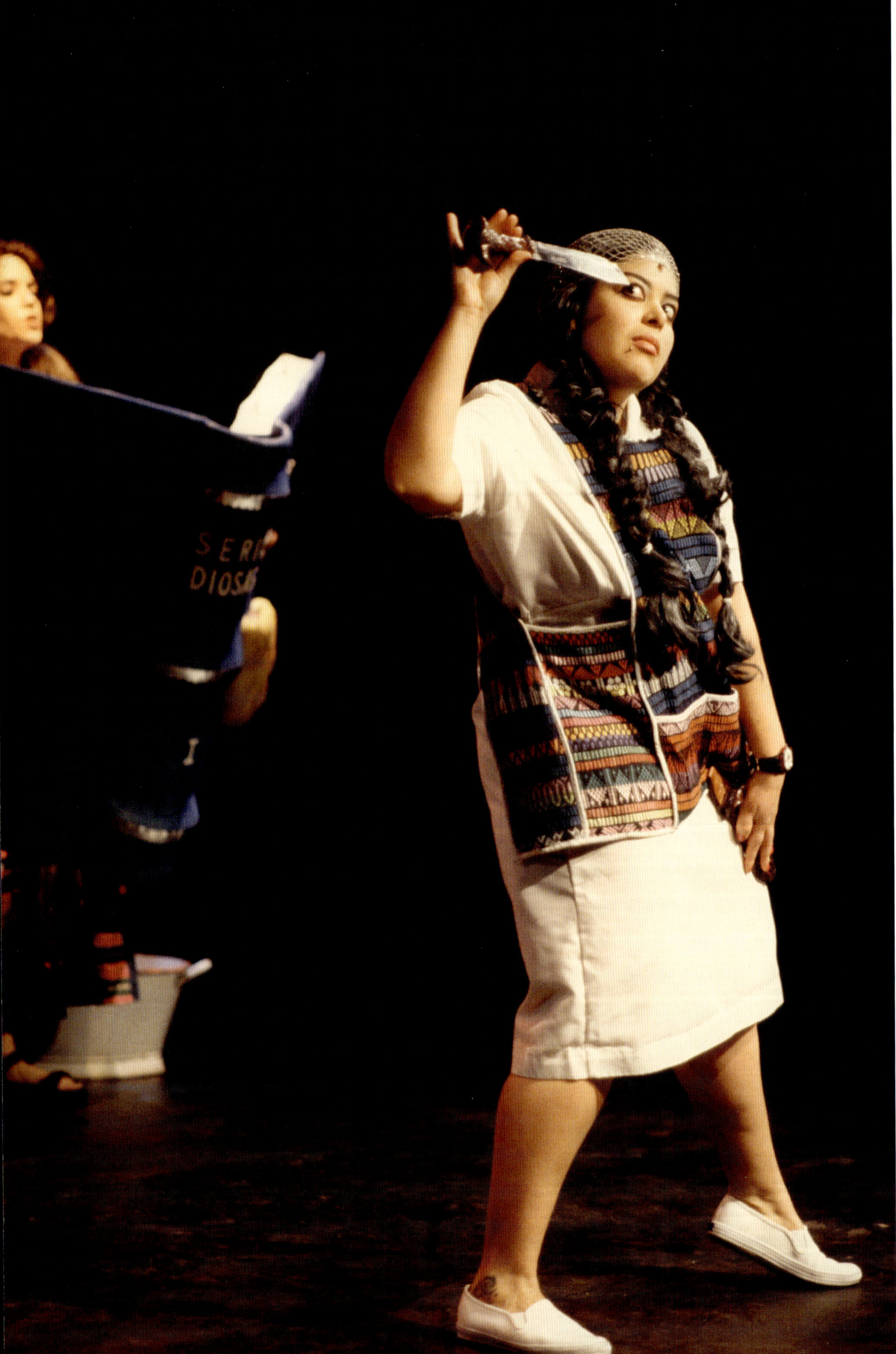
SERA
DIOS

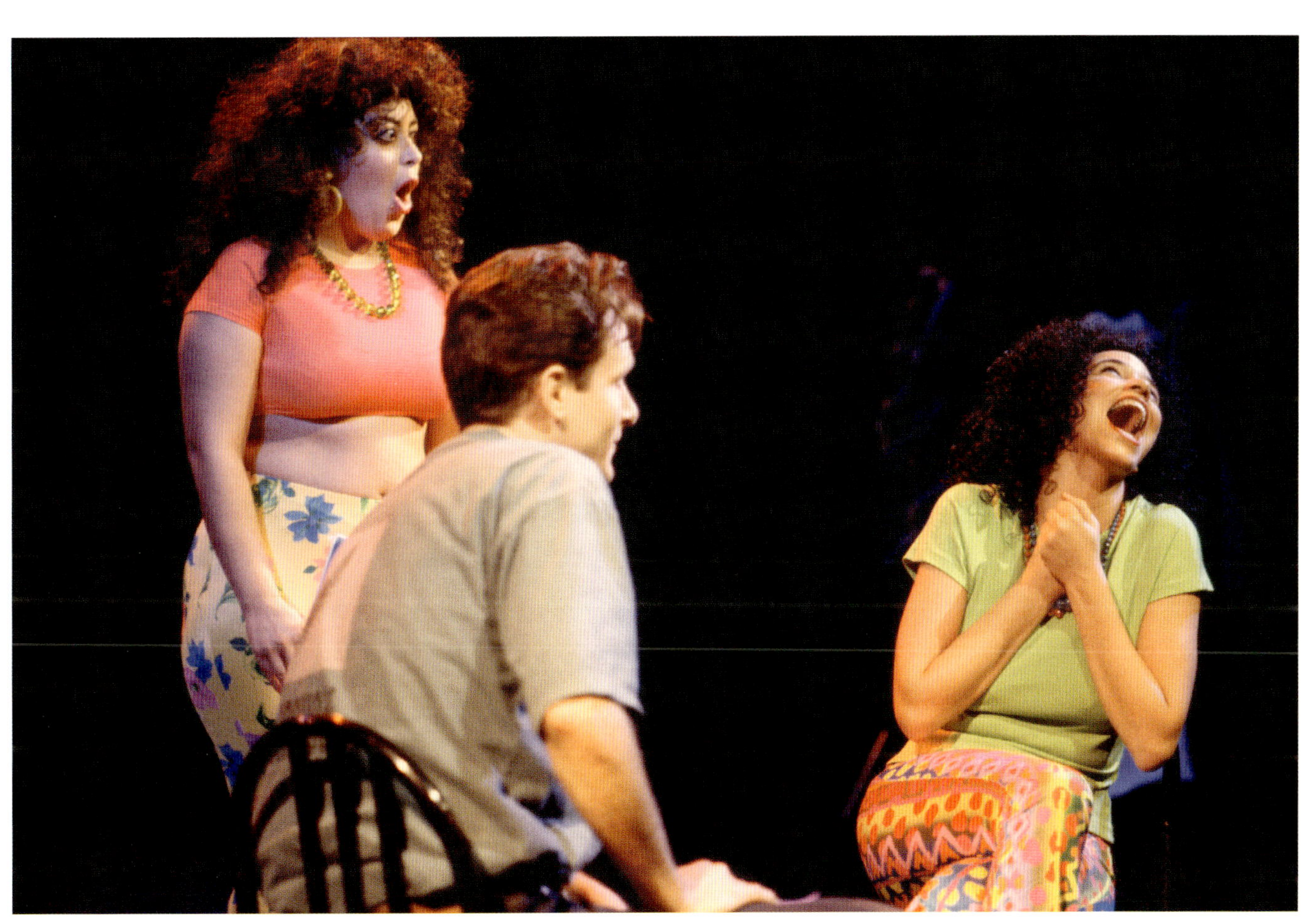

Sudaca Enterprises

(in collaboration with Juan Pablo Ballester, María Elena Escalona, and Vladimir Cuenca)

1997

Conceived as a guerrilla performance by Fusco and Cuban artists Ballester and Escalona, *Sudaca Enterprises*—taking its name from the derogatory term used in Spain to refer to Latinos, translating to "dirty southerner"—was presented at the 1997 ARCO Latino Art Fair in Madrid. Dressed in ski masks and Quechua knit hats, the three performers sold T-shirts with text printed on them that compared the prices of Latin American art in Europe and of art sold at the ARCO fair with the cost of surviving as an undocumented Latin American immigrant in Spain. A fourth performer dressed as a police officer acted as a prop. Over three days, the performers were removed multiple times by the fair's security for not having paid for the space to sell their wares and were stopped from selling inside a booth. Ultimately, they were ejected from the arena for keeping their faces covered. All of the shirts were sold during the fair, and at least two are now in museum collections.

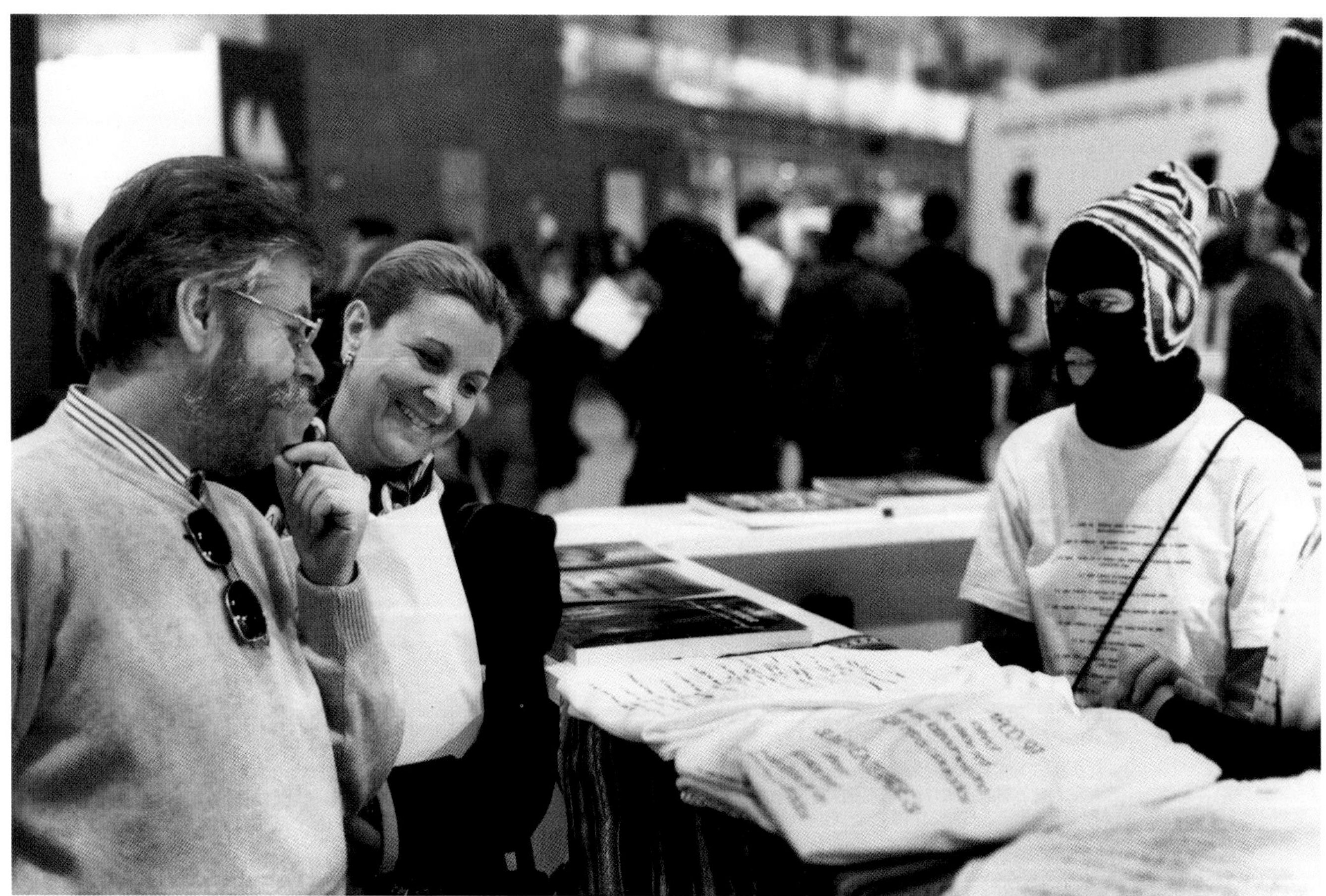

Coco Fusco, María Elena Escalona, Juan Pablo Ballester, and Vladimir Cuenca, *Sudaca Enterprises*, 1997, performance (and overleaf)

SUDACA ENTERPRISES offers a real vision of
Latin America in 300 square centimeters.

SUDACA ENTERPRISES is a project by
Juan Pablo Ballester and Coco Fusco.

What a Botero for the Madrid airport cost:
200,000,000 pesetas.

What a South American pays at that airport to enter Spain:
50,000 ptas.

What you have to have in the bank to obtain Spanish residency:
1,000,000 ptas.

What a fake passport costs:
1,000,000 ptas.

What a fake residence and work permit costs:
500,000 ptas.

What they charge galleries for a square meter at ARCO '97:
17,000 ptas.

What they charge a South American as a deposit for an apartment:
150,000 ptas.

What a Spanish prostitute charges:
15,000 ptas.

What a Cuban jinetera charges a Spanish tourist:
7,000 ptas.

The number of South Americans participating in ARCO '97:
300.

The number of illegal South Americans in Spain:
400,000.

The number of work permits granted to South Americans between 1990 and 1995:
195,330.

The number of "quotas" to be granted in 1997:
10,000.

What the Spanish government pays Lucrecia's family in Sto. Domingo:
10,000 ptas. per month.

Text printed on T-shirts sold during the performance

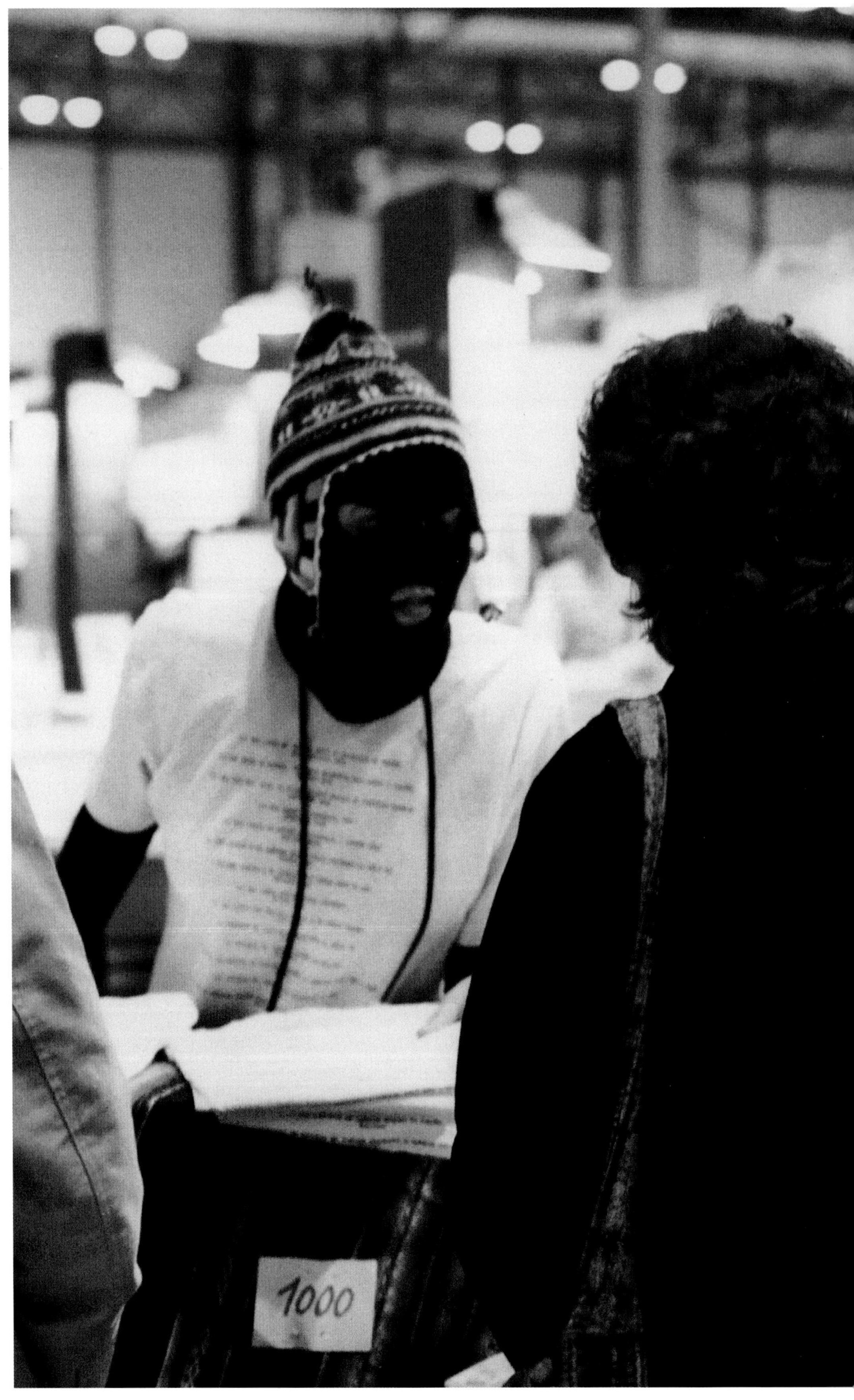

1000

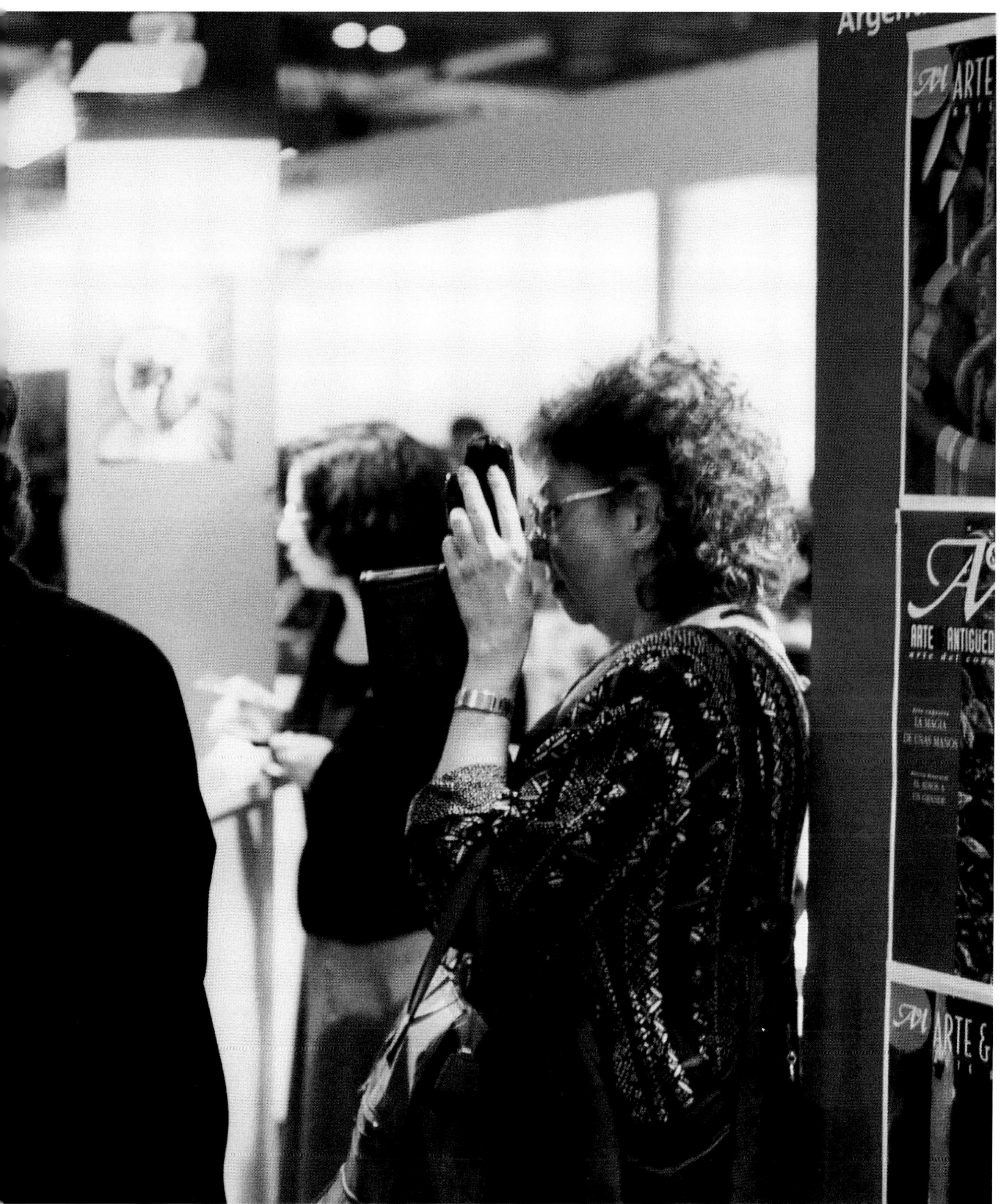
Argen
ARTE
ARTE & ANTIGÜED
arte del co
LA MAGIA
DE UNAS MANOS
EL AMOR A
LO GRANDE
ARTE &

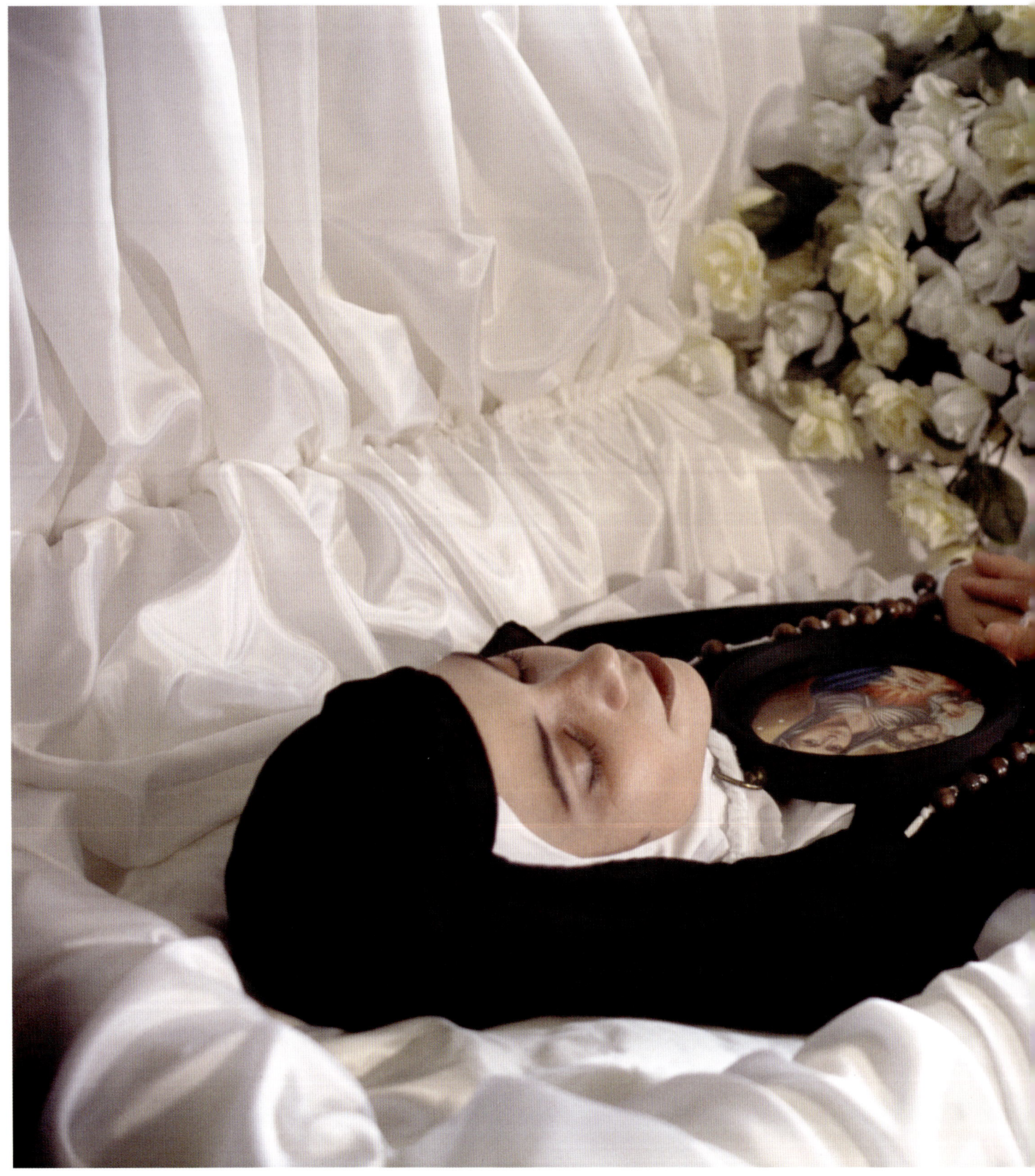

Better Yet When Dead, 1997, performance installation

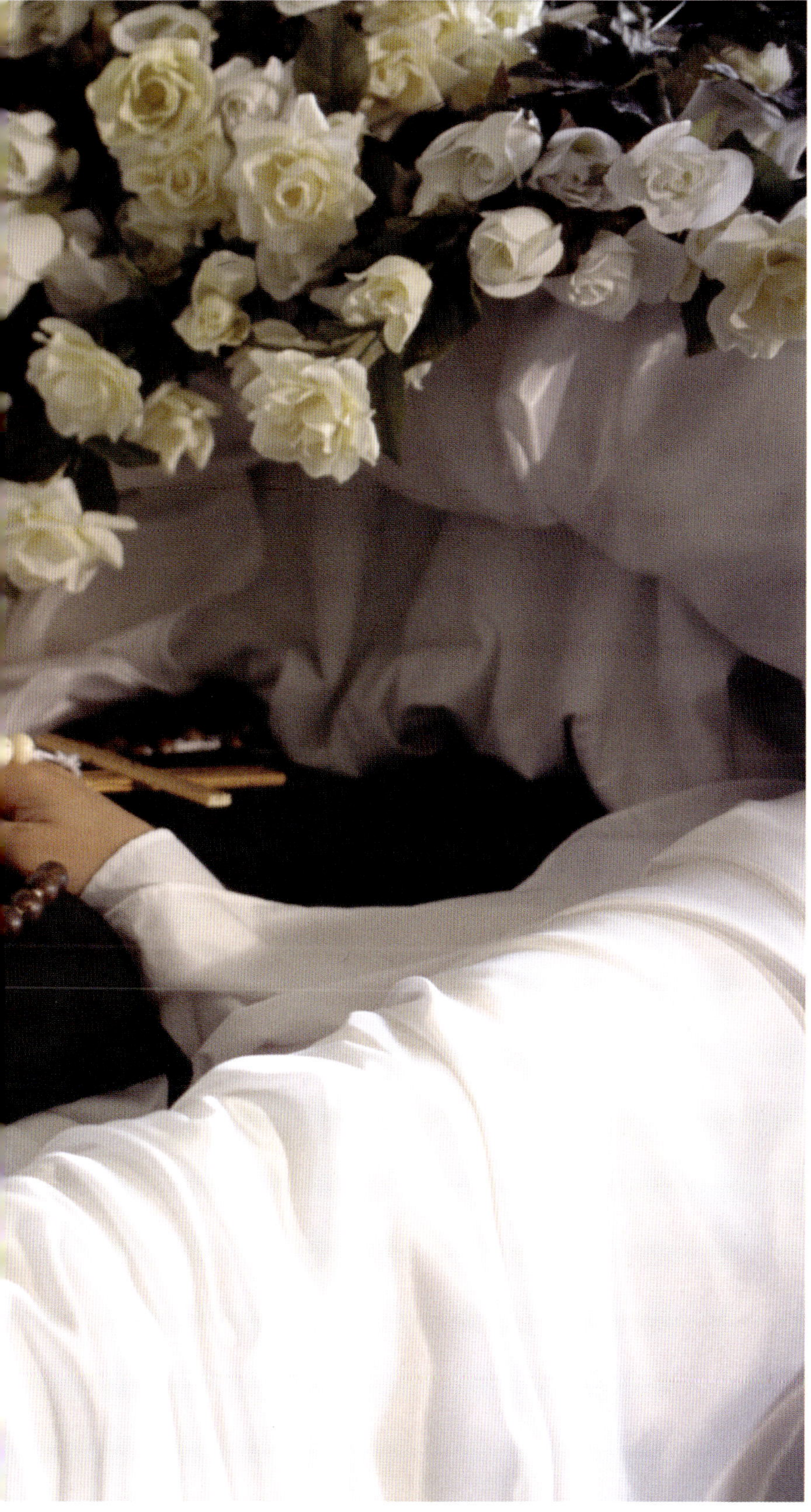

Better Yet When Dead

1997

Better Yet When Dead is a performance and installation examining the paradox of many Latin American women's careers: great invisibility in their lifetime but high value by society after their death. At the International Festival of Art of Medellin and at Toronto's YYZ, Fusco transformed exhibition spaces into funeral parlors and held wakes dedicated to women who became iconic following their untimely deaths. Appearing as a different person each day, from Cuban artist Ana Mendieta (1948–1985) to Mexican American singer-songwriter Selena (1971–1995), Fusco surrounded a coffin with texts that offered pertinent details from each woman's life, along with a written statement from each artist that served as the textual centerpiece. In addition to Selena and Mendieta, the wakes included Mexican painter Frida Kahlo (1907–1954), who only posthumously became a symbol of female artistic martyrdom; Argentinian actress and politician First Lady Evita Perón (1919–1952), whose corpse was hidden by the military due to fear of the power she held over the population even after her death; and Sor Juana Inés de la Cruz (1648–1695), the Mexican nun, writer, philosopher, composer, and poet who was forced by church hierarchy to set down her pen.

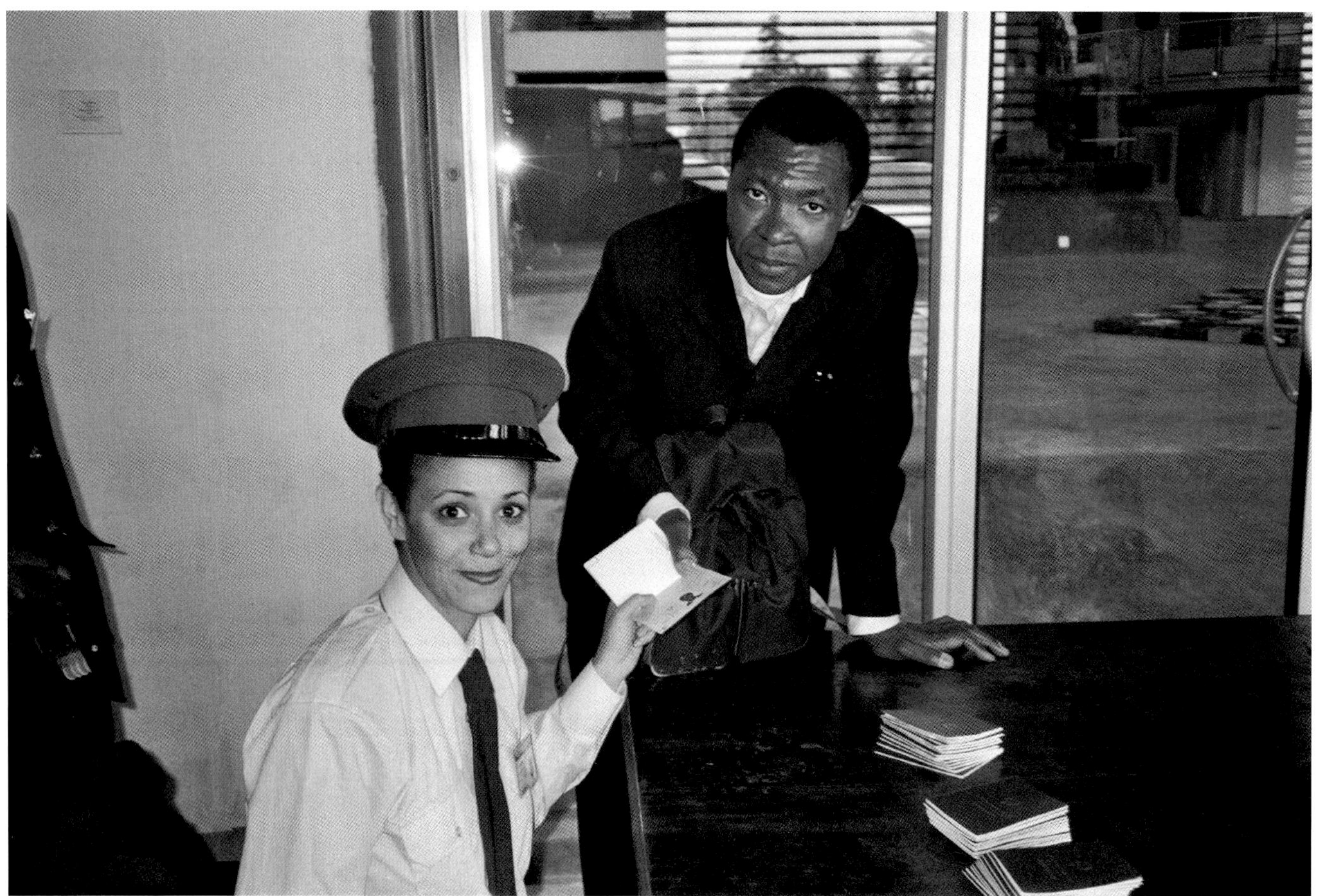

Rights of Passage, 1997, performance

Rights of Passage

1997

A site-specific performance Fusco created for the 1997 Johannesburg Biennale, *Rights of Passage* investigated race, space, and institutional power in post-apartheid South Africa. Dressed in a police uniform, Fusco provided visitors with passbooks that simultaneously served as evidence of payment for entry to the Biennale, an artist's multiple, and residue of the performance. Fusco suggests South Africa's "past" is currently managed via romantic commodification and that "this pack-aging of Blackness, whether it be constructed as a precolonial African identity for tourists, a folkloric preservation of non-hybridized tradition, or a sanitized version of township life, is one of the many socio-cultural mechanisms of repression that characterize contemporary post-apartheid culture." The passbook also functioned as a souvenir, a reminder of a critical moment in the history of demarcation of space in South Africa, of our ambivalent attraction to and repulsion from that past, and of its immanent commodification. For Fusco, *Rights of Passage* evidenced how even the most horrifying historical events can function as a point of attraction, and ultimately, lure global capital investment in order to monetize human suffering.

BODY OF WORK 1990–2022

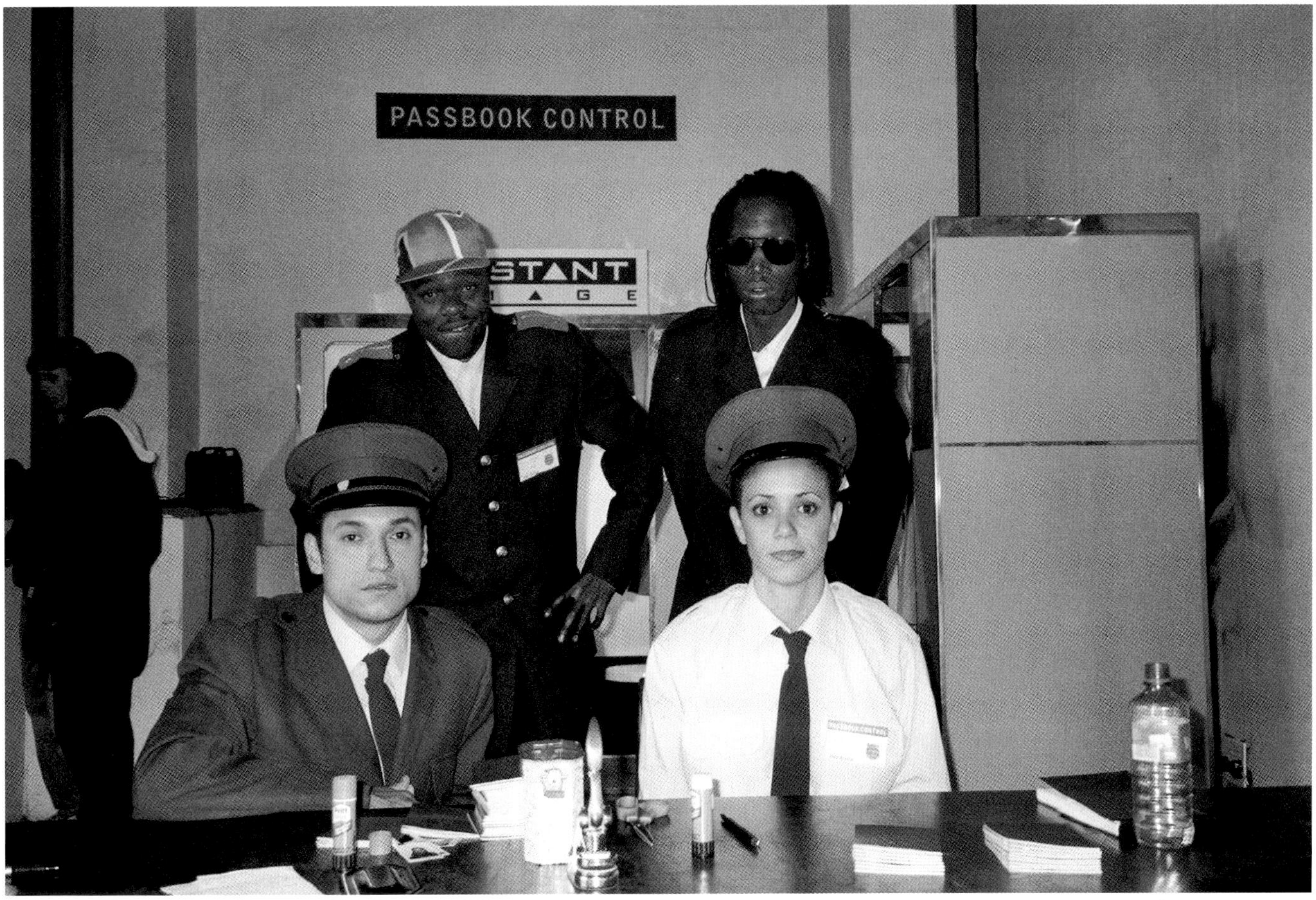

PASSBOOK CONTROL
STANT
AGE

ELECTRICAL
ALL ELECTRICAL
GOOD
PASSBOOK CONTROL

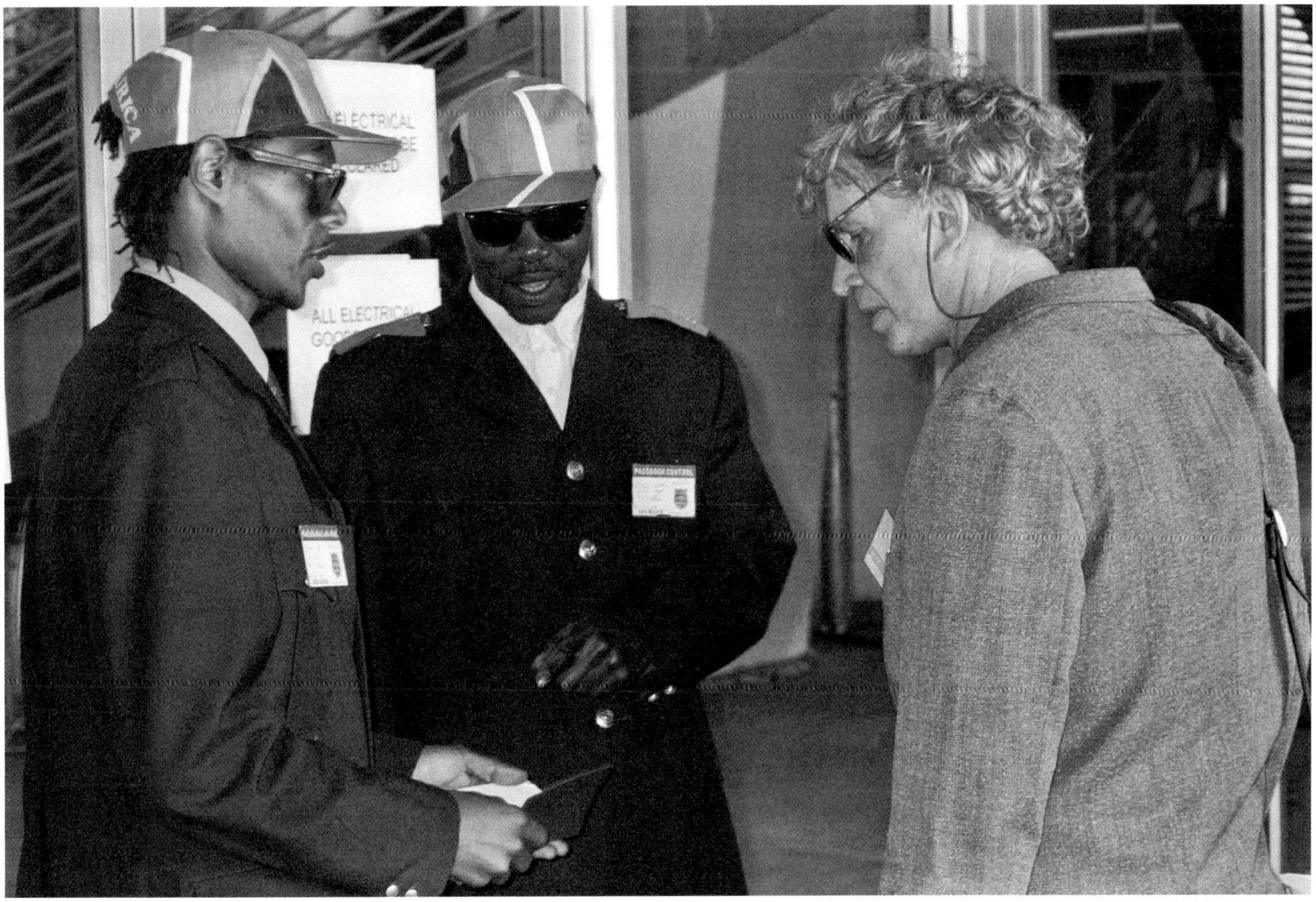

El último deseo (The Last Wish)

1997

The performance is a commentary on the desire of aging Cuban exiles to die in their homeland and the exploitation of that desire by entities seeking to profit from it. Although certain Cuban exiles were granted permission for short visits to their home country after 1979, for many exiles, return to the island was forbidden until after death. When Fusco's grandmother turned 80, she boarded a plane, flew to Barcelona to meet distant cousins, checked into a hotel, laid down, and died in the night. Fusco, who was in Paris at the time, was sent to collect her belongings. When the artist arrived, she discovered her grandmother had only left behind her glasses and a small purse. For *El último deseo* (*The Last Wish*), Fusco staged a Catholic wake inside Havana's Galería Tejadillo 214, the home of artist Tania Bruguera, lying on the floor of a parlor wrapped in a white sheet and ringed with flowers and tea lights. At the room's threshold she posted a sign bearing the performance's title, which refers to her grandmother's unfulfilled "last wish": to be returned, as many other exiles also wished, to Cuba to be buried.

Text accompanying performance:

When my mother and her sisters were younger, they worried about what part of the world they could live in. They hardly ever spoke about returning to their homeland. They had never had riches there to dream of retrieving. But as time goes on and they grow older, they no longer worry about where to are going to live, but about where they will die.

Their mother, my grandmother, was born in Oriente province in 1902. Orphaned as a child, she began to sew professionally at thirteen, helped raise her younger siblings, and was forced to marry before the age of twenty. Supporting her five children as a seamstress and withstanding frequent abuse from her husband, she managed to finish high school at forty. When she saw that her second daughter, my mother, was strong enough to fend for herself, she encouraged her to leave their town and never come back. My mother, then seventeen, took her first train ride to Havana, began to work and study, and in one year brought her mother and siblings to the capital. Eleven years later my mother boarded her first plane and went to the United States with twenty five dollars and a suitcase of clothing my grandmother made for her. Nine years after that, she sent for my grandmother. In all my childhood I never heard her express regret at having left. Yet just after her eightieth birthday, suffering from loss of hearing and memory, she boarded a plane, flew to Barcelona to meet distant cousins, checked into a hotel, lay down, and died in the night.

When I arrived at the hotel three days later, I discovered she had left not a suitcase behind, only her glasses and a small purse.

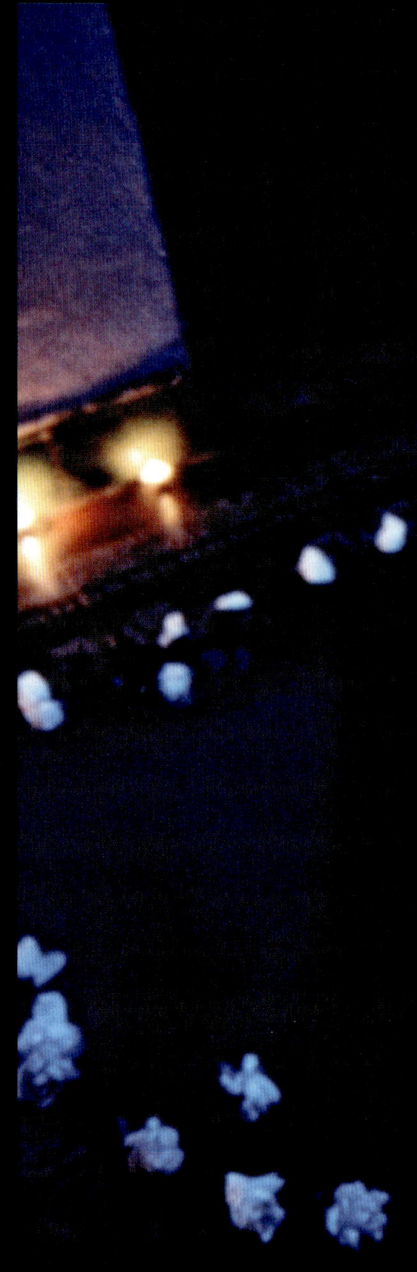

El último Deseo (The Last Wish),
1997, performance

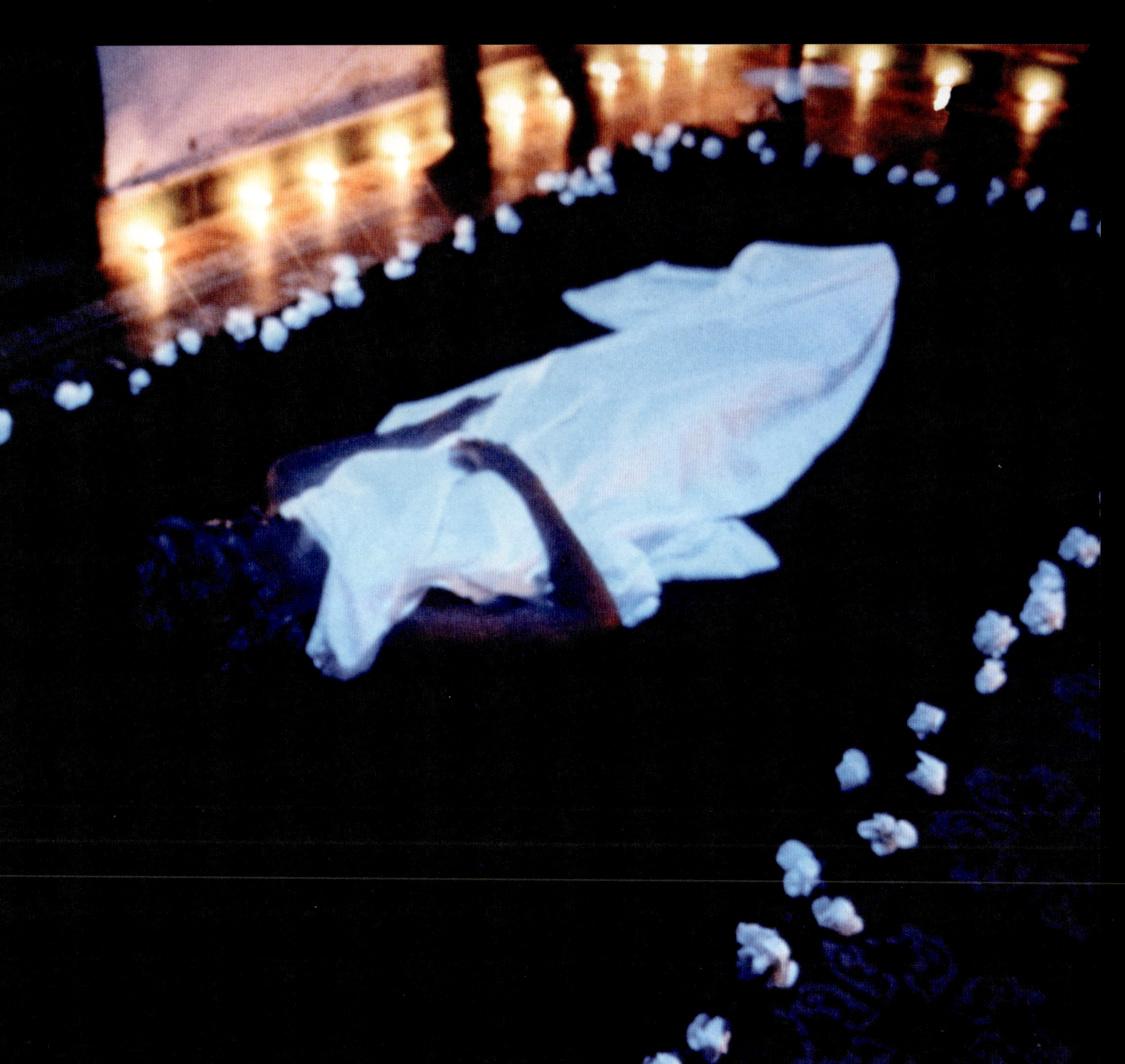

Votos (Vows)

1999–2000

This performance emerges from Fusco's interest in studying how women in Latin America have articulated their desire for intellectual and spiritual life. In the development of *Votos* (*Vows*), Fusco studied the corporeal practices and poetry of Catholic mystics, as well as anthropological writings about the activities of cloistered women in Mexico and Peru during the colonial period, and drew on the practices of *penitents* for her gestures. During the early colonial period, twenty percent of the urban female populations of New Spain and the Viceroyalty of Peru lived in cloisters where they were able to learn to read and to avoid marriage and childbirth. Fusco also found that their highly regimented daily routines, punctuated by the continuous performance of faith, resembled the performances of pioneers in the field of body art in the 1960s and 1970s. *Votos* premiered at the 3rd Annual Performance Festival in Odense, Denmark in September 1999 and was presented at the Washington State University Museum, the Nexus Contemporary Art Center in Atlanta, the Project in Harlem, and in Germany as part of Expo 2000 in August 2000.

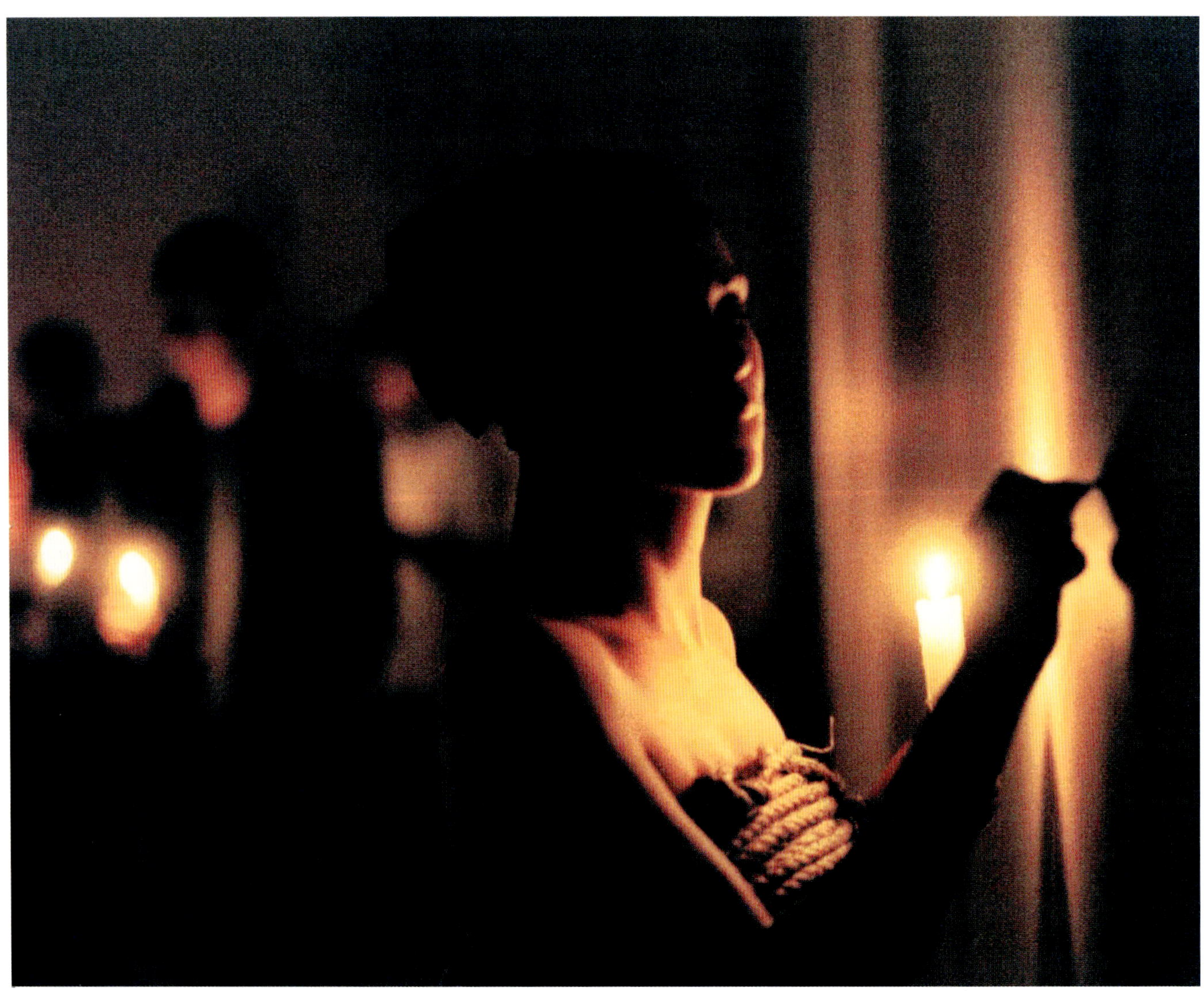

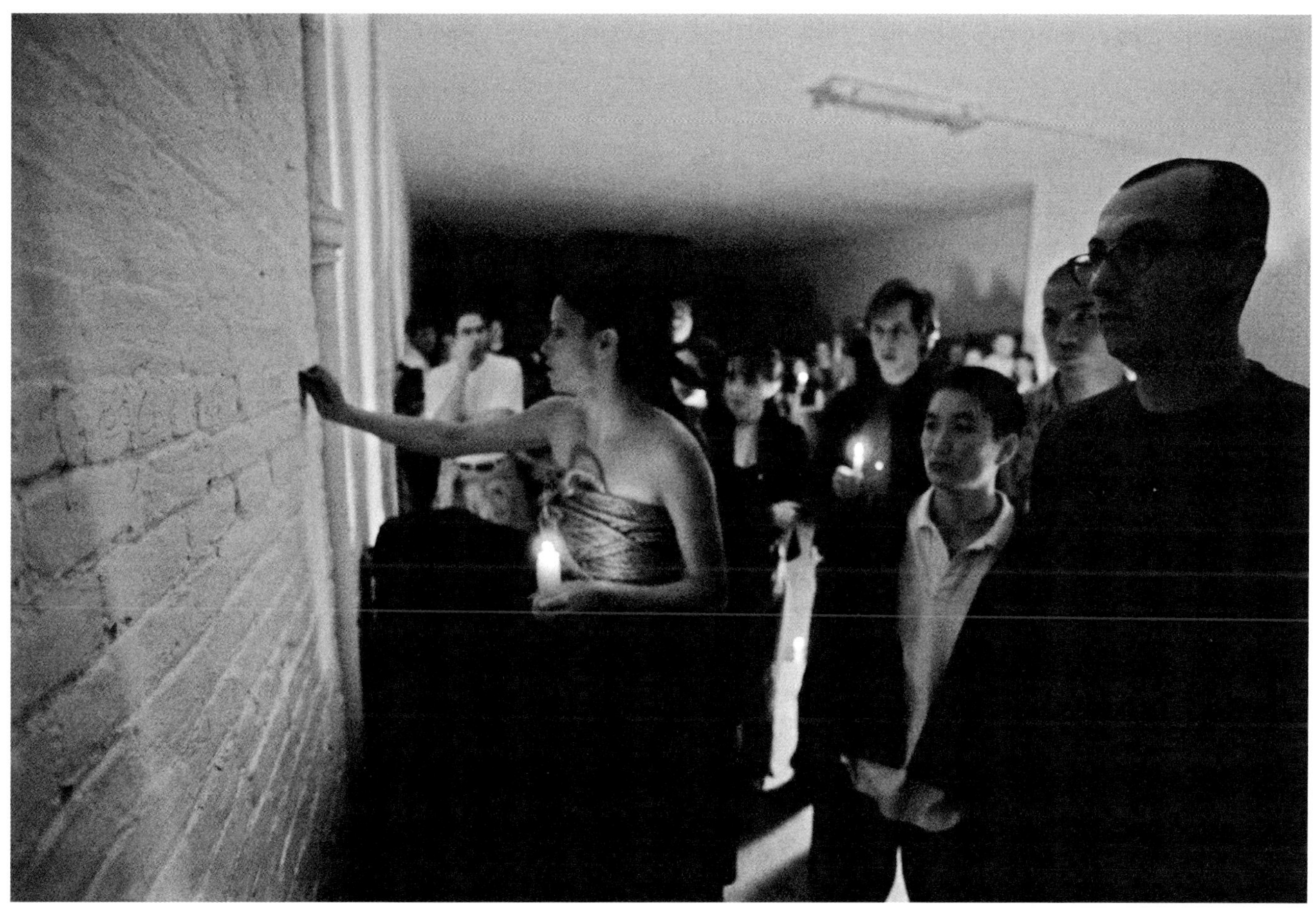

Votos (Vows), 1999–2000, performance

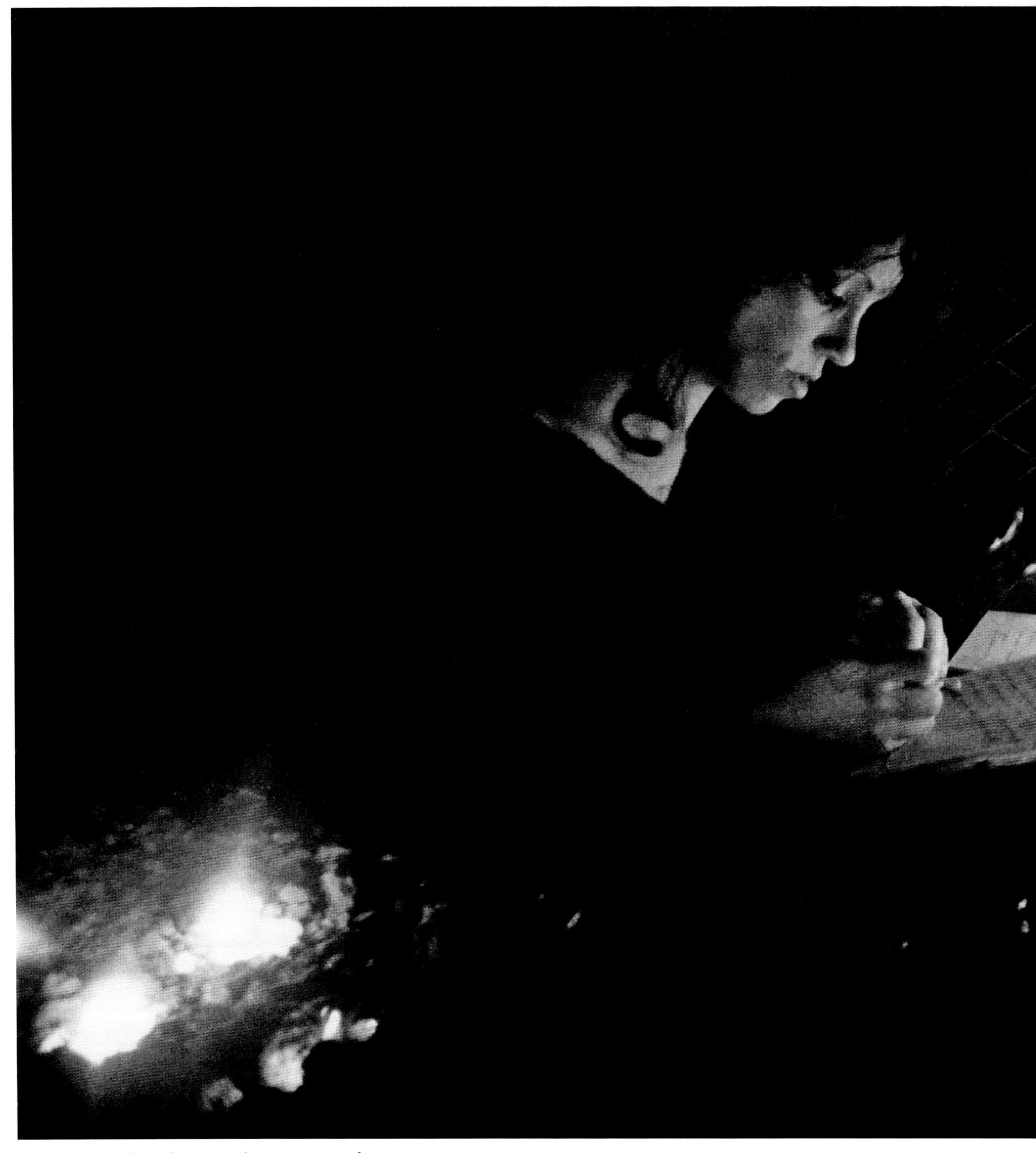

El Evento Suspendido (The Postponed Event), 2000, performance

                    BODY OF WORK 1990–2022

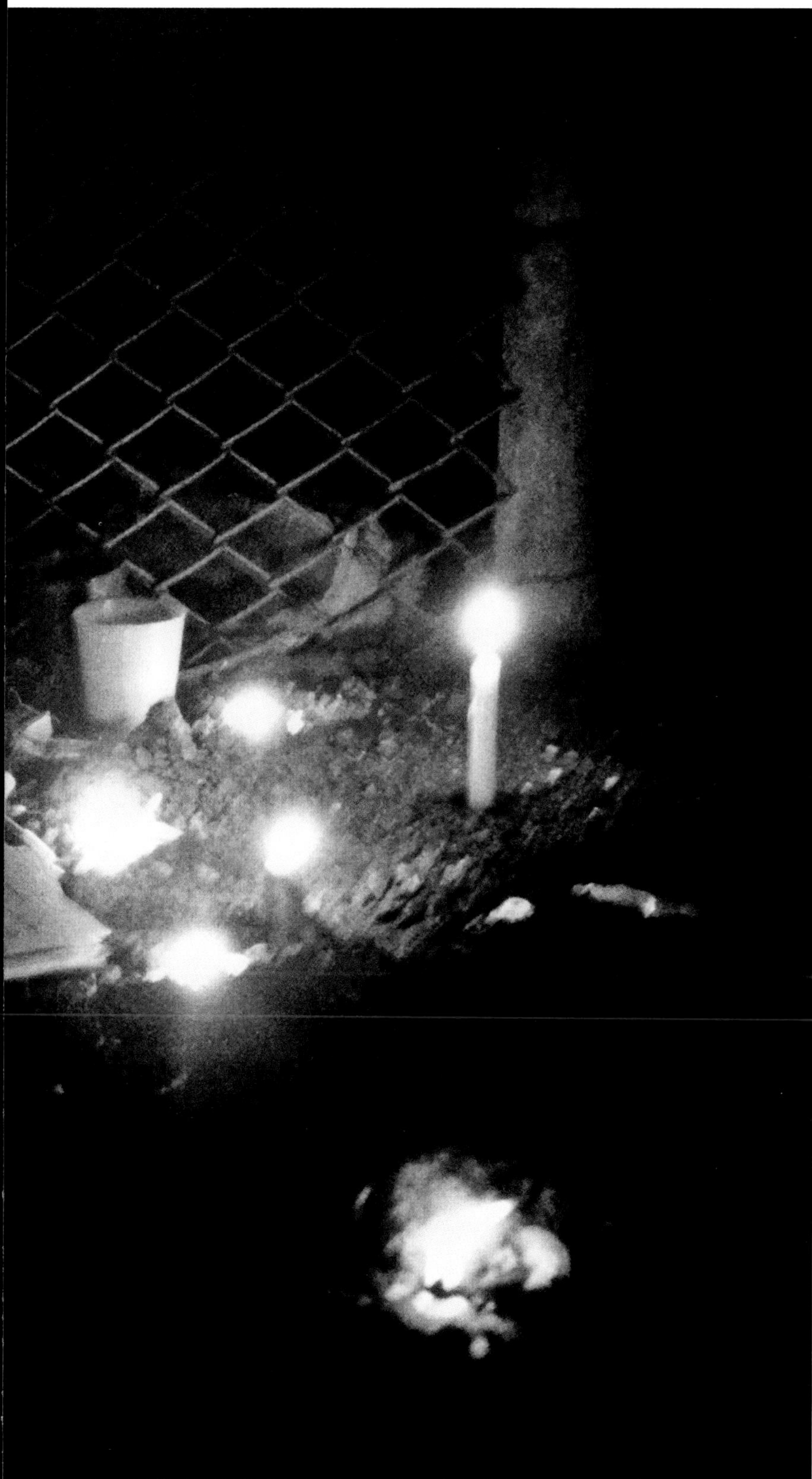

El evento suspendido (The Postponed Event)

2000

For *El evento suspendido* (*The Postponed Event*), a performance staged outside the gallery Espacio Aglutinador in Havana, Fusco was buried upright, chest deep in Cuban soil, for three hours beginning at dusk. Her arms free, she spent that time rewriting a letter in Spanish, over and over, leaving the copies out for members of the audience to take. The letter read:

My dear ones,
I am writing this letter to tell you that I am alive. For many years I feared that if I told the truth you would suffer at the hands of those who buried another woman in my name. I can no longer stand not being able to tell you that I exist. Not a day has passed without my dreaming of you. Fortunately I can say that I recovered from the ordeal that resulted in my departure. I will send more news soon. With love, C.

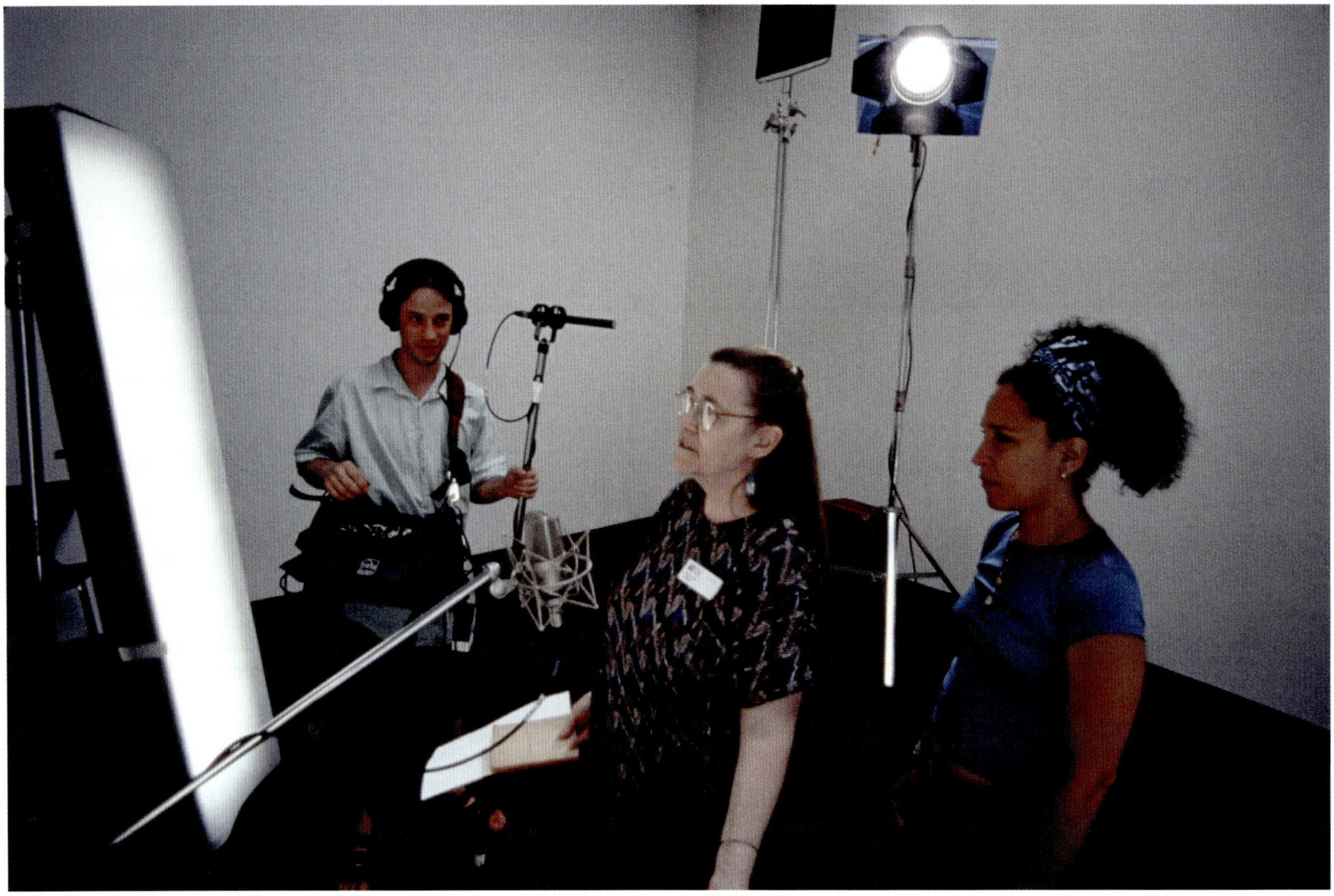

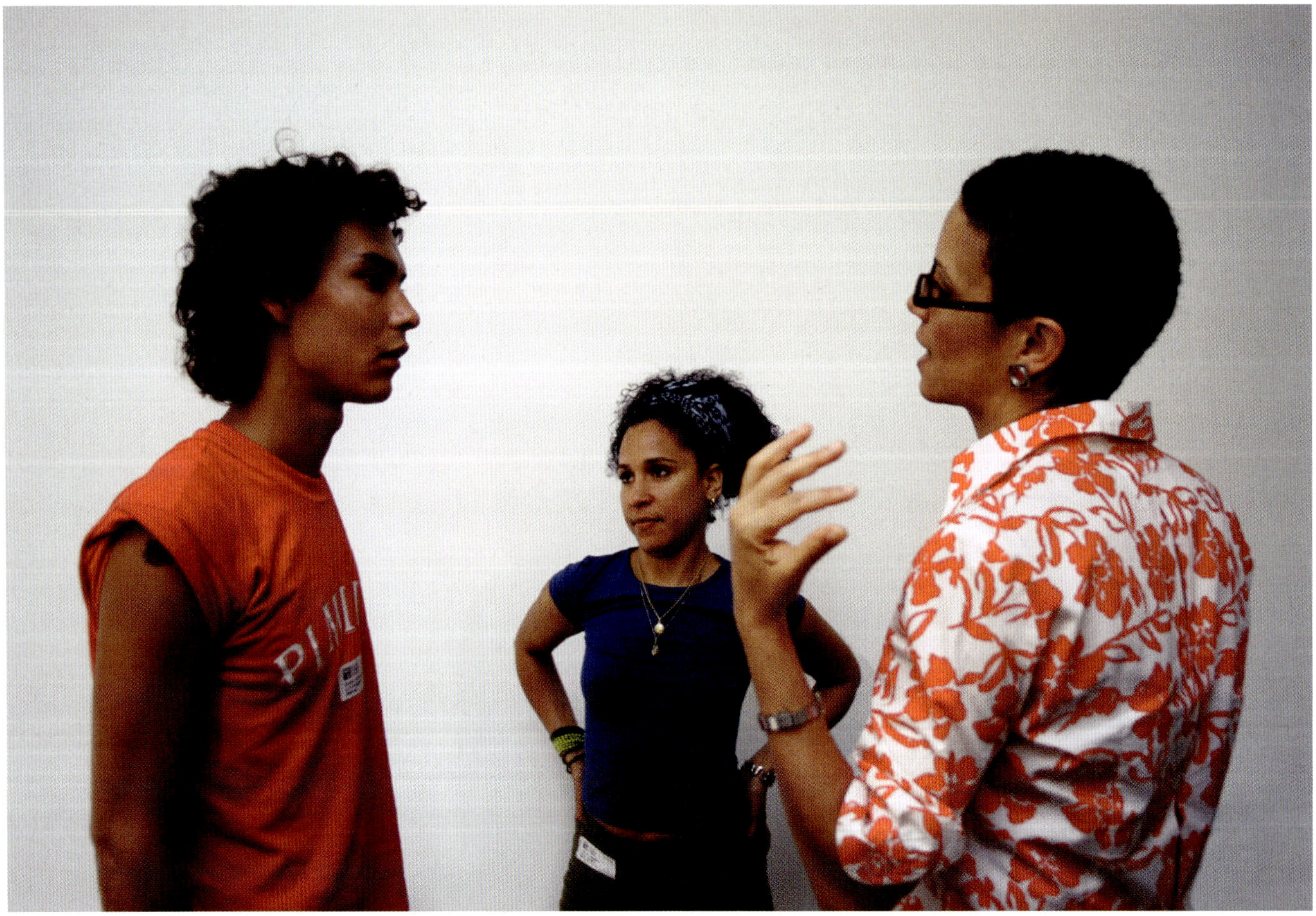

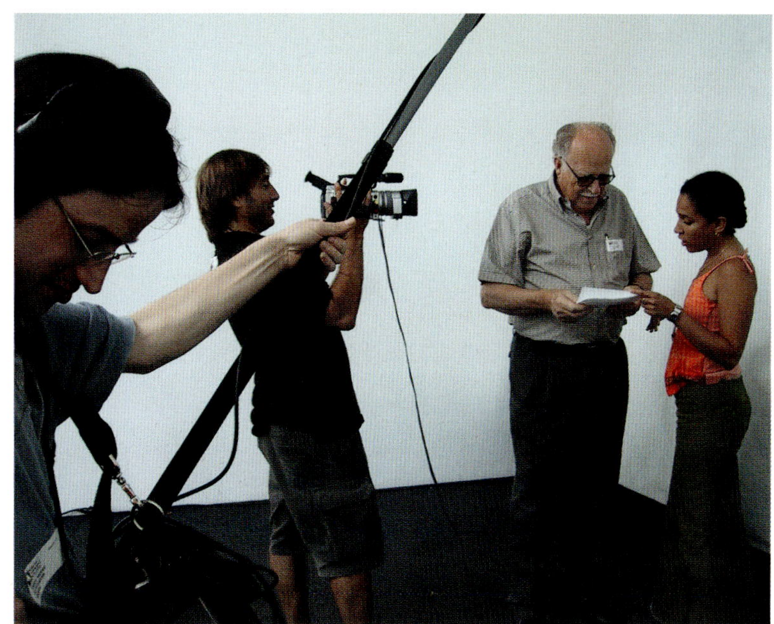

Els Segadors (The Reapers)

2001

This work, commissioned for the exhibition "Unpacking Europe" at Museum Boijmans Van Beuningen in Rotterdam centers on a 2001 decree by the president of Catalunya that the autonomous region's national hymn, "Els Segadors (The Reapers)," be taught in all of the region's public schools as a reaction to mounting anxieties about the impact of immigration on Catalan social integrity. Fusco's video work depicts a diverse range of people singing the hymn and discussing their personal experiences with the language, their feelings about the intricacies of cultural identity, and their relationship to the song. The diversity of experiences expressed in the testimonials, as well as the range of styles in which the hymn is sung, examines how singular notions of national identity distort the social reality of contemporary European societies. As Fusco has stated, "What is extremely difficult to discern is the difference between a historically rooted defense of Catalan identity against encroachment by the Spanish State and burgeoning Catalanist protectionism in the face of hybridizing forces of globalization."

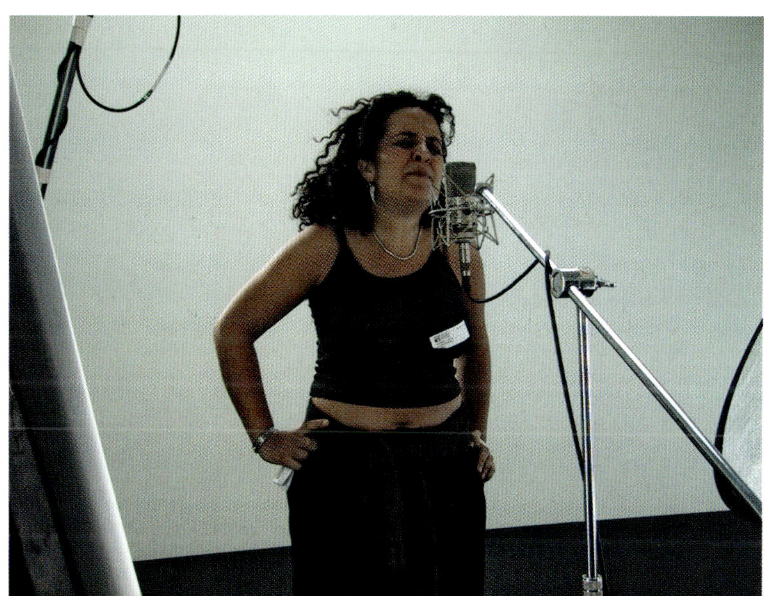

Els Segadors (The Reapers), 2001, video

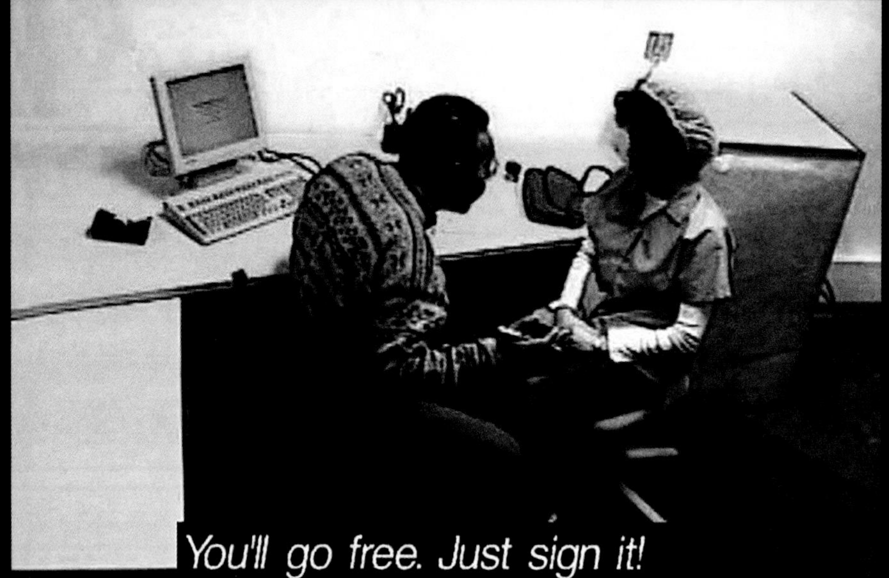

Dolores from 10 to 10

2002

While on a research trip to Tijuana, Mexico, in 1997, Fusco met Delfina Rodriguez, a maquiladora worker who had been accused by her employer of trying to start a union in the plant. In an effort to coerce her into resigning, the manager locked her in a room for twelve hours without food, water, or access to a bathroom or a phone. Rodriguez finally surrendered and signed the letter of resignation. But following her release she reported her ordeal on a live radio show and eventually sued her former employer for violating her civil rights. Her former manager claimed she was insane and accused her of fabricating the story. Management also denied that any security camera footage or eyewitness testimony from coworkers (who were afraid to speak on her behalf) existed, even though it is standard practice to have cameras positioned throughout assembly plants. Fusco was convinced that there must have been cameras recording what happened to her during her internment, so in *Dolores from 10 to 10* she dramatized what she imagined such cameras could have witnessed. The video renders visible the subjugation of a female maquiladora worker and the gender and power dynamics that, to this day, dominate work environments where women are subject to verbal, physical, and sexual abuse.

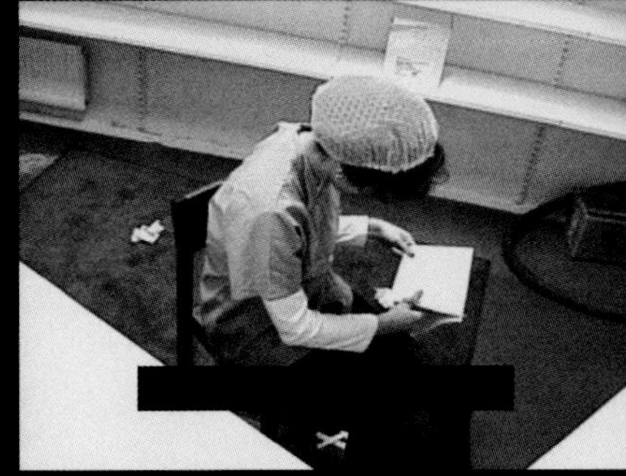
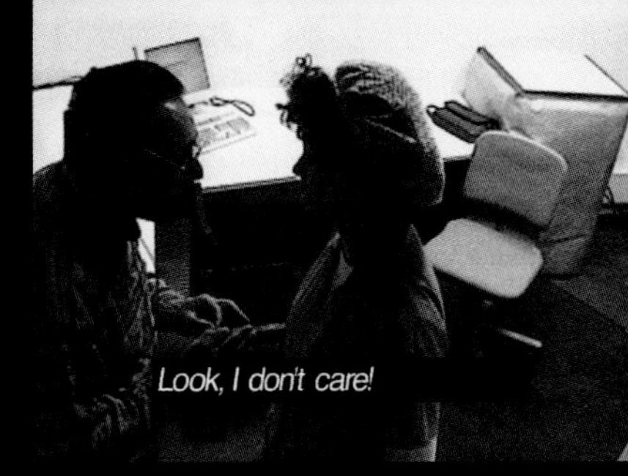

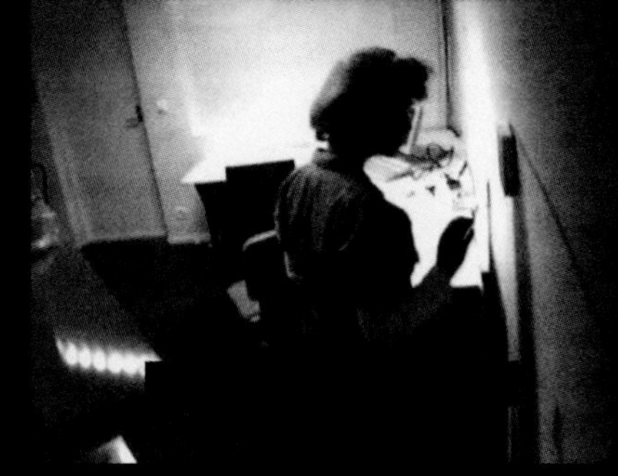
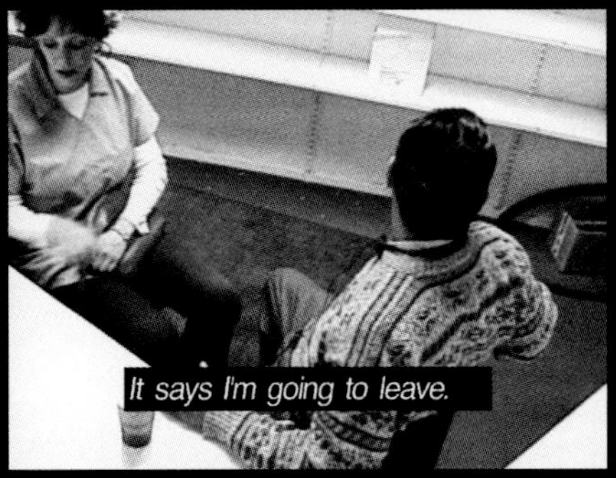

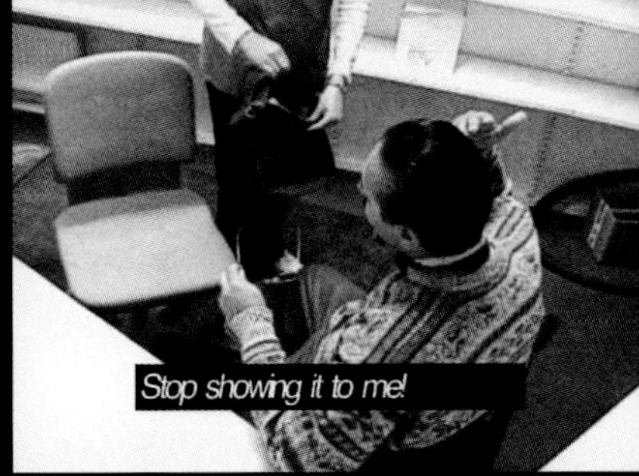

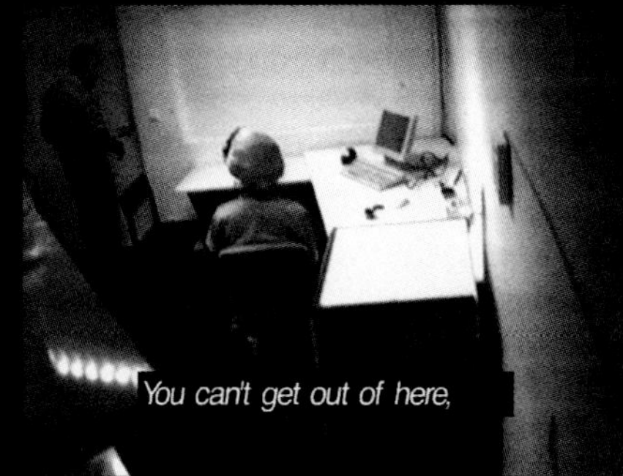

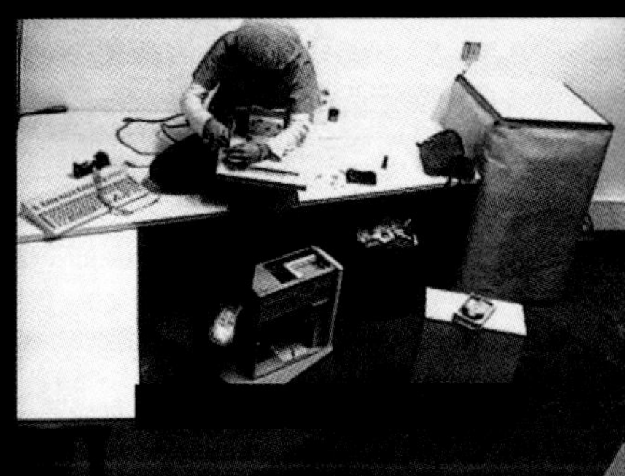
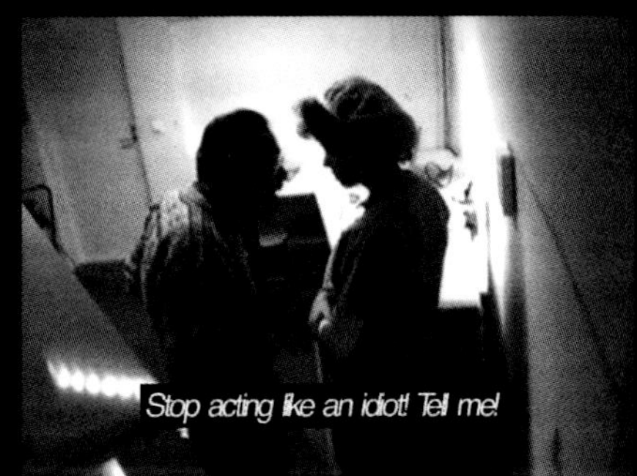

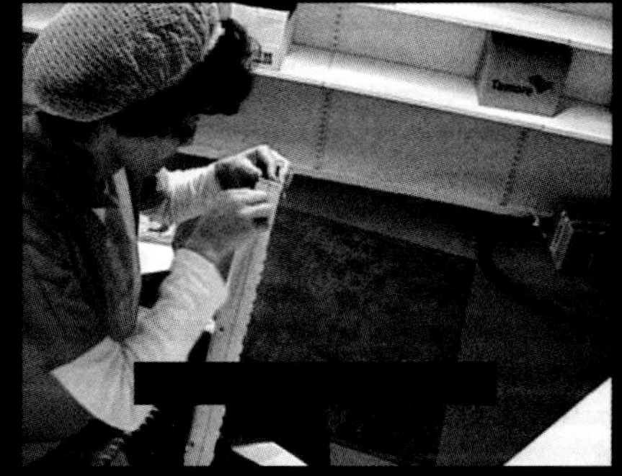
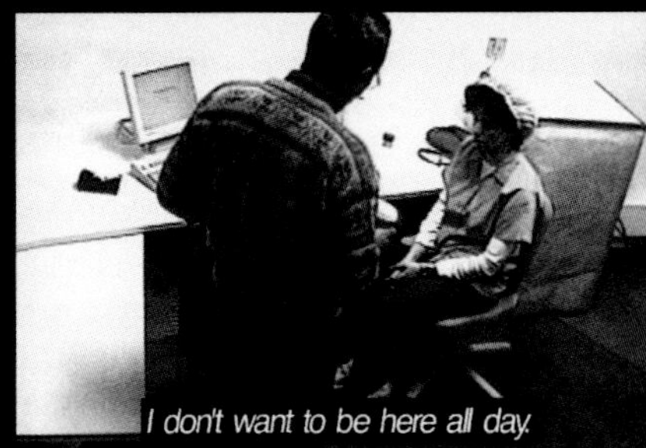

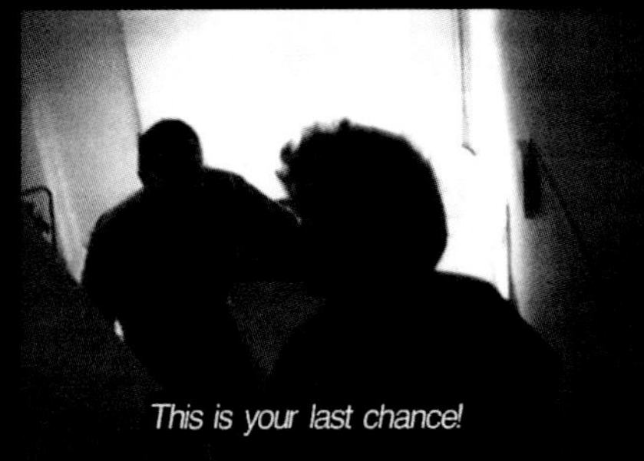

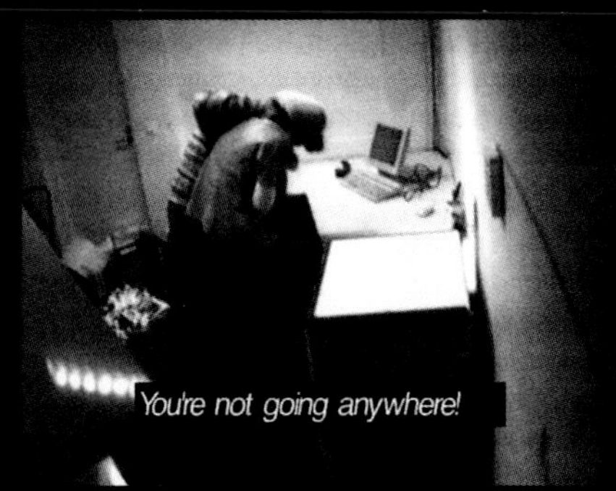

Dolores from 10 to 10, 2002, video installation

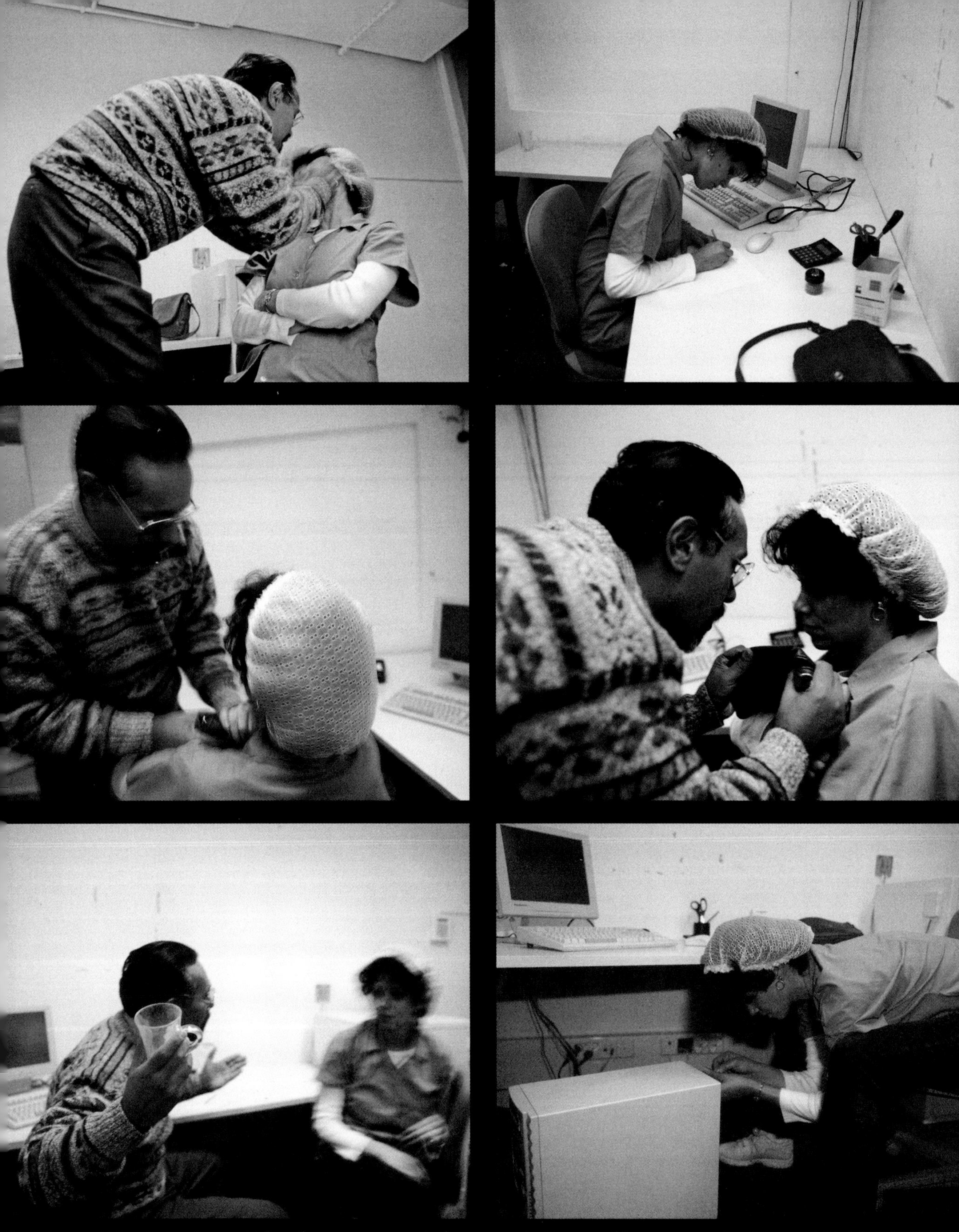

Coco Fusco and Ricardo Dominguez, *Dolores from 10 to 22*, 2001. Performance at the Museum of Contemporary Art Kiasma, Helsinki, Finland.

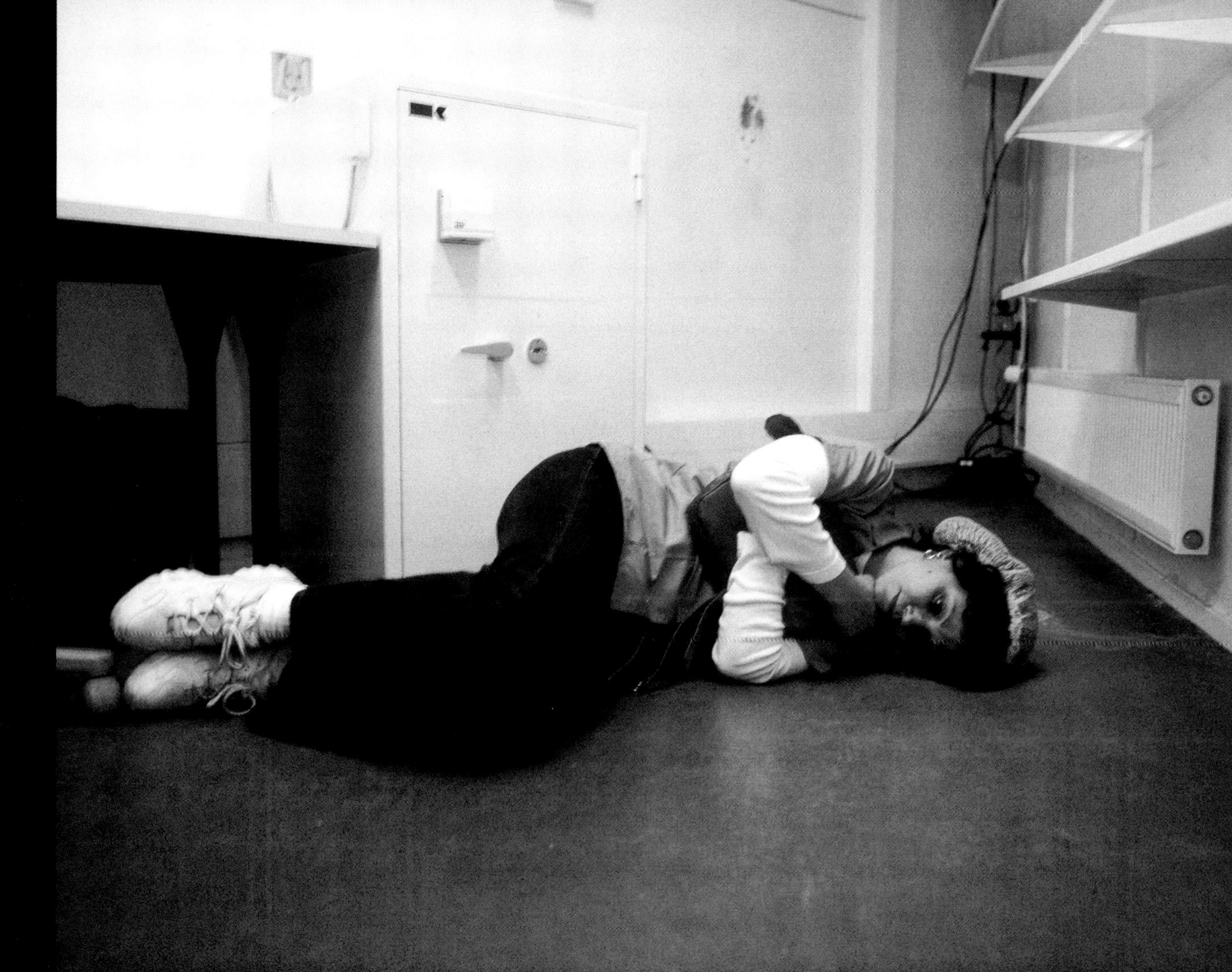

The Incredible Disappearing Woman

2003

In this performance, Fusco questions the intelligibility of political violence in a culture dominated by technological simulation and information saturation. Set within a "live chat" room, the work stages a drama in which three onstage actors are being directed by four unseen characters who appear to be transmitting instructions via the internet. Linking them all is their relationship with Death, embodied as a modern incarnation of the venerated Mexican archetype of *La Pelona* (the bald one), who lies before the characters as both a reminder of their limits and as "the other" inside each of them. The staged scenes address necrophilia fantasies that are loosely based on the true story of an American male artist who traveled to Mexico in the 1970s to rent the body of a dead woman, have sex with her, and document it as art. Fusco invokes this moment in the history of performance to explore what it means to have to play dead in order to live in all its political, technocultural, and gendered implications. As the performers go through the requested sketches, they allude to real-life situations of religious and political repression. However, as low-paid service workers catering to telematic consumers of violence, they dramatize these histories as endlessly rerun games in which actors are "meat puppets." *The Incredible Disappearing Woman* was performed at the In-Transit Festival at the House of World Cultures, Berlin; Institute of Contemporary Arts (ICA), London; the Time-Based Art Festival in Portland, Oregon; and the International Performance Festival in Pancevo, Serbia.

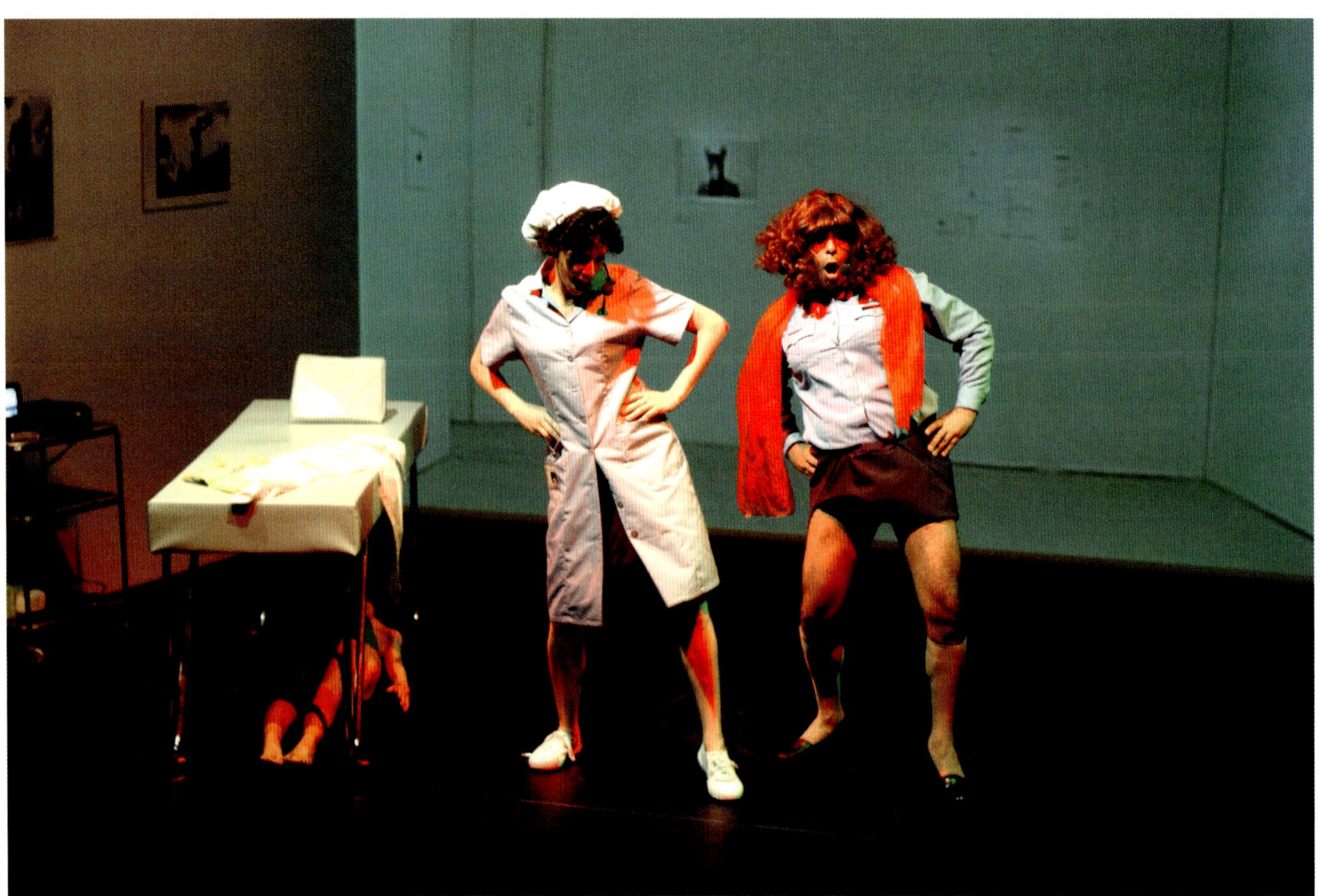

The Incredible Disappearing Woman, 2003, performance featuring Ricardo Dominguez (also overleaf and page 109)

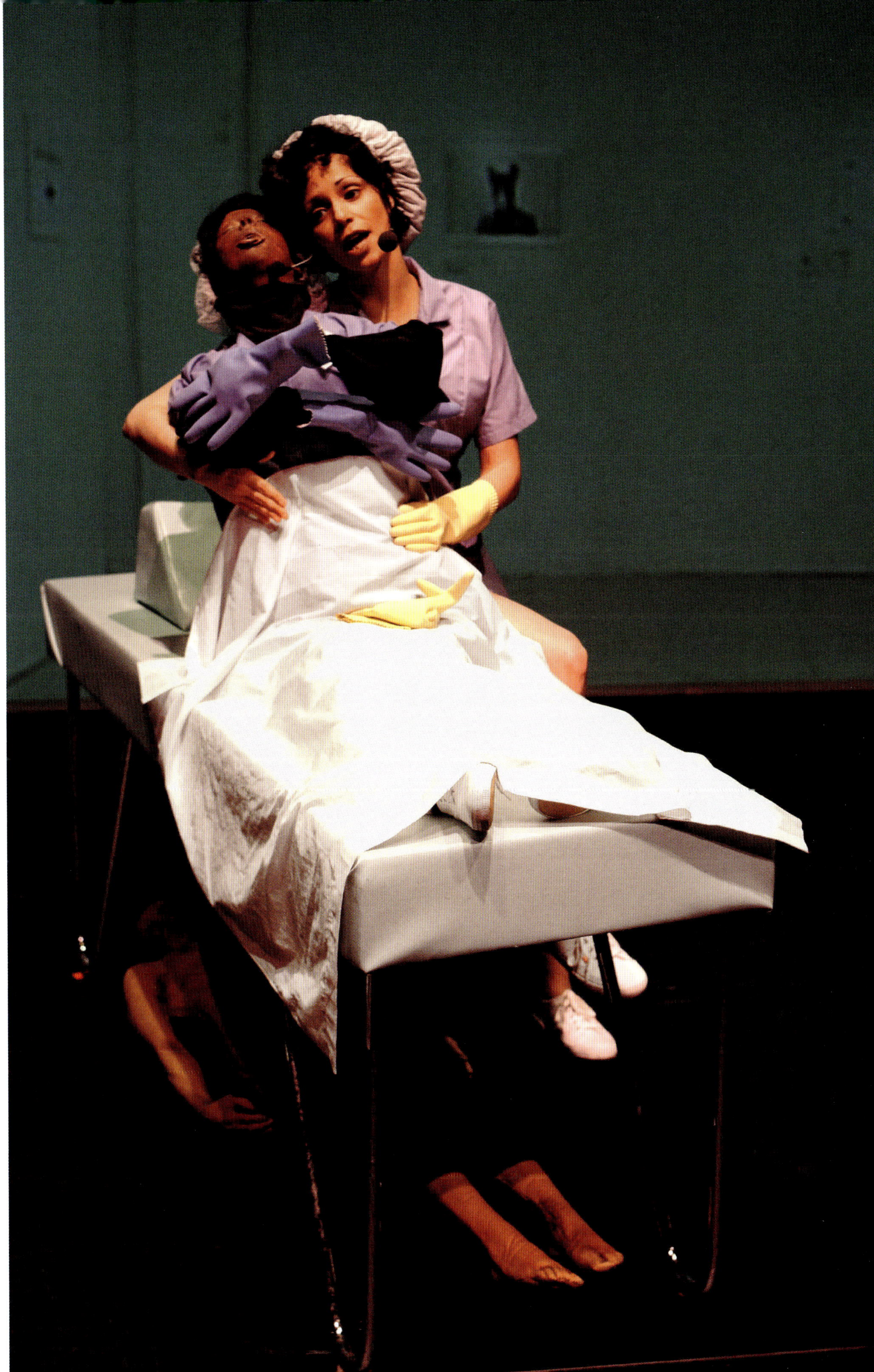

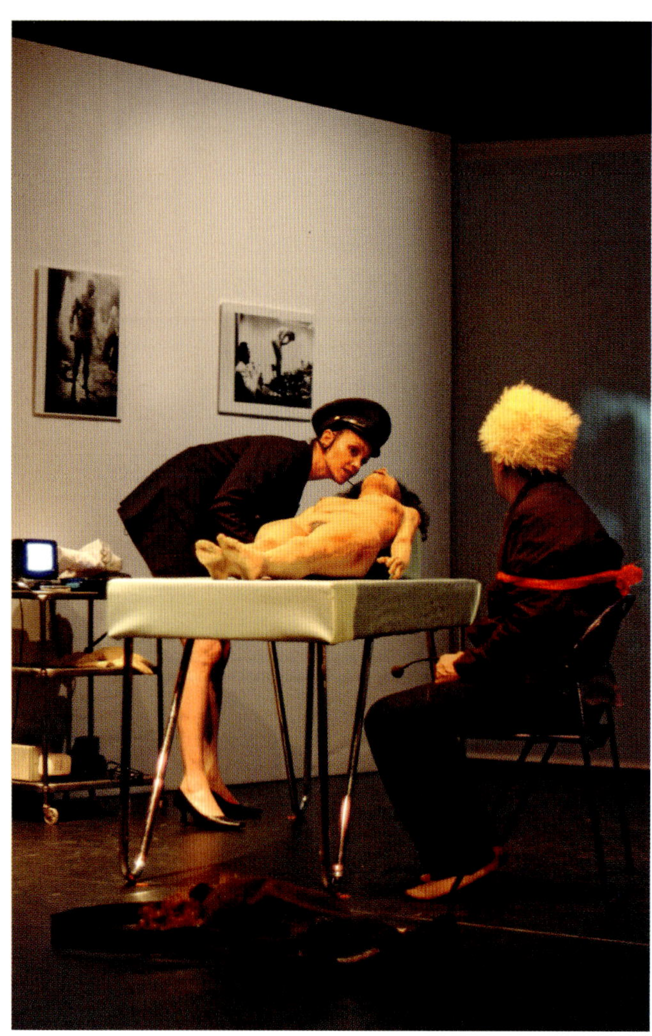

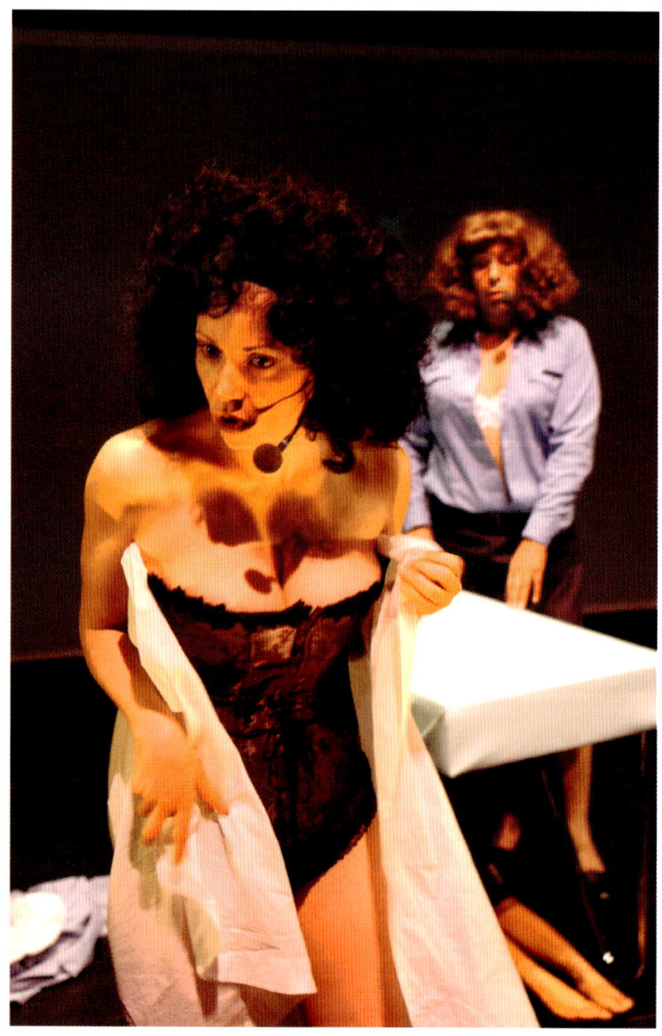

BODY OF WORK 1990–2022

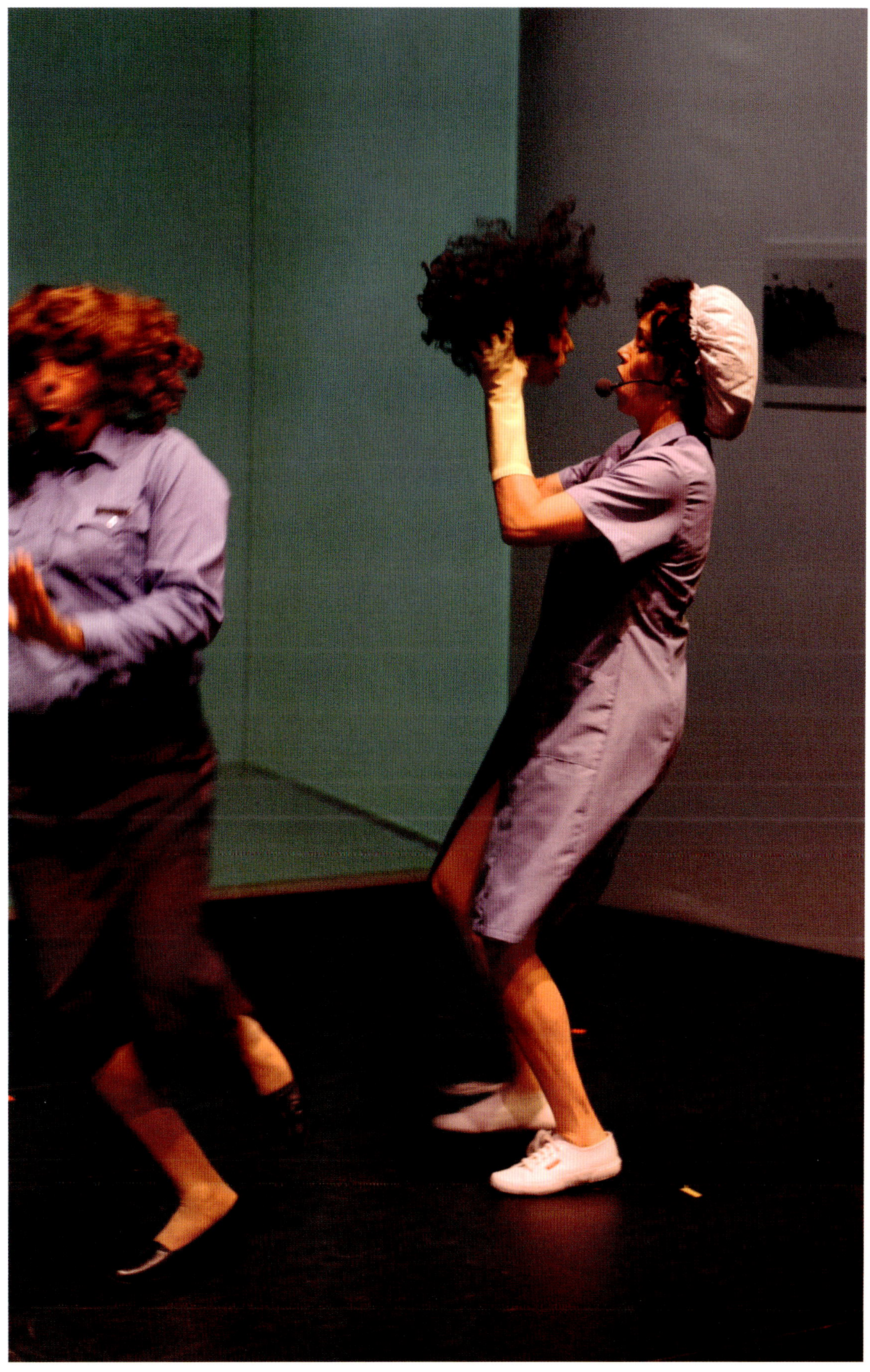

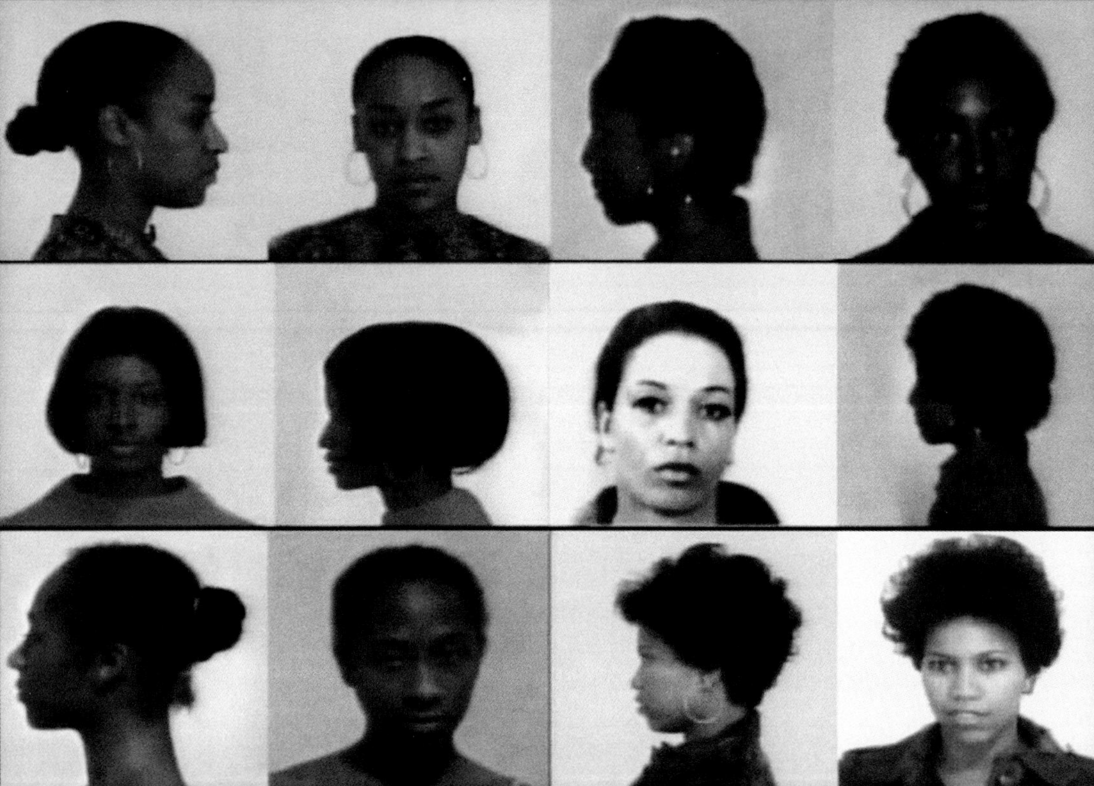

a/k/a Mrs. George Gilbert

2004

a/k/a Mrs. George Gilbert examines the significant role photography played in generating and circulating racial stereotypes during the FBI hunt for Angela Davis, the scholar and political activist who in the 1960s was also one of the most photographed Black women in America. While Davis was a fugitive in 1970 and placed on the FBI's most wanted list, dozens of other Black women with afros were incorrectly identified as Davis and mistakenly arrested by police. Using archival footage and film, Fusco highlights the ways that racialized fantasies about Davis and Black radicals during the 1960s and 1970s interfered with a "scientific" or "objective" use of the photographic image by American law enforcement agencies. Here, Fusco focuses on the ways that the "Angela effect" entails its own undoing—that is, how the hyper-circulation of her image contributed to misrecognition of her person, rather than to her identification.

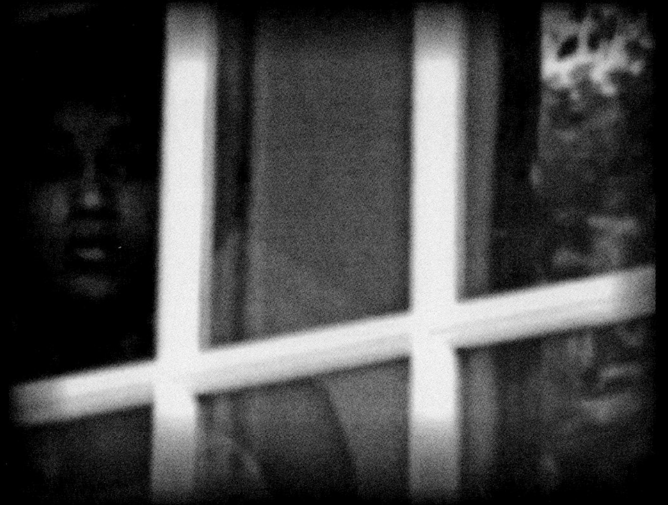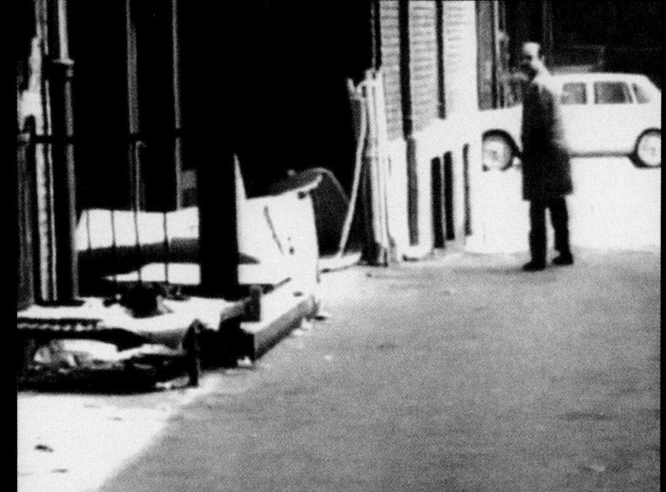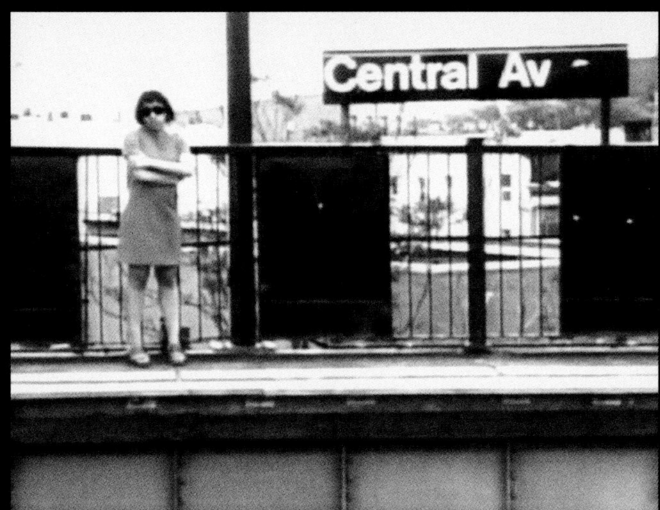

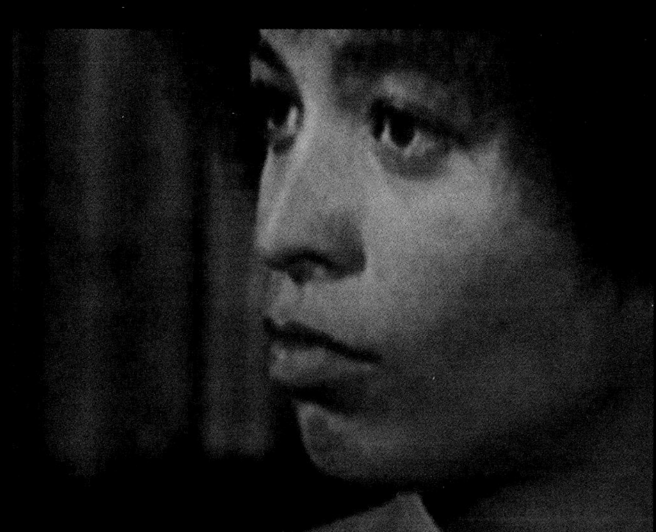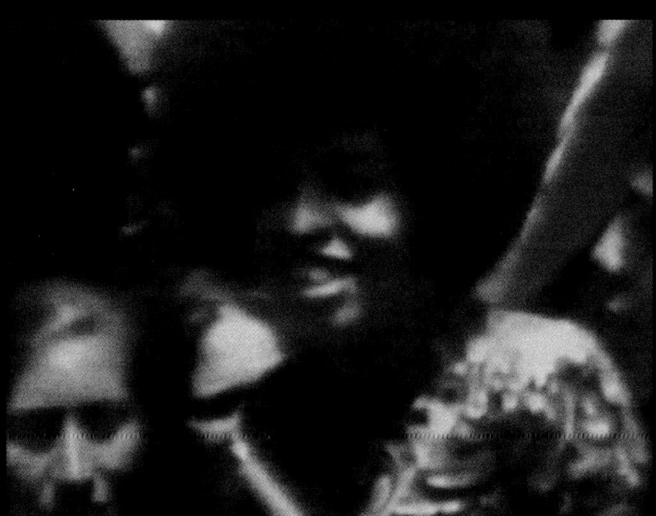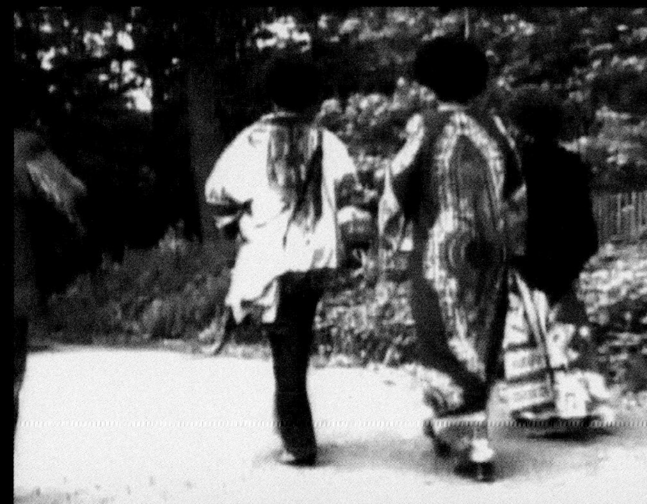

a/k/a Mrs. George Gilbert, 2004, video

These mounted photographs are enlargements of film strips taken with a vintage spy camera from the 1960s, the same apparatus that FBI agents used during that era. While Angela Davis was a fugitive in 1970, scores of other Black women were mistakenly targeted and arrested across the United States by police and FBI agents. *Sightings* commemorates the frenzied, racially driven misidentifications that were made by police and federal agents. It also speaks to the specific targeting and over-policing that ordinary Black citizens experience from "concerned citizens" simply because of their skin color. The misidentification of a Black body, to this day, continues to be rooted in institutionalized racism across all aspects of American society.

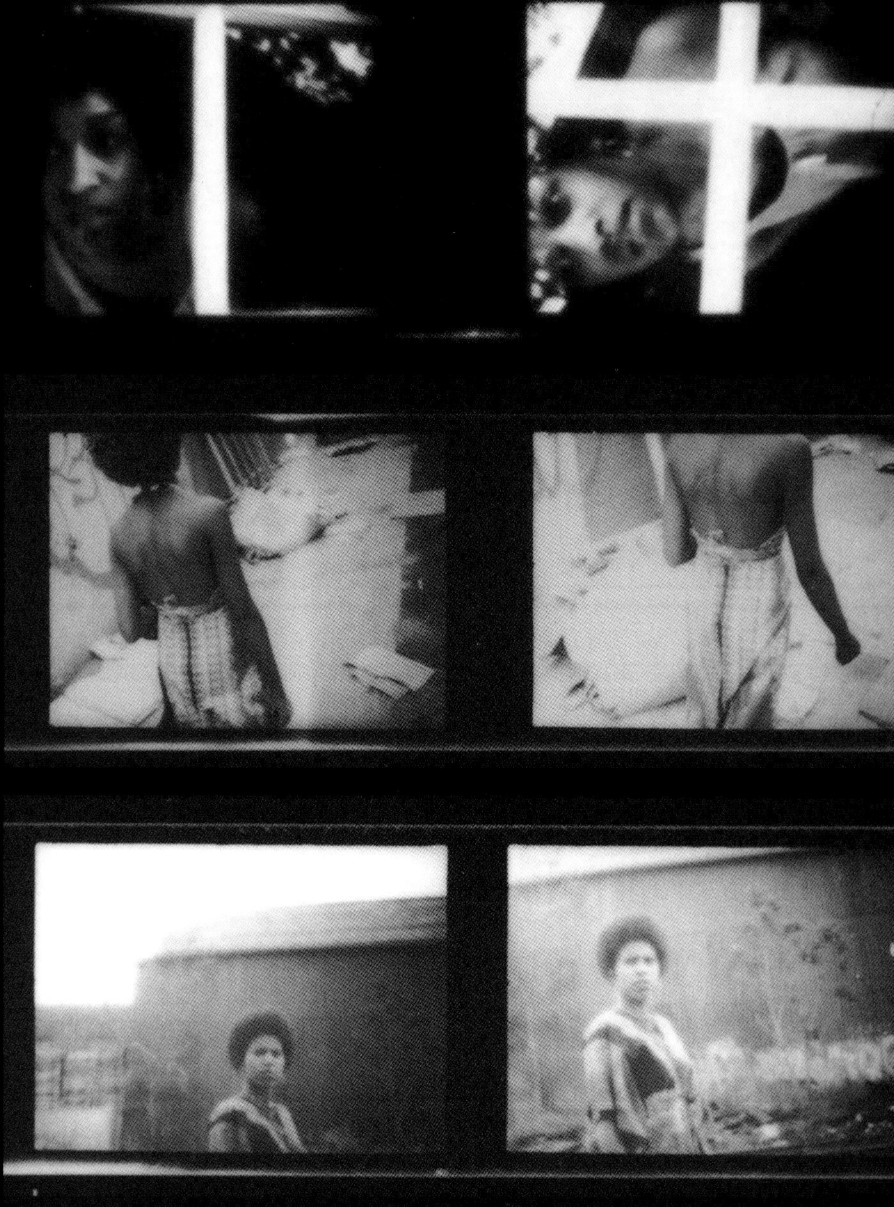

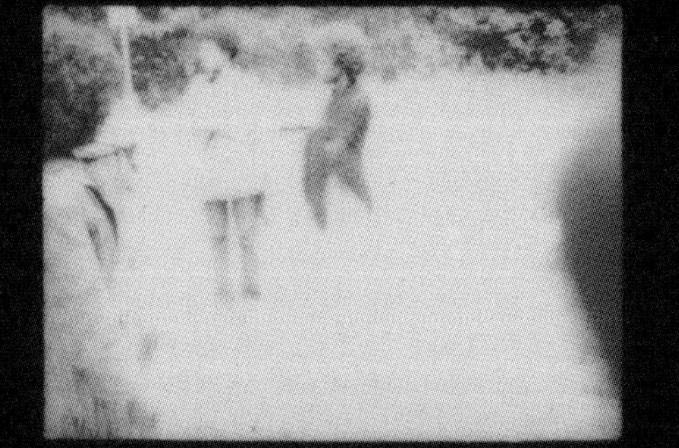

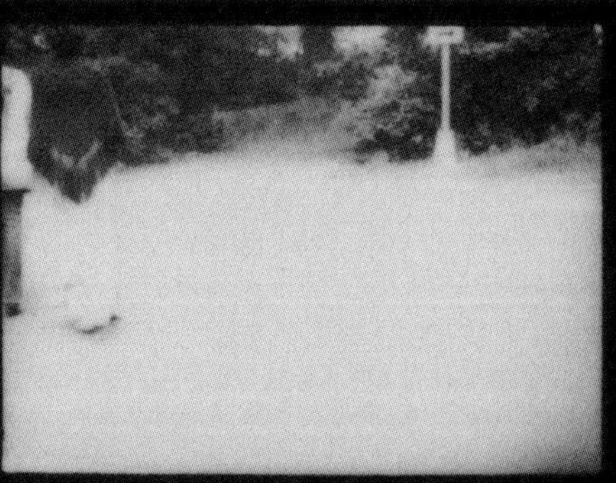

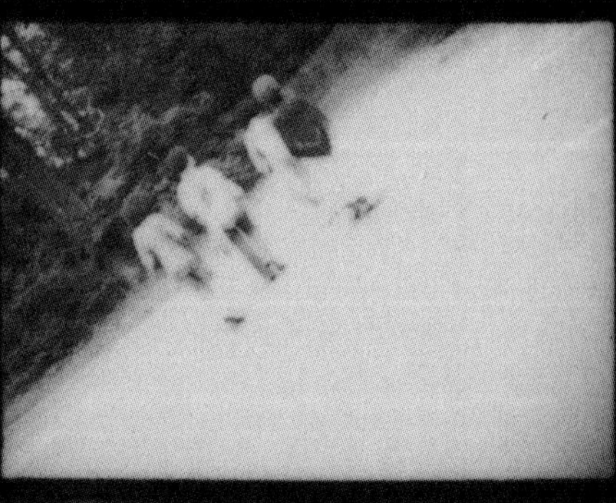

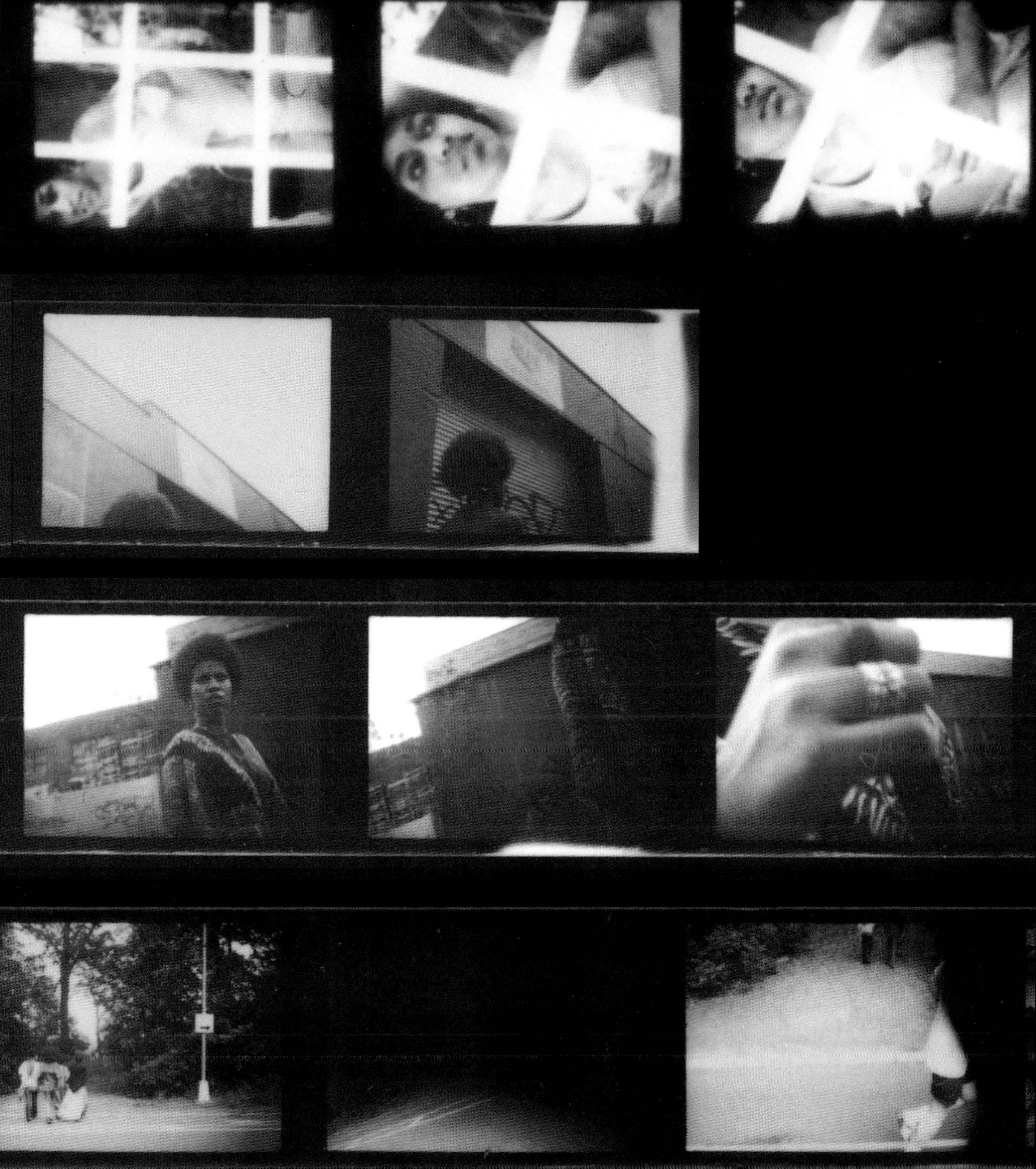

Sightings, 2004, photography

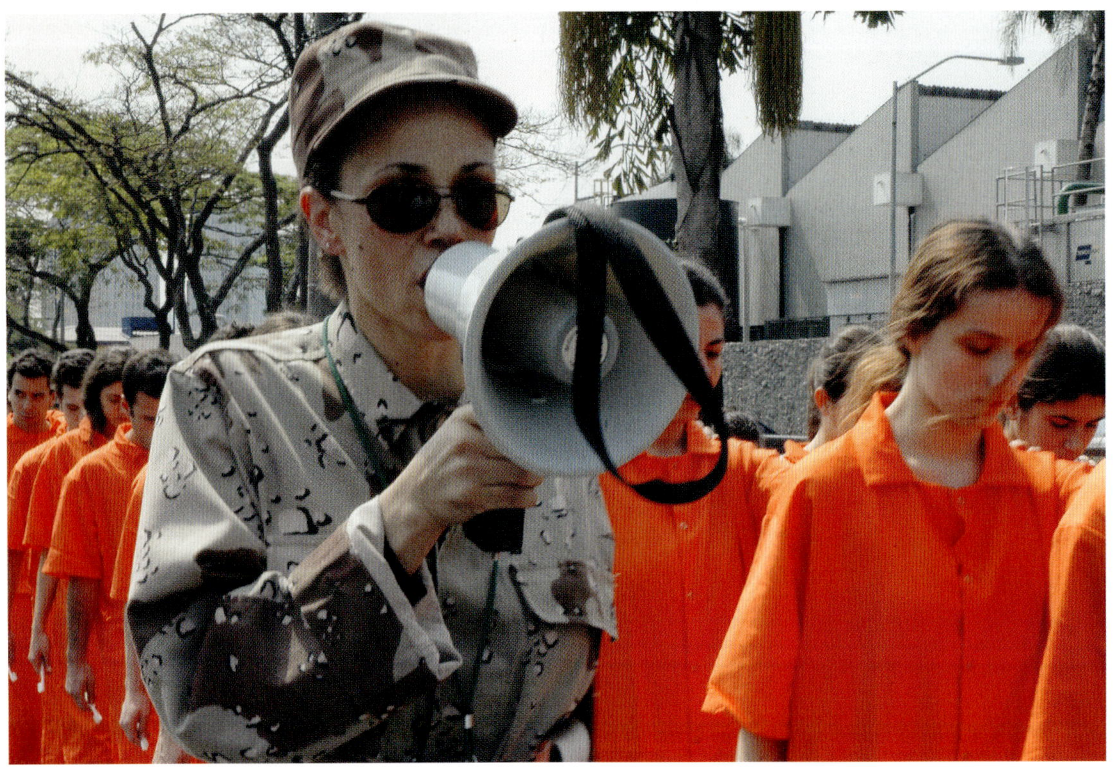

Bare Life Study #1

2005

A street performance presented as part of the VideoBrasil Festival of Electronic Art and Performance, *Bare Life Study #1* inaugurated Fusco's exploration of contemporary military scenarios as intercultural encounters. Drawing on her training in military interrogation with "Team Delta," Fusco stages a public spectacle in front of the US Consulate in São Paulo to portray the modes of subjection that occur inside contemporary American military prisons. In response to reports that American soldiers order prisoners to clean their cells with toothbrushes for hours at a time, Fusco assumes the role of a military policewoman and reenacts the scene of cleaning the ground with a toothbrush with fifty young performers dressed in the orange jumpsuits used by most people incarcerated in American prisons.

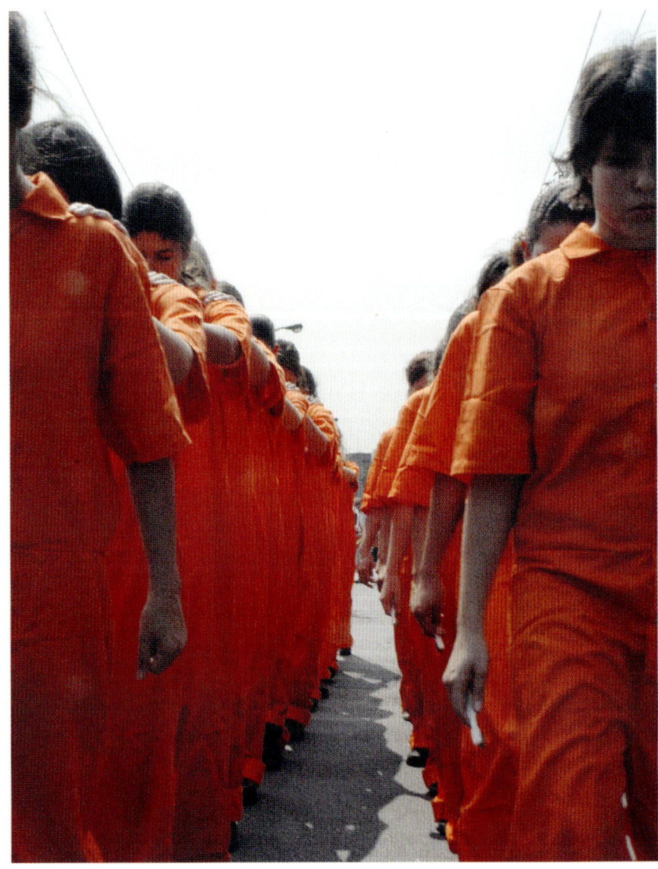

Bare Life Study #1, 2005, performance (also overleaf and page 117)

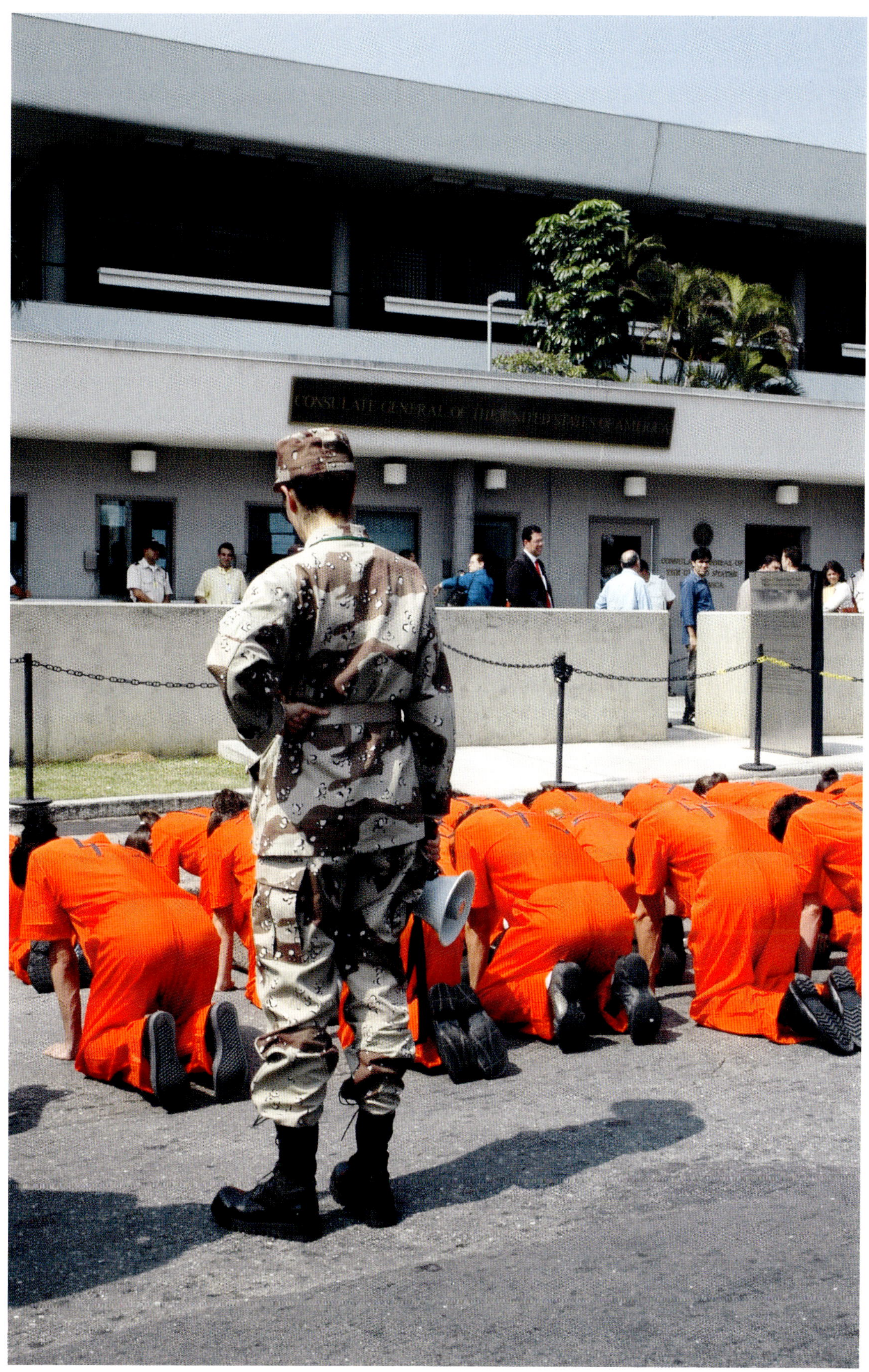

COCO FUSCO

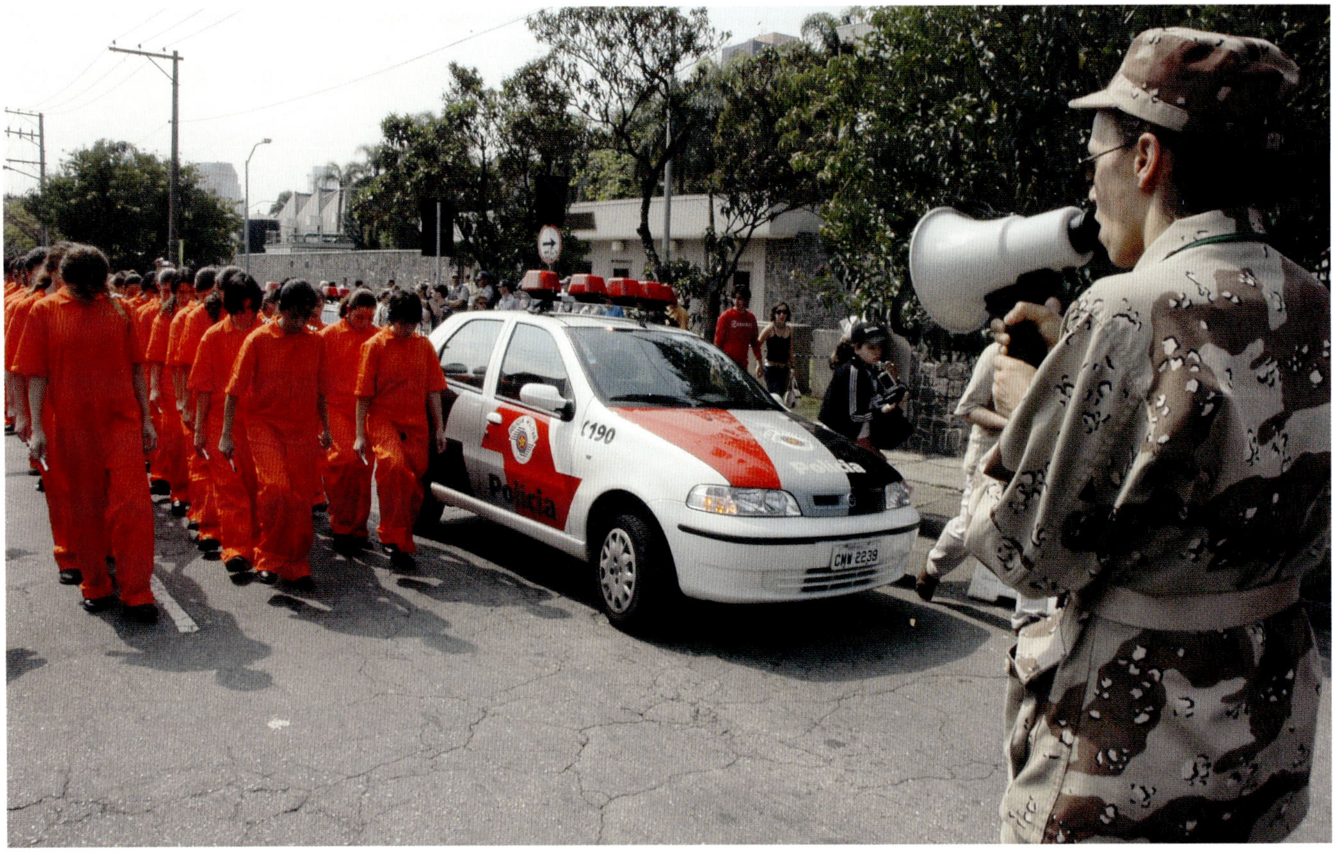

BODY OF WORK 1990–2022

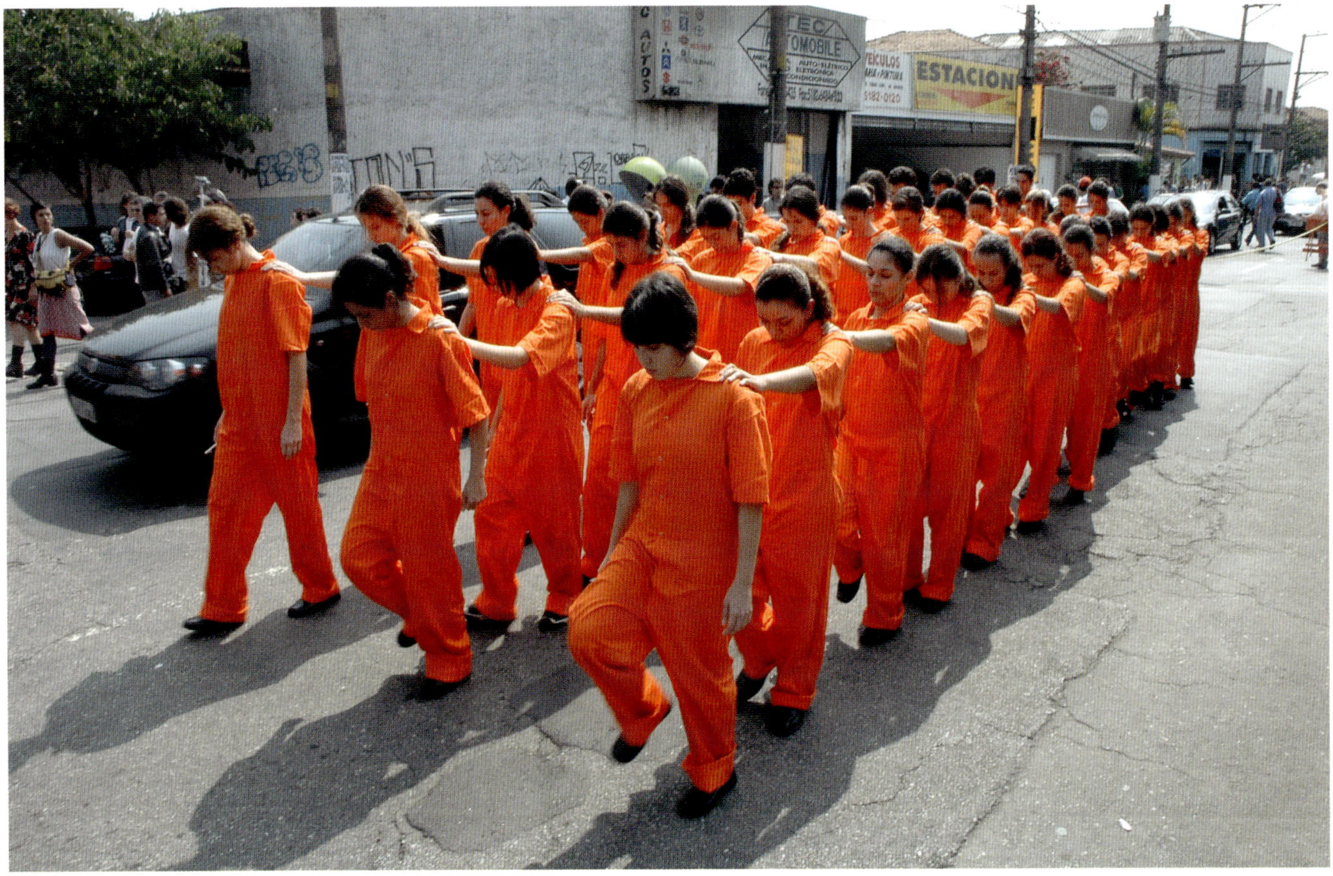

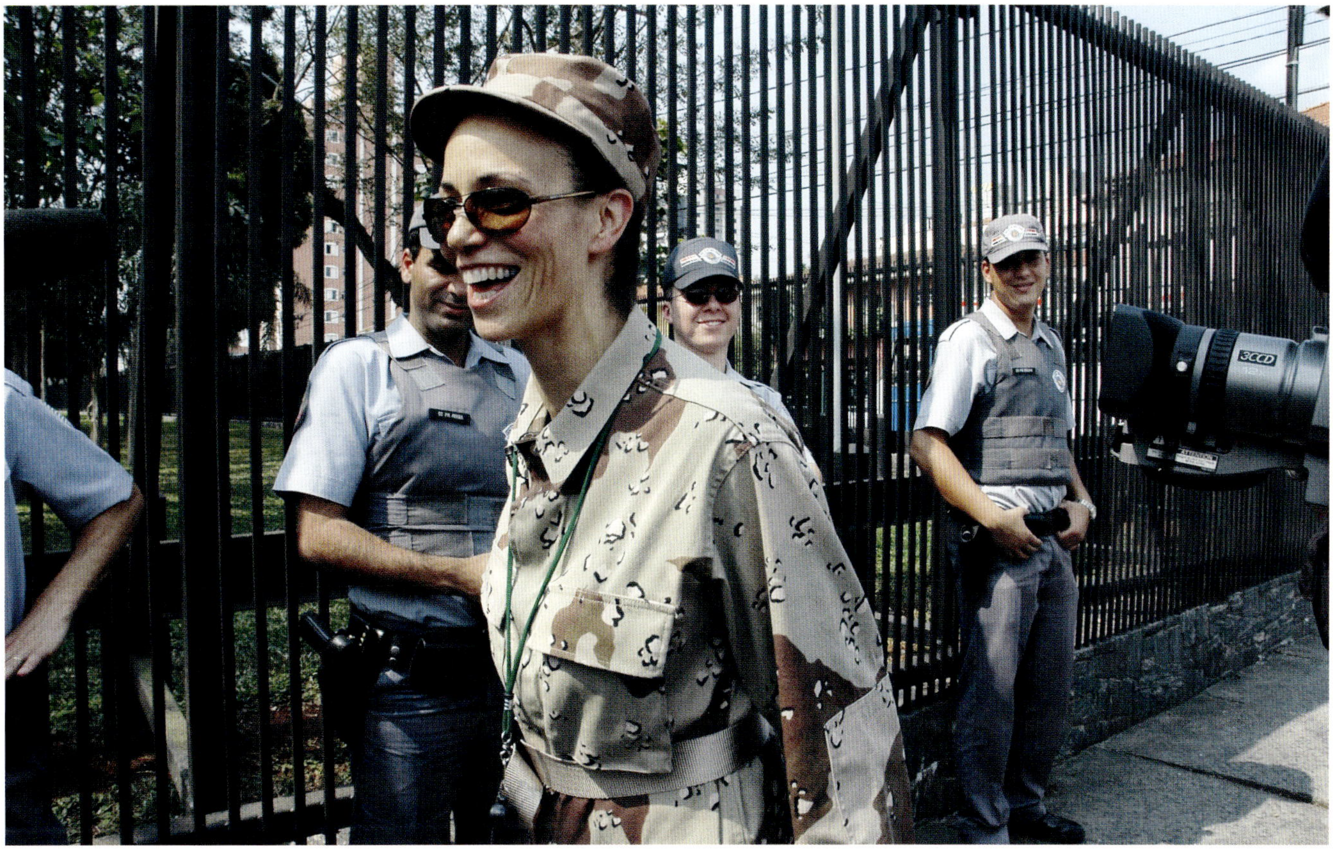

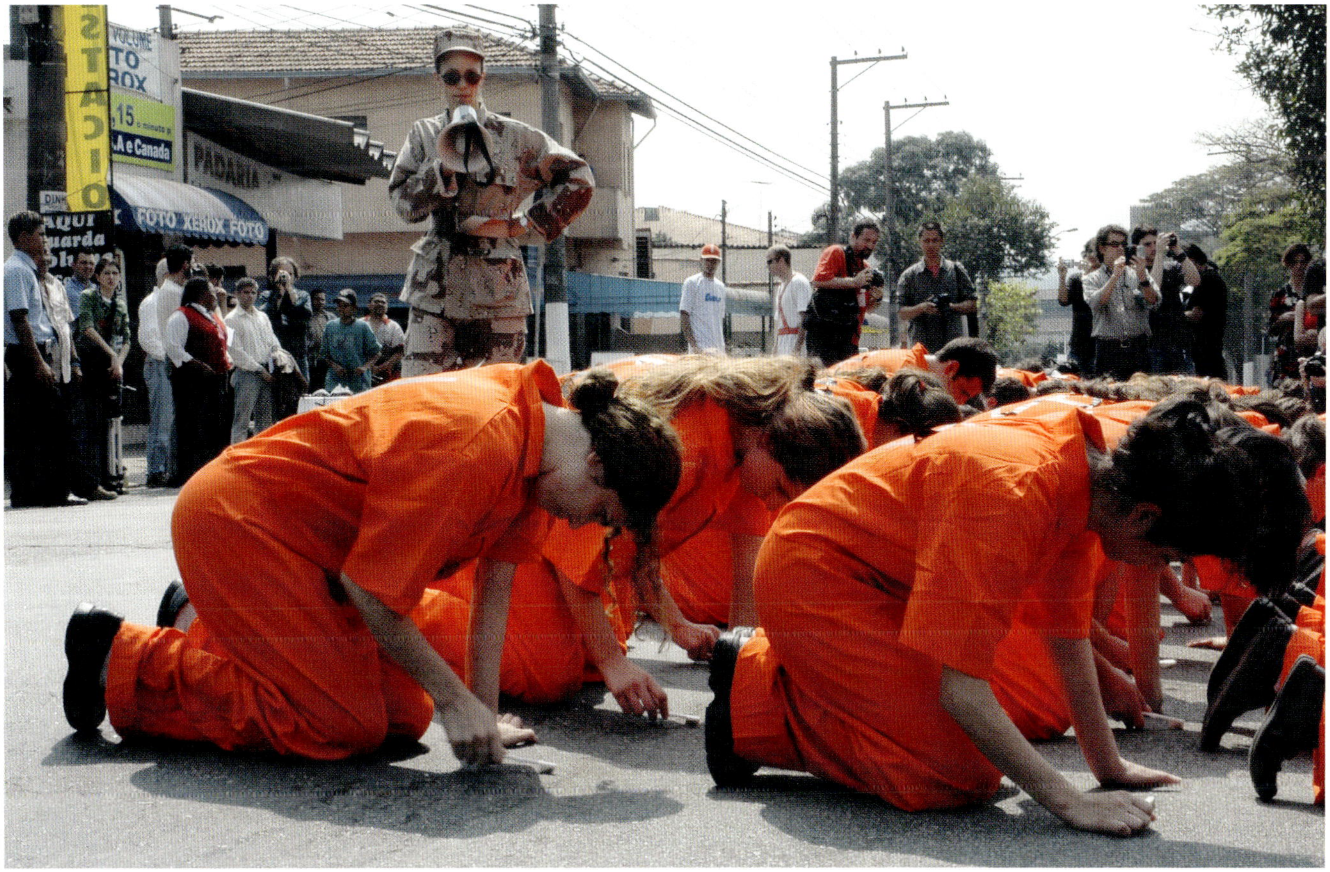

In July 2005, Fusco took a course led by former United States military interrogators designed to teach people in the private sector how to survive as prisoners of war. The course was based on SERE (survival, endurance, resistance, escape) training for US Special Forces and would enable her to learn about interrogation techniques. For *Operation Atropos*, Fusco invited a group of six women to join her and filmed the workshop documenting their experience, which involved an immersive simulation of the experience of prisoners of war. The women were ambushed, captured, strip-searched, thrown in an outdoor pen, and subjected to several interrogations. Afterwards, the women were invited into a classroom scenario where the tactics used against them were analyzed and they were taught how to employ the same strategies. The work was screened at Palais de Tokyo in Paris and the Royal Ontario Museum in Toronto in 2006 and the 2008 Whitney Biennial.

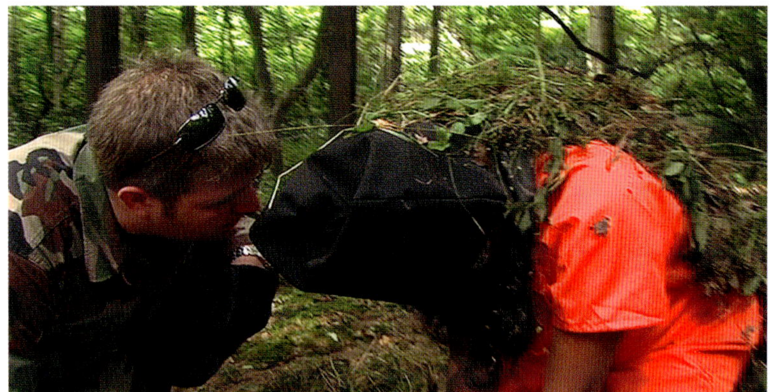

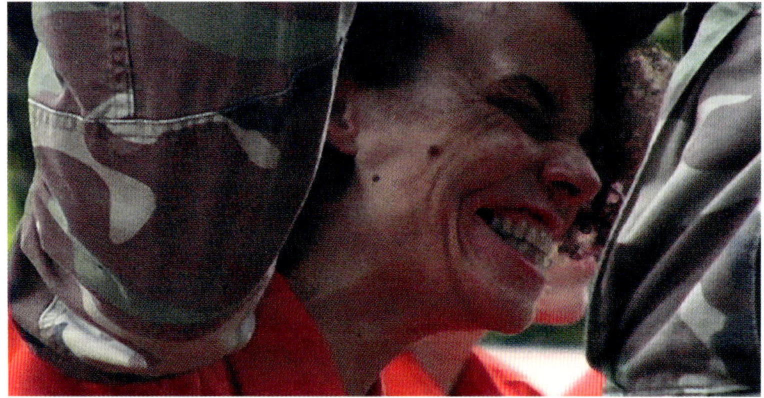

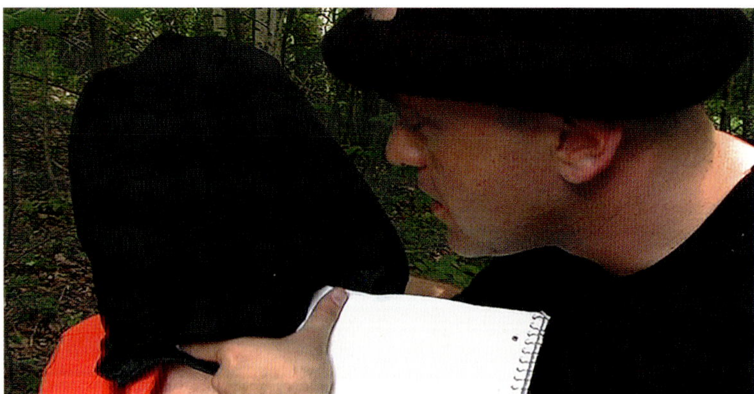

Operation Atropos, 2006, video

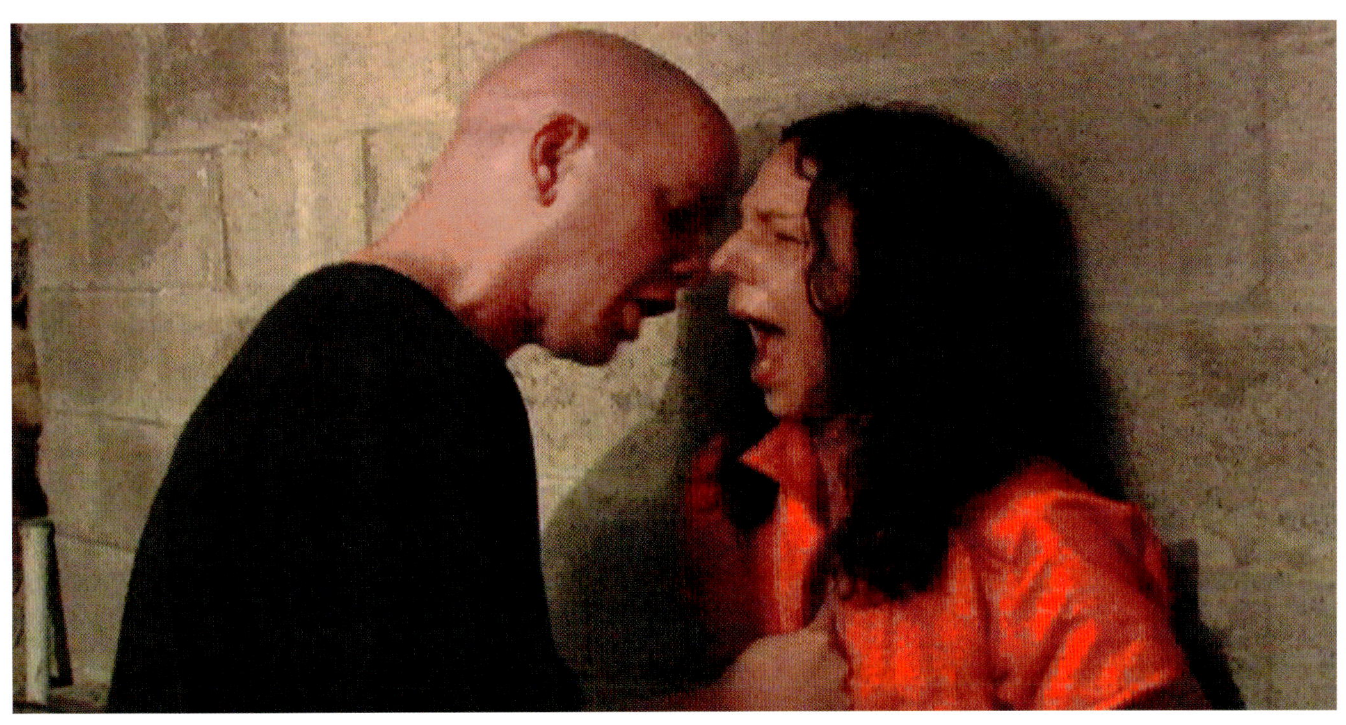

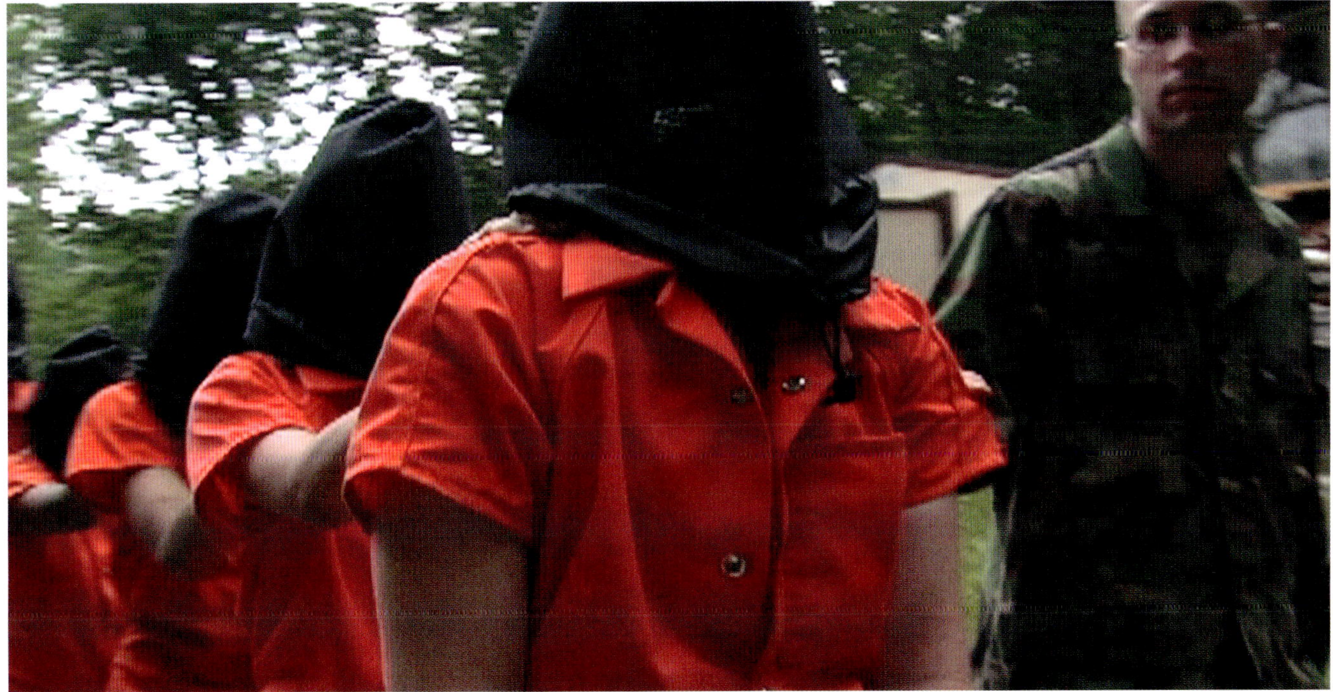

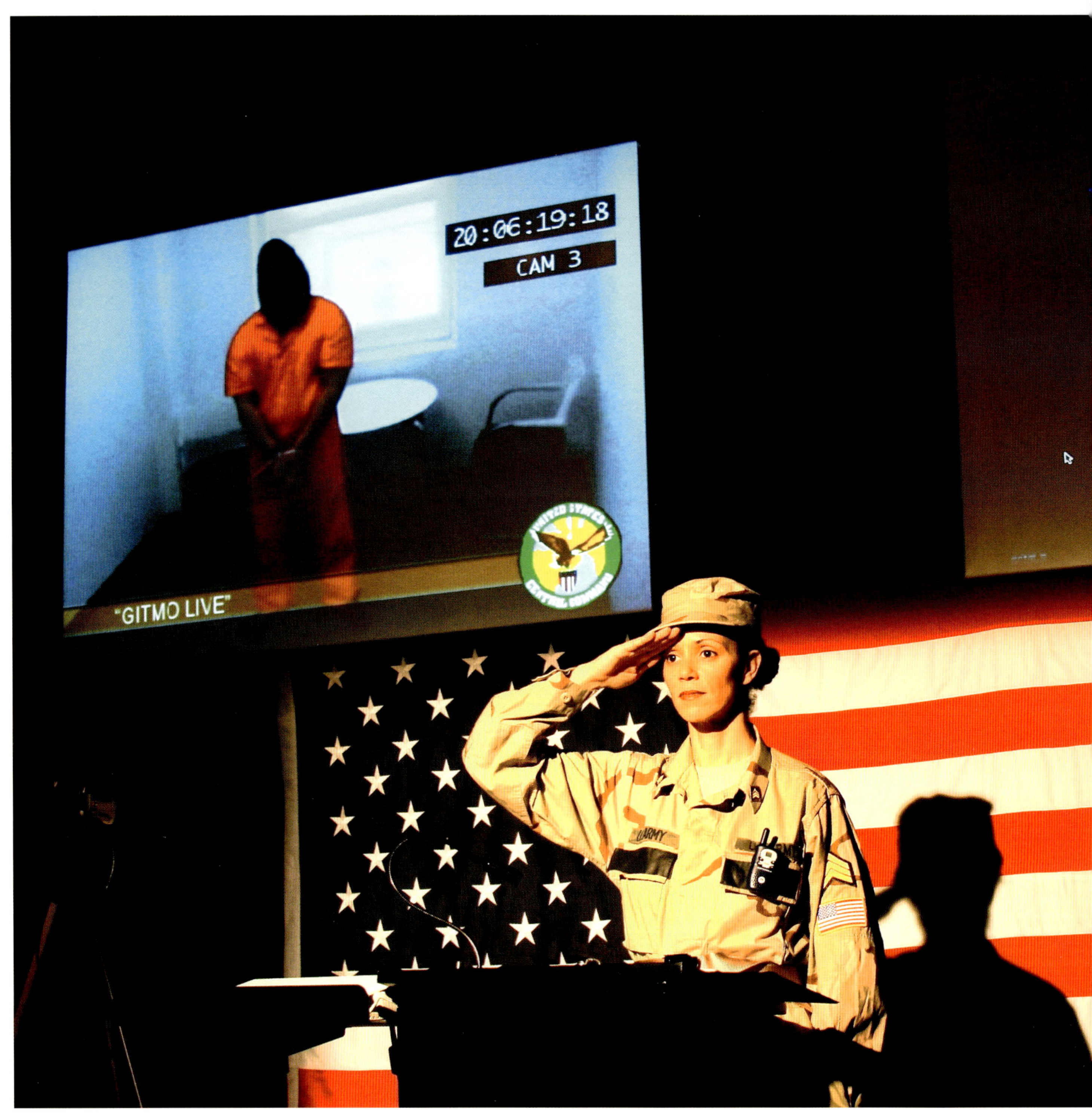

A Room of One's Own: Women and Power in the New America, 2006–08, performance

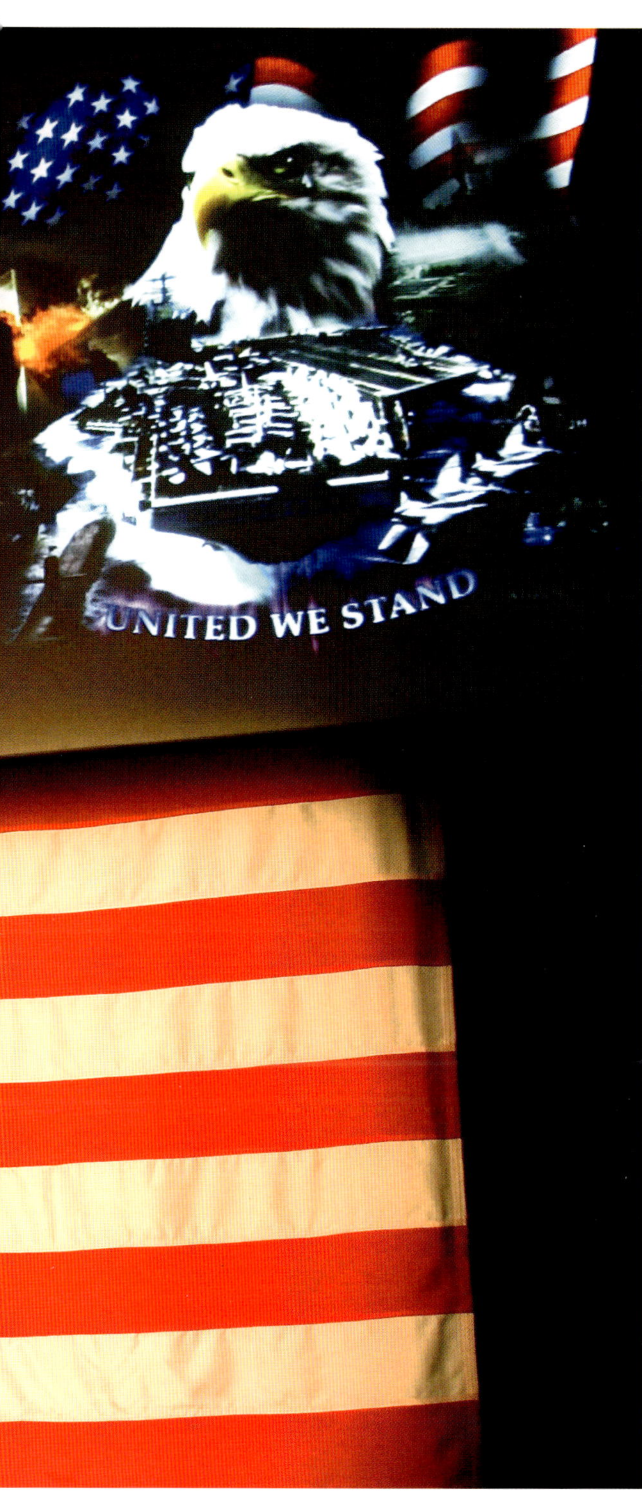

A Room of One's Own: Women and Power in the New America

2006–08

A Room of One's Own: Women and Power in the New America is a performance-lecture about the expanding role of American women in the War on Terror that premiered at The Kitchen in New York as Part of Performa 05, was included in the 2008 Whitney Biennial, and has been performed in London, Oslo, and Auckland. Fusco assumes the persona of a female graduate of a military intelligence school and a seasoned interrogator who briefs the audience on the rationales for using sexual innuendo as a tactic for extracting information from Islamic fundamentalists. The presentation stresses how a career in military intelligence represents great opportunities to emancipated women of the 21st century who have finally shed their victimhood. Taking its title from British novelist Virginia Woolf's notion that every woman needs a room of her own in order to manifest her strengths, Fusco ironically suggests that the contemporary American woman has found such a room in the military. Sardonically, she suggests that the War on Terror offers an unprecedented opportunity for women, as the US provides the space and support women need to prove they are powerful forces in the struggle for democracy.

Buried Pigs with Moros

2008

This exhibition continues Fusco's exploration of the ways that the War on Terror exploited existing racial and cultural stereotypes about Muslims. This mixed-media installation and exhibition features documents and artifacts related to the US occupation of the Philippines in the early 20th century, when the military contended with rebellious *juramentados*, Muslim holy warriors who pledged to kill Christians. The exhibition explores the life of a myth about the mass execution of insurrectionists intended to quell Islamic insurgents that emerged from the first American war against Muslims—the Moro Rebellion. According to military lore, General Pershing ordered that *juramentados* captured in that rebellion be executed with bullets dipped in pig's blood and that the dead be buried facing away from Mecca, thereby defiling them. The exhibition's centerpiece is *Lecture by Dr. Larry Forness* (2008), a dramatic reading of the transcript of a lecture that was delivered at the American Military University in 2005 by a former Marine and military consultant on the most expedient methods of torture, in which it was suggested that this tactic should be revived. *Buried Pigs with Moros* was presented at the Project Gallery, New York in 2008.

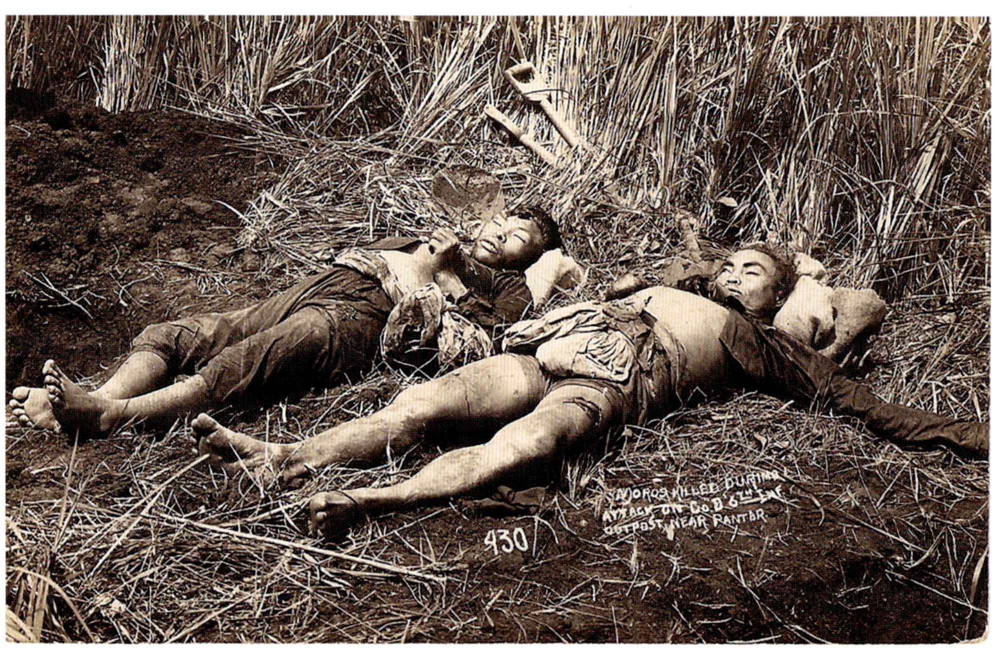

Buried Pigs with Moros, 2008, installation (details)

course there is nothing to be done, but I understand it has long been a custom to bury juramentados with pigs when they kill Americans. This I think a good plan, for if anything will discourage the juramentado it is the prospect of going to hell instead of to heaven. You can rely on me to stand by

Detail from General Pershing's letter

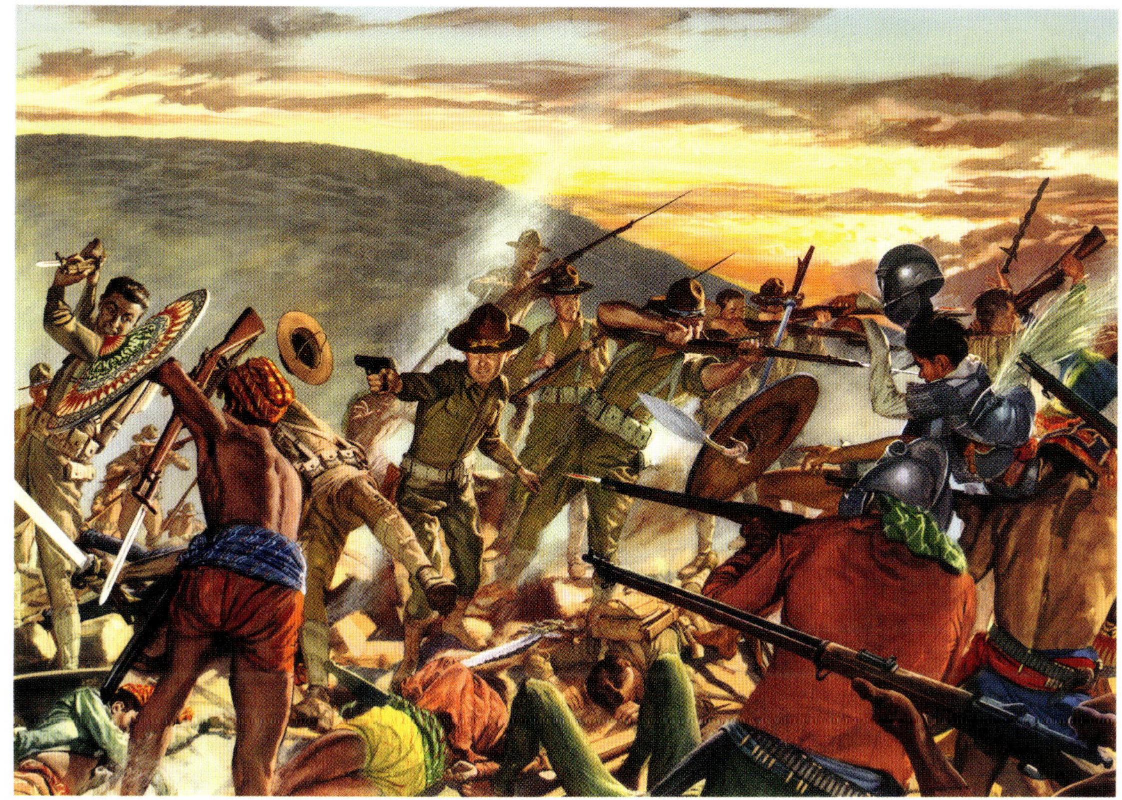

KNOCKING OUT THE MOROS
THE U. S. ARMY IN ACTION
The four-day battle of Bagsak Mountain on Jolo Island in the Philippines took place from 11 to 15 June 1913. Americans of the 8th Infantry and the Philippine Scouts, personally led by Brigadier General John J. Pershing, brought to an end years of bitter struggle against the Moro pirates. These Bolo men, outlaws of great physical endurance and savage fighting ability,
were well organized under their Datus or chiefs. They had never been conquered during several centuries of Spanish rule in the Philippines. The U.S. Army .45-caliber pistol was developed to meet the need for a weapon with enough striking power to stop fanatical charges of lawless Moro tribesmen in hand-to-hand fighting.
INSTRUCTIONS FOR FRAMING
DEPARTMENT OF THE ARMY POSTER NO. 21-48
U.S. GOVERNMENT PRINTING OFFICE : 2004 0 - 312-230; QL 2
CUT ON THIS LINE FOR FRAMING
NO. 12.— HISTORY OF THE UNITED STATES ARMY.
This poster is one of a series to be published to dramatize the history and accomplishments of the United States Army from the American Revolution and may be used as a supplemental aid when discussing these accomplishments. It is suitable for framing and preserving for permanent display in dayrooms, clubs, and offices of the Army. The overall size is 20 by 24 inches. A 1-inch black frame is recommended for uniformity of the series.
Distribution.— Active Army: Tech Svc (1); AFF (10); OS Maj Comd (15); Base Comd (2); MDW (5); A (10); CHQ (2); Div (5); Brig (2); Regt (2); Sep Bn (2); Bn (1); Co (1); FT (5); Sch (2); PMS&T (1); Dep (1); GH (5); Pers Cen (5); PRGR (1); Dspln Bks (1); Rct Sta (1); Div Engr (1); Dist (1); Tng Div (1); DISTRIBUTION WILL NOT BE MADE TO UNITS IN KOREA. NG: None. Army Reserve: Special. For explanation of distribution formula see SR 310-90-1.

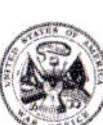

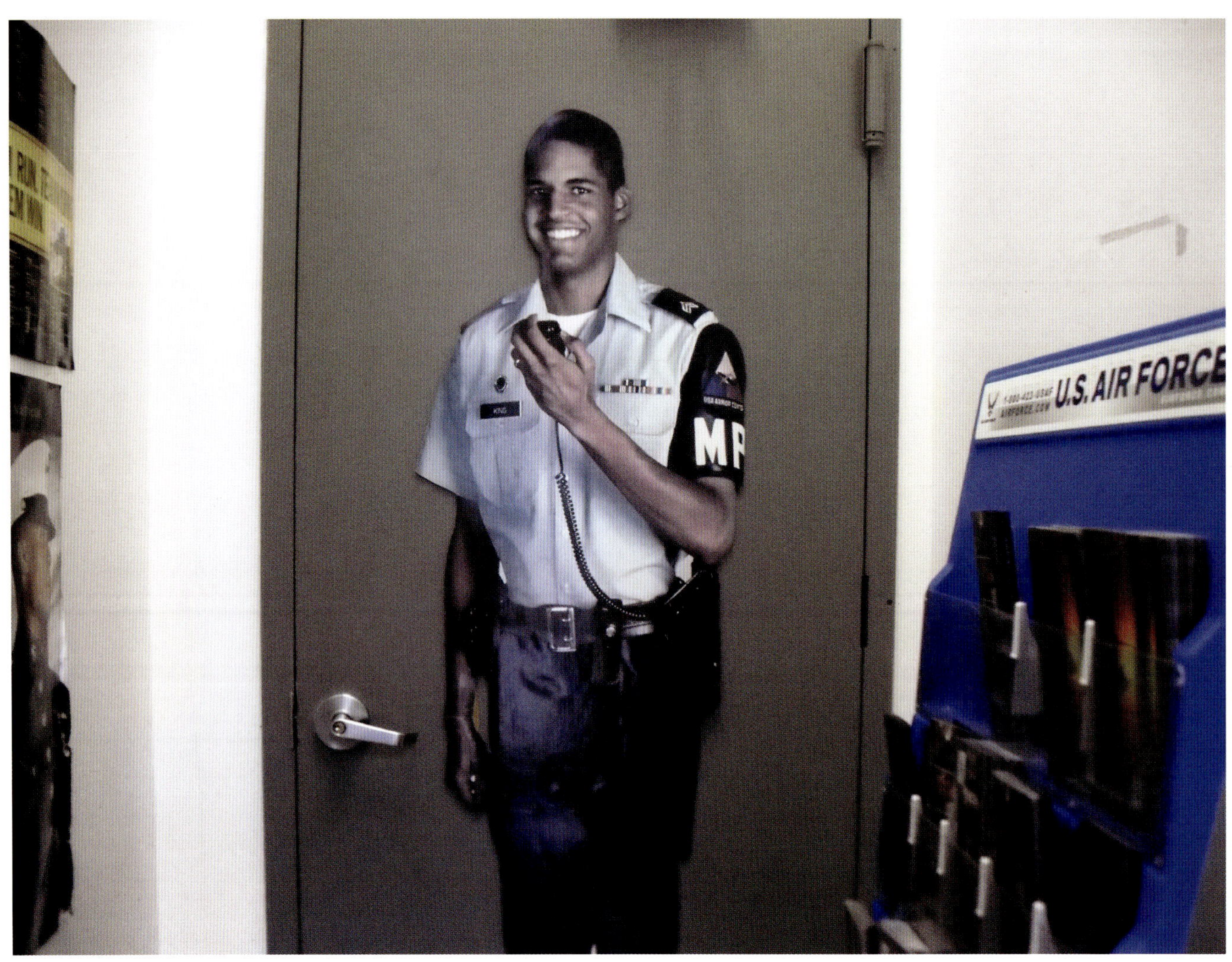

Harlem Postcards

2008

In 2008, Fusco was invited to participate in the Studio Museum's *Harlem Postcards*, an ongoing project that, beginning in 2004, has engaged contemporary artists of diverse backgrounds to reflect on Harlem as a site of cultural activity, political vitality, visual stimuli, artistic contemplation, and creative production. For her contribution, Fusco chose to document the activities at the US Army Recruiting Center on 125th Street, whose location underscores how the military's recruitment strategies specifically target young adults in communities of color. However, since neither the Army nor the recruiters would give Fusco permission to photograph any part of the recruiting process or center, she resorted to taking photos surreptitiously through reflections in the windows, of vacated desks, and of brochures and posters tucked away behind closed doors.

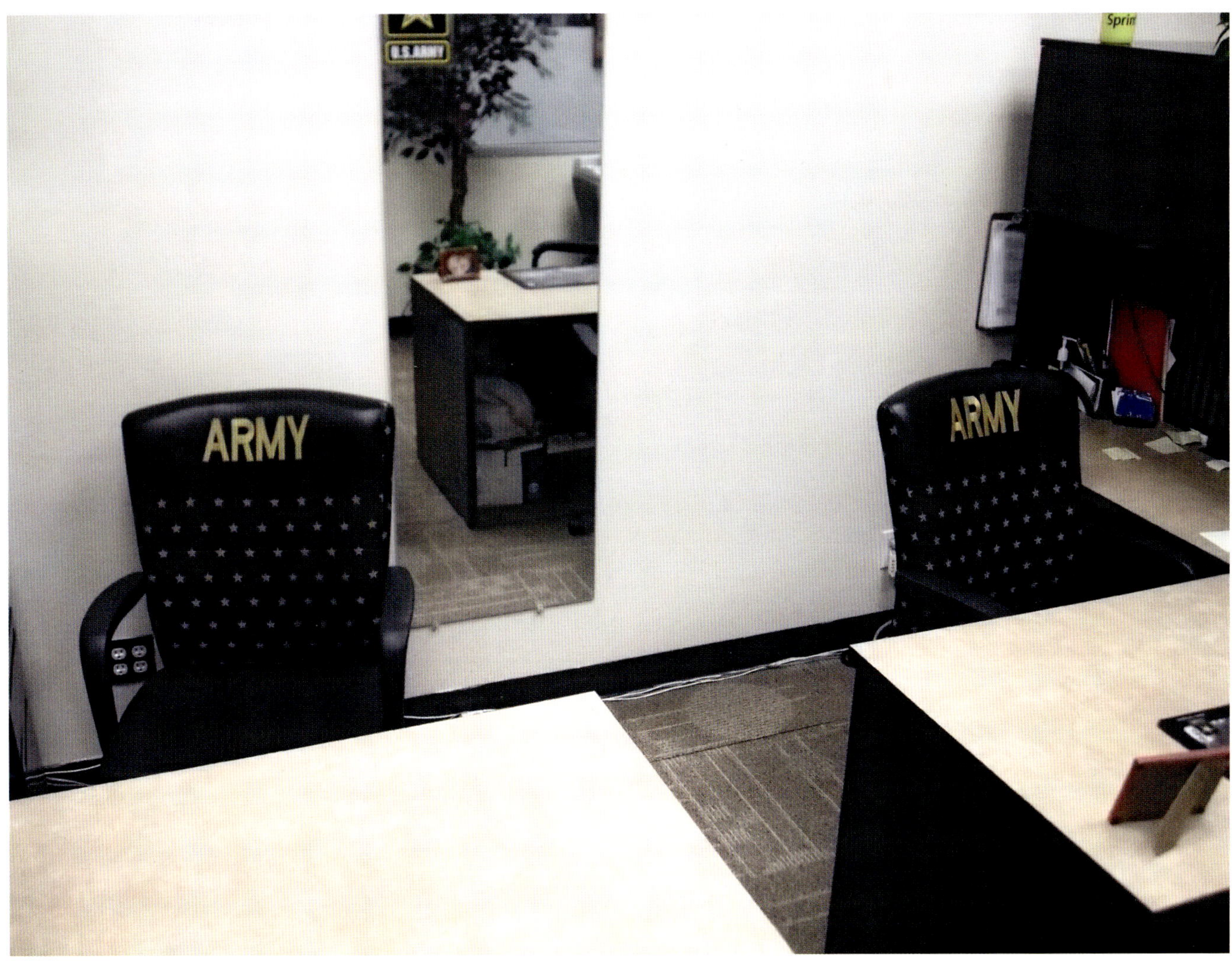

Harlem Postcards, 2008, photography

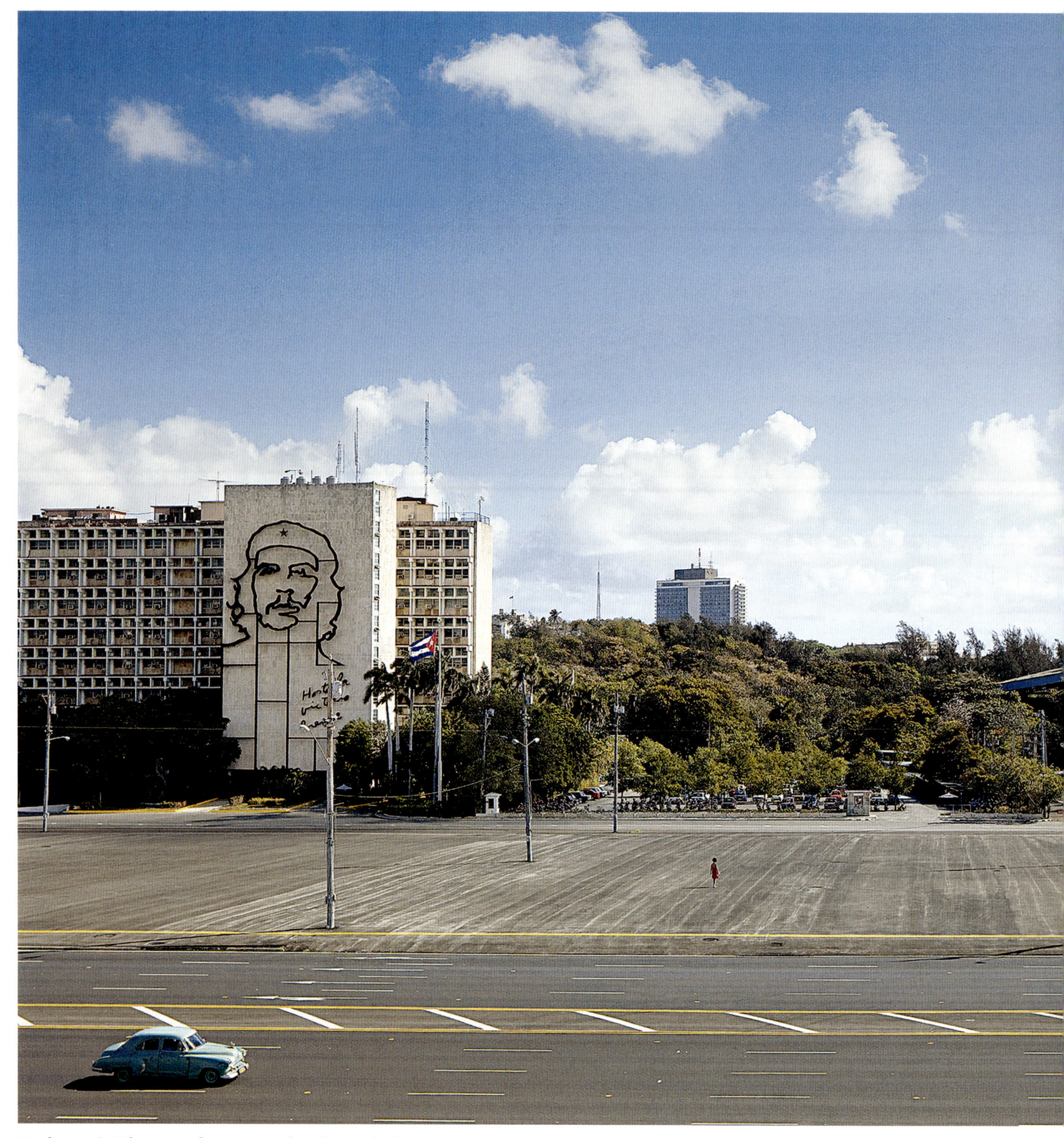

La plaza vacía (The Empty Plaza), 2012, video (also overleaf and page 129)

La plaza vacía
(The Empty Plaza)
2012

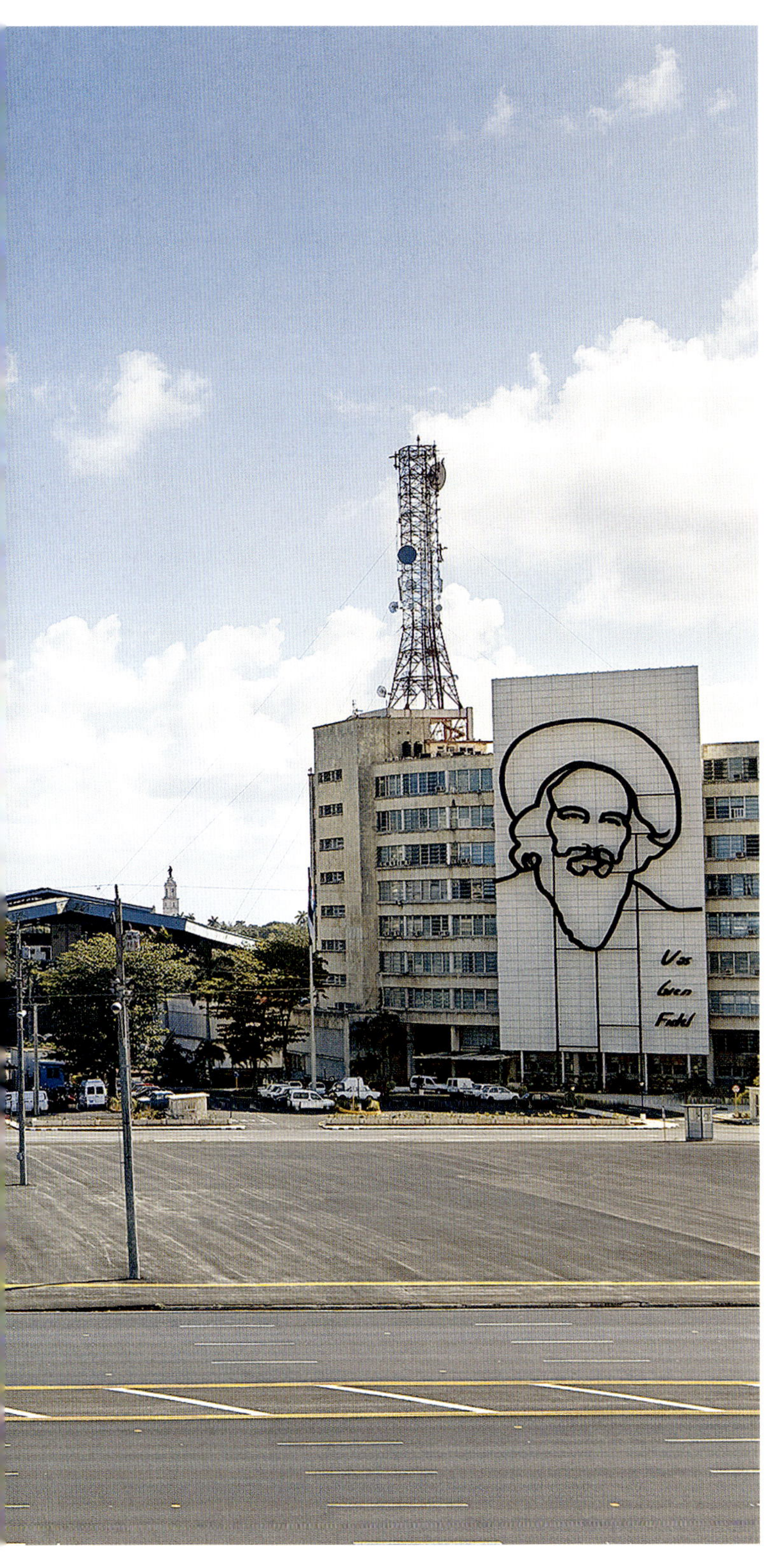

Inspired by Arab Spring protests of 2011, Fusco took note of discussions among Cubans about why it was that their plazas were left vacant. In *La plaza vacía* (*The Empty Plaza*), Havana's Plaza de la Revolución becomes the protagonist in the artist's meditation on public space, revolutionary promise, and memory. Intermittent close-up views bring the expansive plaza's architecture into sharp focus while long shots documenting Fusco's passage through the vacant square are punctuated by archival footage of post-revolutionary Cuba. The video narration is written by Cuban journalist Yoani Sánchez, who describes what appears and does not appear in view. "The absence of the public in some plazas seemed just as resonant and provocative as the presence in others," Fusco recalls. "Cuba's Plaza of the Revolution is one such place—a stark, inhospitable arena where all the major political events of the past half-century have been marked by mass choreography, militarized displays, and rhetorical flourish. I decided to create a piece about that legendary site—an empty stage filled with memories, through which every foreign visitor passes, while nowadays many, if not most, Cubans flee."

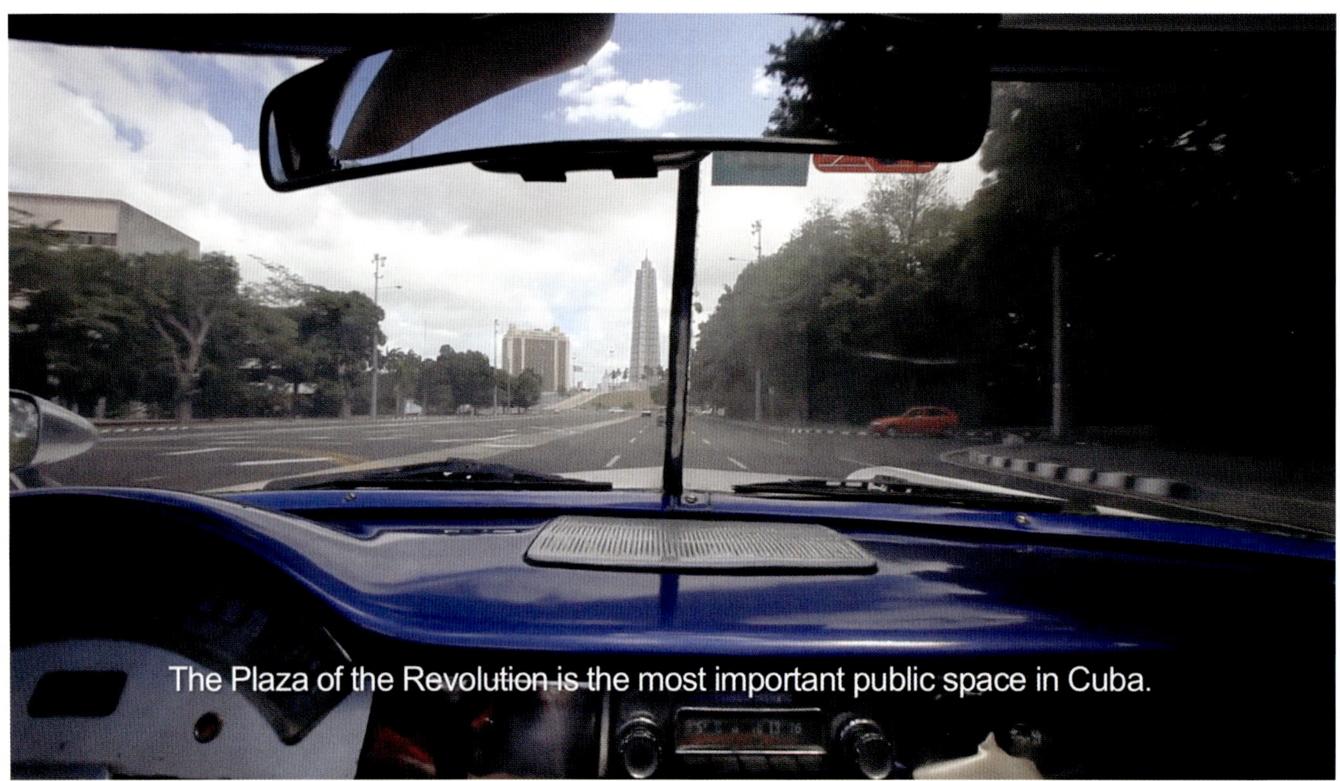

The Plaza of the Revolution is the most important public space in Cuba.

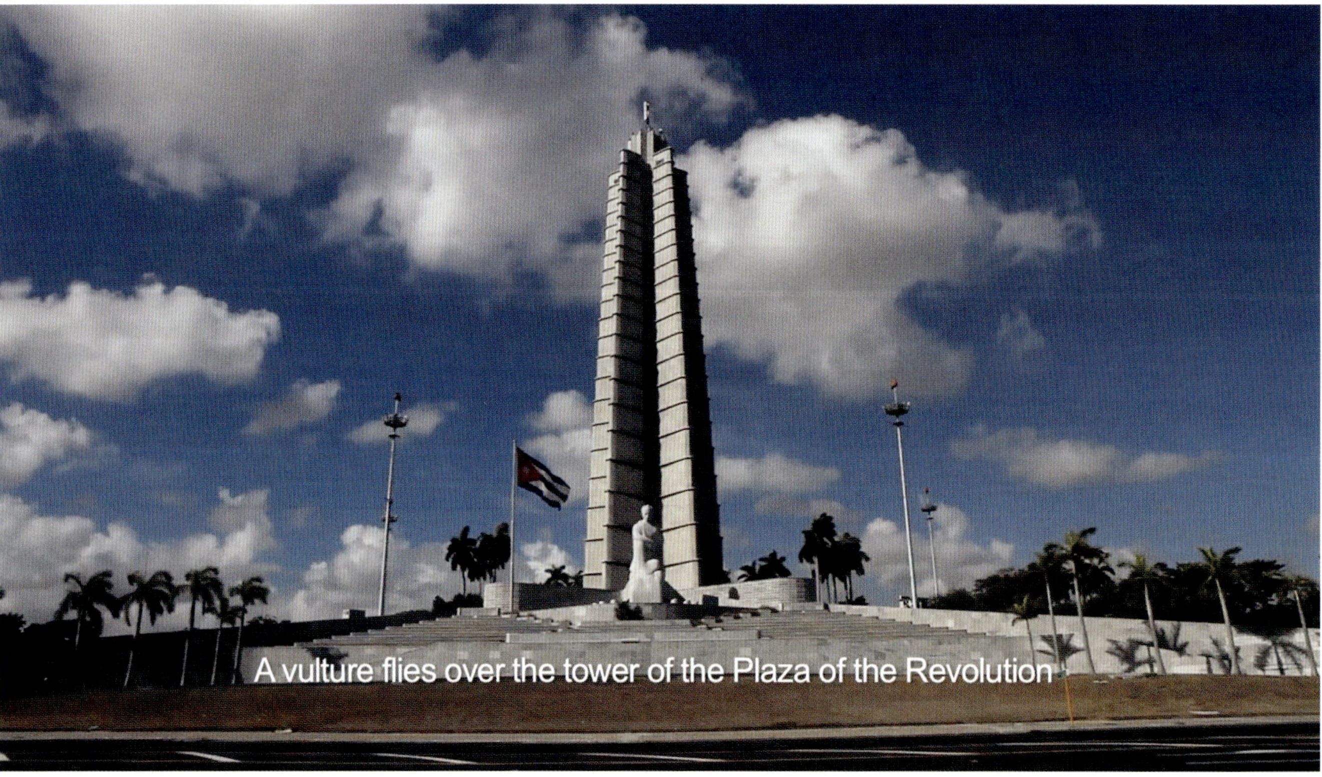

A vulture flies over the tower of the Plaza of the Revolution

BODY OF WORK 1990–2022

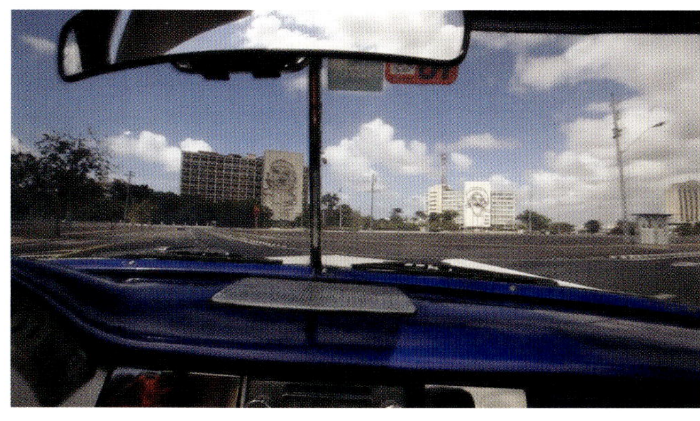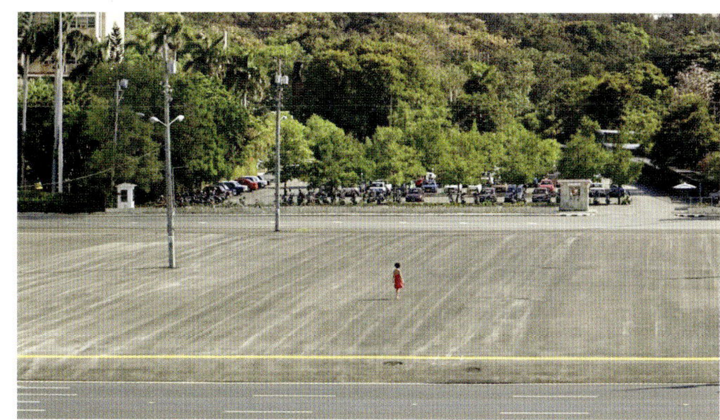

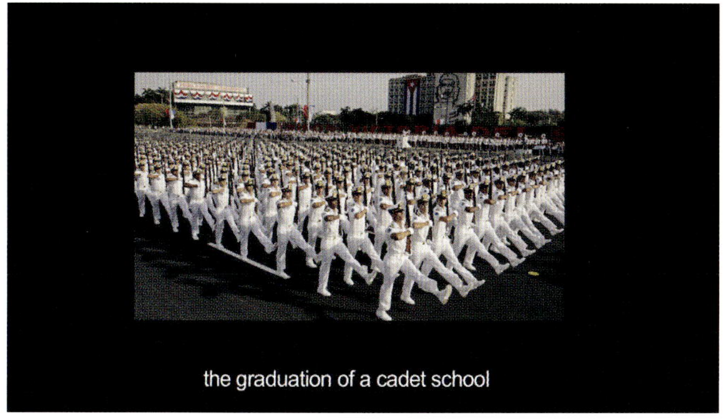
the graduation of a cadet school

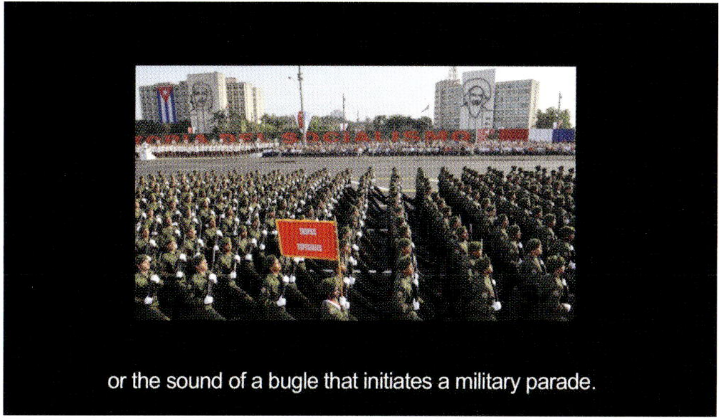
or the sound of a bugle that initiates a military parade.

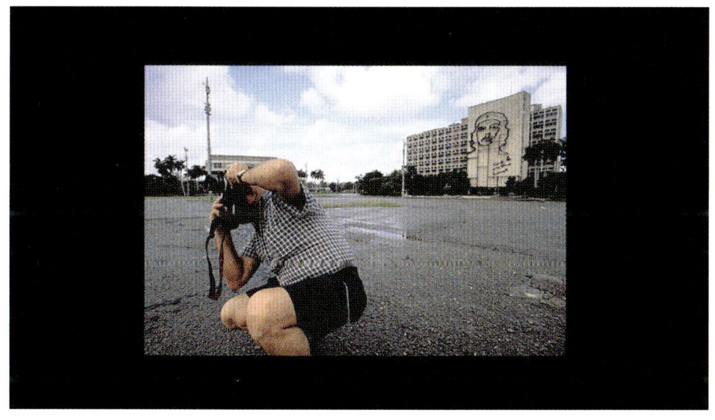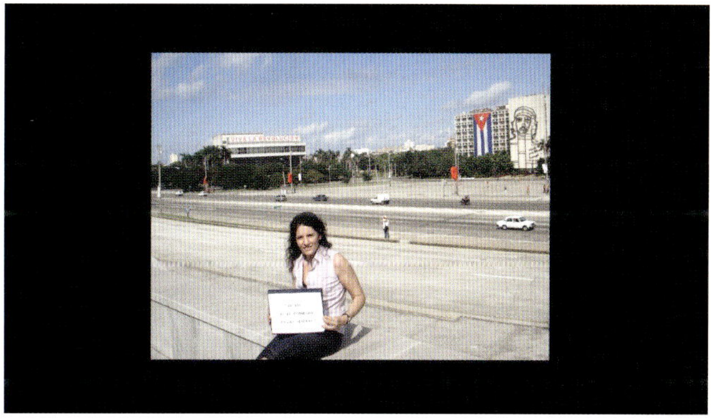

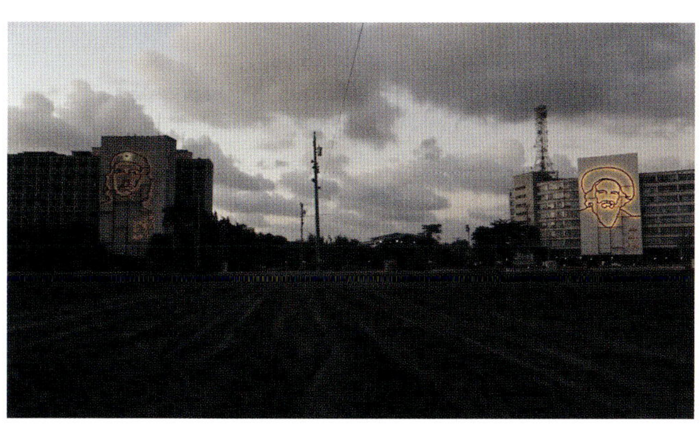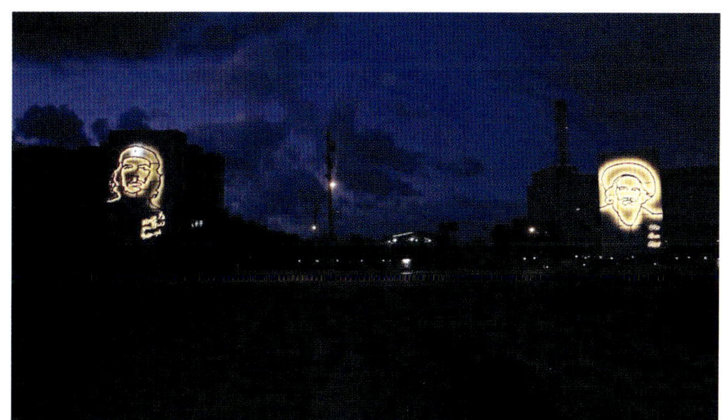

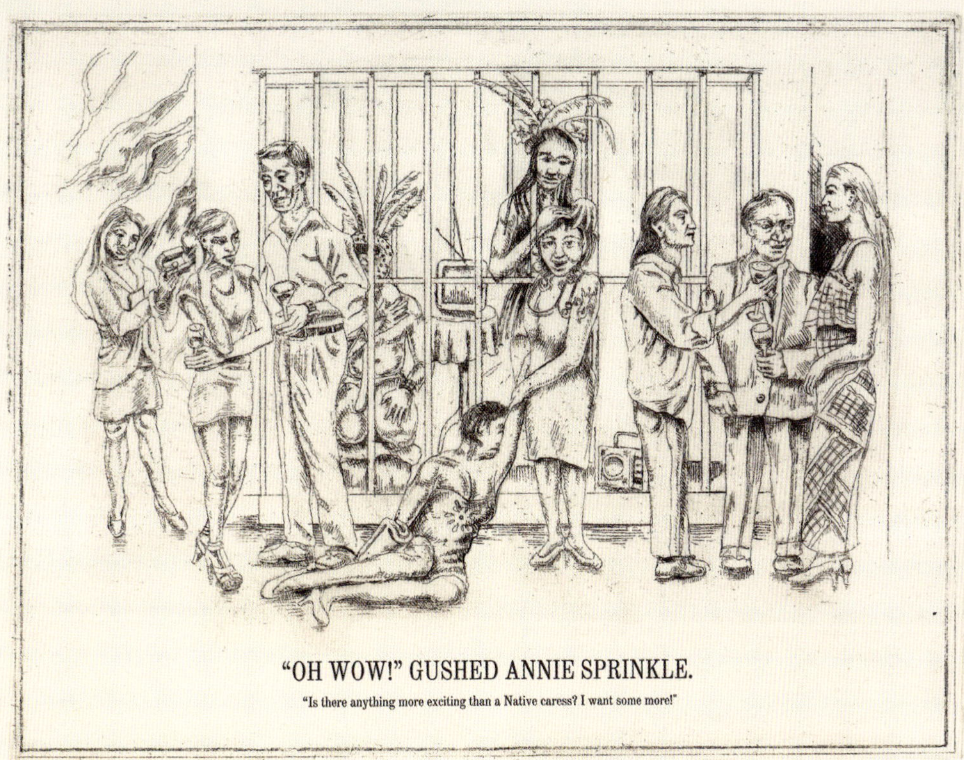

The Undiscovered Amerindians

2012

For the twentieth anniversary of Coco Fusco and Guillermo Gómez-Peña's *Two Undiscovered Amerindians Visit the West* (1992–94), Fusco produced a series of commemorative engravings rendered in the style of 19th-century caricatures, each illustrating Fusco's recollections of audience responses to the performance through a humorous yet unsettling narrative, exposing the residue of colonial stereotypes in contemporary culture. While looking back at the original response to the performance, *The Undiscovered Amerindians* underscores how remnants of colonial attitudes persist in today's society.

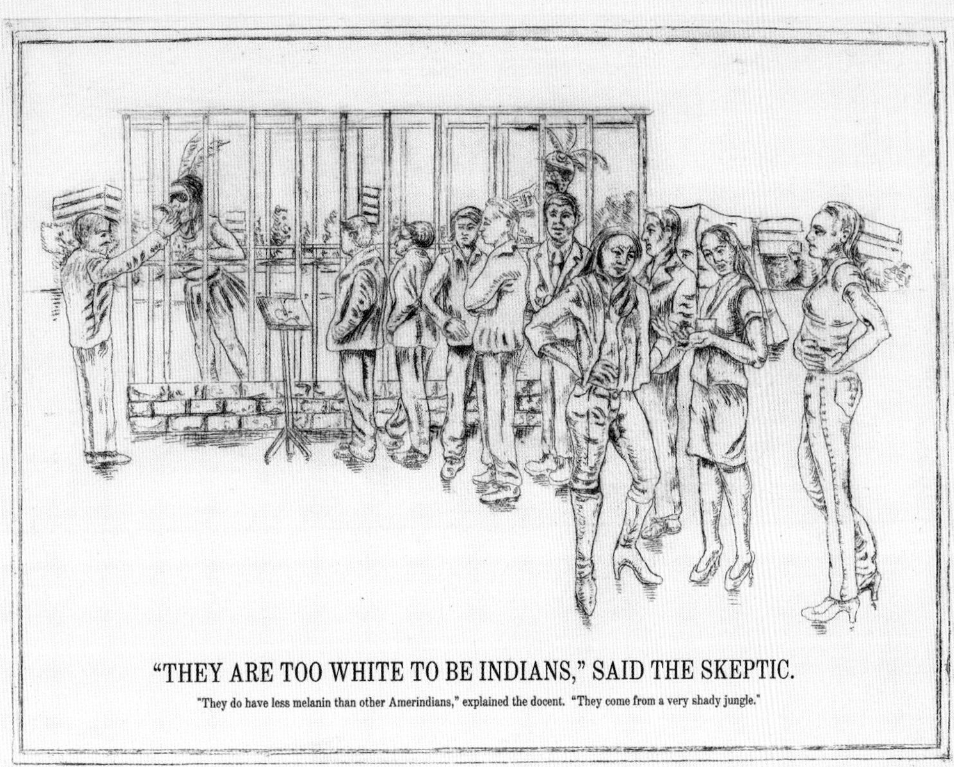

The Undiscovered Amerindians, 2012, letterpress and intaglio prints on paper in 10 parts,
18¼ × 21 in. (46.48 × 53.34 cm) each (also overleaf and pages 133–35)

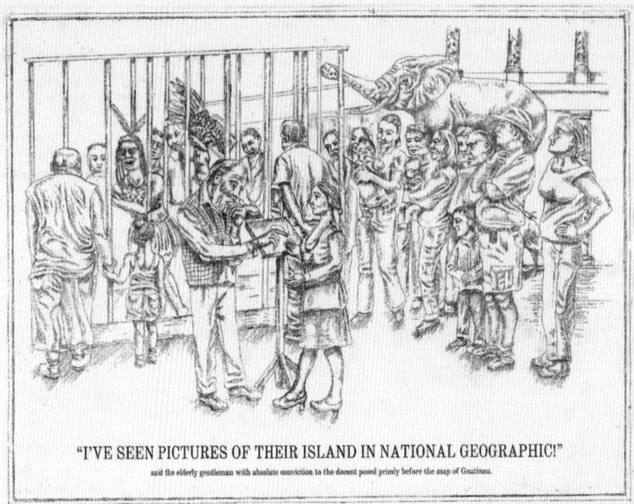

"I'VE SEEN PICTURES OF THEIR ISLAND IN NATIONAL GEOGRAPHIC!"
said the elderly gentleman with absolute conviction to the docent posed primly before the map of Guatinau.

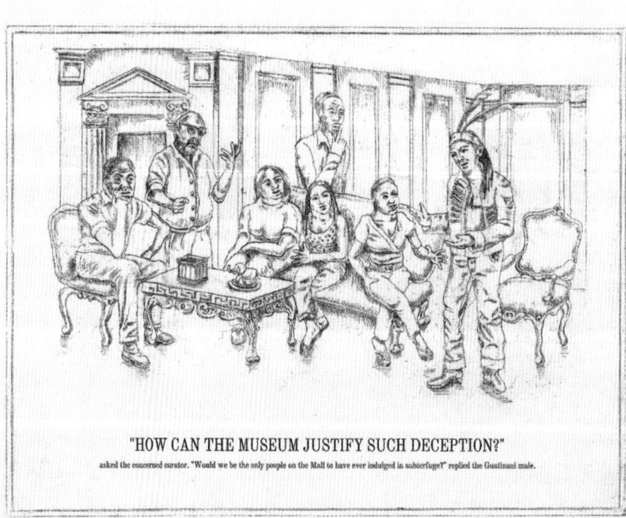

"HOW CAN THE MUSEUM JUSTIFY SUCH DECEPTION?"
asked the concerned curator. "Would we be the only people on the Mall to have ever indulged in subterfuge?" replied the Guatinaui male.

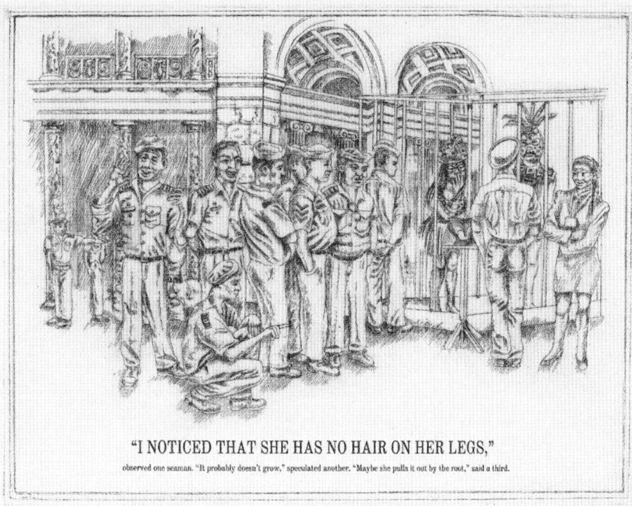

"I NOTICED THAT SHE HAS NO HAIR ON HER LEGS,"
observed one seaman. "It probably doesn't grow," speculated another. "Maybe she pulls it out by the root," said a third.

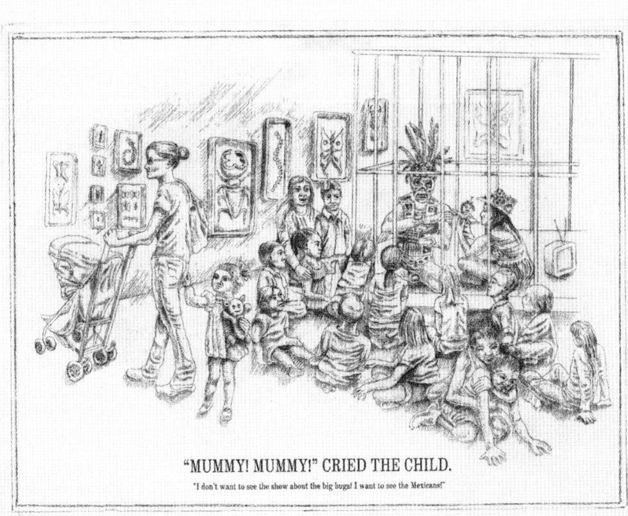

"MUMMY! MUMMY!" CRIED THE CHILD.
"I don't want to see the show about the big bugs! I want to see the Mexicans!"

COCO FUSCO

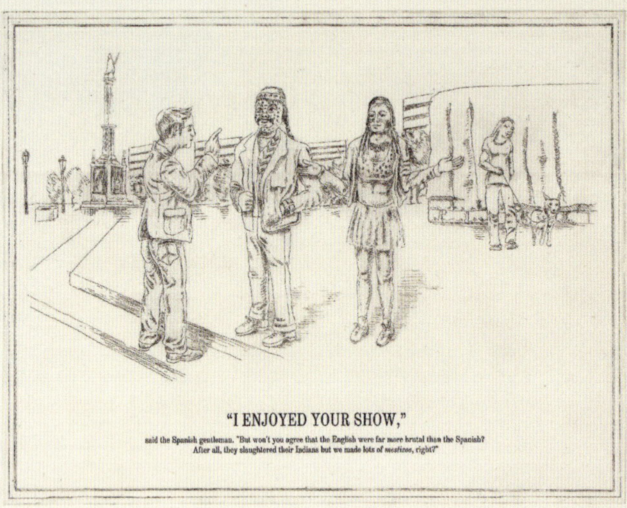

"I ENJOYED YOUR SHOW,"

said the Spanish gentleman. "But won't you agree that the English were far more brutal than the Spanish? After all, they slaughtered their Indians but we made lots of *mestizos*, right?"

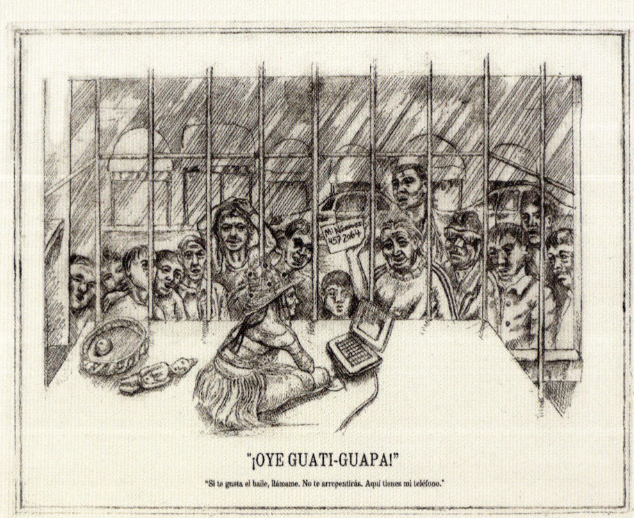

"¡OYE GUATI-GUAPA!"

"Si te gusta el baile, llámame. No te arrepentirás. Aquí tienes mi teléfono."

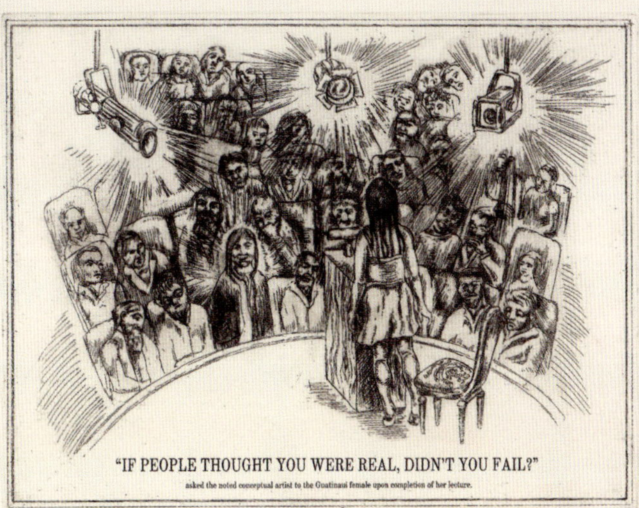

"IF PEOPLE THOUGHT YOU WERE REAL, DIDN'T YOU FAIL?"

asked the noted conceptual artist to the Guatinaui female upon completion of her lecture.

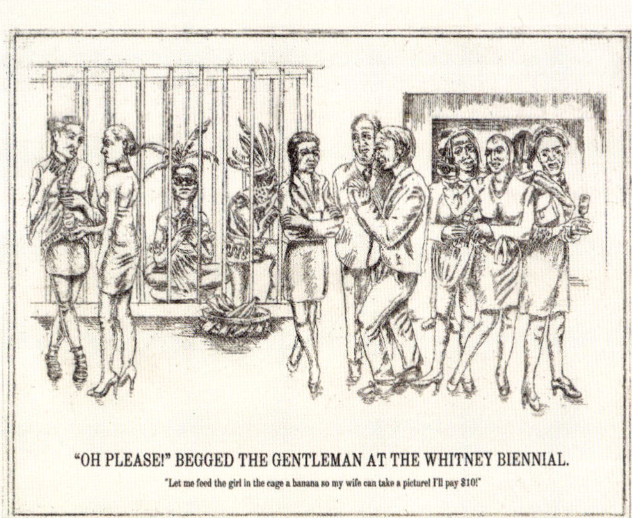

"OH PLEASE!" BEGGED THE GENTLEMAN AT THE WHITNEY BIENNIAL.

"Let me feed the girl in the cage a banana so my wife can take a picture! I'll pay $10!"

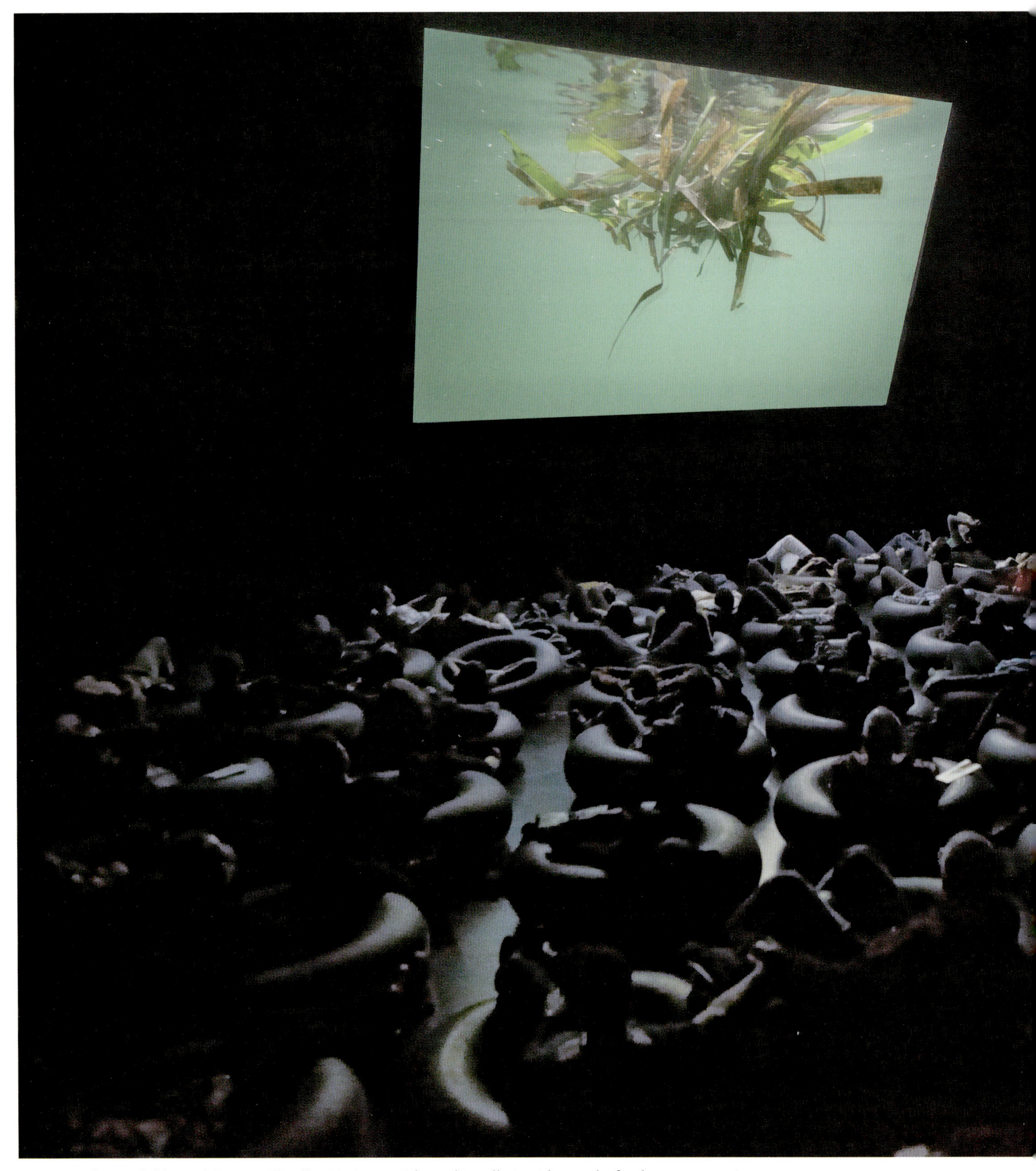

Y entonces el mar te habla (And the Sea Will Talk to You), 2012, video and installation (also overleaf and pages 140–41)

  BODY OF WORK 1990–2022

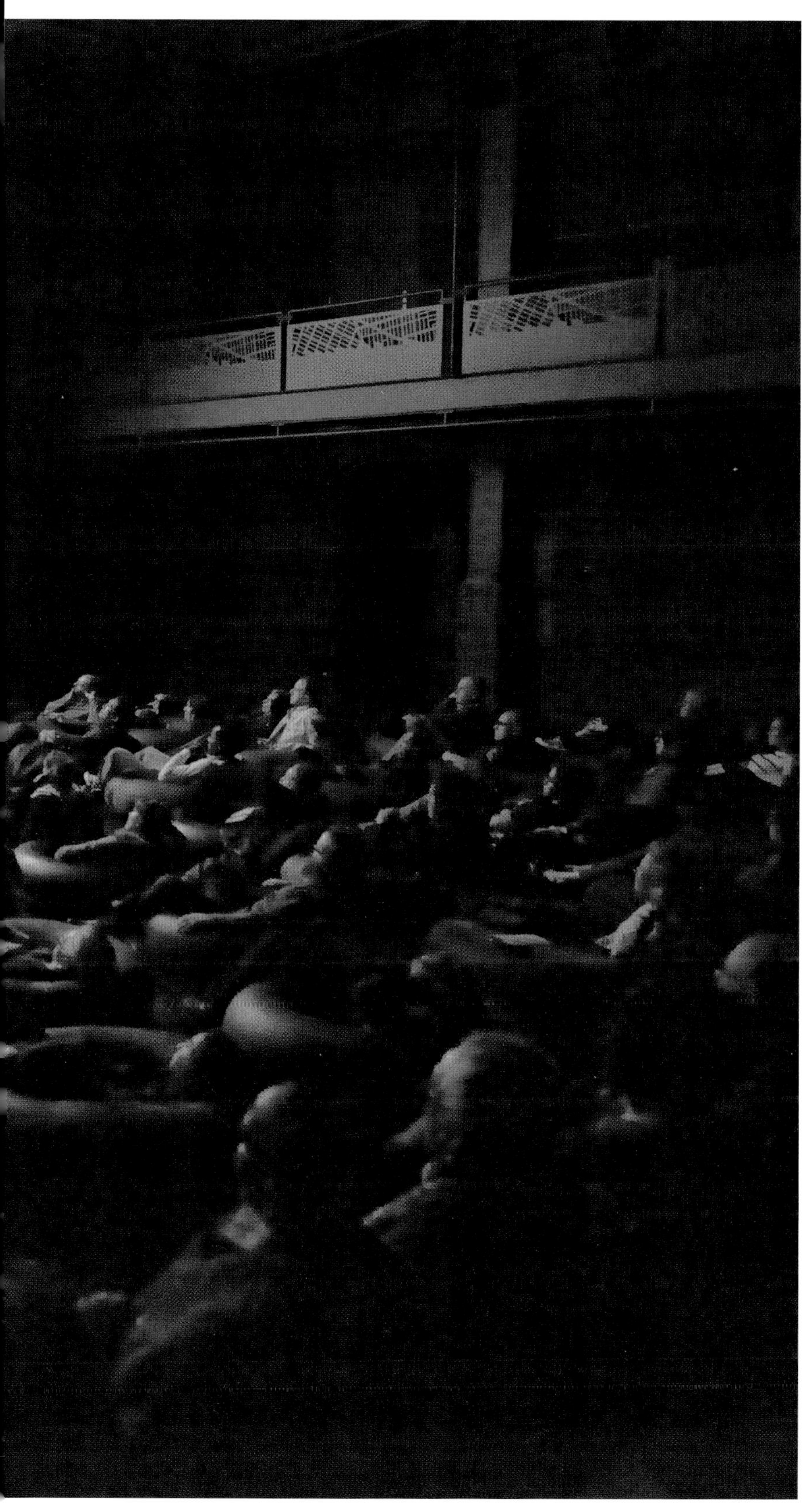

Y entonces el mar te habla (And the Sea Will Talk to You)

2012

Y entonces el mar te habla (And the Sea Will Talk to You) is a filmic engagement with the Florida Strait, a body of water that divides two warring countries and is an omnipresent symbolic reference in Cuban poetry. Considering the strait as a cemetery, Fusco weaves together Cuban poetry about the waters surrounding Cuba, first-hand testimony of rafter journeys from Cuba to the US through the Straits of Florida, with her own adventure surreptitiously bringing her mother's ashes back to Cuba. These evocations of being adrift are set against images of the Caribbean Sea and skies. The audience, seated in inner tubes, is given a simulated experience reminiscent of the challenging journey between the two countries.

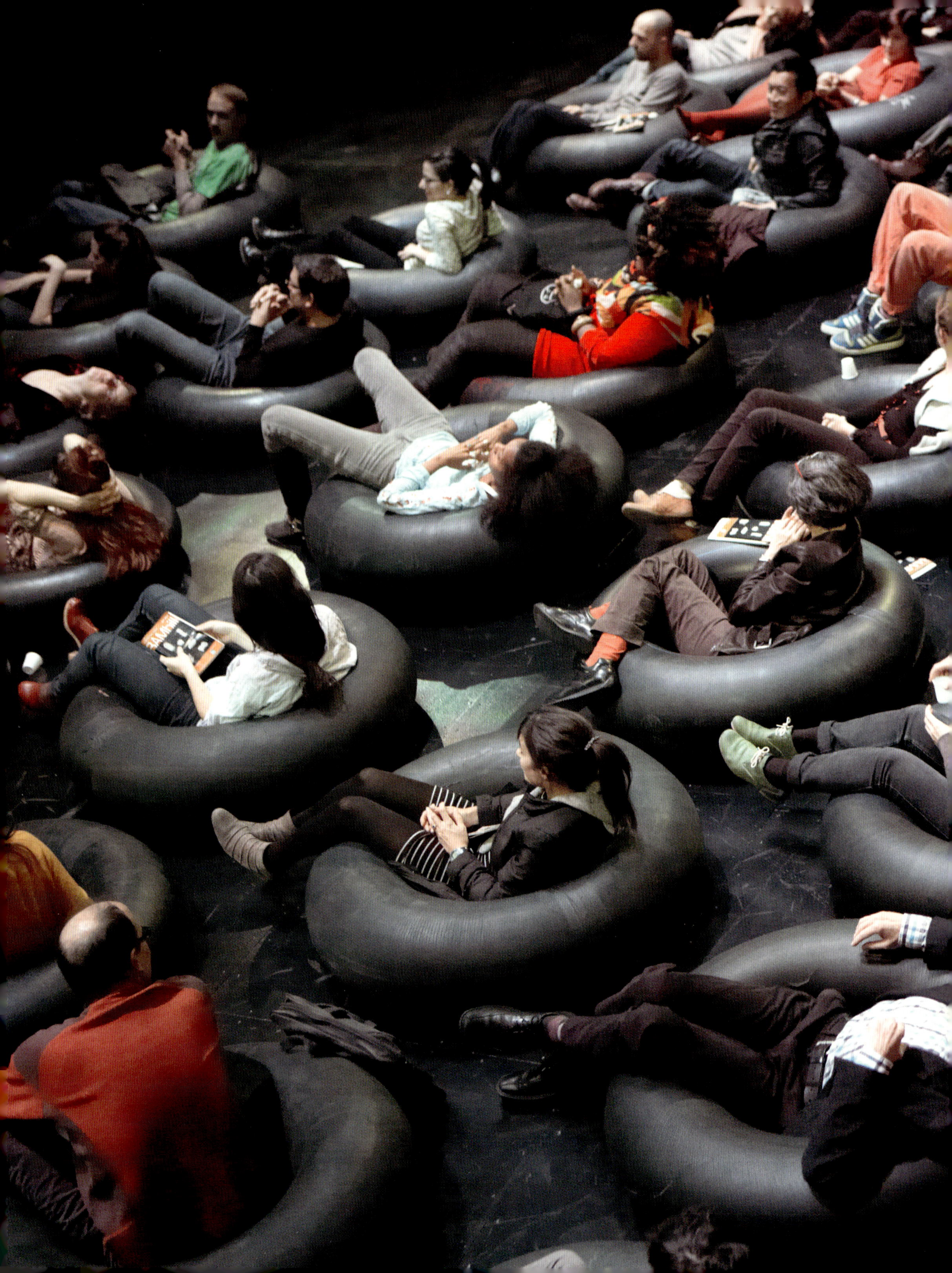

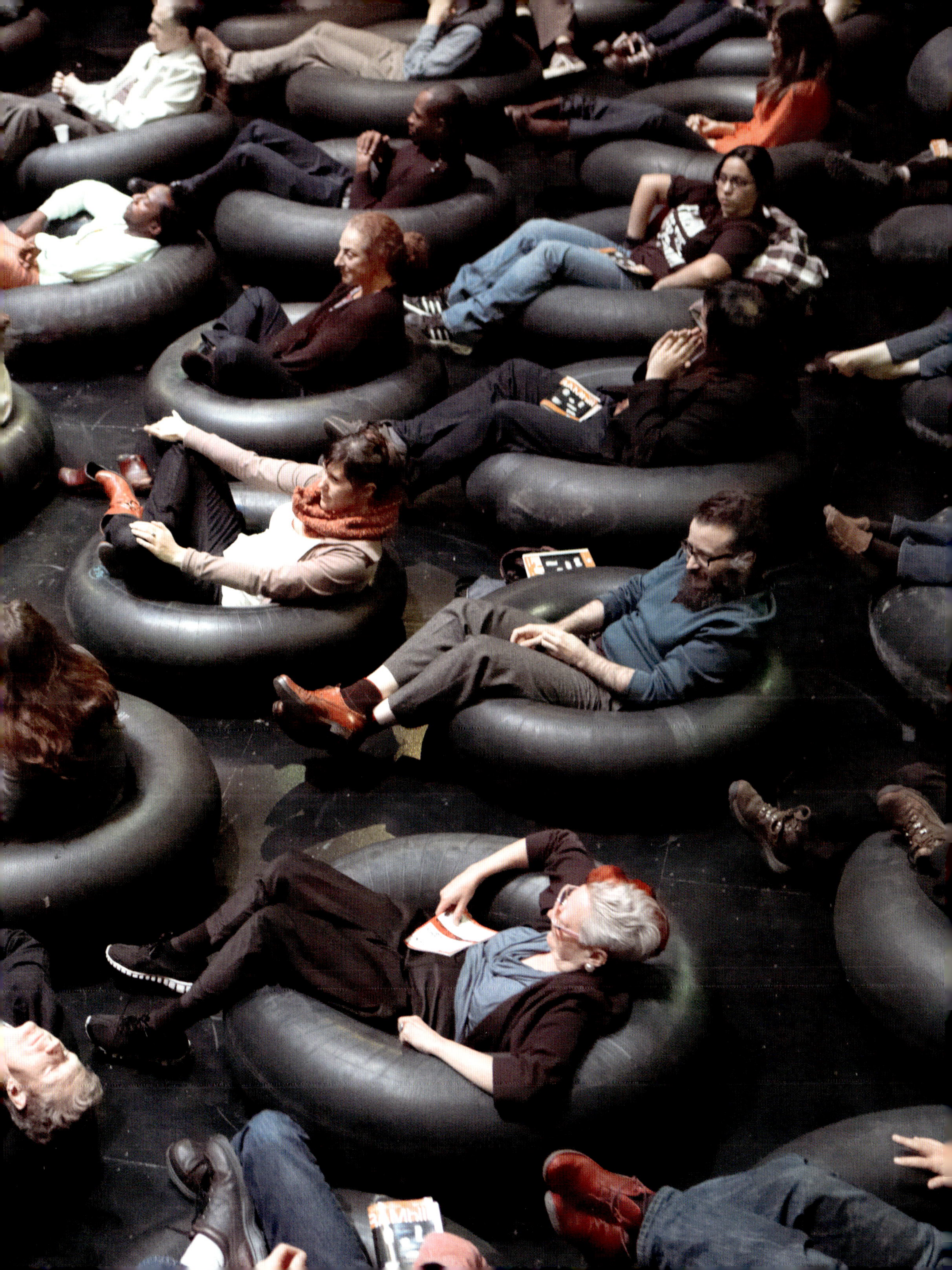

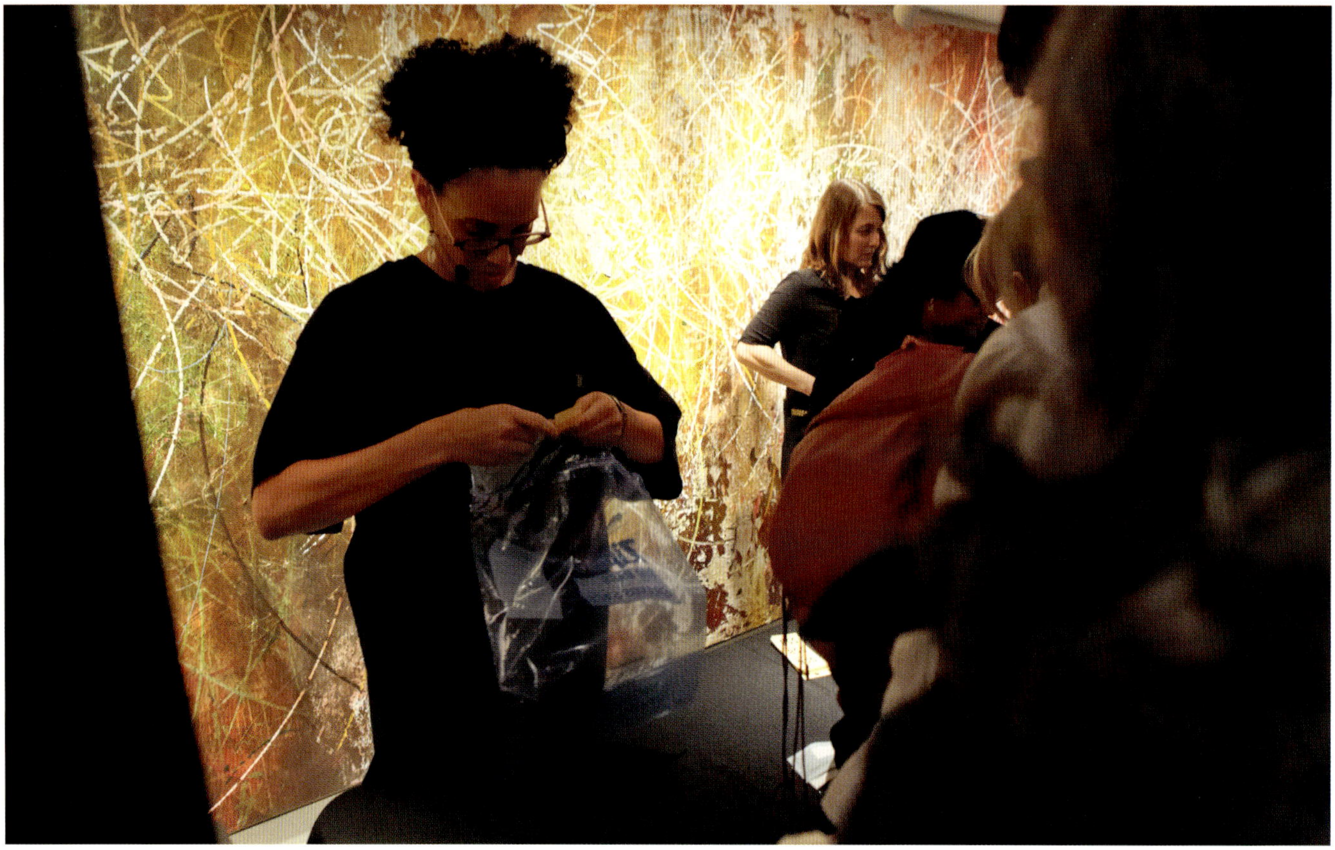

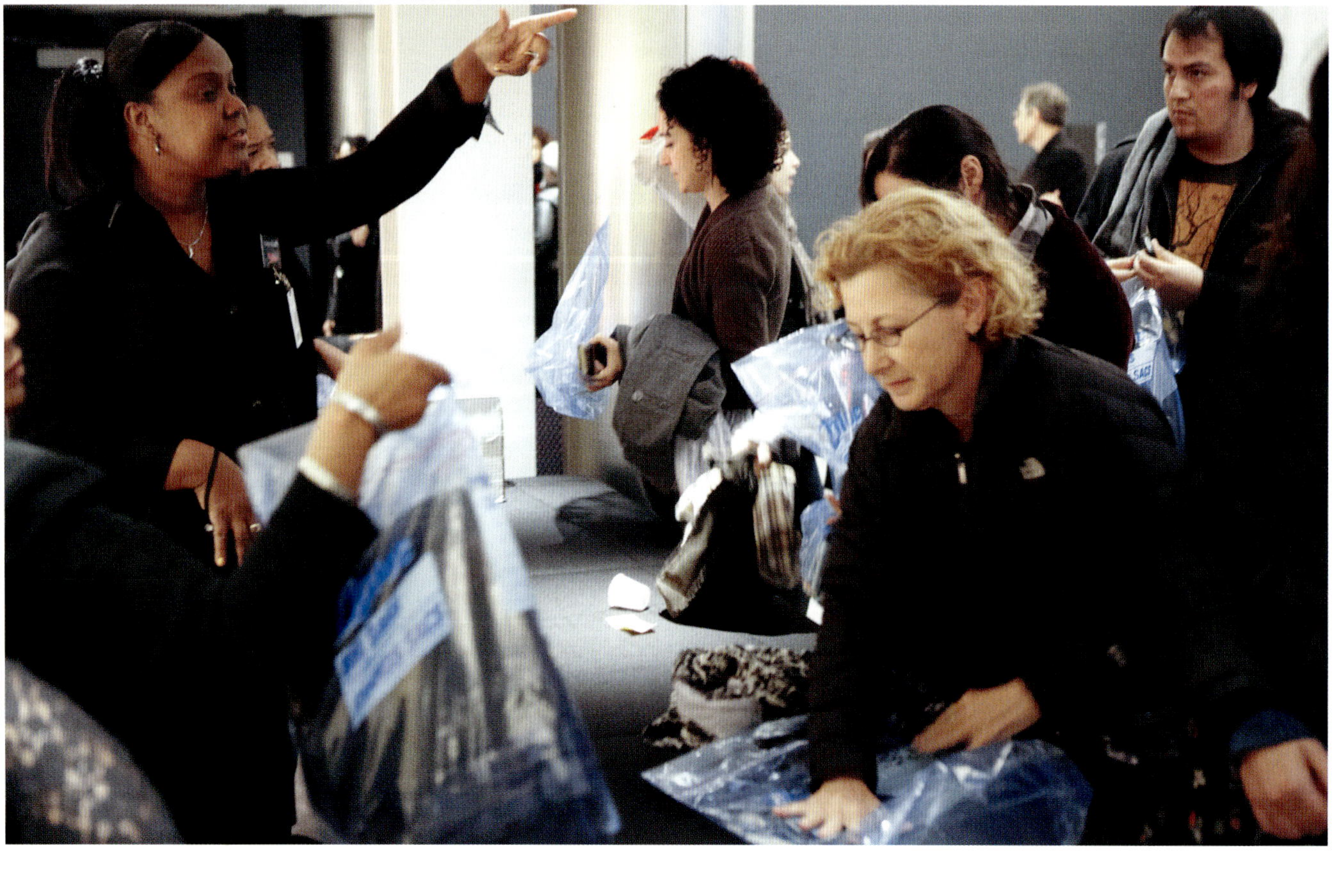

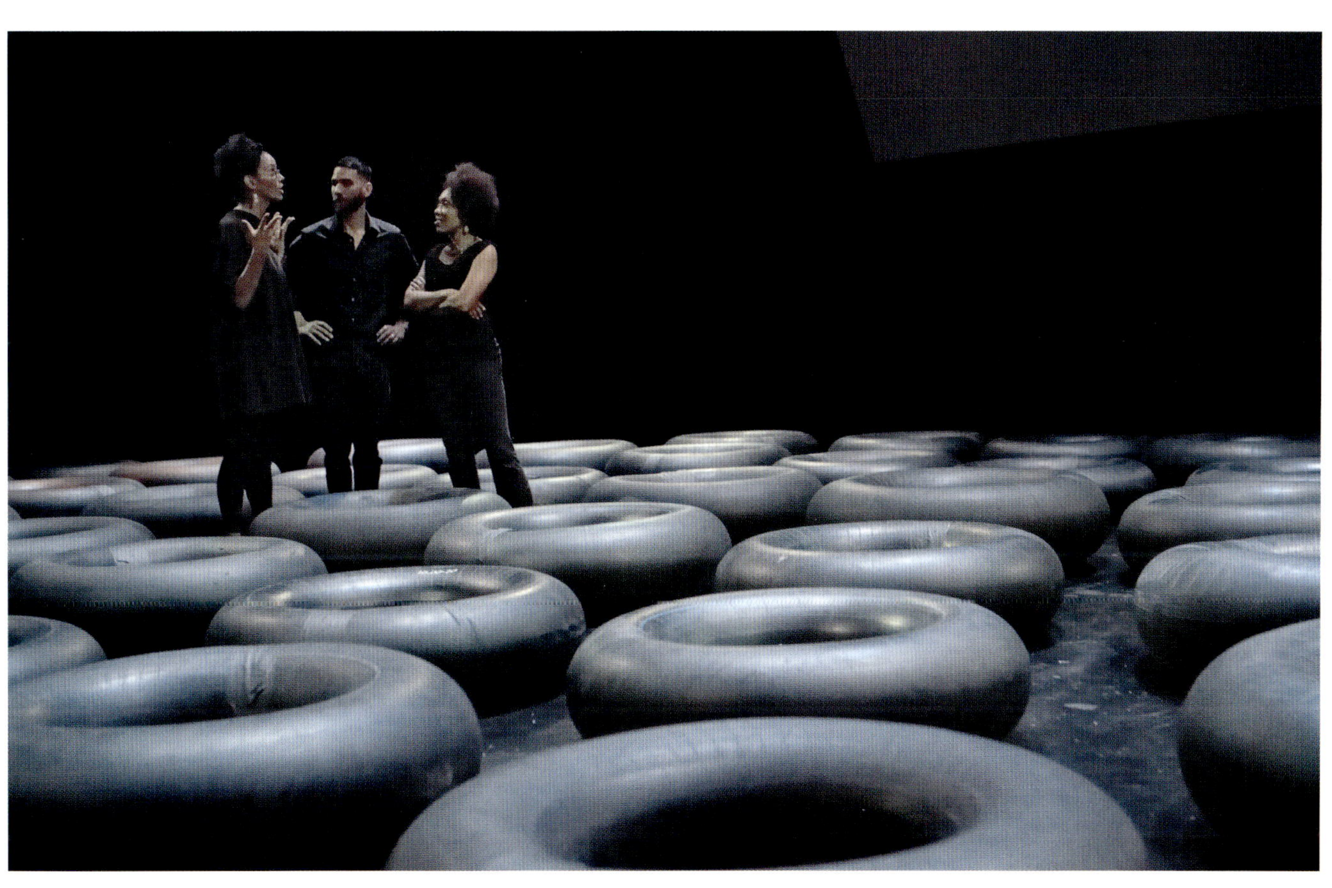

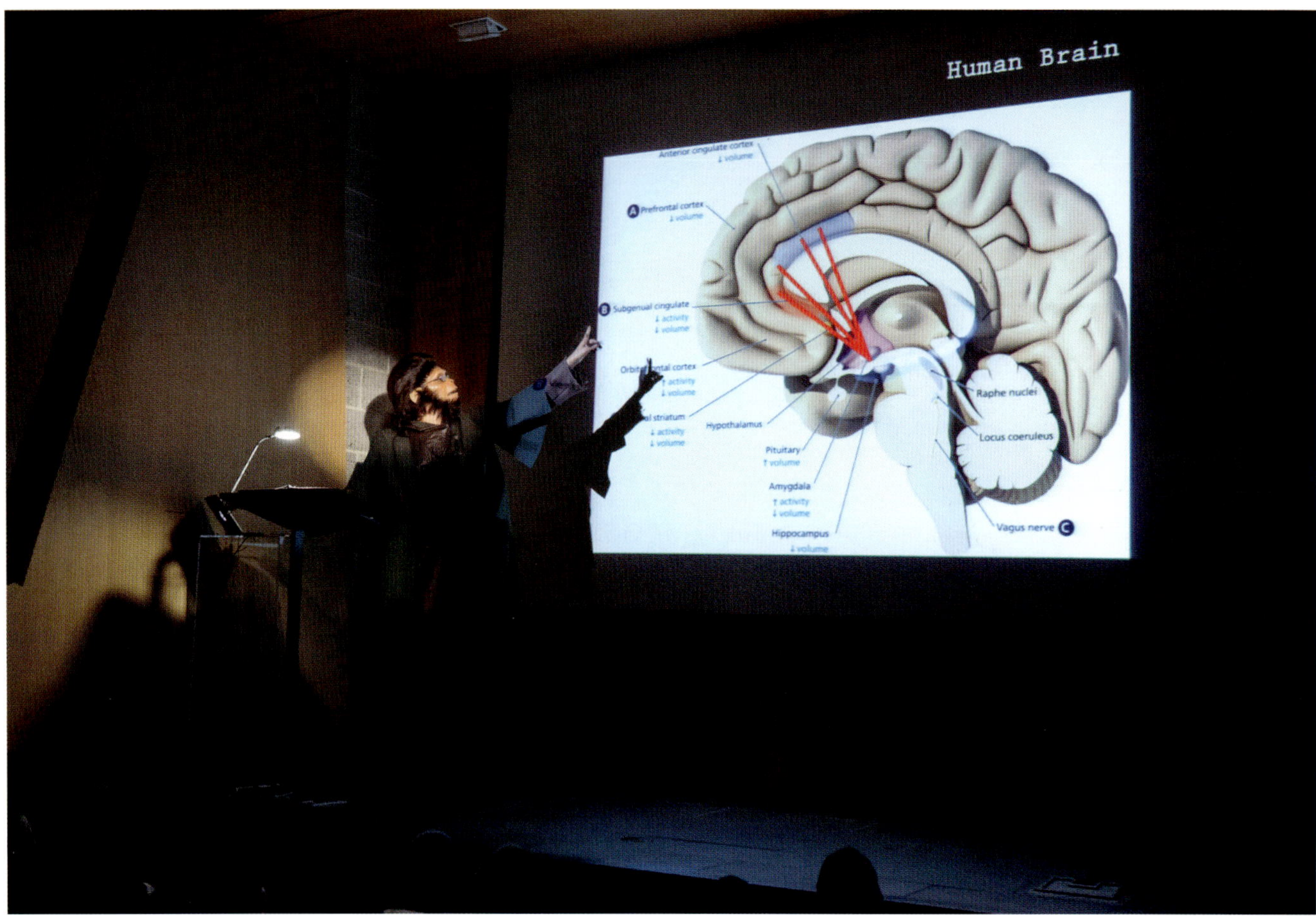

Observations of Predation in Humans: A Lecture by Dr. Zira, Animal Psychologist, 2013–16, performance

Observations of Predation in Humans: A Lecture by Dr. Zira, Animal Psychologist

2013–16

Commissioned by The Studio Museum in Harlem for its presentation of the exhibition, "Radical Presence: Black Performance in Contemporary Art," Fusco assumes the role of Dr. Zira, the chimpanzee psychologist from *Planet of the Apes*, who has traveled back in time to pay our civilization a visit. Fusco adapts the original story in which Dr. Zira was killed by 20th-century humans when she traveled back in time to encounter them. Instead, Fusco has Zira go into hiding, observing humans from afar. The decision by the human scientific community in the 21st century to recognize nonhuman animals as sentient allows her to come out of hiding and share her observations of human predation, based on her many years of research, with a lecture followed by a question and answer session with a live audience. Fusco employs the language of animal psychology in this performance to shed light on the aggressive practices of Wall Street bankers that led to the 2008 economic meltdown.

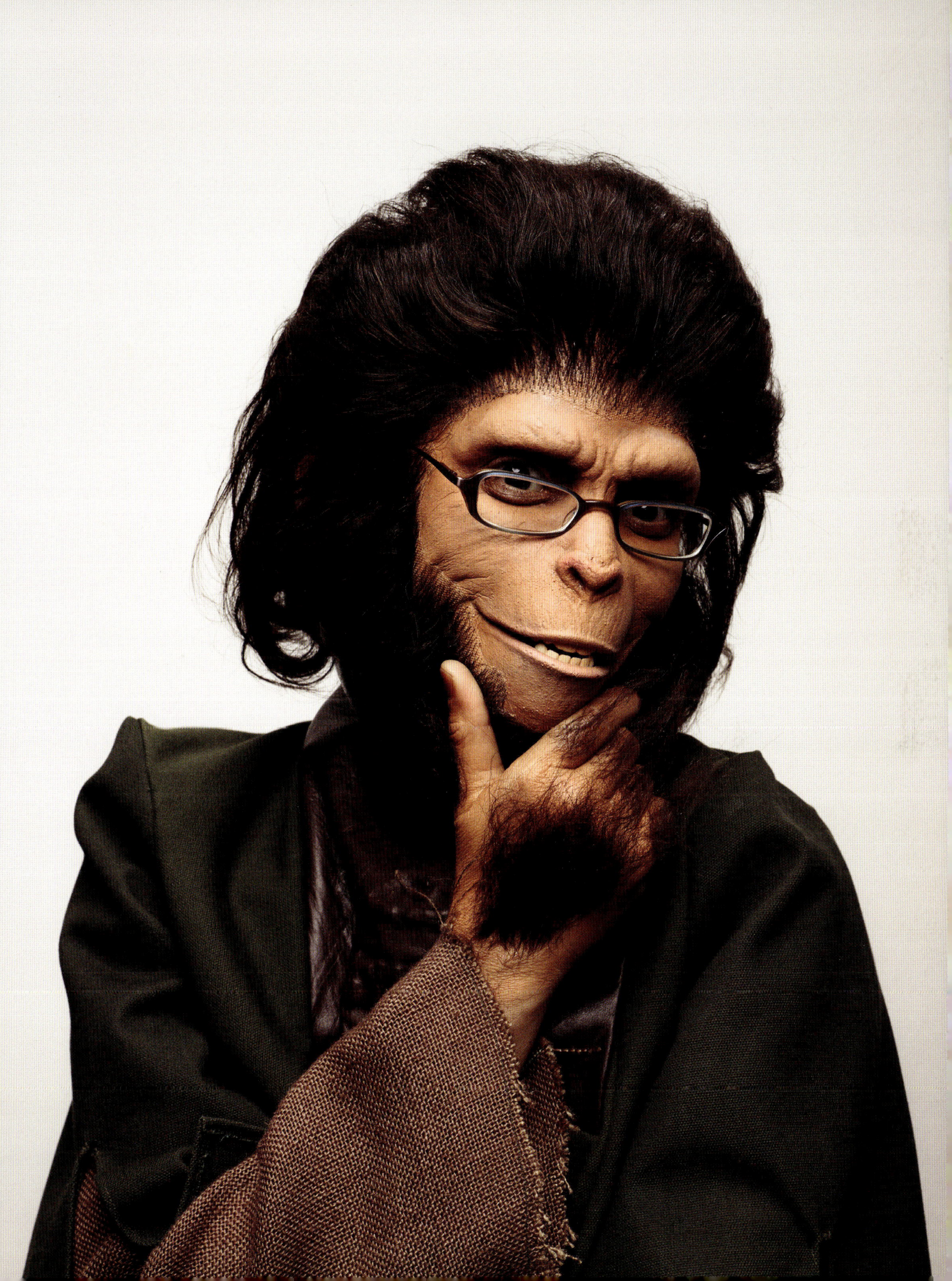

Eu sou um consumidor (I Am a Consumer)

2014

This participatory performance, commissioned by the 2014 Trans-performance Festival in Rio de Janeiro, was inspired by the *rolezinhos* carried out by young Brazilians of color. In 2013, in response to conditions of social apartheid that make it impossible for them to enter shopping malls, those sacrosanct sites of consumption, without suffering harassment from police and private security, hundreds of youth began invading high-end shopping malls in Rio de Janeiro and São Paulo. Brazilian judges responded by ruling that their actions constituted illegal interference with commerce. For the performance, Fusco organized thirty Brazilian youths to enter the Leblon Shopping Mall in Rio de Janeiro with T-shirts, of her own creation, emblazoned with the phrase "I Am a Consumer" on the front and "Don't Arrest Me" on the back. They proceeded *en masse* to the top floor where they pur-chased and consumed ice cream and were followed and monitored by private security despite the presence of video cameras and production staff.

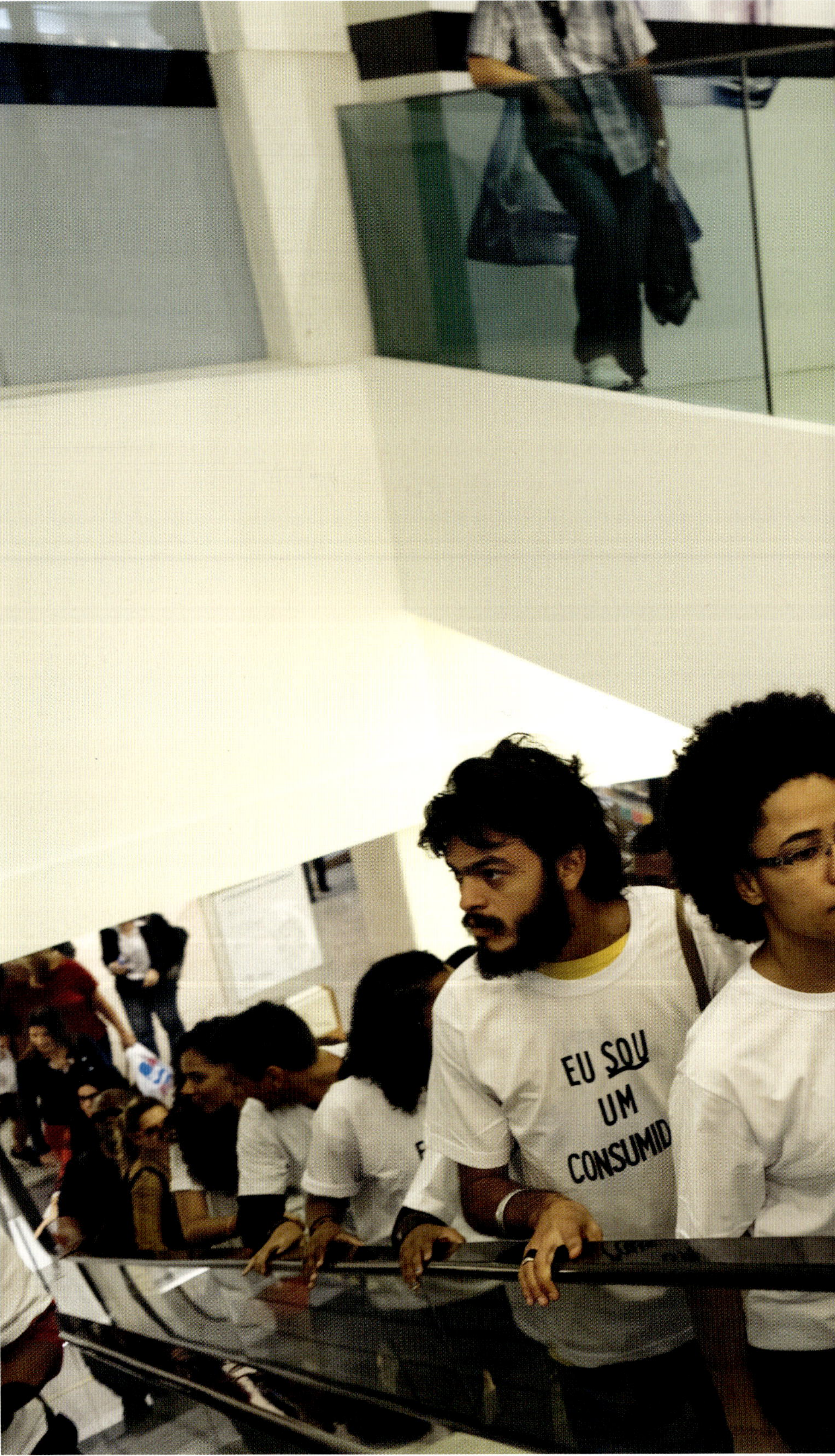

Eu sou um consumidor (I Am a Consumer), 2014, performance (also overleaf and pages 148–49)

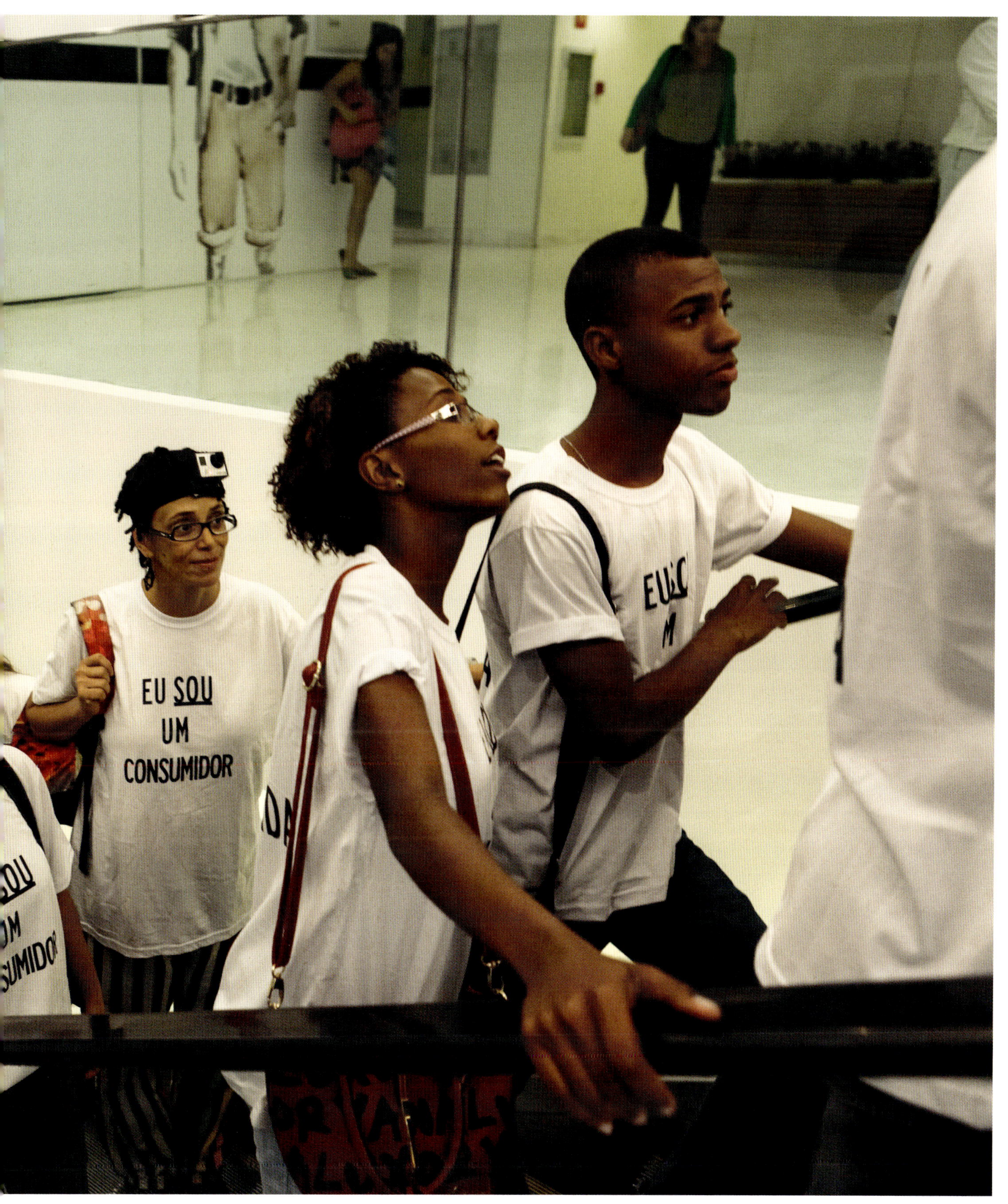

EU SOU
UM
CONSUMIDOR

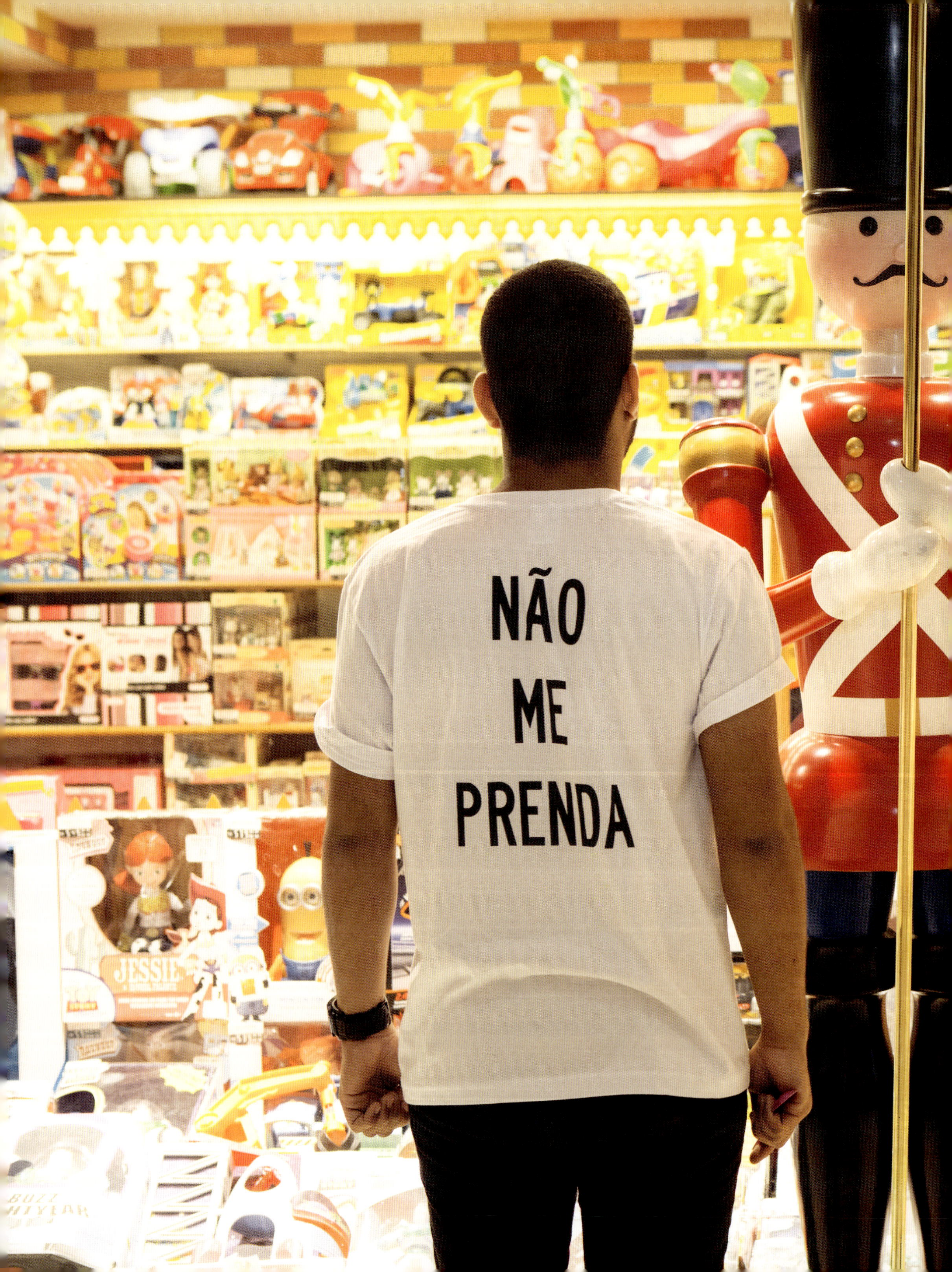
NÃO
ME
PRENDA

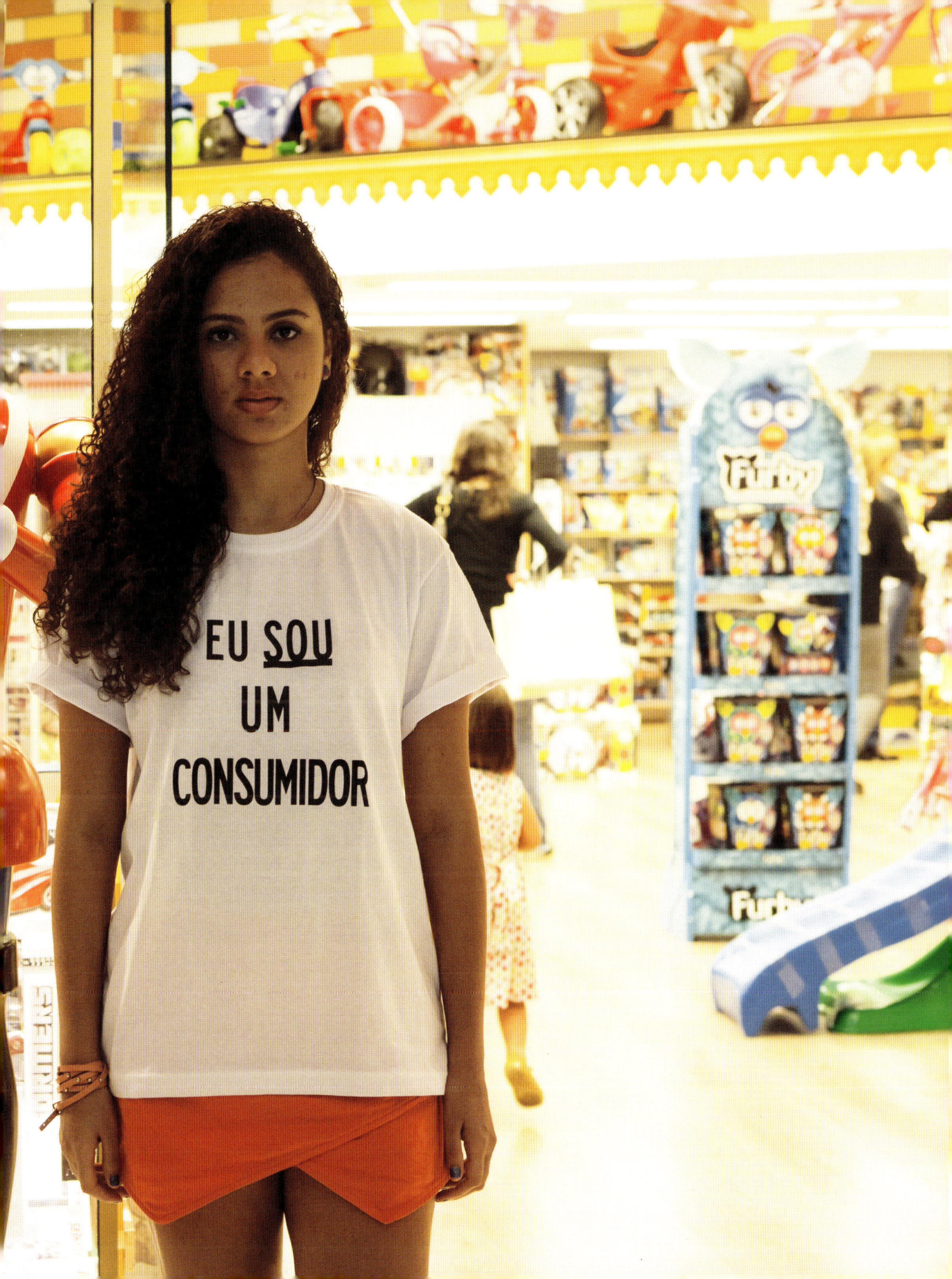

EU SOU
UM
CONSUMIDOR

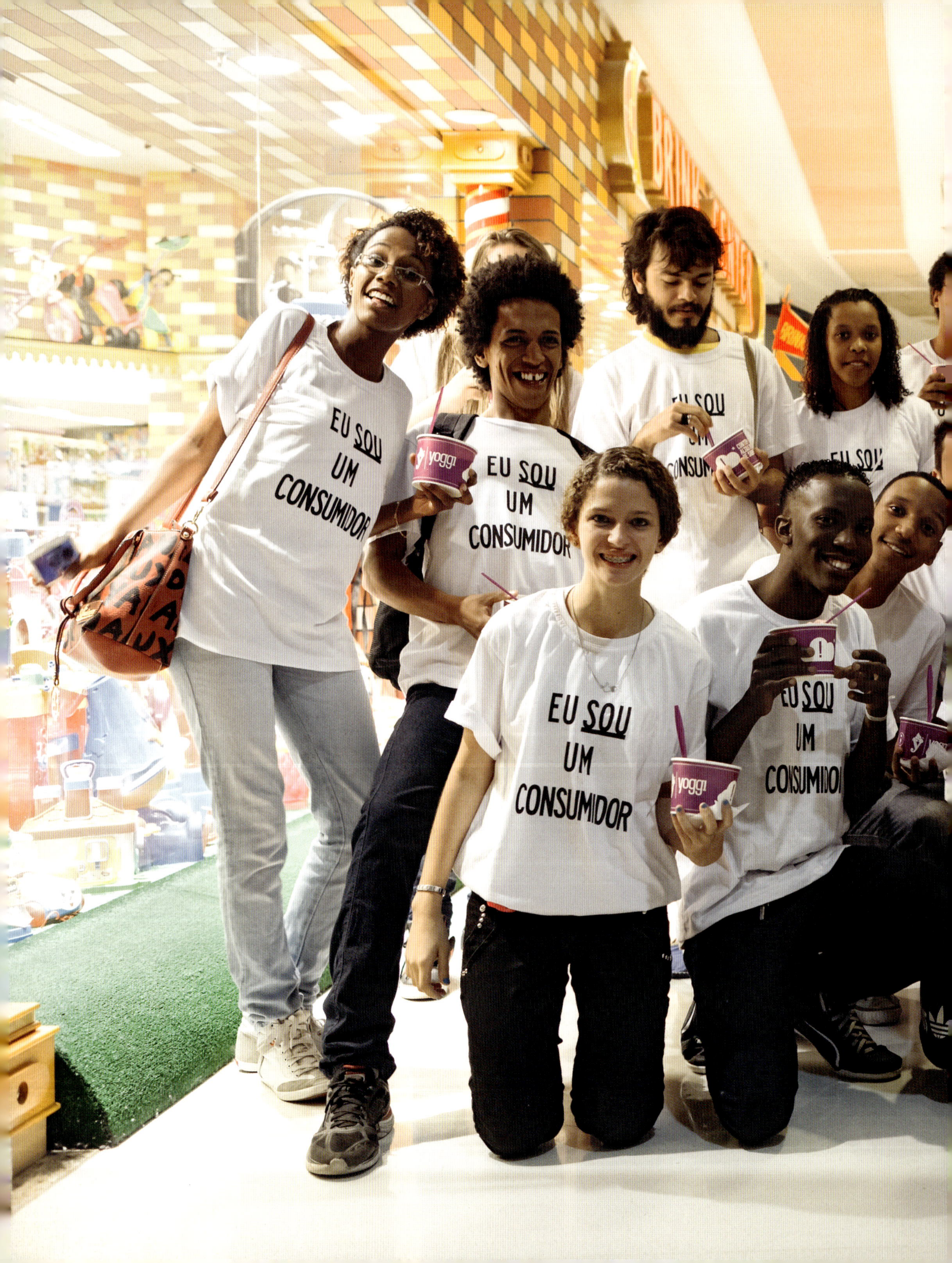

EU SOU UM CONSUMIDOR
EU SOU UM CONSUMIDOR
EU SOU UM CONSUMIDOR
EU SOU UM CONSUMIDOR
EU SOU UM CONSUMIDOR
yoggi

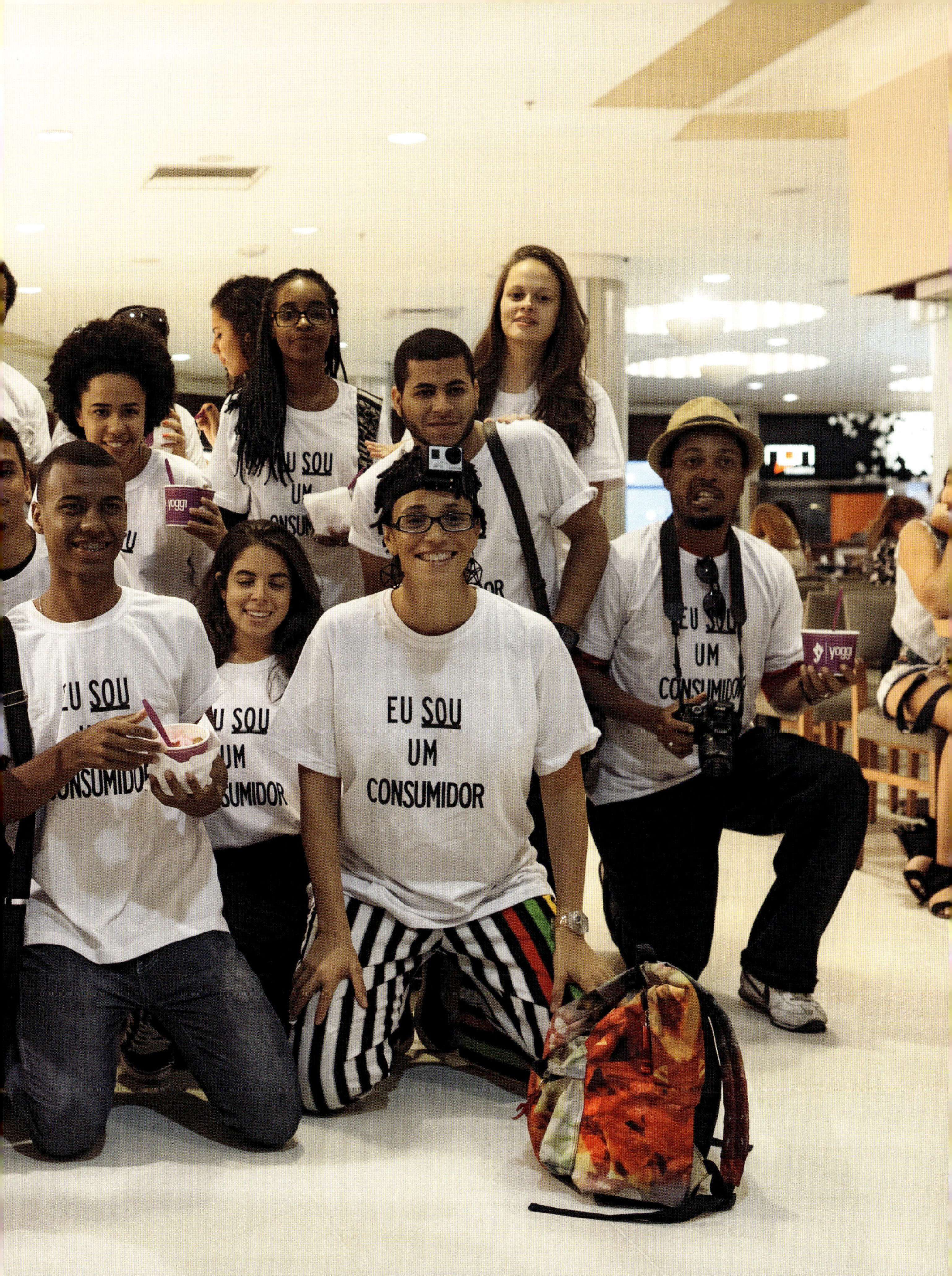

EU SOU UM CONSUMIDOR
EU SOU UM CONSUMIDOR
EU SOU UM CONSUMIDOR
EU SOU UM CONSUMIDOR
yogg!
yogg!

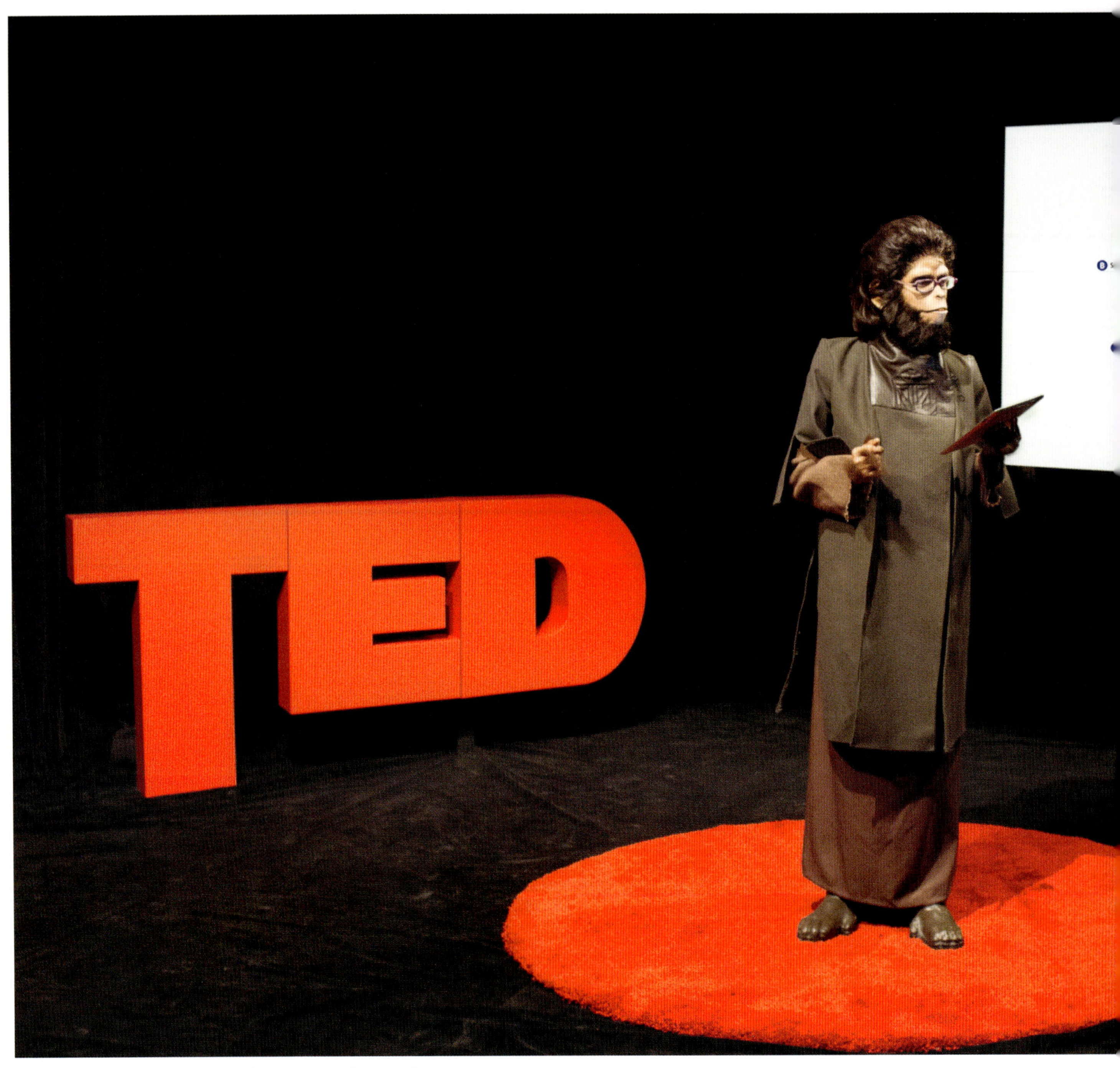

TED Ethology: Primate Visions of the Human Mind, 2015, video

                    BODY OF WORK 1990–2022

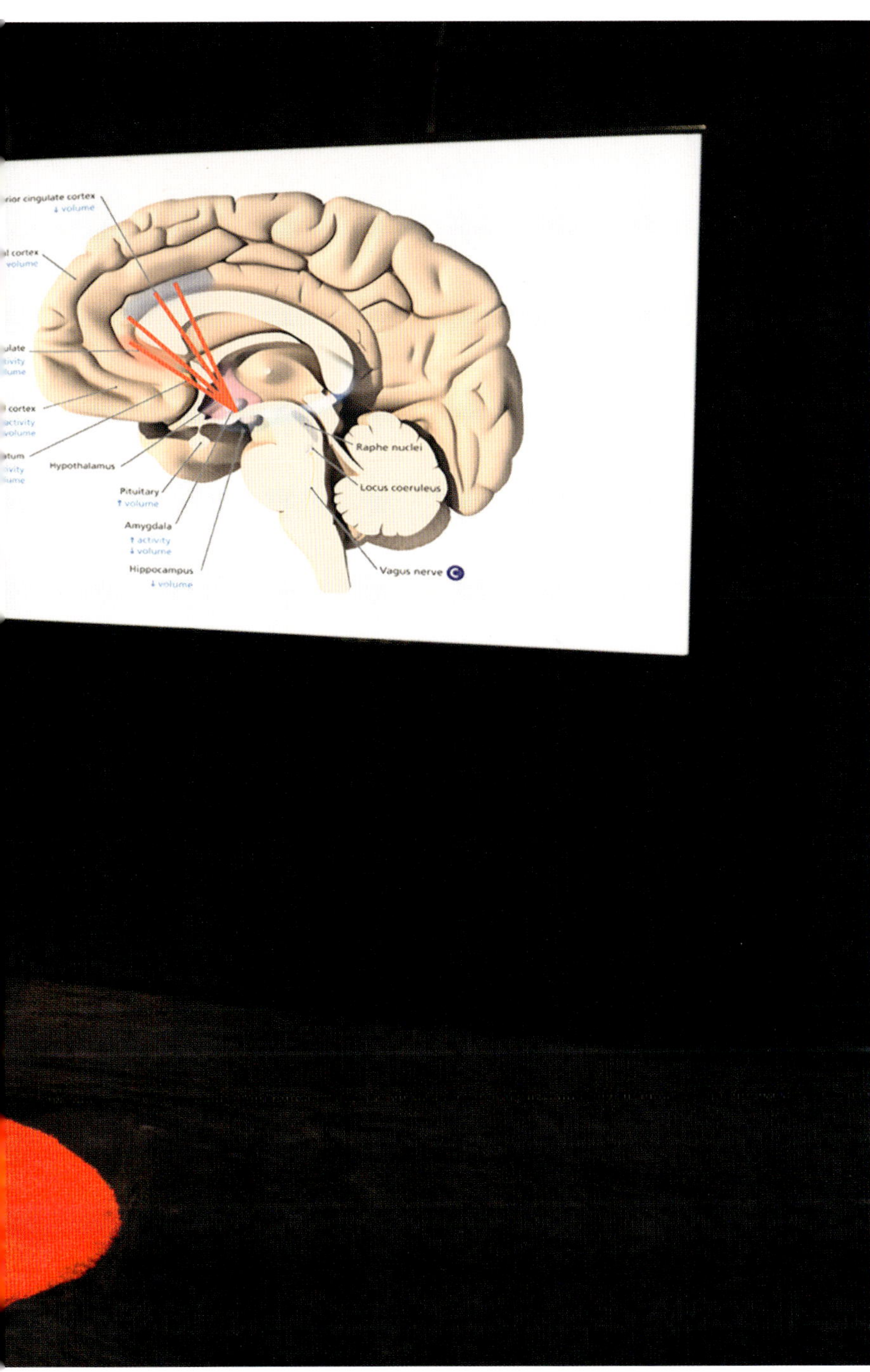

TED Ethology: Primate Visions of the Human Mind

2015

In *TED Ethology: Primate Visions of the Human Mind*, Fusco creates a simulated TED talk, again reviving and embodying the fictional chimpanzee animal psychologist Dr. Zira from the *Planet of the Apes* films of the late 1960s and early 1970s. After twenty years in hiding, the chimp psychologist returns to share her observations about the predatory practices of *Homo sapiens*. Dr. Zira's filmed lecture draws from primatology, neuroscience, and evolutionary biology to address human aggression and predatory behavior for the accumulation of resources in post-industrial societies.

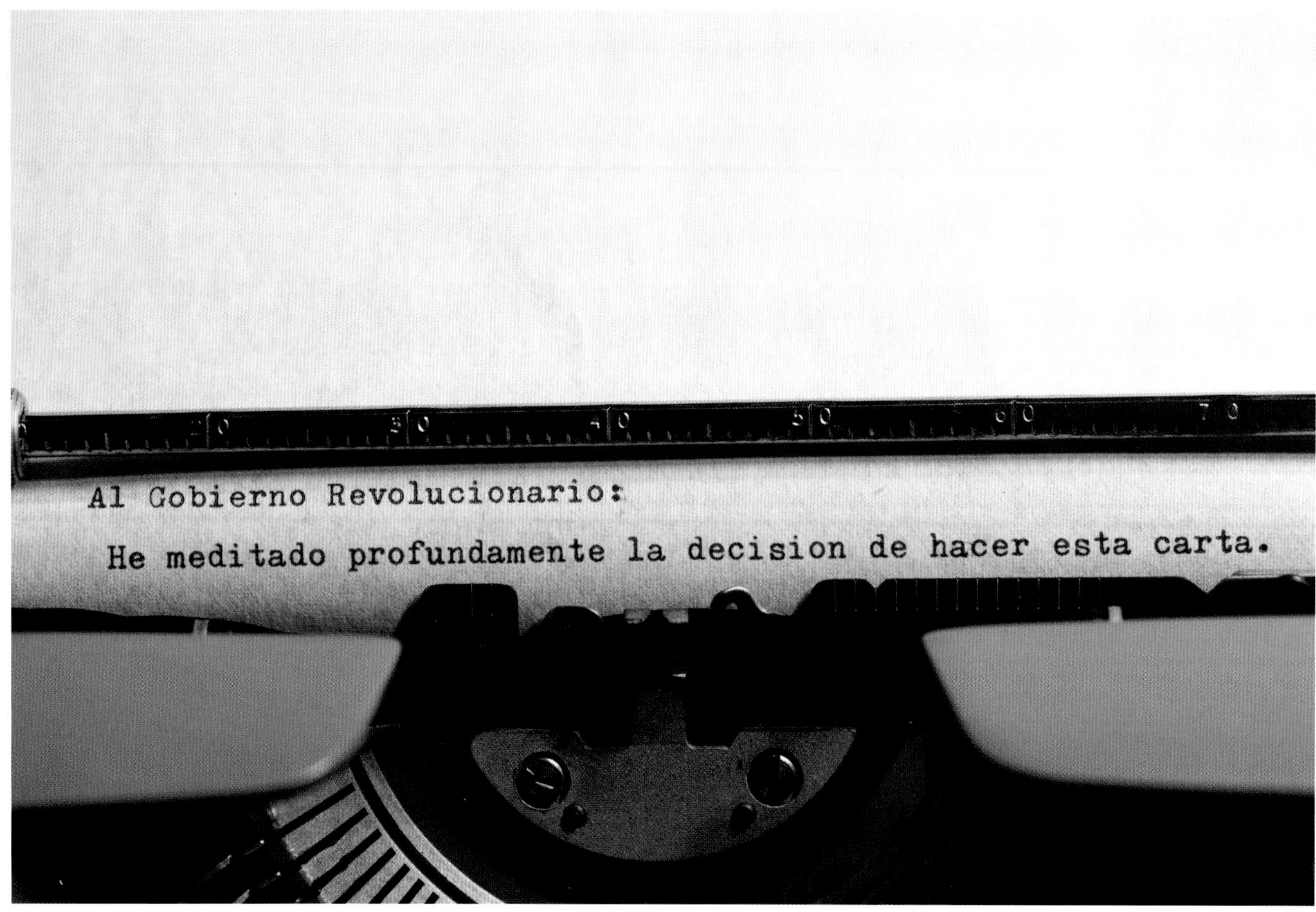

La confesión (The Confession), 2015, video. The text reads: "To the revolutionary government: I have thought deeply about writing this letter."

La confesión (The Confession)

2015

Created on the occasion of the 56th Venice Biennale, curated by Okwui Enwezor, *La confesión* (*The Confession*) reflects on one of the most significant crises in the intellectual history of the Cuban Revolution—the arrest and forced confession of poet Heberto Padilla, who publicly stated that he was a counterrevolutionary. Padilla's confession, which was pronounced in April 1971 after he was held for five weeks in Villa Marista prison, shifted the terms of the international leftist community, and the role of culture in revolution, and reconfigured the relationship between European intellectuals and Cuba's nationalism. The video reconstructs the story of Padilla's fall from grace and its repercussions throughout the world using archival fragments, readings of Padilla's poems, and an excerpt of the filmed confession that emerged forty years after the event.

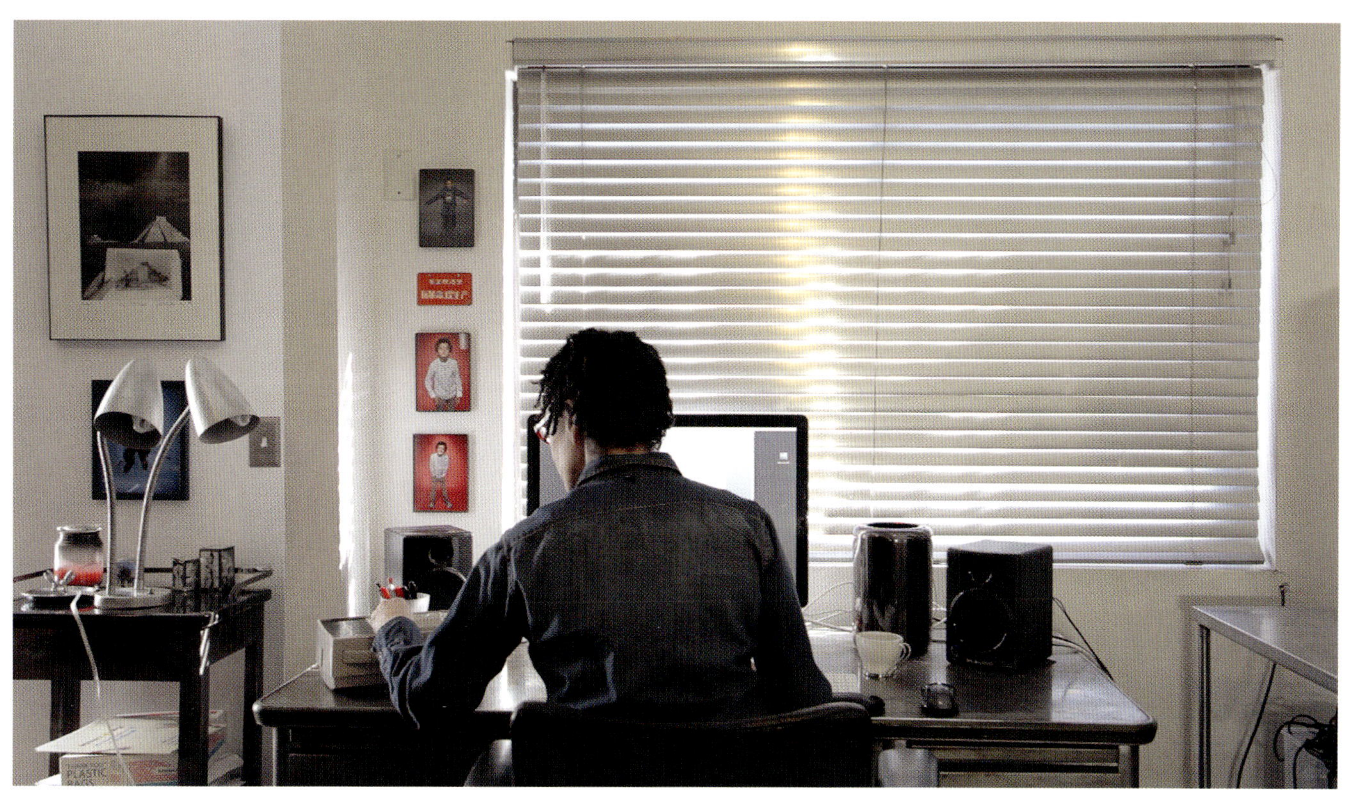

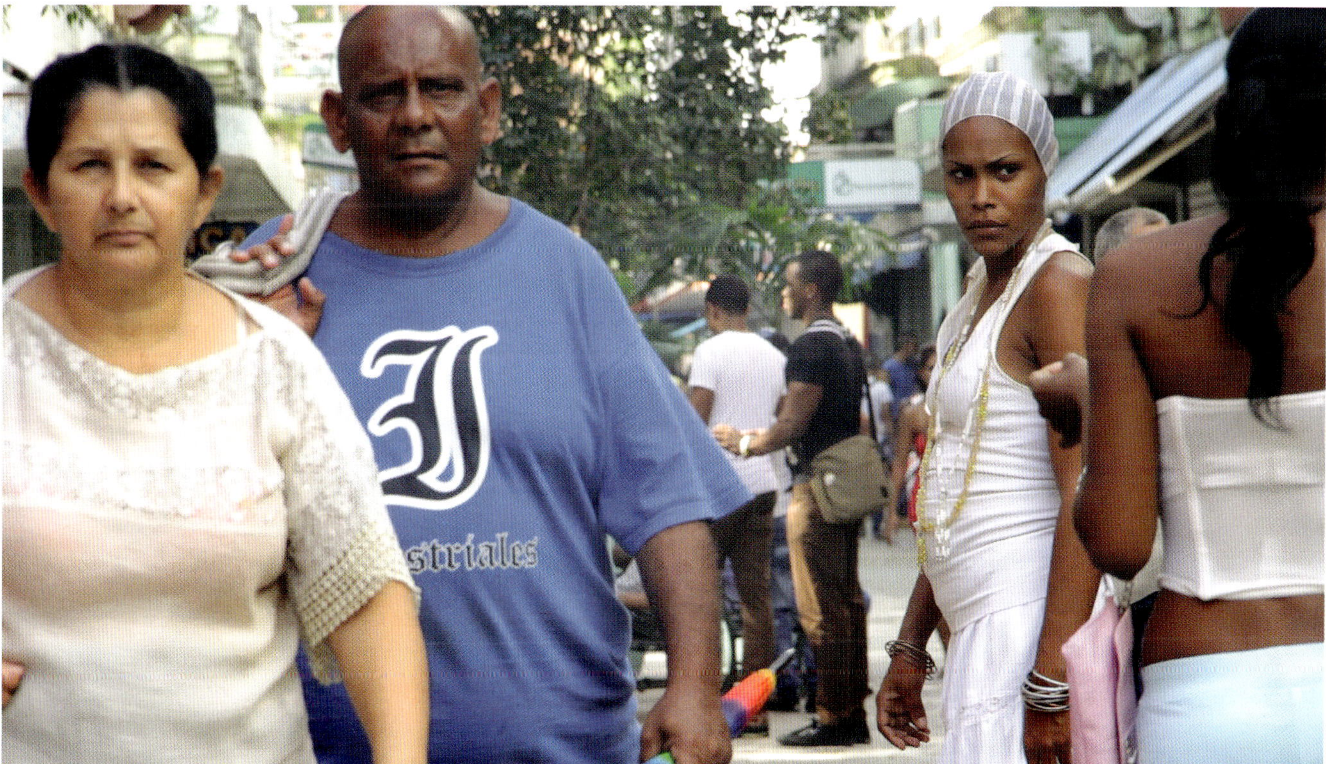

La confesión (The Confession), 2015, video (also overleaf and pages 155–57)

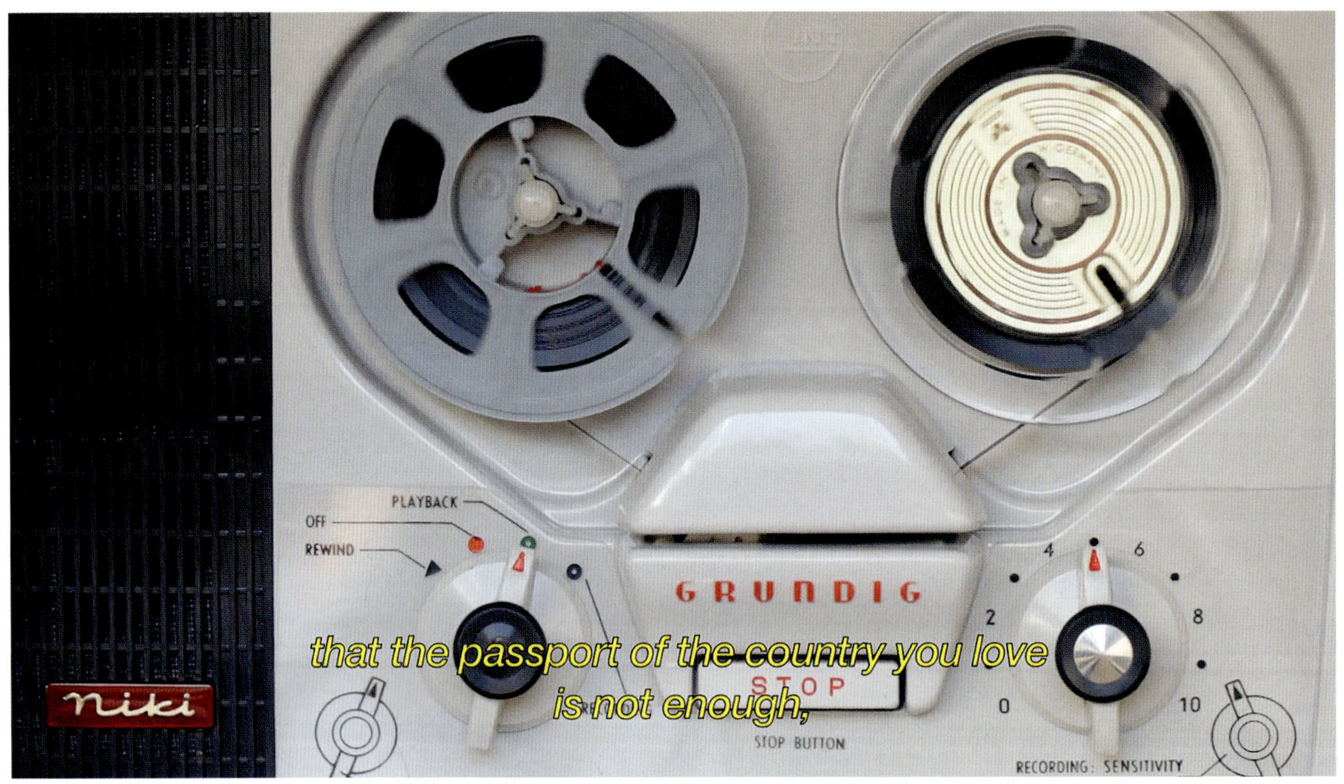

niki
PLAYBACK
OFF
REWIND
GRUNDIG
STOP
STOP BUTTON
4   6
2   8
0   10
RECORDING: SENSITIVITY
that the passport of the country you love
is not enough,

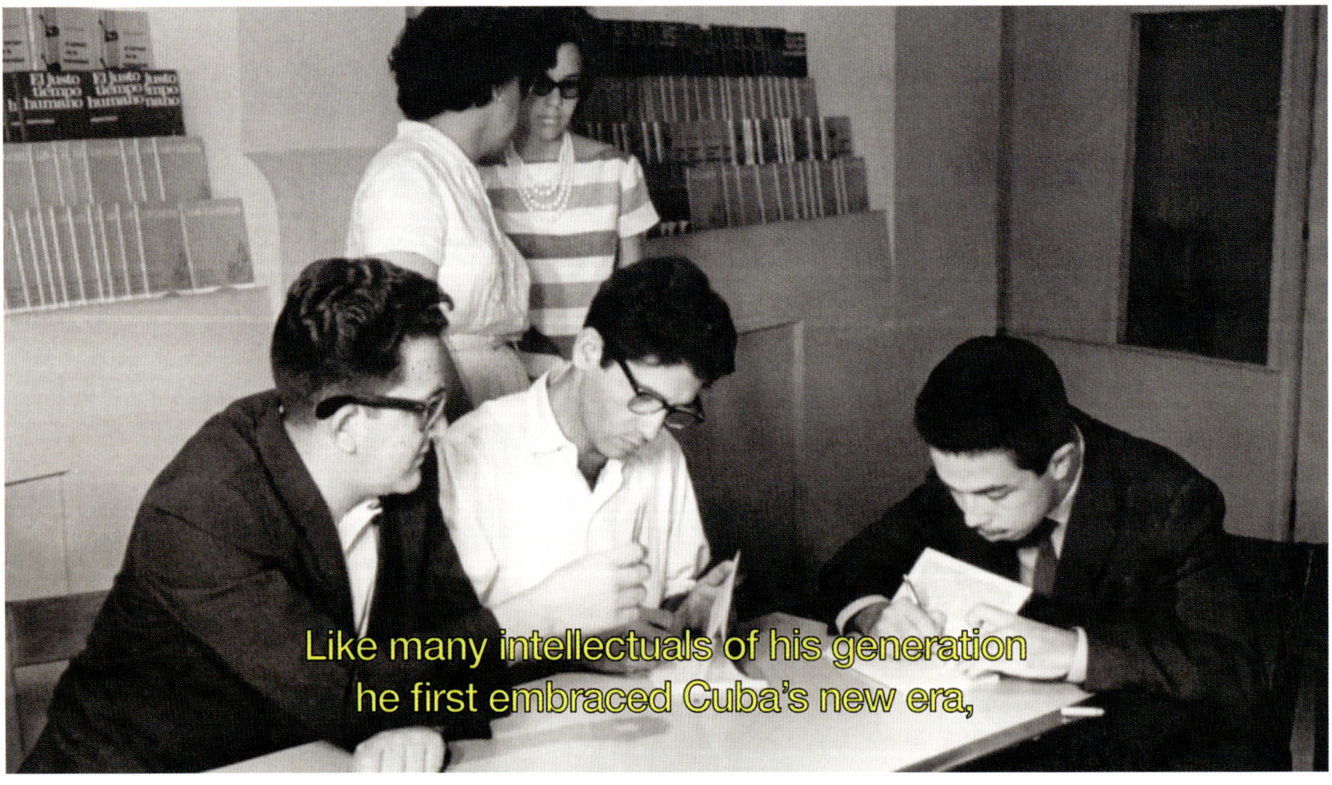

El justo
tiempo
humano
Like many intellectuals of his generation
he first embraced Cuba's new era,

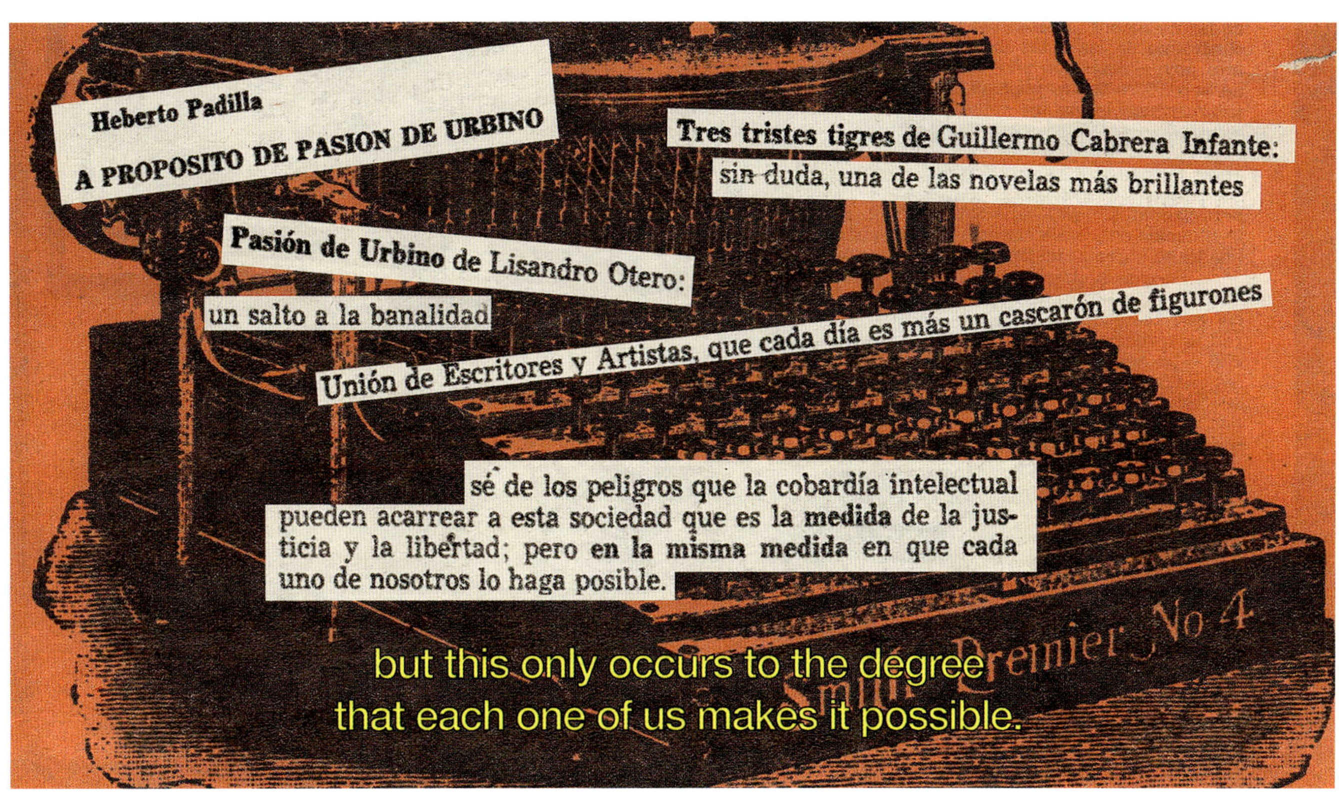

Heberto Padilla
A PROPOSITO DE PASION DE URBINO

Tres tristes tigres de Guillermo Cabrera Infante:
sin duda, una de las novelas más brillantes

Pasión de Urbino de Lisandro Otero:
un salto a la banalidad

Unión de Escritores y Artistas, que cada día es más un cascarón de figurones

sé de los peligros que la cobardía intelectual
pueden acarrear a esta sociedad que es la medida de la jus-
ticia y la libertad; pero en la misma medida en que cada
uno de nosotros lo haga posible.

Smith Premier No 4

but this only occurs to the degree
that each one of us makes it possible.

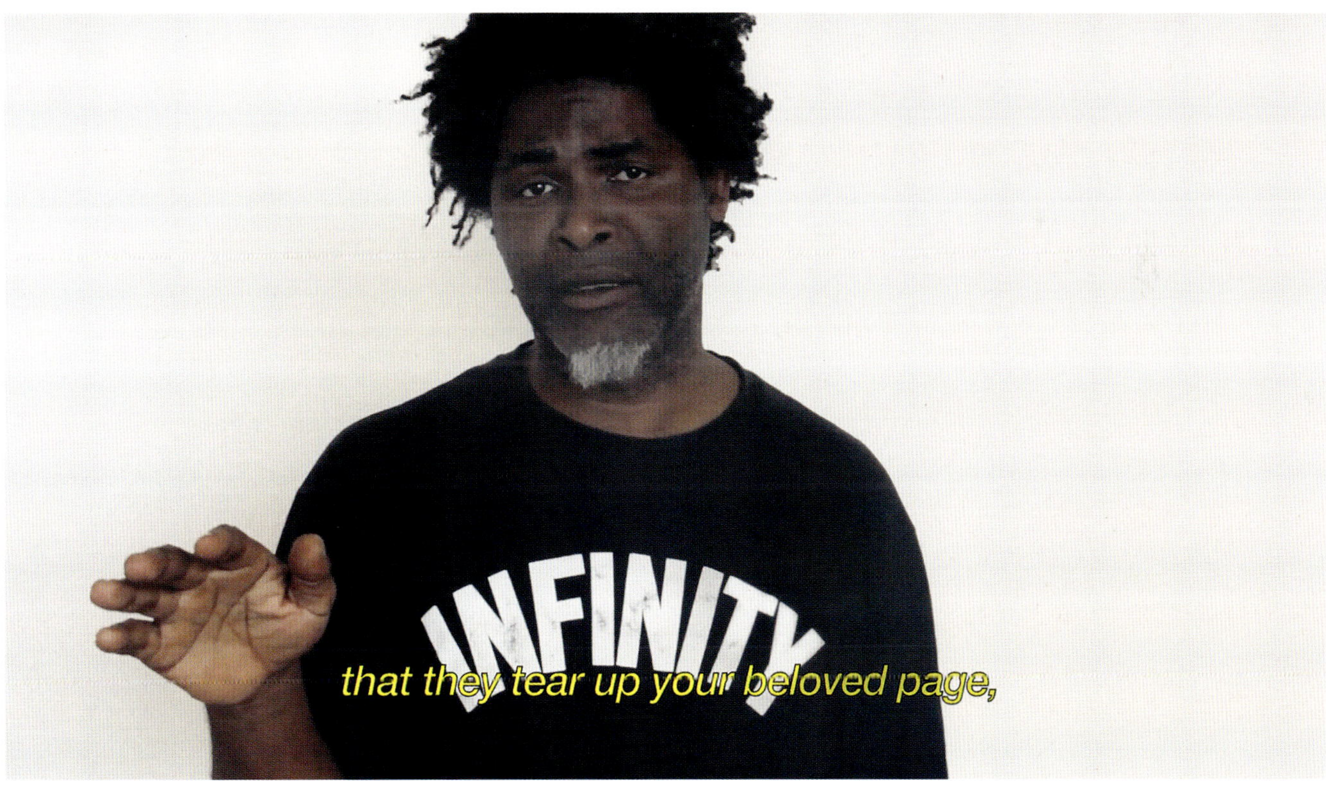

INFINITY
that they tear up your beloved page,

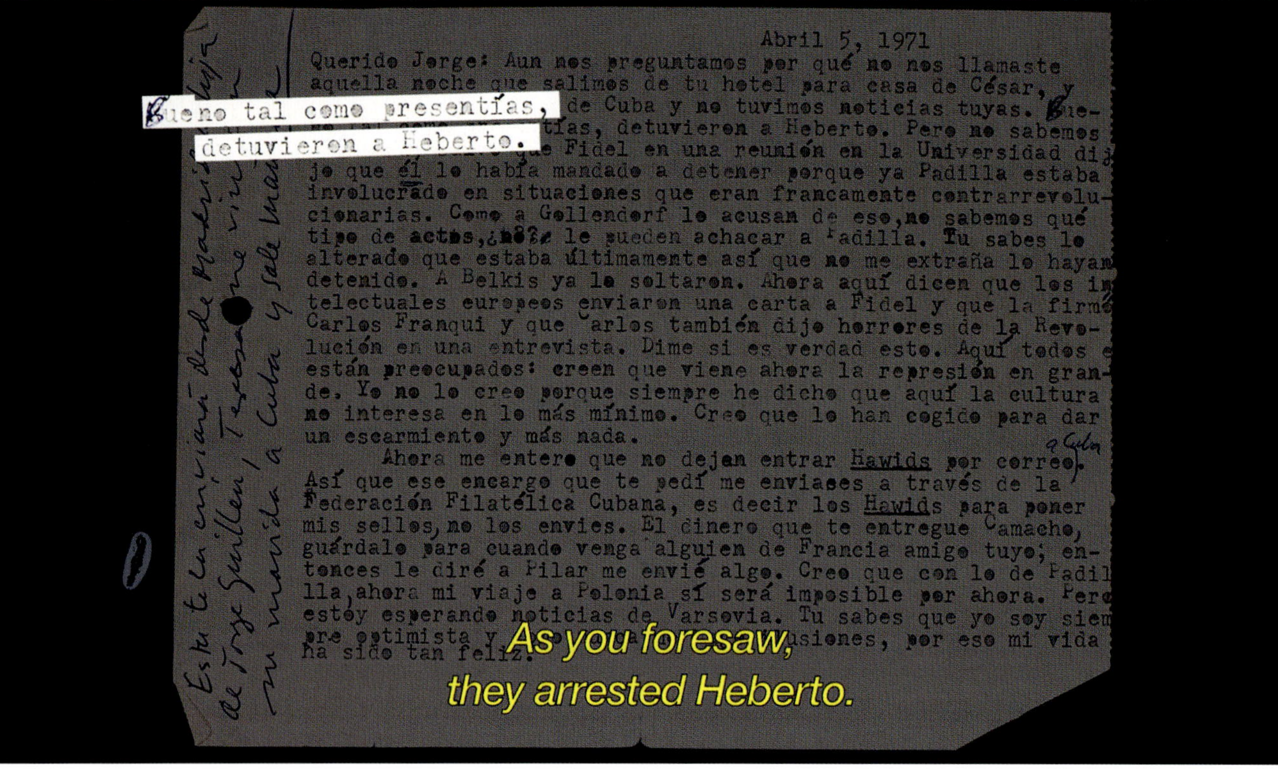

De todos modos, había decidido renunciar al comité y a dictar ese curso, desde que leí la confesión de Heberto Padilla y los despachos de Prensa Latina sobre el acto de la UNEAC en el que los compañeros Belkis Cuza Male, Pablo Armando Fernández, Manuel Díaz Martínez y César López hicieron su autocrítica.

*after I read Heberto Padilla's confession and
the reports from Prensa Latina*

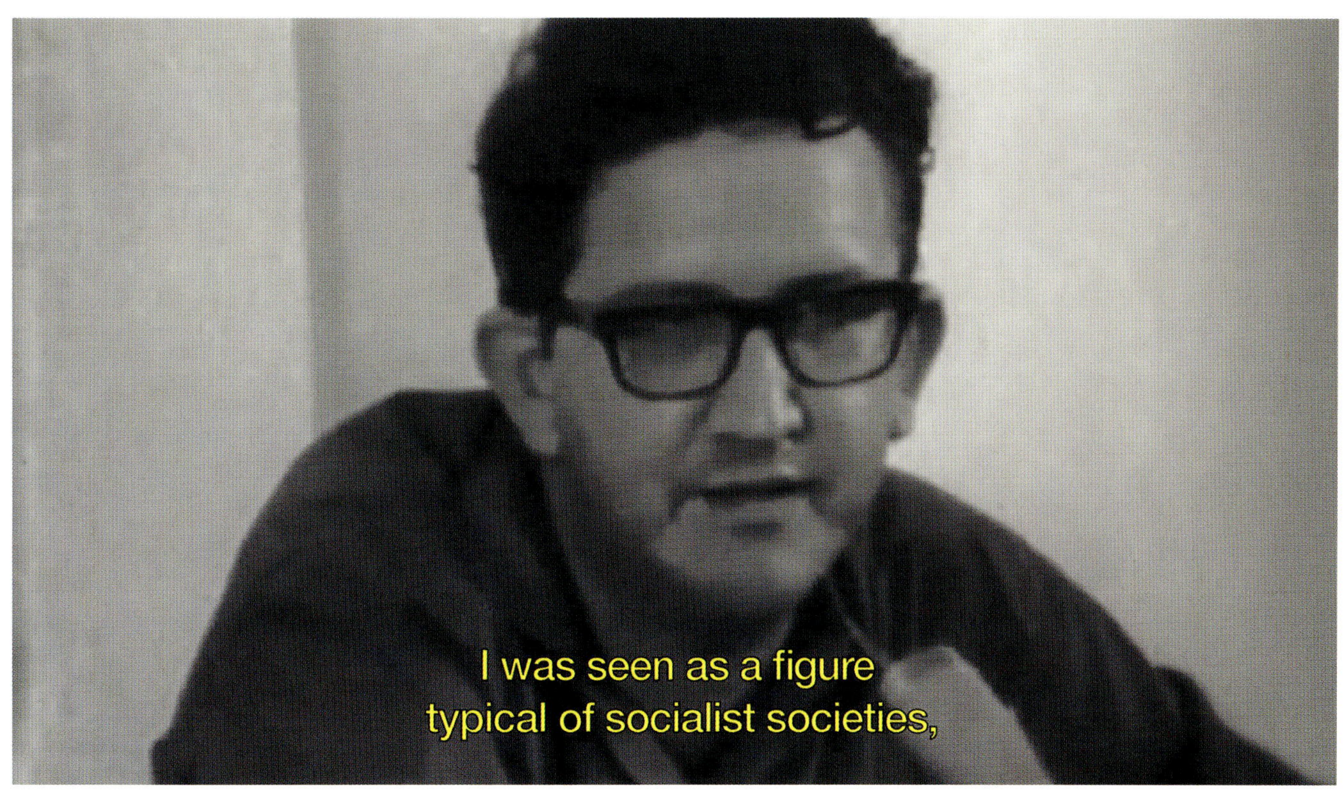

Mayo 15, 1971

Querido amigo: Es una lástima que Padilla no leyese las páginas de Las
ilusiones perdidas de nuestro Balzac donde Herrera aconseja al joven Lu-
ciano cuando éste está sumido en la desesperación y pronto a acometer
una locura. Quizá entonces reconocería que es un ingenuo y que en este
mundo siempre esos ingenuos pagan sus indiscreciones. Bueno, ya pasó la
tormenta. El se hizo su autocrítica y ha sido perdonado. lución fue
bien generosa con él. La Revolución fue bien generosa con él.
el daño que le ha hecho a muchos de sus amigos. Lo vi antes de irse para
Santa María a pasarse una semana y está muy bien. Belkis también está muy
alegre y tal parece que no ha pasado nada. Pronto todo este desagradable
episodio se olvidará porque después de todo la literatura es un asunto
bastante sin He presented his self-criticism nos preocupa va
bastante bien. Ya es and was pardoned. si no llueve mucho creo que
llegaremos a la meta que mucho falta nos hace falta, pero mucho.

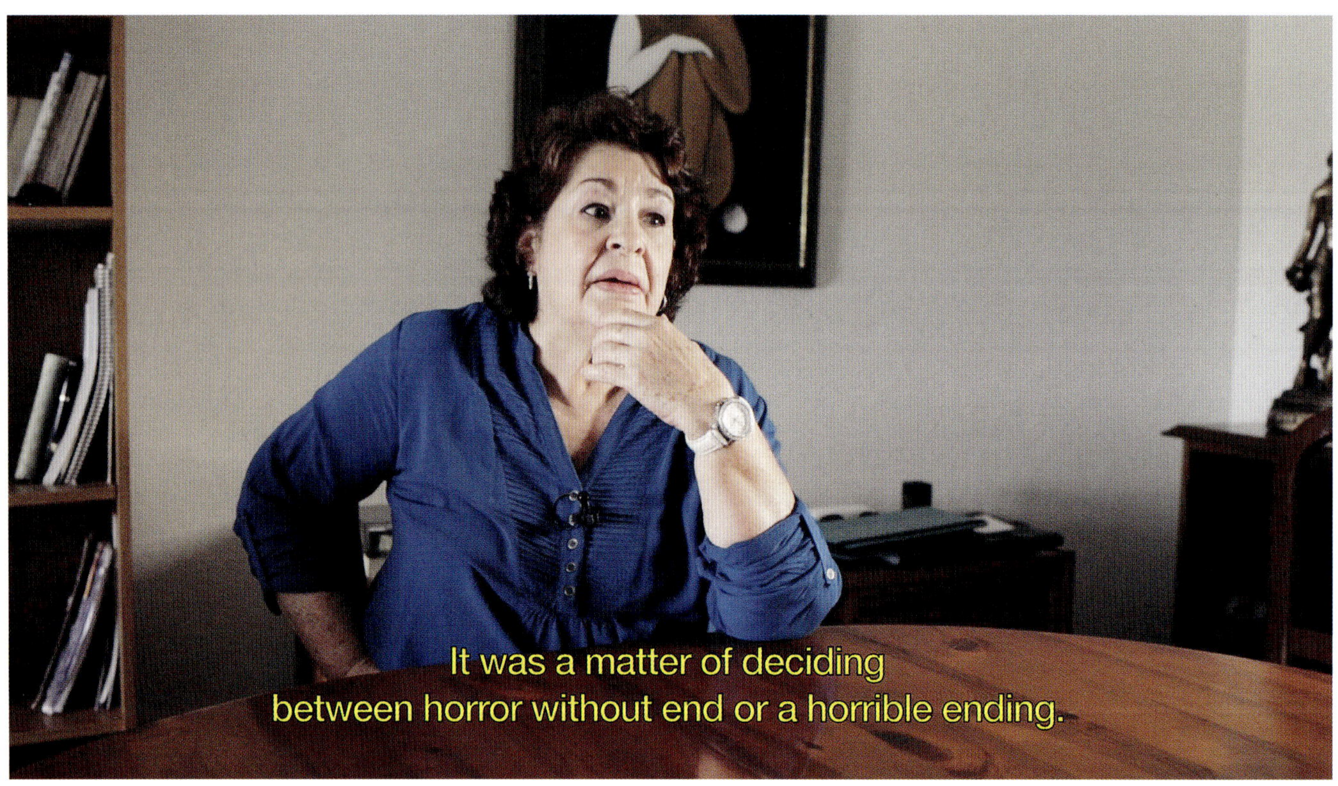

La botella al mar de María Elena
(The Message in a Bottle from María Elena)

2015

This video addresses the case of Cuban poet María Elena Cruz Varela, winner of the 1989 National Poetry Prize, who in 1991 spearheaded an effort by ten Cuban intellectuals to issue a public document calling for political reforms. This Declaration of the Cuban Intellectuals addressed the critical situation the country faced following the dissolution of the Soviet Union, the fall of Communism in Eastern Europe, and the dramatic drop in imports and trade. Cruz Varela was besieged by mobs and imprisoned for her efforts. In the video, Fusco counterposes the poet's recollections of the events with those of the Communist party militant who led the mob attacks.

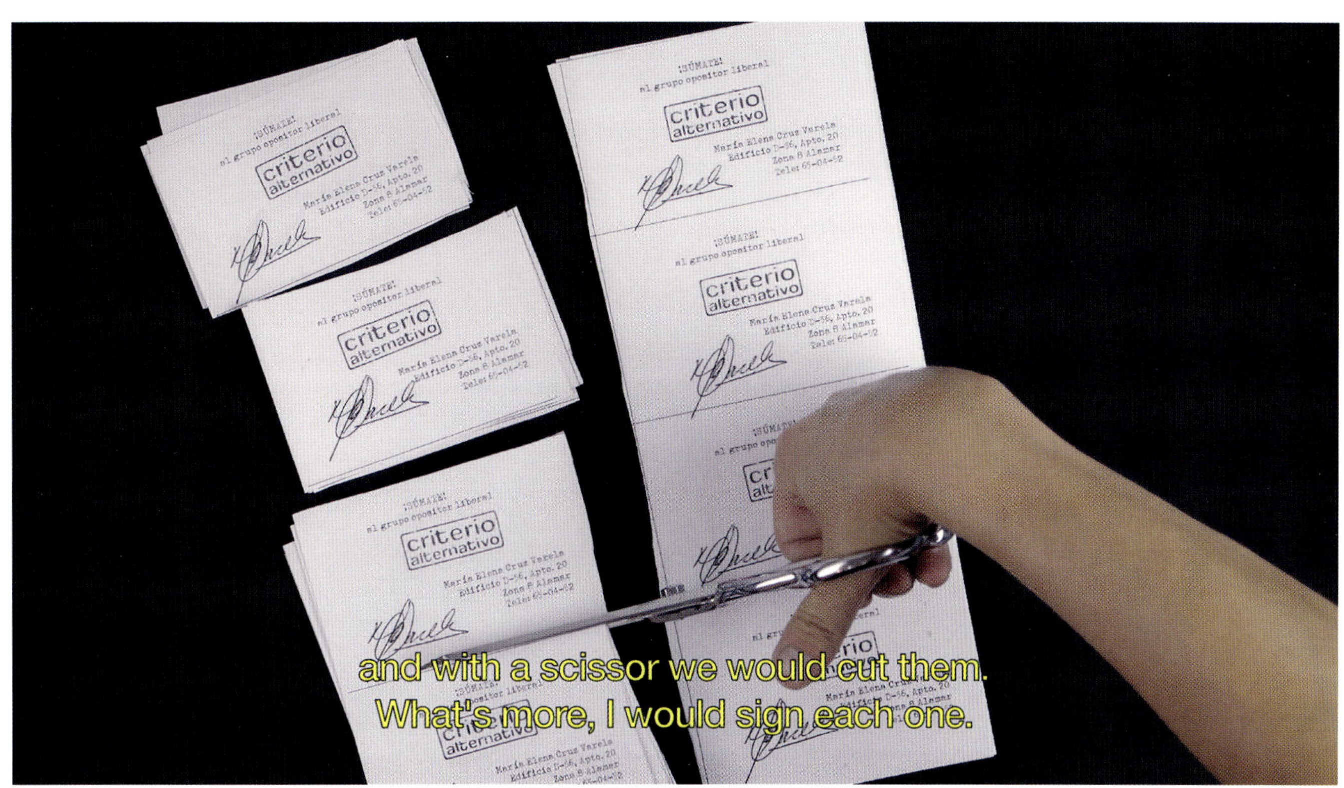

La botella al mar de María Elena (The Message in a Bottle from María Elena), 2015, video (also overleaf and pages 161–63)

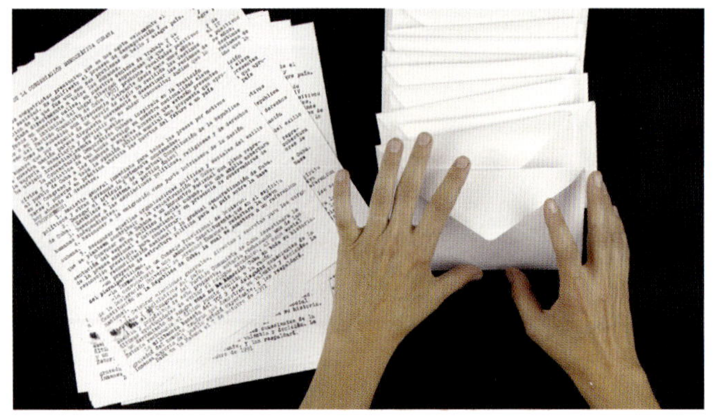

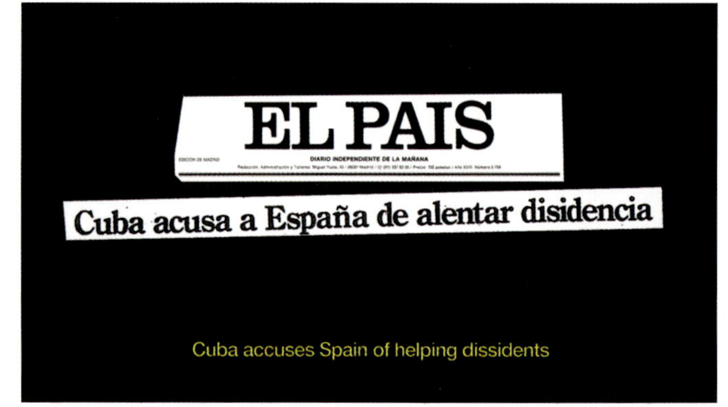
EL PAIS
Cuba acusa a España de alentar disidencia
Cuba accuses Spain of helping dissidents

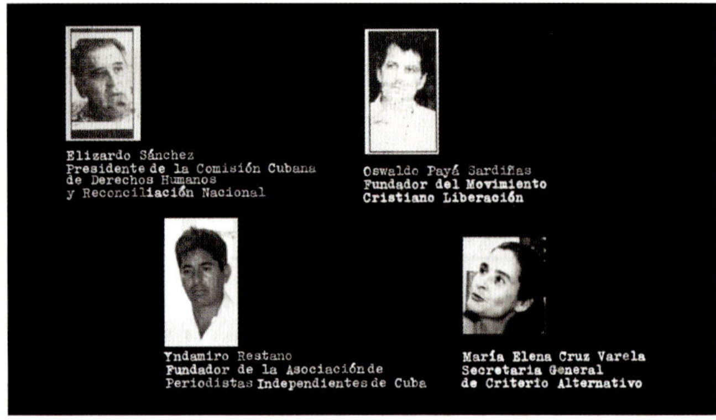
Elizardo Sánchez
Presidente de la Comisión Cubana
de Derechos Humanos
y Reconciliación Nacional

Oswaldo Payá Sardiñas
Fundador del Movimiento
Cristiano Liberación

Yndamiro Restano
Fundador de la Asociación de
Periodistas Independientes de Cuba

María Elena Cruz Varela
Secretaria General
de Criterio Alternativo

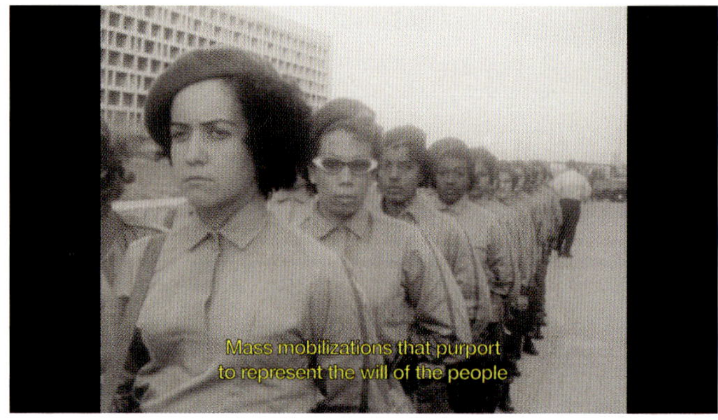
Mass mobilizations that purport
to represent the will of the people

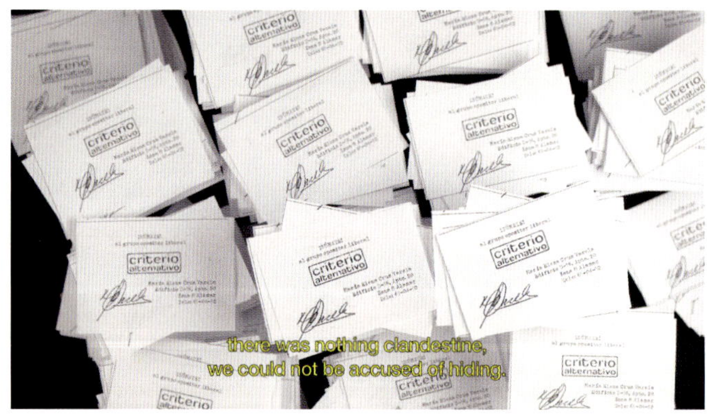
La disidente cubana María Elena
Cruz Varela está sitiada en su aparta-
mento del barrio habanero de Alamar
por turbas que no permiten la
entrada o salida de nadie.

Cuban dissident Maria Elena Cruz Varela is
under siege in her apartment in Alamar

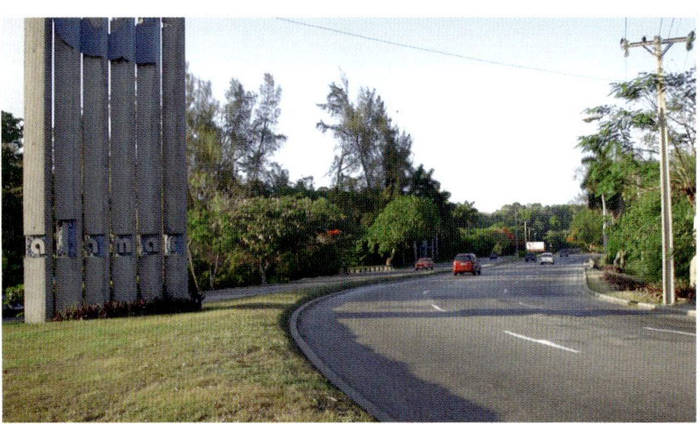
there was nothing clandestine,
we could not be accused of hiding.

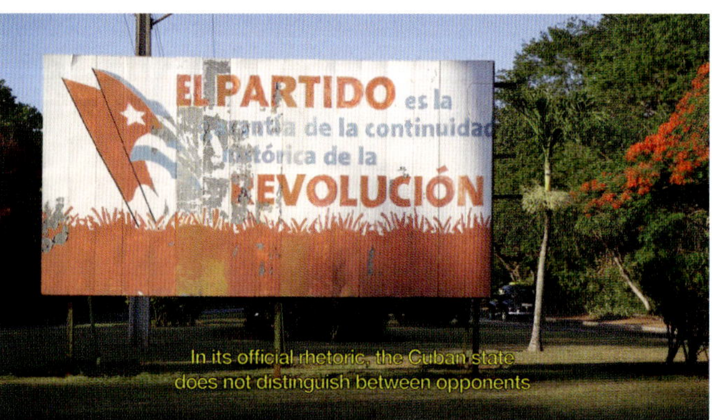
EL PARTIDO es la
garantía de la continuidad
histórica de la
REVOLUCIÓN

In its official rhetoric, the Cuban state
does not distinguish between opponents

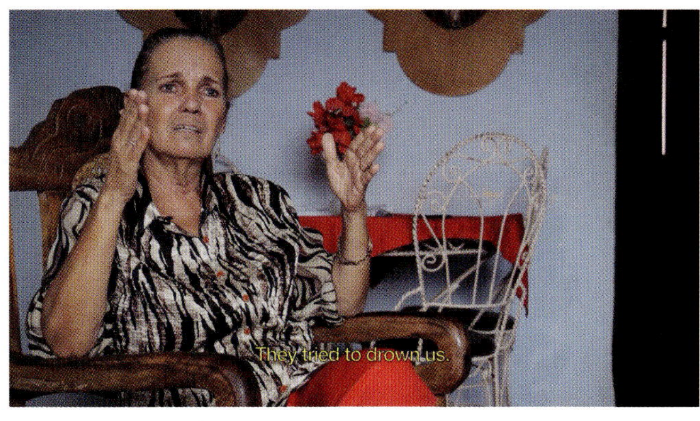
They tried to drown us.

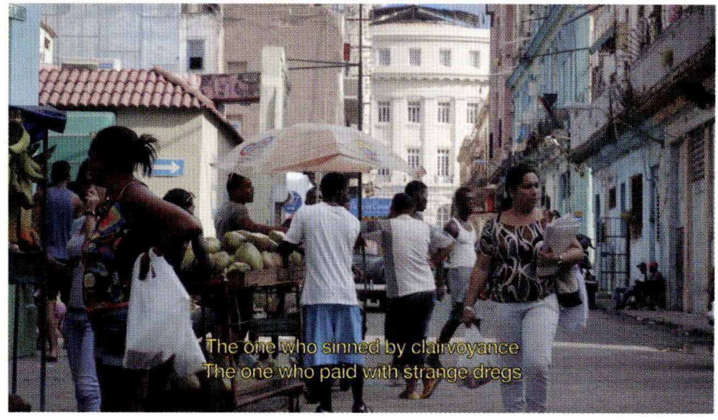
The one who sinned by clairvoyance
The one who paid with strange dregs

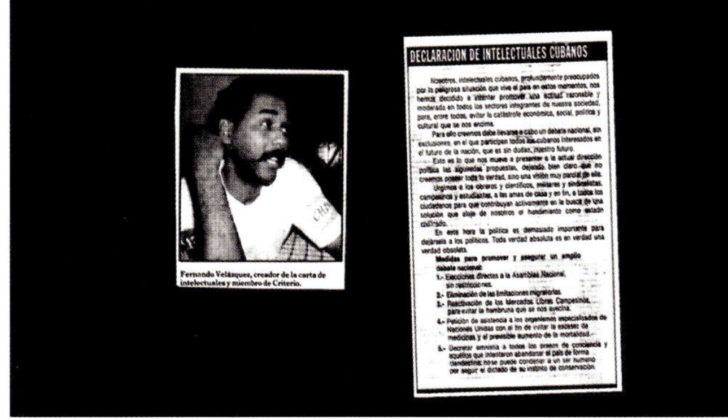
DECLARACION DE INTELECTUALES CUBANOS
Fernando Velázquez, creador de la carta de
intelectuales y miembro de Criterio.

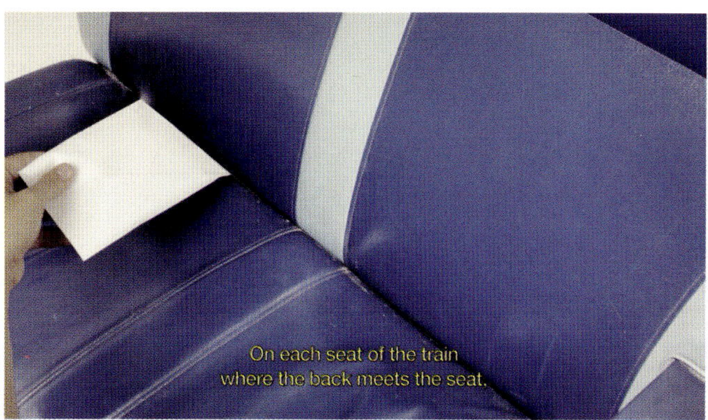
On each seat of the train
where the back meets the seat,

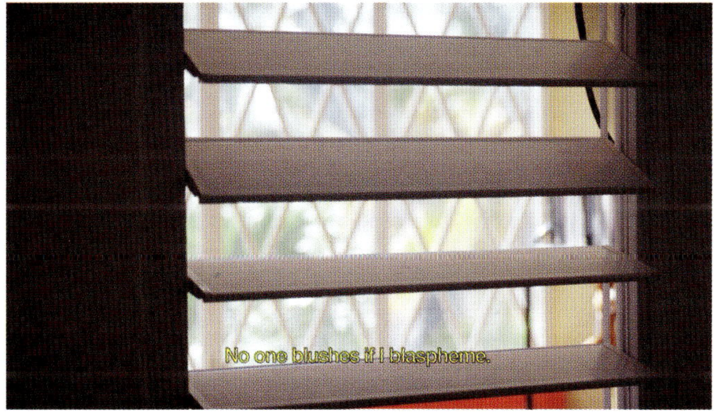
No one blushes if I blaspheme.

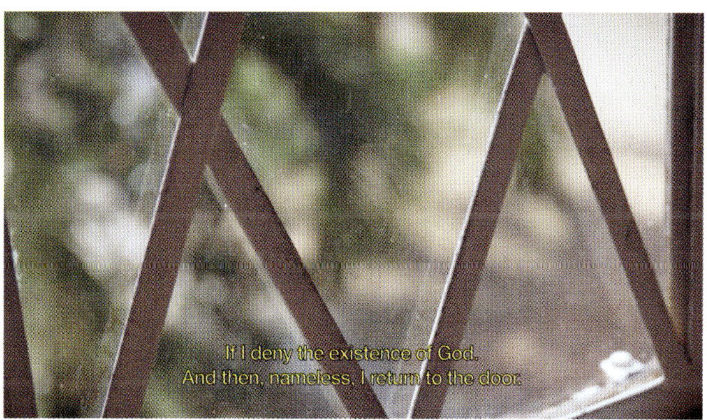
If I deny the existence of God,
And then, nameless, I return to the door.

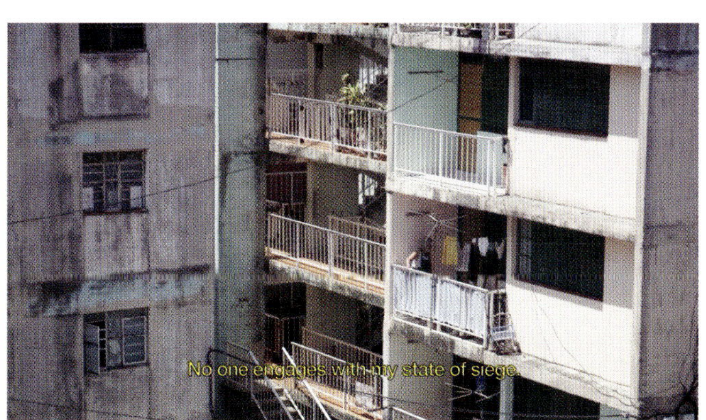
No one engages with my state of siege.

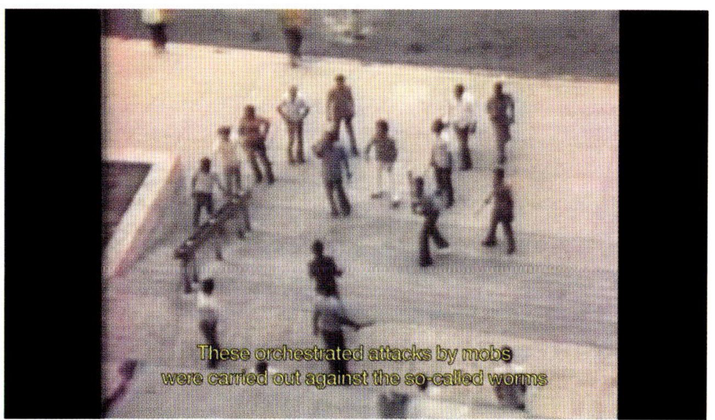
These orchestrated attacks by mobs
were carried out against the so-called worms

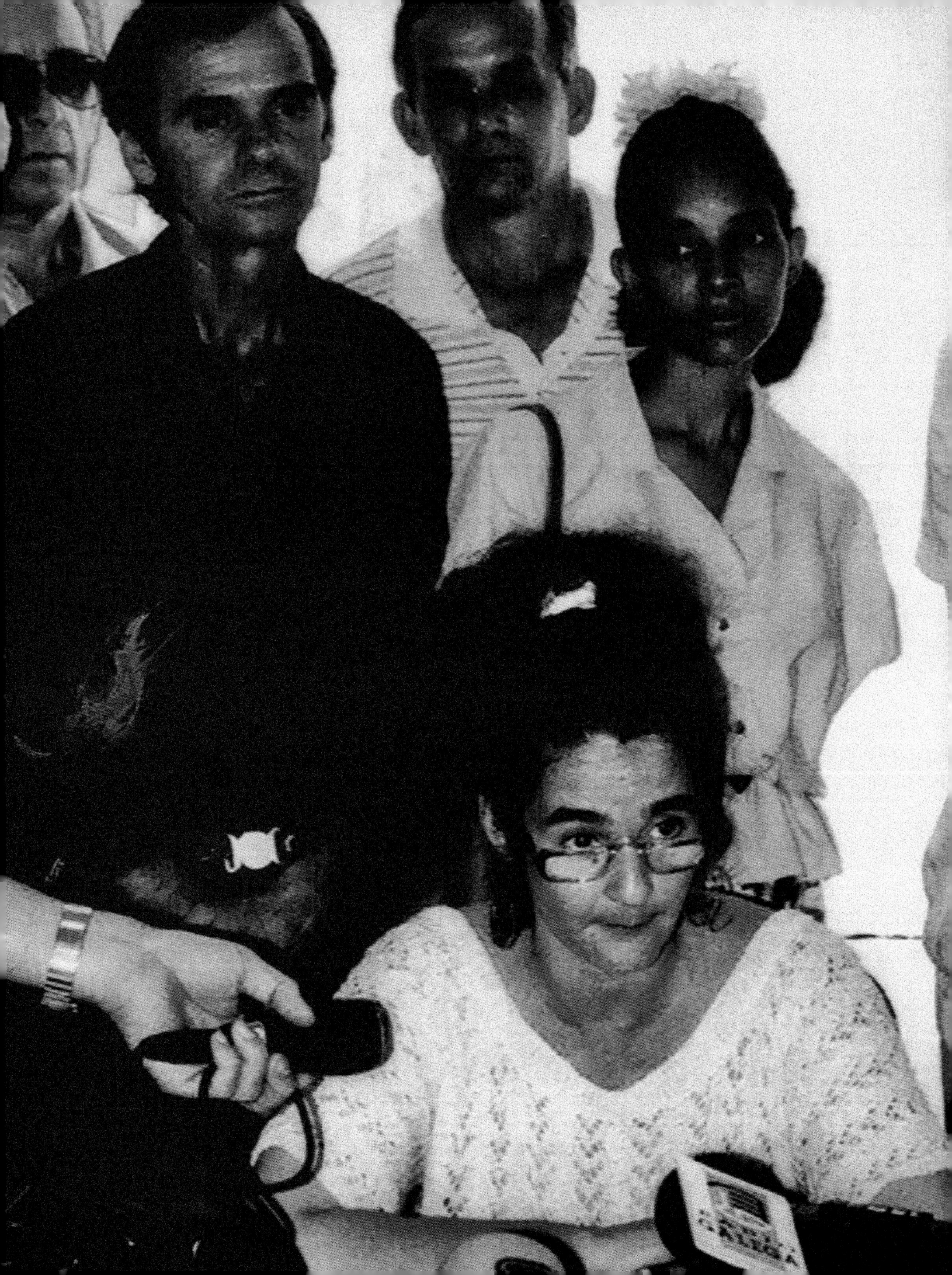

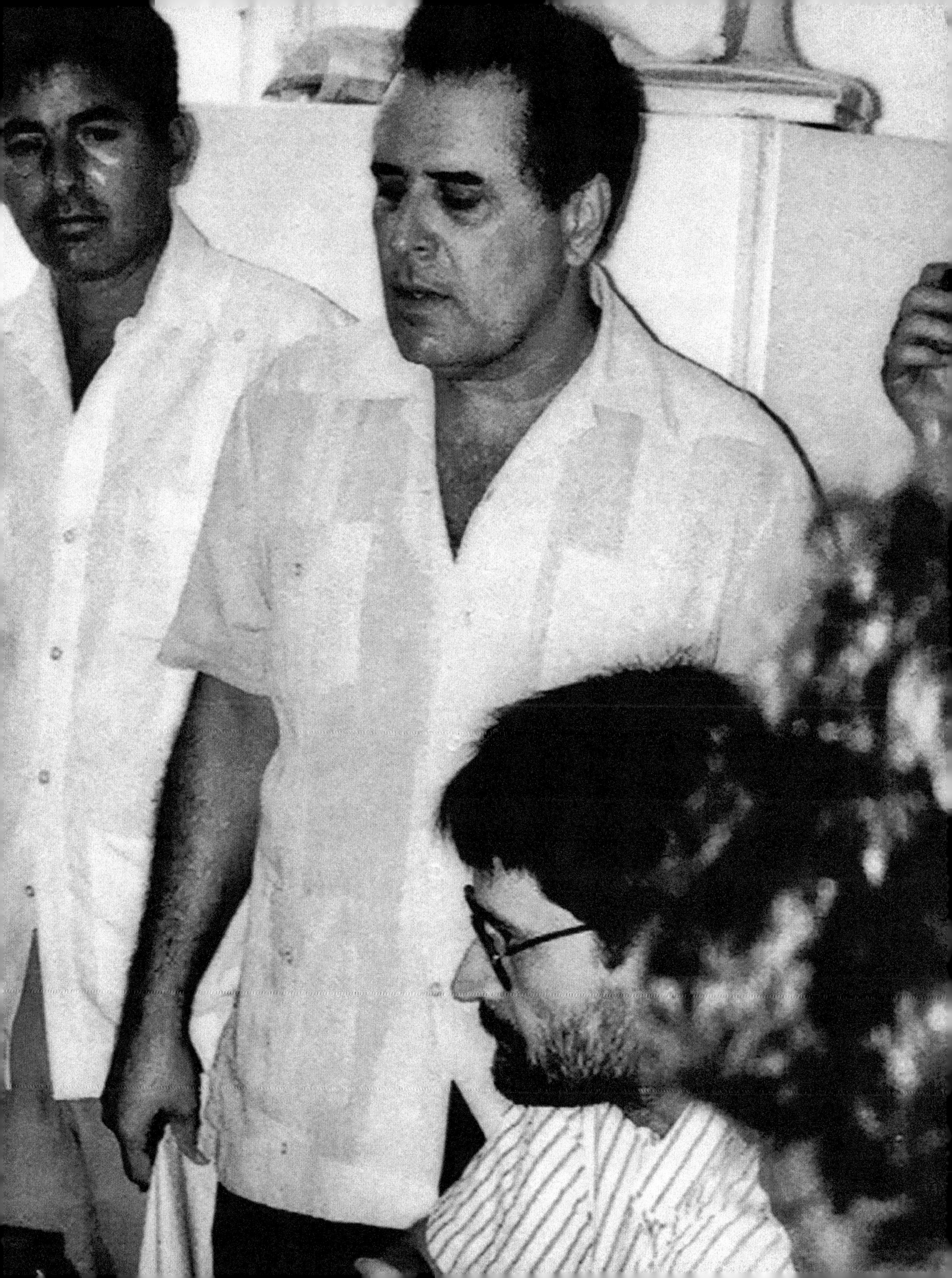

DGICL-2901 - (Confidencial)

DOCUMENTO I

Política a desarrollar por el INSTITUTO CUBANO DEL LIBRO ante aquellos intelectuales (y su obra) que han asumido una postura de abierta hostilidad hacia la Revolución Cubana por el caso Heberto Padilla

Ante la detención de Heberto Padilla -por actividades -- francamente contrarrevolucionarias- un grupo de intelectuales europeos y latinoamericanos (muchos de éstos últimos residentes en capitales europeas), han asumido una actitud de abierta hostilidad hacia la Revolución Cubana, -actitud que en un primer momento se manifestó en la firma del documento que le fuera enviado al Primer Ministro del Gobierno Revolucionario, Comandante Fidel Castro; en la firma de un segundo documento, también dirigido al compañero Fidel, ya en fecha posterior a la terminación del Congreso Nacional de Educación y Cultura; en la redacción de un documento enviado por intelectuales mexicanos y en varias declaraciones que han hecho algunos de estos intelectuales en la prensa de México, y en otras revistas latinoamericanas.

Después de analizados los documentos hemos visto cómo algunos de estos intelectuales son firmantes del primero y segundo documentos enviados a nuestro gobierno; firmantes, también, de la carta de México y han hecho, además, declaraciones contra nuestra Revolución. Es decir, que en al-

---

DGICL-2901 - (Confidencial)   2.

gunos de dichos intelectuales se produce una abierta, activa y manifiesta hostilidad hacia nuestra revolución y gobierno. Hay otros que habiendo firmado el primer documento, no han firmado ninguno de los otros dos, ni han hecho declaración alguna contra nuestra revolución, en una actitud, si se quiere, expectante, pues han hecho público reconocimiento de haber sido injustos en sus ataques o haberse retractado de los mismos.

Ante esta situación, se impone hacer una valoración del nivel de participación que han tenido los intelectuales comprometidos en este caso, que, indiscutiblemente, no es la misma en todos. Por esta razón pensamos que, si existen distintos grados de participación entre unos y otros intelectuales, es necesario hacer las distinciones pertinentes ante cada caso.

Hay uno que nos llama particularmente la atención y es el de Jesús Silva Herzog, del que pensamos ya había sido víctima --aún su decrepitud- de aquellos intelectuales contrarrevolucionarios que se han aprovechado de esta situación para buscar, en apoyo de su documento, una firma como la de Silva Herzog.

Consideramos importante destacar todo el odio contrarrevolucionario que se esconde en los firmantes del segundo documento enviado desde París al compañero Fidel, en el que, con una virulencia increíble, se ataca a nuestra revolución,

---

DGICL-2901 - (Confidencial)   3.

acusándola de métodos draconianos para "arrancar" a Heberto Padilla su carta autocrítica. Debe tenerse en cuenta que ya en esa fecha había concluido el Congreso Nacional de Educación y Cultura y Fidel hablaba en su clausura, por lo que puede considerarse este documento como una respuesta a ellos.

Planteada la situación en estos términos, cabe preguntarse: ¿Cuál debe ser la política del Instituto Cubano del Libro con relación a la actitud de estos intelectuales? y ¿cuál la actitud frente a su obra?

Pensamos que debemos plantearnos la acción a desarrollar, en los siguientes términos:

1. No editar obra alguna de los firmantes de estos documentos, ni de los que hayan hecho declaraciones contra la revolución y el gobierno cubanos.

2. En el caso de aquellos autores cuya obra --de valores reconocidos -, por su magnitud y calidad los trasciende y desde ahora podemos afirmar que les sobrevivirá, dejar que sea la historia quién la juzgue y determine, casuísticamente, si merece editarse o no, en el futuro, partiendo del criterio de que la creación artística, literaria o científica es patrimonio de la Humanidad y no de sus creadores.

3. Hacer la distinción obligada, dados los distintos grados de actividad demostrados, entre unos y otros casos y ana-

---

DGICL-2901 - (Confidencial)   4.

lizar la situación de aquellos que han hecho declaraciones reconociendo lo equívoco de las posiciones asumidas o señalando no ser firmantes de los documentos mencionados.

4. En cuanto a exportación, sacar de los fondos exportables las obras de dichos autores, no vendiendo en el exterior obra alguna de estos intelectuales. De igual forma proceder con los catálogos de exportación, suprimiendo de ellos las obras que se dejarán de vender.

5. En cuanto a distribución nacional, quitar de la venta si fuere necesario, títulos que sean obra de estos autores. Consideramos que esto debe hacerse con la obra de aquellos que han asumido una franca postura anticubana. Es posible que muchos de estos títulos se encuentren ya agotados en las librerías de venta o intercambio, pero en el caso de quedar algunos, retirarlo.

6. Que, como un modo de preservar las obras que, por su valor, lo merezcan, aquellos títulos que se retiren de la venta, salas de Lectura o librerías de intercambio, sean enviados a las bibliotecas del país, para su conservación y uso necesario.

7. En cuanto a los catálogos generales de nuestras Editoriales, que se encuentran en proceso de preparación y en los que deberá aparecer reflejada la obra de estos intelectuales, detener la confección de los mismos en espera del

---

DGICL-2901 - (Confidencial)   5.

desarrollo de los acontecimientos, dejando pendiente la decisión al respecto, que deberá ser tomada en cuanto a las condiciones lo permitan.

8. En la misma forma que hoy acordamos no editar, no vender en el exterior, no incluir en catálogos y quitar de la venta la obra de estos intelectuales, consideramos que, en el futuro y ante una situación distinta a la que hoy enfrentamos, debe actuarse en consecuencia y, caso por caso, ir determinando qué autores y qué obras de aquellos autores que hubieran variado su actitud hacia nuestro gobierno y revolución, editaremos, sobre todo pensando que algunos de estos intelectuales puedan haber sido arrastrados, mediante la mentira, a suscribir los documentos mencionados que atacan al Gobierno Revolucionario y a la Revolución cubana. En pocas palabras: actuar mañana con el mismo rigor con que hoy lo hacemos y hacerlo a tono con la realidad.

La Habana, 23 de mayo de 1971
AÑO DE LA PRODUCTIVIDAD

DGICL-2901 (Confidencial)

DOCUMENTO II

Algunas consideraciones en torno a la circulación interna (Distribución Nacional) de los títulos de autores referidos

1. En posesión de la lista de autores entrar a una congelación en la distribución de los títulos en existencia --(Paralizados en estos momentos). Recomendamos la posibilidad de concentrar en un sólo almacén todos estos títulos para su conservación.

2. Una vez recopilada la información que en estos momentos se procesa convocar a una reunión con todos los Delegados Provinciales, donde podamos informar de todos estos problemas y podamos oír la situación real de existencias de estos títulos en las diferentes provincias, esto es, en cuales esta presente en almacén y en cuales están totalmente distribuidas anteriormente.

En esta reunión se fijaría claramente que no procederemos a recoger ningún material distribuido a Salas de Lectura, Bibliotecas y Salas de Intercambio, recomendando que en el caso de estas últimas y por una observación directa de cada Delegado se vayan extrayendo lentamente de la circulación.

DGICL-2901 (Confidencial)   2.

3. Plantearnos finalmente que algunas cantidades de estos títulos se destinen nuevamente a Bibliotecas especialmente la Biblioteca Nacional (Habana) y provinciales y las Bibliotecas Centrales de las Universidades, Escuelas del Partido, etc.

4. Concentrar en un sólo lugar, los Catálogos recientemente editados por la Serie Arte y Literatura, que no fueron distribuidos anteriormente y que se encuentran en: Centro de Exposición, Serie Editorial y Almacén Nacional.

La Habana, 23 de mayo de 1971
AÑO DE LA PRODUCTIVIDAD

DGICL-2901 (Confidencial)

DOCUMENTO III

Algunas consideraciones en torno a la importación de publicaciones de autores referidos

1. Opinamos que independientemente de la posición adoptada en mayor o menor intensidad por un grupo numeroso de autores, nuestro país deberá importar en cantidades discretas los diferentes títulos que a partir de este instante fueran editados. Fundamentamos este planteamiento en:

1.1. Considerar toda obra de estos autores en todo caso en la categoría de información; no importamos cantidades de las mismas.

1.2. Necesidad de una valoración mantenida de sus obras que nos permitan analizar la profundidad de la obra la cual podrá o no sobrevivir a su autor.

1.3. Inteligencia comercial con respecto a las Editoriales extranjeras que las publican. Sin dudas nuestro organismo maneja el comercio internacional de publicaciones y consecuentemente puede manejar criterios en torno a nuestras relaciones con determinadas editoriales.

1.4. Posición inteligente ante los observadores extranjeros que puedan manejar una posición de cierre to-

---

DGICL-2901 (Confidencial)   2.

tal. Hasta aquí nuestro país ha realizado siempre compras masivas fundamentalmente en libros técnicos, por lo que incluso la compra discreta no entraría en contradicción con la posición adoptada hasta aquí.

2. Consideramos importante que una vez aceptado el aspecto anterior se hace imprescindible la fijación de algunos criterios con respecto a quienes.

En nuestra opinión debemos normar el que no todos los organismos del país adquieran publicaciones de estos autores, sin embargo proponemos que esta medida sea de carácter interno, esto es, cualquier organismo de los que no queden comprendidos y los que puedan añadirse, no recibirían ningún tipo de información, sino nosotros internamente procederíamos a tachar o eliminar esa importación, brindándole al final del plan la información de que los materiales (en unión de todos los demás títulos que generalmente no podemos servir) no servidos quedan cancelados.

Organismos que proponemos puedan realizar importaciones en cantidades discretas:
Instituto Cubano del Libro (Series Editoriales que correspondan y niveles de Dirección)
con
MINFAR - Dirección Política
MININT - Dirección Política
MINREX - Dirección que corresponda

CONFIDENCIAL, AUTORES FIRMANTES

2015

This mixed-media installation is the fruit of Fusco's ongoing research on Cuba and collaboration with University of Florida professor Lillian Guerra. Working with archival materials related to the international controversy generated by the forced confession of poet Heberto Padilla, Fusco created twenty-one facsimiles of official memorandums and letters from 1971 found by Guerra in the archives of the Cuban Ministry of Culture. The texts detail orders and methods by which to censor publications by intellectuals deemed "anti-Cuban" due to their open disagreement with the government's detainment of Padilla and their skepticism regarding the motives of Padilla's ensuing "confession" that he had betrayed the revolution. The facsimiles [see the Appendix for translations], forged assiduously with vintage typewriters and letterpress printing, are presented alongside original editions of books by Padilla's supporters such as Gabriel García Márquez, Julio Cortázar, and Mario Vargas Llosa—publications that were originally printed and then censored in Cuba. This installation functions as an archive of a key historical moment that redefined the Cuban revolutionary government's relationship with progressive intellectuals of that era, both inside the island and out. As the artist says, "A state may produce the absence of its own archive while retaining its own contents for a future exercise of force."

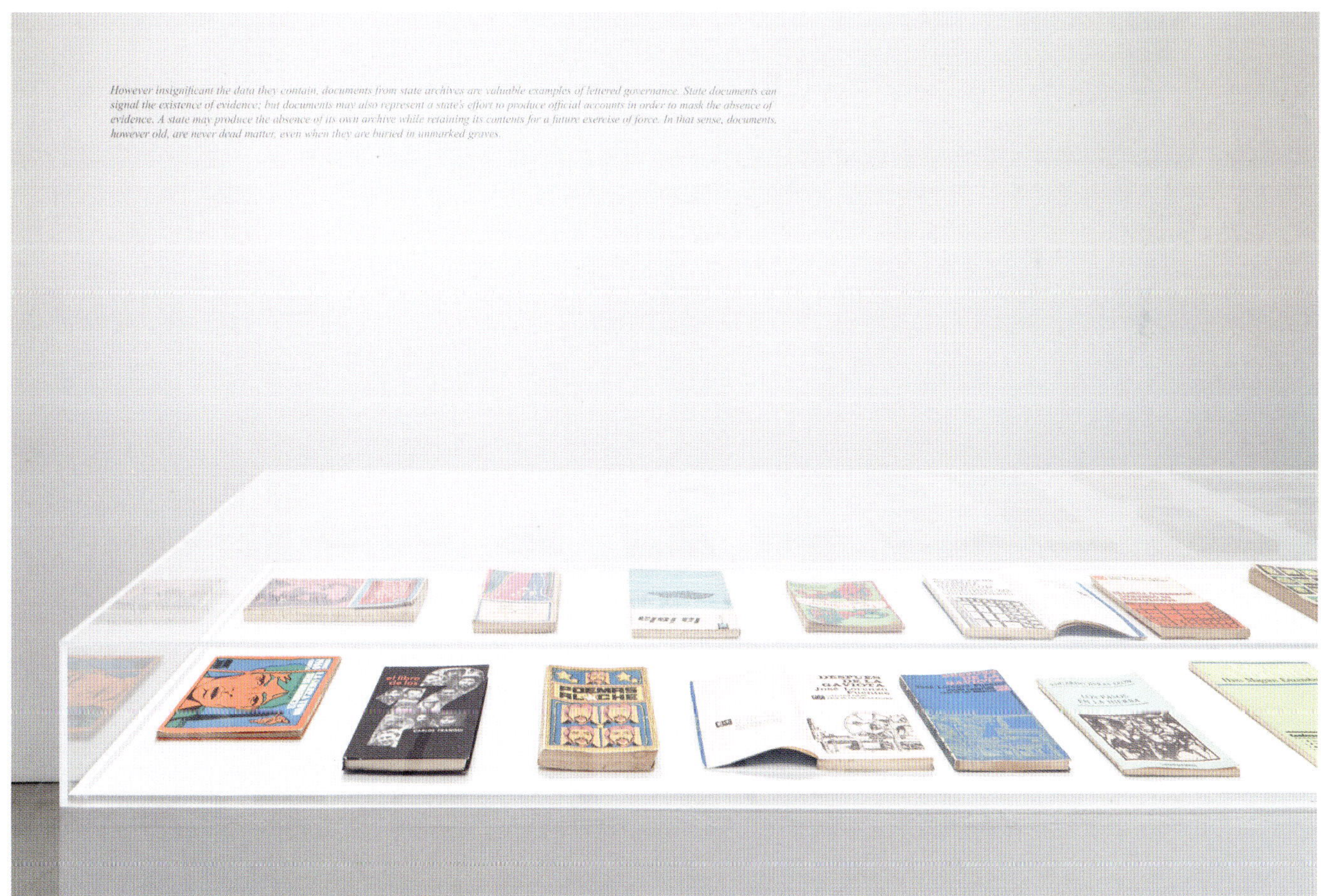

CONFIDENCIAL, AUTORES FIRMANTES, 2015, installation (also overleaf and pages 167–71)

MEMORANDUM

A: **Co. René Roca** DGICL-2852 FECHA **21 de mayo de 1971**
Director Grupo III CONFIDENCIAL "AÑO DE LOS 10 MILLONES"

ASUNTO: DE: **Oficina Dirección General.**

Te instruyo para que des las órdenes pertinentes para retirar con -
caracter urgente del comercio internacional, así como de las listas
y catálogos de nuestro organismo las siguientes obras y autores, en
las próximas horas agregaremos nuevos nombres y títulos, así como -
tomaremos las decisiones con respecto a la circulación nacional.

JUAN PAUL SARTRE

    Sarte visita a Cuba
    Tintorero, el secuestrado de Venecia
    Las Palabras
    ¿Qué es la literatura? Tomos I y II
    Cuestiones del método

MARIO VARGAS LLOSA

    Los cachorros

JULIO CORTAZAR

    Rayuela
    Cuentos
    Sobre Julio Cortázar
      (Cuadernos Casa)

JORGE SEMPRUN

    El largo viaje

CARLOS FRANQUI

    El libro de los 12

CARLOS FUENTES

    Aura

ITALO CALVINO

    Las dos mitades del vizconde

MARGARITA DURAS

    Días enteros en las ramas

LUIS GOYTISOLO

    La isla

GABRIEL GARCIA MARQUEZ

    Cien años de soledad
    Gabriel García Márquez (valoración múltiple, Casa)

TO: Comrade René Roca   DGICL — 2852   DATE: May 21 1971
Director Group III   CONFIDENTIAL   General Management Office

SUBJECT:

I instruct you so that you give the pertinent orders for the urgent removal of the following names and authors from international commerce and from the lists and catalogues of our organization. In the coming hours we will be adding new names and titles, and will also be making decisions regarding national circulation.

JEAN PAUL SARTRE
Sartre Visits Cuba
The Captive of Venice, Tintoretto
The Words
What is Literature? Volumes I and II
The Search for Method

MARIO VARGAS LLOSA
The Cubs

JULIO CORTAZAR
Hopscotch
Stories
About Julio Cortazar (Casa Notebooks)

JORGE SEMPRUN
The Long Journey

CARLOS FRANQUI
The Book of the Twelve

ITALO CALVINO
The Cloven Viscount

MARGUERITE DURAS
Whole Days in the Trees

LUIS (sic) GOYTISOLO
The Island

GABRIEL GARCIA MARQUEZ
One Hundred Years of Solitude
Gabriel Garcia Marquez (Casa, Multiple Views)

INSTITUTO DEL LIBRO
CALLE 19. 1002
VEDADO
LA HABANA
TELF 30.5531

MEMORANDUM

A: _______________________ DGICL-2852 FECHA _______________
"AÑO DE LOS 10 MILLONES"

ASUNTO: _______________ DE: _______________

VARGAS LLOSA, CORTAZAR, FUENTES, OTROS
      Quince relatos de América Latina

JAN KOTT

      Shakespeare, nuestro contemporáneo

NICANOR PARRA

      Poemas

EDUARDO HERAS LEON

      Los pasos en la hierba

NORBERTO FUENTES

      Condenados de condado

En caso de existir algún obstáculo para ello o tener alguna obser
vación en contra te ruego me lo informes a la mayor brevedad, así
como las medidas a tomar con las existencias de los mismos. Estas
medidas deben ser tomadas con la mayor discreción posible para no
levantar "polvoreada" al respecto.

Revolucionariamente

Rolando Rodríguez
Director General

cc: Miguel Rodríguez, Director Editorial
    Eduardo Neira,   Relaciones Internacionales

VARGAS LLOSA, CORTAZAR, FUENTES, OTHERS
    Fifteen Stories from Latin America

JAN KOTT
    Shakespeare, Our Contemporary

NICANOR PARRA
    Poems

EDUARDO HERA LEON
    The Steps on the Grass

NORBERTO FUENTES
    The Condemned of the County

If there are obstacles to or comments against carrying out these instructions I ask that you please inform me as quickly as possible, as well as letting me know about the measures to be taken with the warehoused stock of these works. These measures should be taken with the highest degree of discretion possible so as not to create a ruckus about the issue.

Revolutionarily,

Rolando Rodríguez
General Manager

cc: Miguel Rodríguez, Editor in Chief
     Eduardo Neira, International Relations

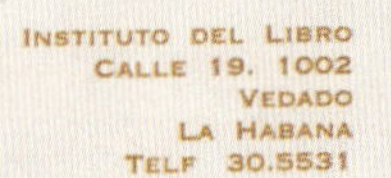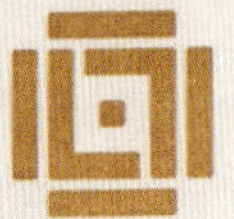

MEMORANDUM

CONFIDENCIAL

A: Co. Rolando Rodríguez
Director General

FECHA: 22 de mayo de 1971
"Año de la Productividad"

DE: Dpto. Relaciones Internacionales

ASUNTO:

Compañero:

Ampliando nuestro memo del pasado día 19, a continuación te rela-
cionamos los títulos de los libros que recomendamos se valore el-
retiro circulación de los mismos. Quisiéramos aclararte que por -
no existir una lista total de libros editados por el organismo, -
no confiamos que la misma esté completa aún.

1. Poemas al Che

2. Nueva poesía española

3. La ruta de Hernán Cortés - Benítez

4. Límites y potencialidades del movimiento de Mayo - ANDRE
GORZ

5. El llano en llamas - JUAN RULFO

6. Pedro Páramo

7. Tropismos - N. SARRAUTE

8. Breve historia de la revolución mexicana - SILVA HERZOG

9. Las Casas y Trujillo - HANS MAGNUS - ENZENBERGER

10. Juan Rulfo - Valoración Múltiple

11. OCTAVIO PAZ

12. CLARIDAD ALEGRIA

13. R. ROSSANDA

Revolucionariamente,

PATRIA O MUERTE
¡VENCEREMOS!

sl

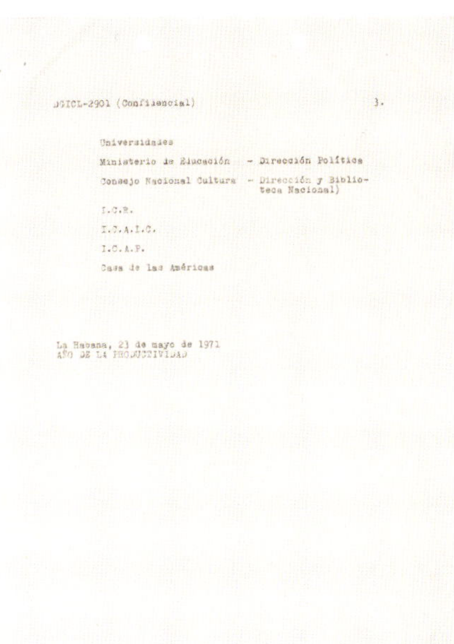

DGICL-2901 (Confidencial)   3.

Universidades

Ministerio de Educación   - Dirección Política

Consejo Nacional Cultura   - Dirección y Biblio-
                             teca Nacional)

I.C.R.

I.C.A.I.C.

I.C.A.P.

Casa de las Américas

La Habana, 23 de mayo de 1971
AÑO DE LA PRODUCTIVIDAD

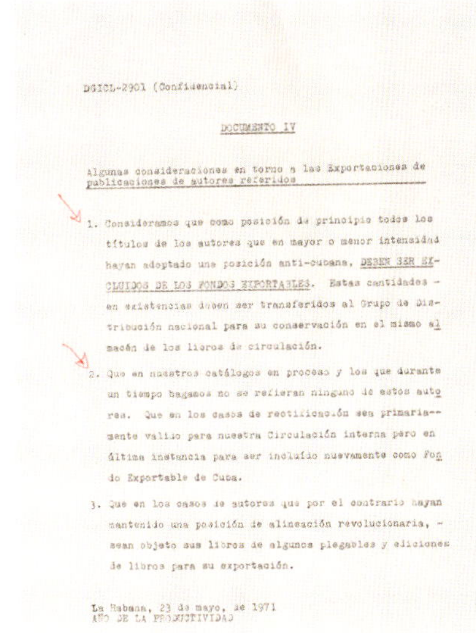

DGICL-2901 (Confidencial)

DOCUMENTO IV

Algunas consideraciones en torno a las Exportaciones de
publicaciones de autores referidos

1. Consideramos que como posición de principio todos los
títulos de los autores que en mayor o menor intensidad
hayan adoptado una posición anti-cubana, DEBEN SER EX-
CLUIDOS DE LOS FONDOS EXPORTABLES. Estas cantidades -
en existencias deben ser transferidos al Grupo de Distribución nacional para su conservación en el mismo al
macén de los libros de circulación.

2. Que en nuestros catálogos en proceso y los que durante
un tiempo hagamos no se refieran ninguno de estos auto
res. Que en los casos de rectificación sea primaria--
mente valido para nuestra Circulación interna pero en
última instancia para ser incluido nuevamente como Fon
do Exportable de Cuba.

3. Que en los casos de autores que por el contrario hayan
mantenido una posición de alineación revolucionaria, -
sean objeto sus libros de algunos plegables y ediciones
de libros para su exportación.

La Habana, 23 de mayo, de 1971
AÑO DE LA PRODUCTIVIDAD

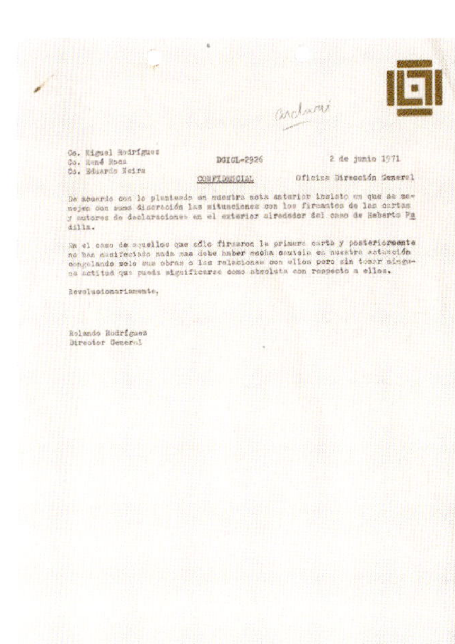

Co. Miguel Rodríguez
Co. René Roca   DGICL-2926   2 de junio 1971
Co. Eduardo Neira
              CONFIDENCIAL   Oficina Dirección General

De acuerdo con lo planteado en nuestra nota anterior insisto en que se ma-
nejen con suma discreción las situaciones con los firmantes de las cartas
y autores de declaraciones en el exterior alrededor del caso de Heberto Pa
dilla.

En el caso de aquellos que sólo firmaron la primera carta y posteriormente
no han manifestado nada mas debe haber mucha cautela en nuestra actuación
congelando solo sus obras o las relaciones con ellos pero sin tomar ningu-
na actitud que pueda significarse como absoluta con respecto a ellos.

Revolucionariamente,

Rolando Rodríguez
Director General

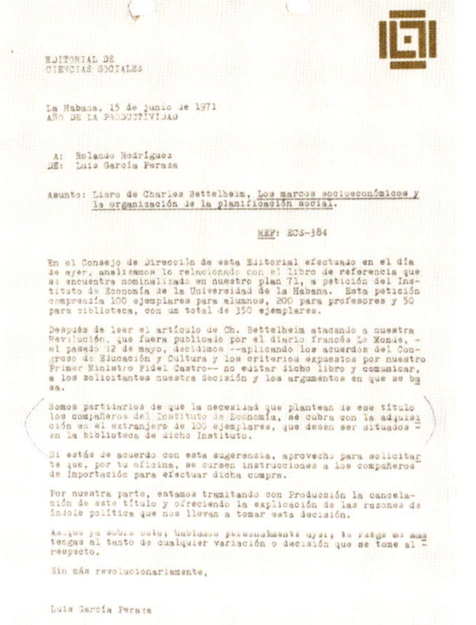

EDITORIAL DE
CIENCIAS SOCIALES

La Habana, 15 de junio de 1971
AÑO DE LA PRODUCTIVIDAD

A: Rolando Rodríguez
DE: Luis García Peraza

Asunto: Libro de Charles Bettelheim, Los marcos socioeconómicos y
la organización de la planificación social.

REF: ECS-384

En el Consejo de Dirección de este Editorial efectuado en el día
de ayer, analizamos lo relacionado con el libro de referencia que
se encuentra nominalizado en nuestro plan 71, a petición del Instituto de Economía de la Universidad de la Habana. Esta petición
comprendía 100 ejemplares para alumnos, 200 para profesores y 50
para biblioteca, con un total de 350 ejemplares.

Después de leer el artículo de Ch. Bettelheim atacando a nuestra
Revolución, que fuera publicado por el diario francés Le Monde, -
el pasado 12 de mayo, decidimos --aplicando los acuerdos del Congreso de Educación y Cultura y los criterios expuestos por nuestro
Primer Ministro Fidel Castro-- no editar dicho libro y comunicar,
a los solicitantes nuestra decisión y los argumentos en que se ba
sa.

Somos partidarios de que la necesidad que plantean de ese título
los compañeros del Instituto de Economía, se cubra con la adquisi
ción en el extranjero de 100 ejemplares, que deben ser situados -
en la biblioteca de dicho Instituto.

Si estás de acuerdo con esta sugerencia, aprovecho para solicitar
te que, por tu oficina, se cursen instrucciones a los compañeros
de Importación para efectuar dicha compra.

Por nuestra parte, estamos tramitando con Producción la cancelación de este título y ofreciendo la explicación de las razones de
índole política que nos llevan a tomar esta decisión.

Aunque ya sobre esto, hablamos personalmente ayer, te ruego me mag
tengas al tanto de cualquier variación o decisión que se tome al -
respecto.

Sin más revolucionariamente,

Luis García Peraza

c/c: Archivo,
     Consecutivo

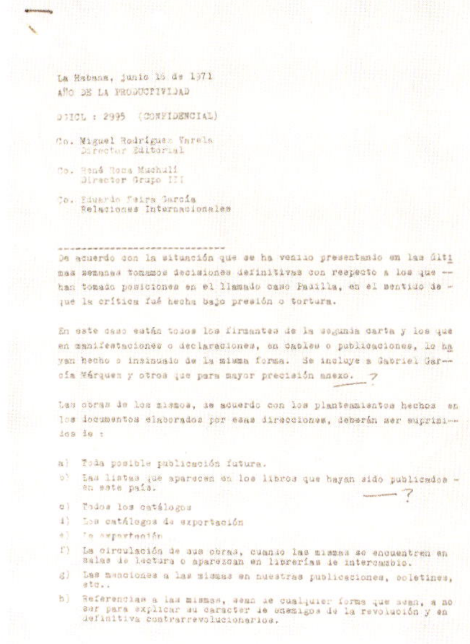

La Habana, junio 15 de 1971
AÑO DE LA PRODUCTIVIDAD

DGICL : 2995 (CONFIDENCIAL)

Co. Miguel Rodríguez Varela
     Director Editorial

Co. René Roca Machulí
     Director Grupo III

Co. Eduardo Neira García
     Relaciones Internacionales

De acuerdo con la situación que se ha venido presentando en las últi
mas semanas tomamos decisiones definitivas con respecto a los que --
han tomado posiciones en el llamado caso Padilla, en el sentido de -
que la crítica fué hecha bajo presión o tortura.

En este caso están todos los firmantes de la segunda carta y los que
en manifestaciones o declaraciones, en cables o publicaciones, lo ha
yan hecho o insinuado de la misma forma. Se incluye a Gabriel García Márquez y otros que para mayor precisión anexo.

Las obras de los mismos, de acuerdo con los planteamientos hechos en
los documentos elaborados por esas direcciones, deberán ser suprimi-
dos de :

a) Toda posible publicación futura.
b) Las listas que aparecen en los libros que hayan sido publicados -
   en este país.
c) Todos los catálogos
d) Los catálogos de exportación
e) La exportación
f) La circulación de sus obras, cuando las mismas se encuentren en
   salas de lectura o aparezcan en librerías de intercambio.
g) Las menciones a las mismas en nuestras publicaciones, boletines,
   etc..
h) Referencias a las mismas, sean de cualquier forma que sean, a no
   ser para explicar su caracter de enemigos de la revolución y en
   definitiva contrarrevolucionarios.

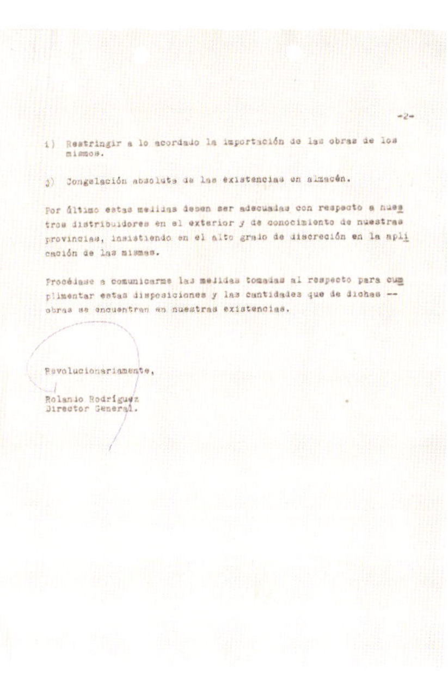

-2-

i) Restringir a lo acordado la importación de las obras de los
   mismos.

j) Congelación absoluta de las existencias en almacén.

Por último estas medidas deben ser adecuadas con respecto a nues
tros distribuidores en el exterior y de conocimiento de nuestras
provincias, insistiendo en el alto grado de discreción en la apli
cación de las mismas.

Procédase a comunicarme las medidas tomadas al respecto para cum
plimentar estas disposiciones y las cantidades que de dichas --
obras se encuentren en nuestras existencias.

Revolucionariamente,

Rolando Rodríguez
Director General.

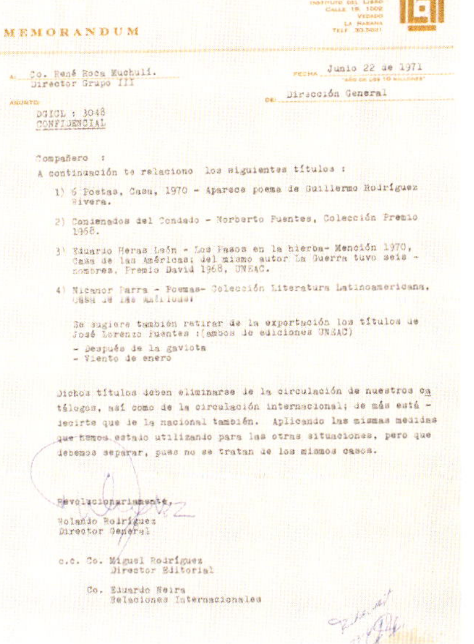

MEMORANDUM

INSTITUTO DEL LIBRO
CALLE 19 1002
VEDADO
LA HABANA
TELF 30-5631

A: Co. René Roca Machulí.   FECHA: Junio 22 de 1971
   Director Grupo III   AÑO DE LOS 10 MILLONES

                                   DE: Dirección General
ASUNTO:
   DGICL : 3048
   CONFIDENCIAL

Compañero :

A continuación te relaciono los siguientes títulos :

   1) 6 Poetas, Casa, 1970 - Aparece poema de Guillermo Rodríguez
      Rivera.

   2) Condenados del Condado - Norberto Fuentes, Colección Premio
      1968.

   3) Eduardo Heras León - Los Pasos en la hierba- Mención 1970,
      Casa de las Américas; del mismo autor La Guerra tuvo seis -
      nombres. Premio David 1968, UNEAC.

   4) Nicanor Parra - Poemas- Colección Literatura Latinoamericana.
      Casa de las Américas;

      Se sugiere tambien retirar de la exportación los títulos de
      José Lorenzo Fuentes :(ambos de ediciones UNEAC)
      - Después de la gaviota
      - Viento de enero

Dichos títulos deben eliminarse de la circulación de nuestros ca
tálogos, así como de la circulación internacional; de más está -
decirte que de la nacional también. Aplicando las mismas medidas
que hemos estado utilizando para las otras situaciones, pero que
debemos separar, pues no se tratan de los mismos casos.

Revolucionariamente,

Rolando Rodríguez
Director General

c.c. Co. Miguel Rodríguez
     Director Editorial

     Co. Eduardo Neira
     Relaciones Internacionales

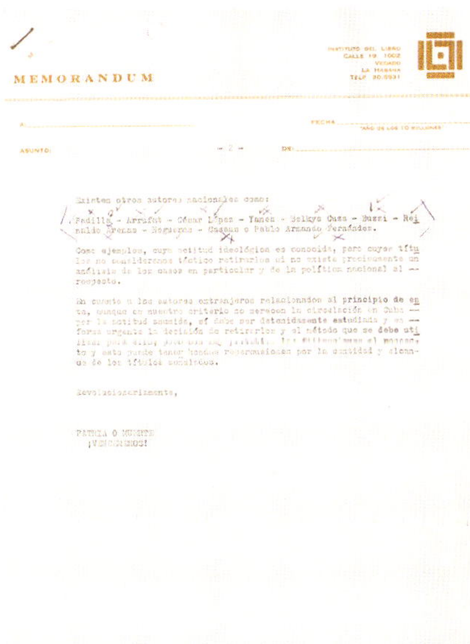

etc..

h) Referencias a las mismas, sean de cualquier forma que sean, a no
   ser para explicar su caracter de enemigos de la revolución y en
   definitiva contrarrevolucionarios.

MEMORANDUM

INSTITUTO DEL LIBRO
CALLE 19 1002
VEDADO
LA HABANA
TELF 30-5631

A: FECHA: AÑO DE LOS 10 MILLONES
ASUNTO: - 2 -   DE:

Existen otros autores nacionales como:

Padilla - Arrufat - César López - Yanes - Belkys Cuza - Buzzi - Rei
naldo Arenas - Nogueras - Casaus o Pablo Armando Fernández.

Como ejemplos, cuya actitud ideológica es conocida, pero cuyos títu
los no consideramos táctico retirarlos si no existe precisamente un
análisis de los casos en particular y de la política nacional al --
respecto.

En cuanto a los autores extranjeros relacionados al principio de es
ta, aunque en nuestro criterio no merecen la circulación en Cuba --
por la actitud asumida, sí debe ser detenidamente estudiada y en --
forma urgente la decisión de retirarlos y el método que se debe uti
lizar para ello; poco aconsejable... el momen
to y esto puede tener hondas repercusiones por la cantidad y alcan
ce de los títulos señalados.

Revolucionariamente,

PATRIA O MUERTE
  ¡VENCEREMOS!

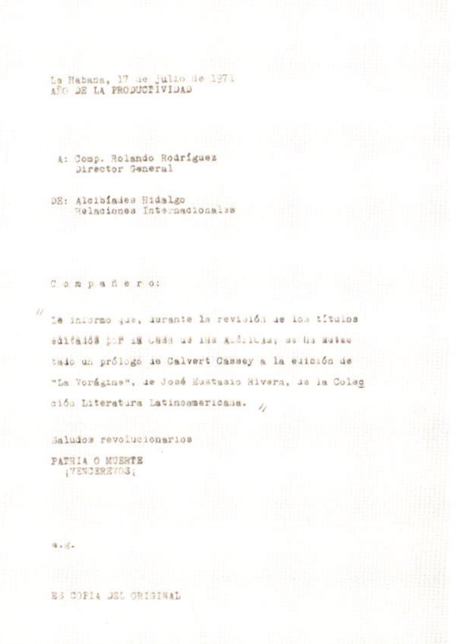

La Habana, 17 de julio de 1971
AÑO DE LA PRODUCTIVIDAD

A: Comp. Rolando Rodríguez
   Director General

DE: Alcibíades Hidalgo
    Relaciones Internacionales

Compañero:

" Le informo que, durante la revisión de los títulos
editados por la Casa de las Américas, se ha adver-
tido un prólogo de Calvert Casey a la edición de
"La Vorágine", de José Eustasio Rivera, de la Colec
ción Literatura Latinoamericana. "

Saludos revolucionarios
PATRIA O MUERTE
  ¡VENCEREMOS!

a.g.

ES COPIA DEL ORIGINAL

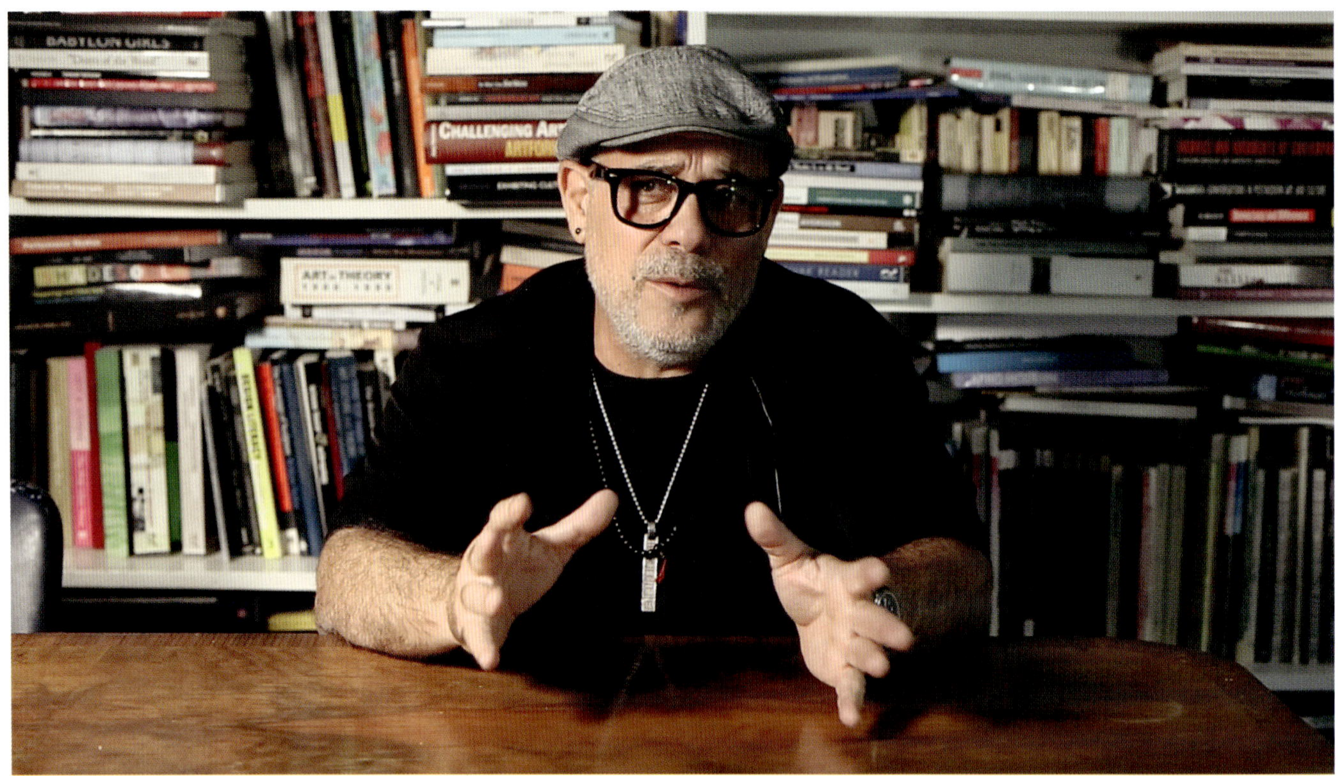

The Art of Intervention:
The Performances of JuanSí González

2016

This documentary video explores the ground-breaking street performances of Cuban artist JuanSí González during the 1980s. A pioneer of social practice, González transformed public spaces in Havana into laboratories for unsettling exchanges between artists and the public, culminating in a series of works that questioned the role of art in a socialist society. His experiments provoked surprise from his peers and suspicion from state authorities. For this video, JuanSí sat down with Fusco to reflect on the relevance of those performances for the development of contemporary art on the island. The video also features rare archival footage of Cuban performance art from the 1980s.

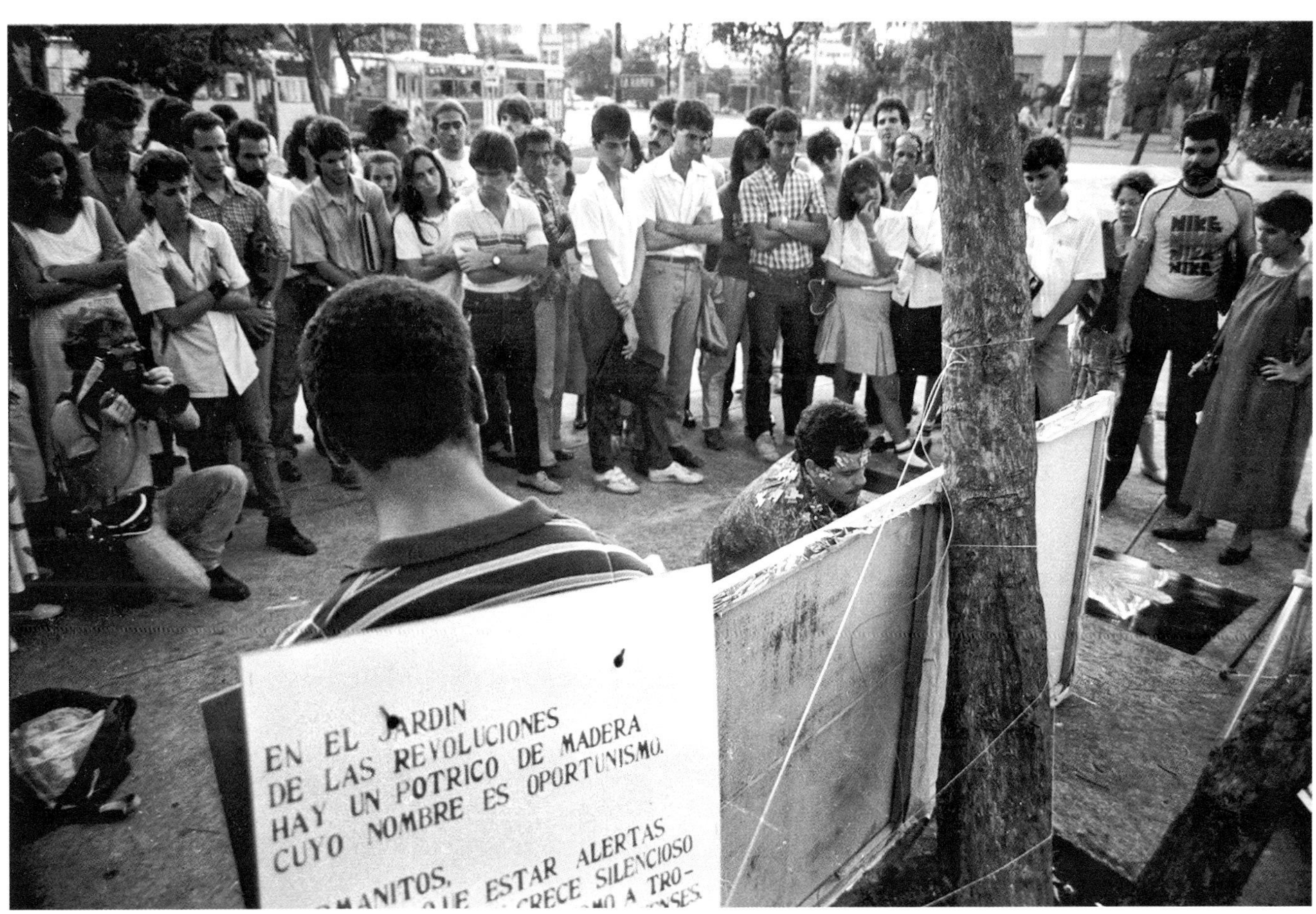

The Art of Intervention: The Performances of JuanSí González, 2016, video

Words May
Not Be Found

2017

Words May Not Be Found is a performance that premiered at the KW Institute for Contemporary Art in Berlin in 2017, and also took place in Stuttgart, and in Elsinore, Denmark. More than a century after the German military campaign in South West Africa (now Namibia), the conflict that emerged in response to an insurrection by the Nama and Herero peoples remains a source of collective trauma for both nations. The traumatic nature of this history is due both to the scale of violence that was carried out against civilians and to the efforts to suppress the sole document that contained Namibian testimony relating to the conflict. This work, in which Fusco performs together with a group of participants chosen at each locale, focuses on the struggle over the words of the native informants. For nearly three decades, she has delved into historical records and colonial archives to create works that tease out subtexts and the counter-narratives embedded in them. In *Words May Not Be Found*, she seeks to draw out parallels between colonial and contemporary perceptions of non-western "others."

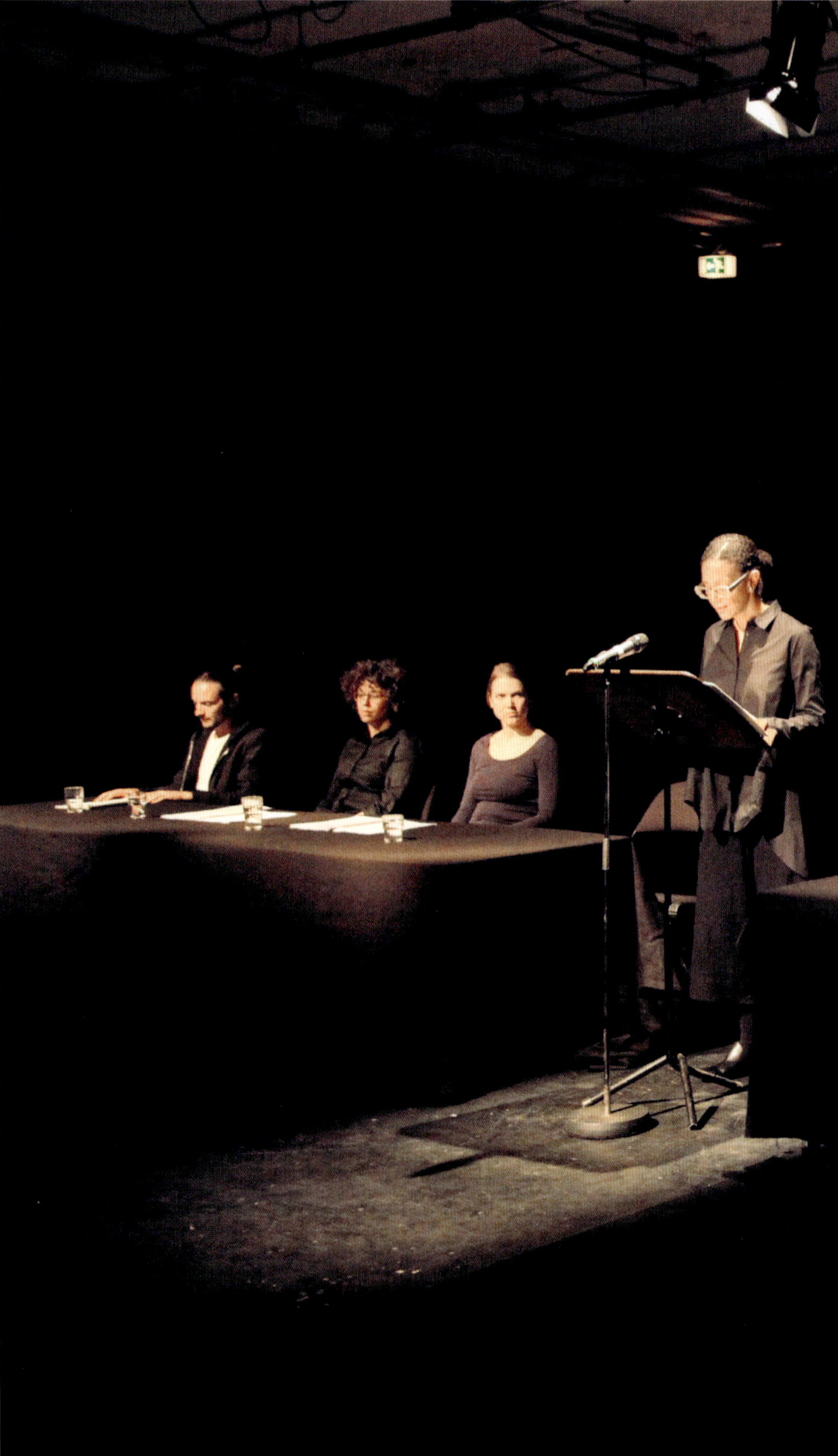

Words May Not Be Found, 2017, performance (and overleaf)

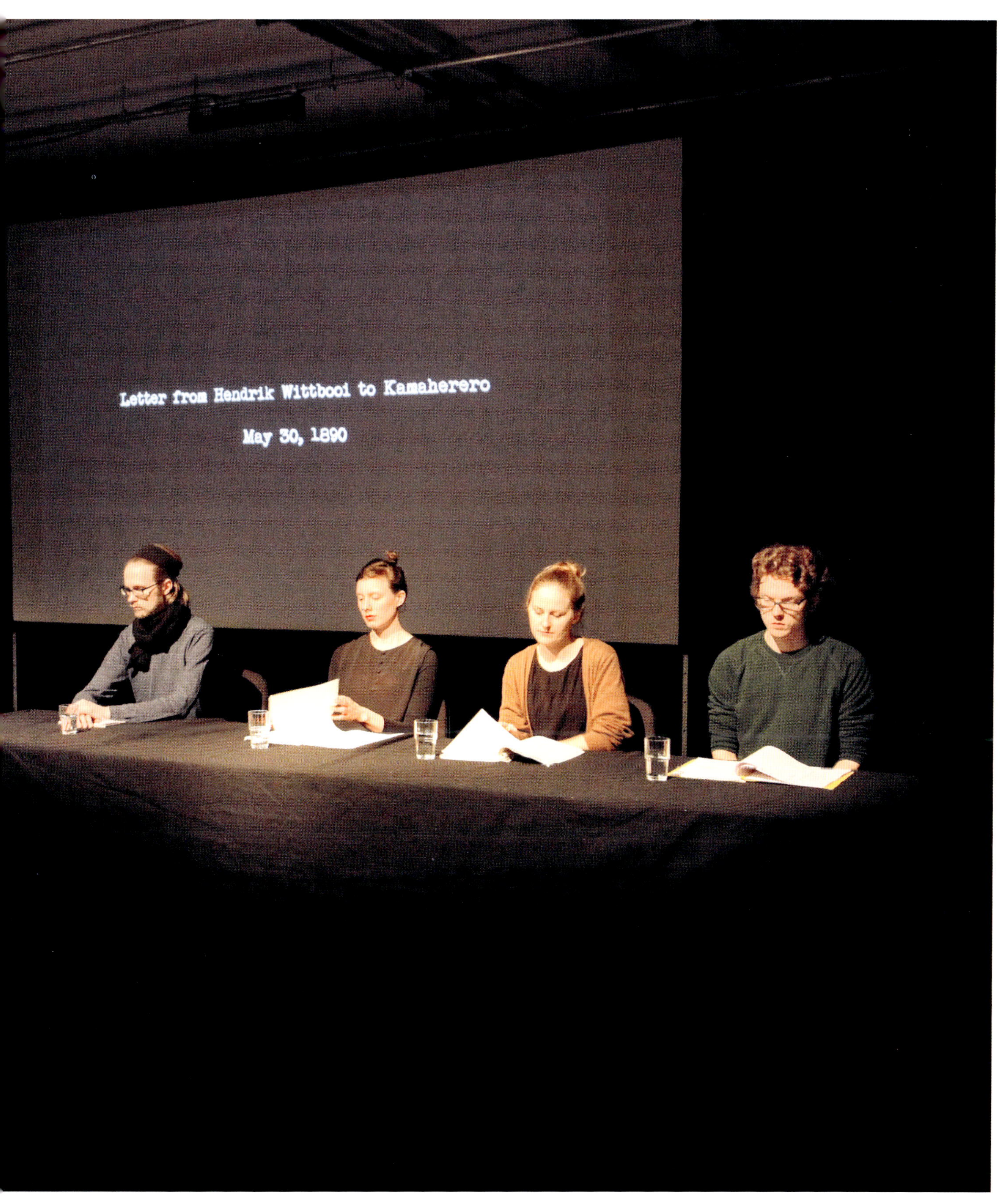

Letter from Hendrik Wittbooi to Kamaherero

May 30, 1890

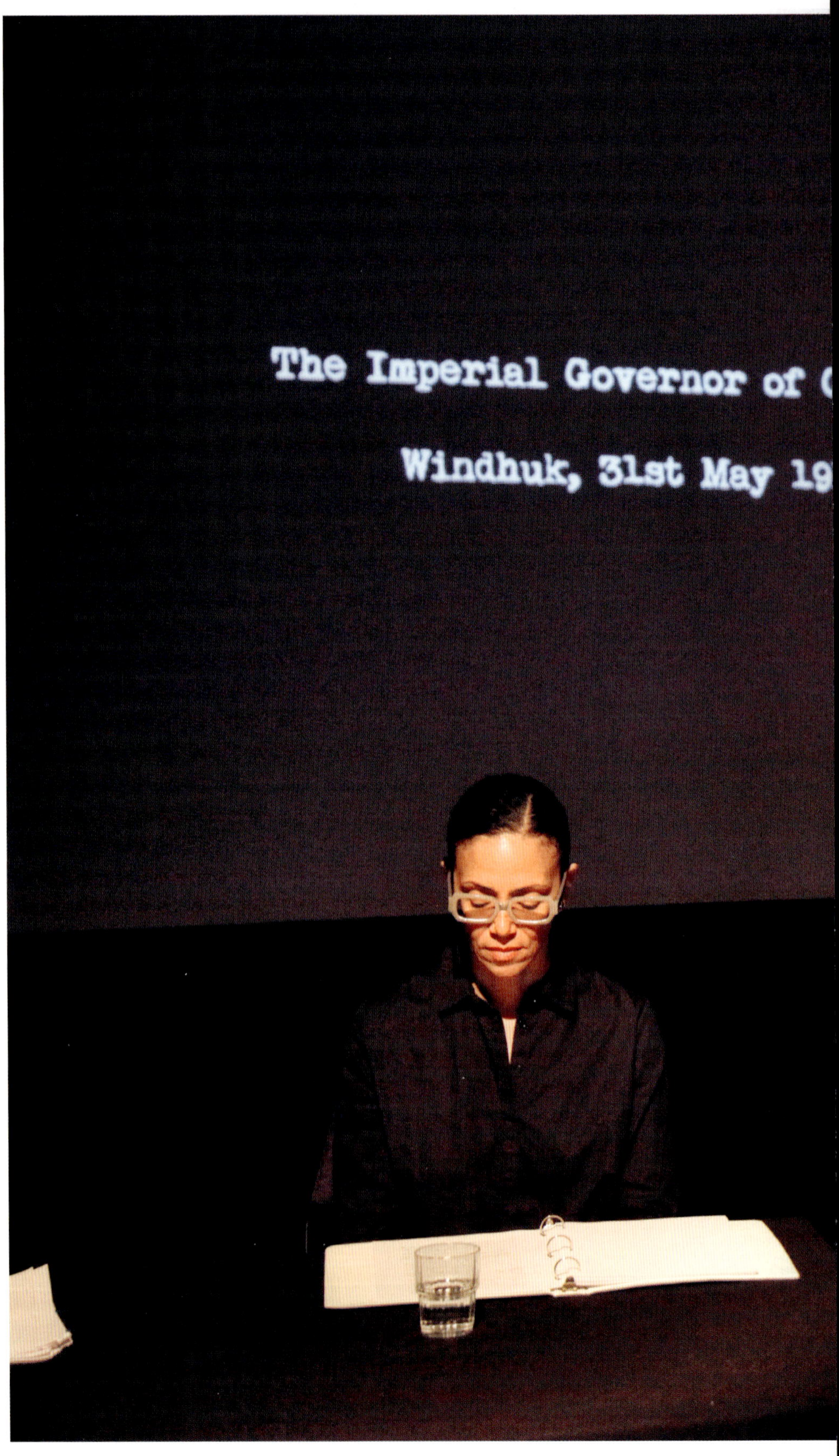

BODY OF WORK 1990–2022

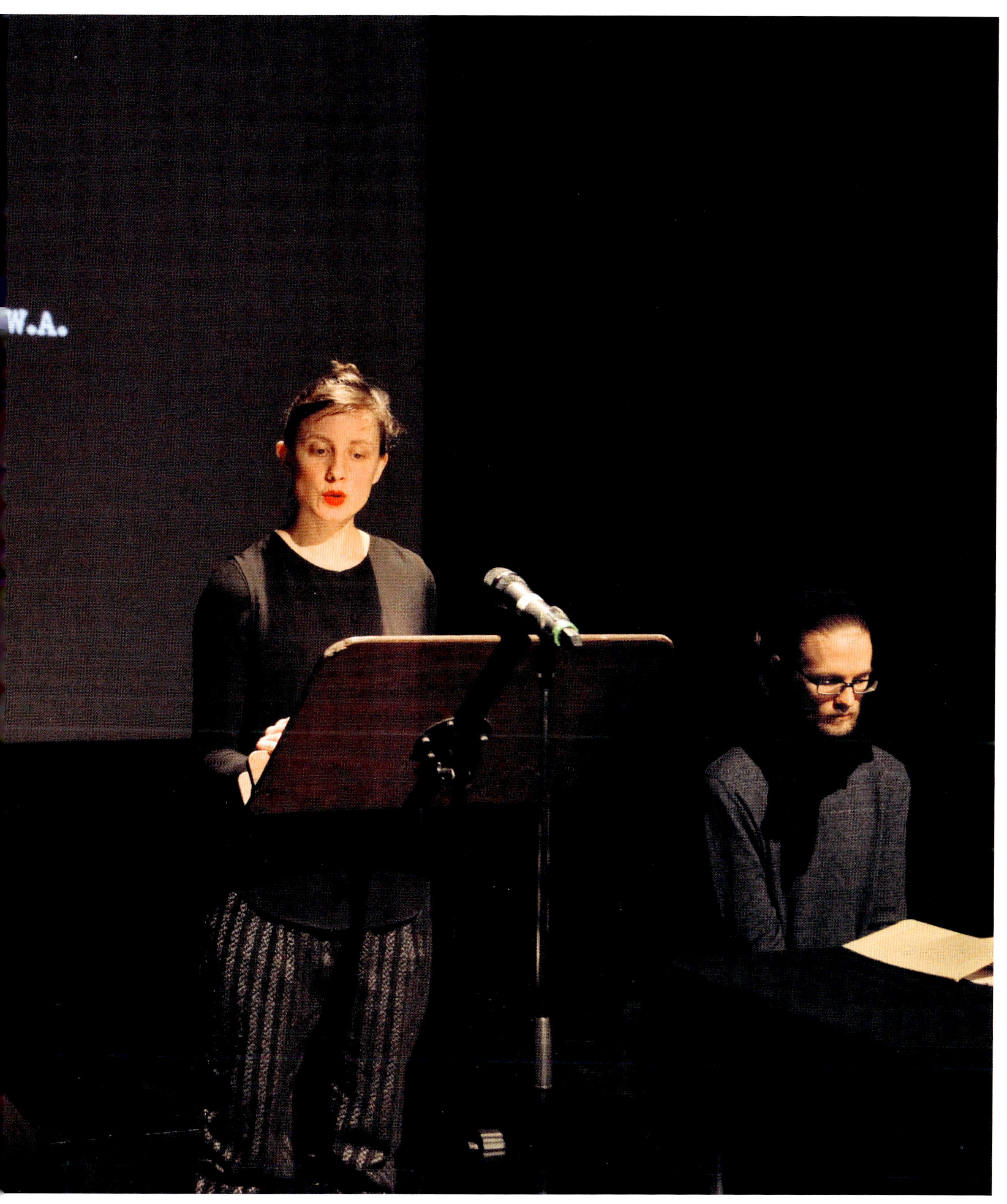

COCO FUSCO

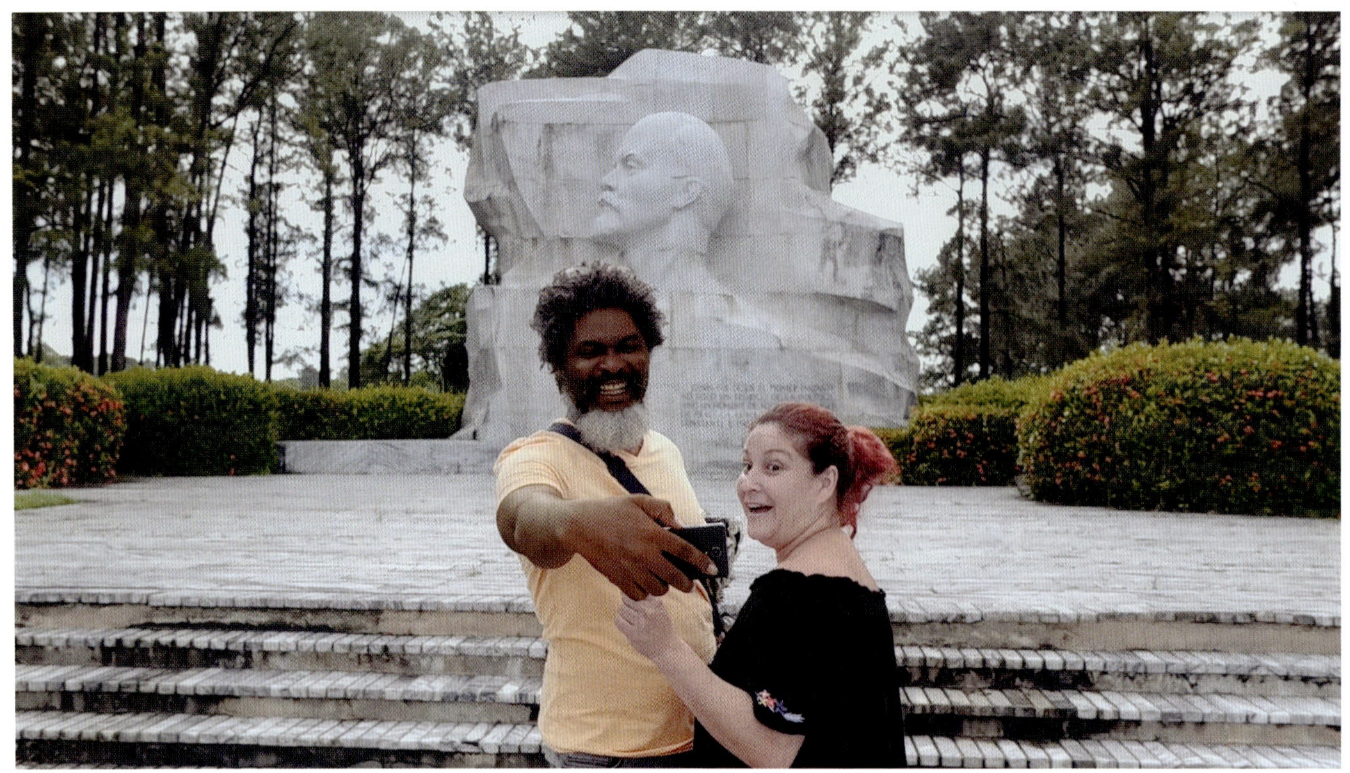

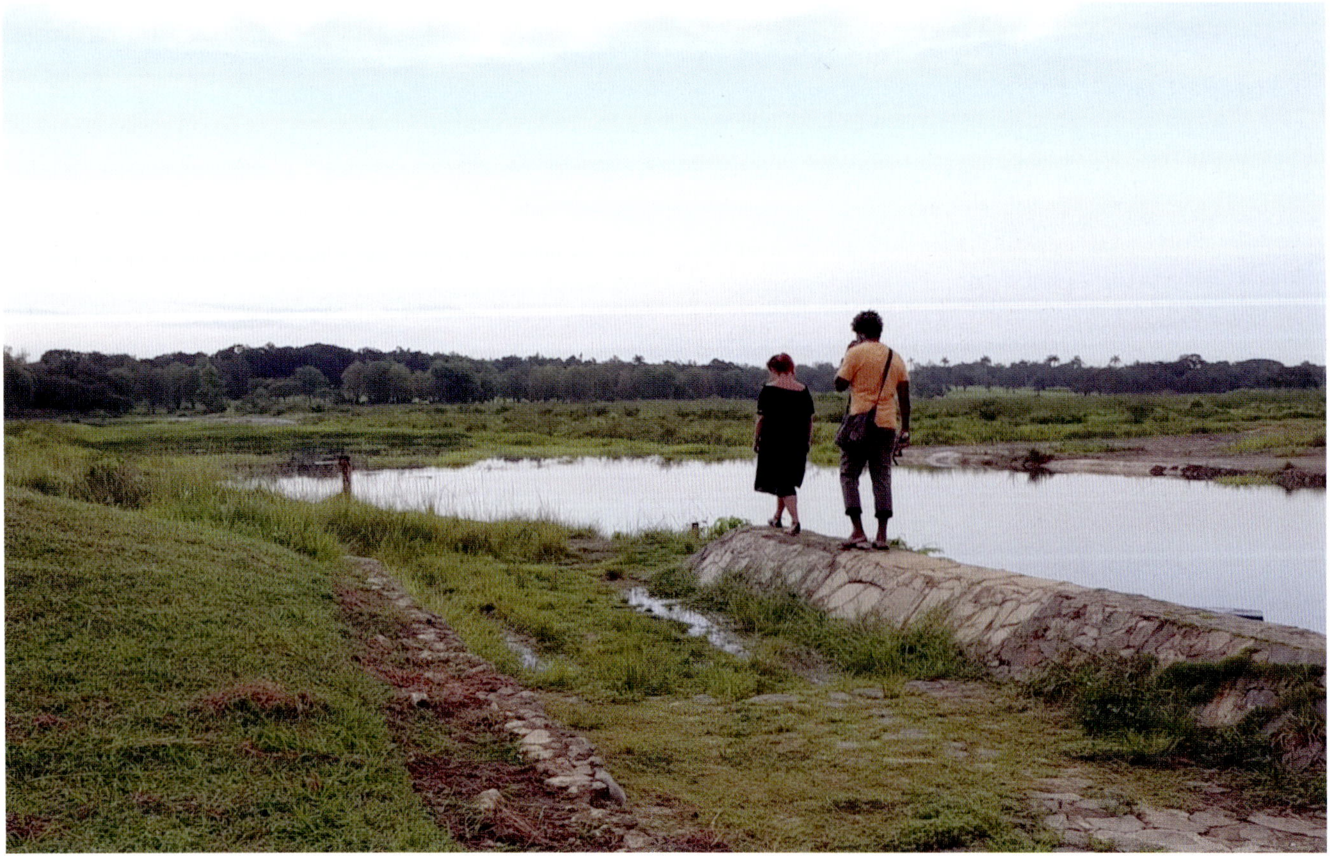

Vivir en junio con la lengua afuera (To Live in June with Your Tongue Hanging Out), 2018, video

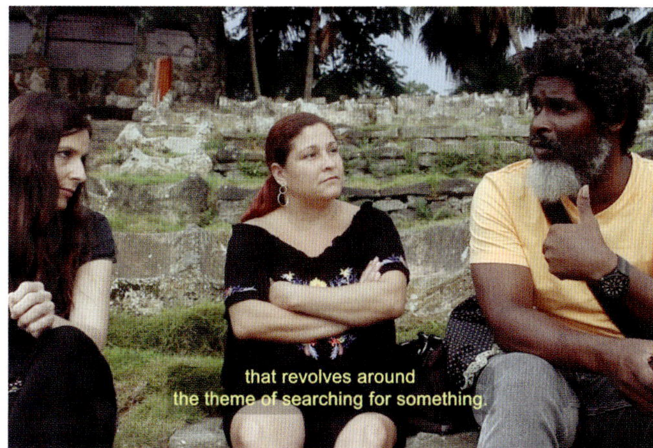

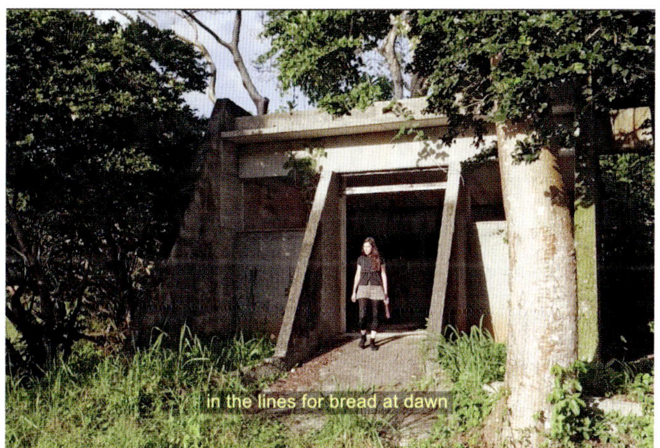

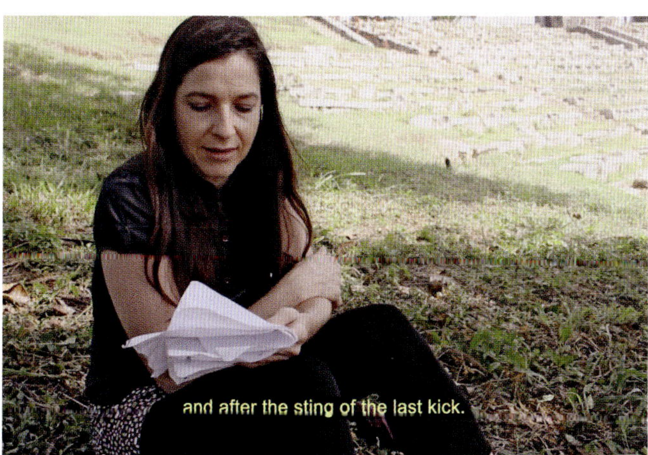

Vivir en junio con la lengua afuera (To Live in June with Your Tongue Hanging Out)

2018

In *Vivir en junio con la lengua afuera* (*To Live in June with Your Tongue Hanging Out*), Fusco returns to the site of fugitive author Reinaldo Arenas's refuge, Havana's Lenin Park, to restore a sense of historical memory to what is now a virtual ruin. Though he supported the Cuban revolution as a young man, Arenas spent much of his adult life on the island as a *persona non grata* because of his open homosexuality and politically dissident views. While his work was banned inside the country, his manuscripts were smuggled out by friends and won prizes abroad. During the 1970s, Arenas organized secret literary gatherings in this park to share his writings with friends and colleagues. He escaped arrest in 1974, spending months in the park as a fugitive and drafting his memoir, *Before Night Falls*. With the help of journal entries written by a friend of Arenas, Fusco was able to locate and film in the spot where Arenas hid, wrote, and fished for food. In the film, three Cuban artists attempt to commit to memory one of Arenas's most famous poems about yearning for a homeland that has been ripped away from those who fought to free it.

The Tin Man of the Twenty-First Century

(in collaboration with Chico MacMurtrie)

2018

The Tin Man of the Twenty-First Century offers a satirical commentary on America's most talked about public figure, calling on audiences to consider the role of monumental sculpture in representing history: the ten-foot depiction of former President Donald Trump resembles the tin woodsman from *The Wizard of Oz*. While the film character may have been overly sentimental, his behavior can also be interpreted as petulant and self-centered, adding another layer of symbolism to the sculpture. "The November 2016 election was a watershed moment for me," Fusco explains. "I sensed that our country would be changed forever. A very different concept of presidential power was ushered in, one that has affected every aspect of social, political and cultural life in America and the rest of the world."

Coco Fusco and Chico MacMurtrie, *The Tin Man of the Twenty-First Century*, 2018, sculpture (and overleaf)

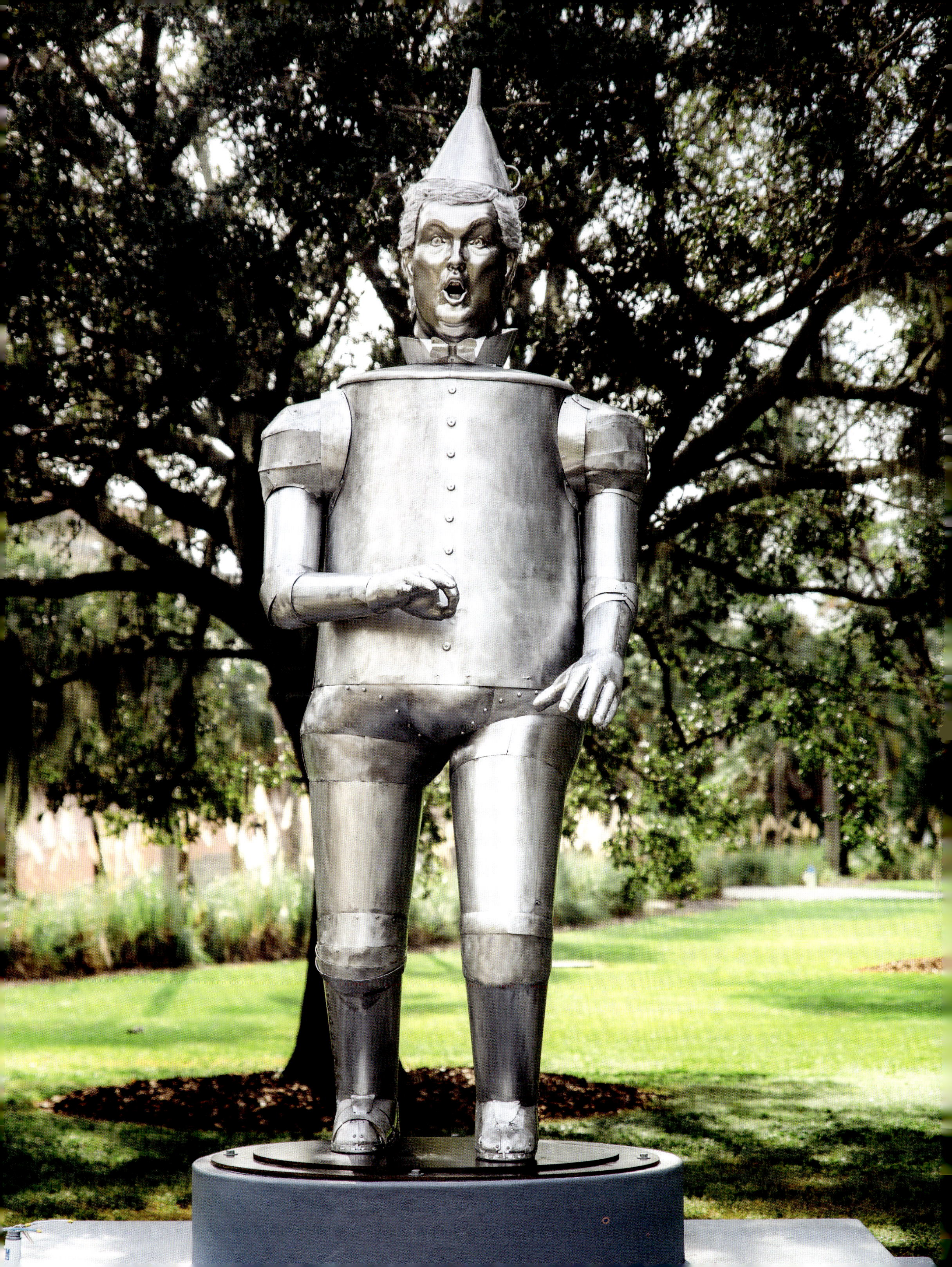

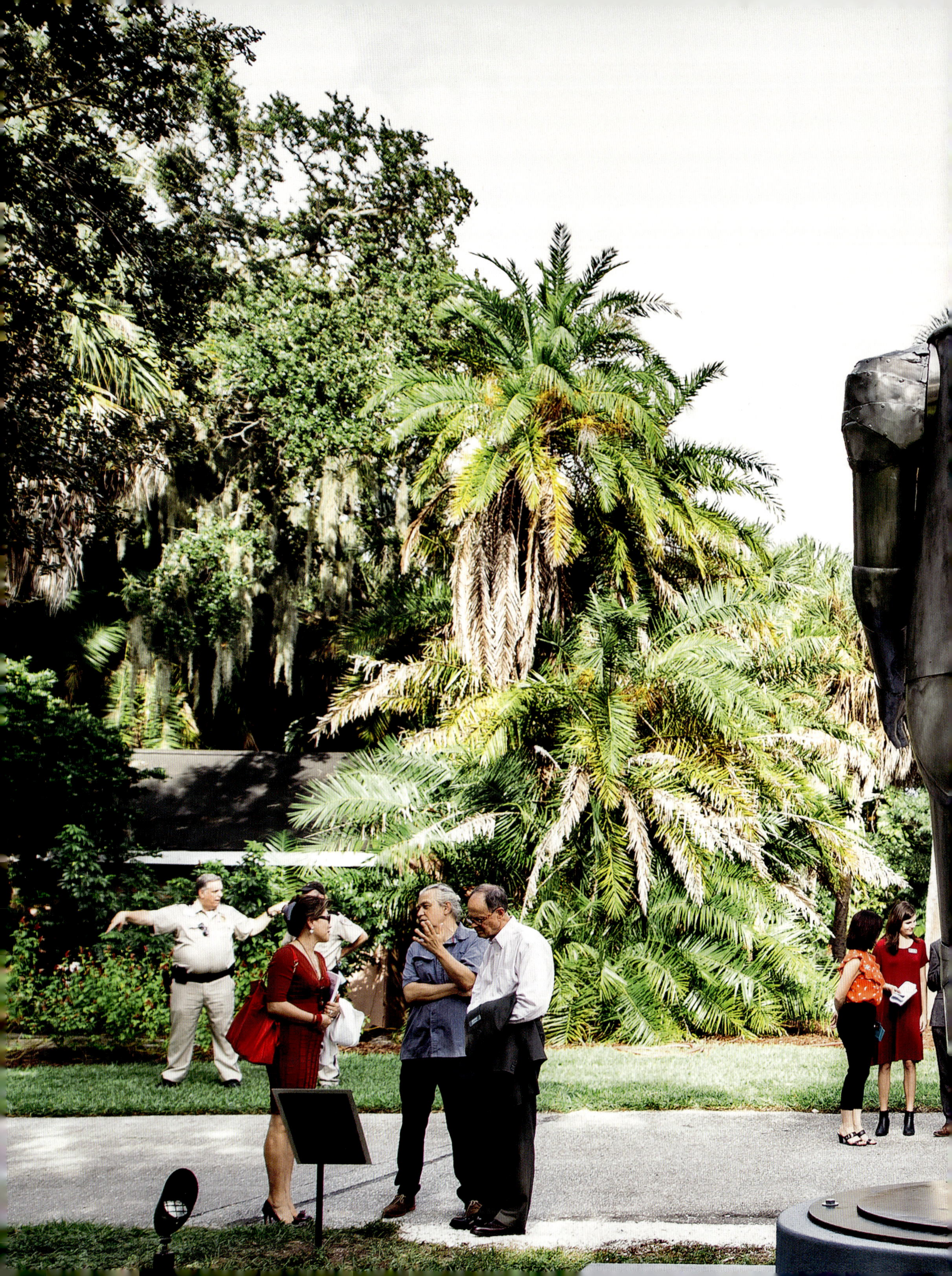

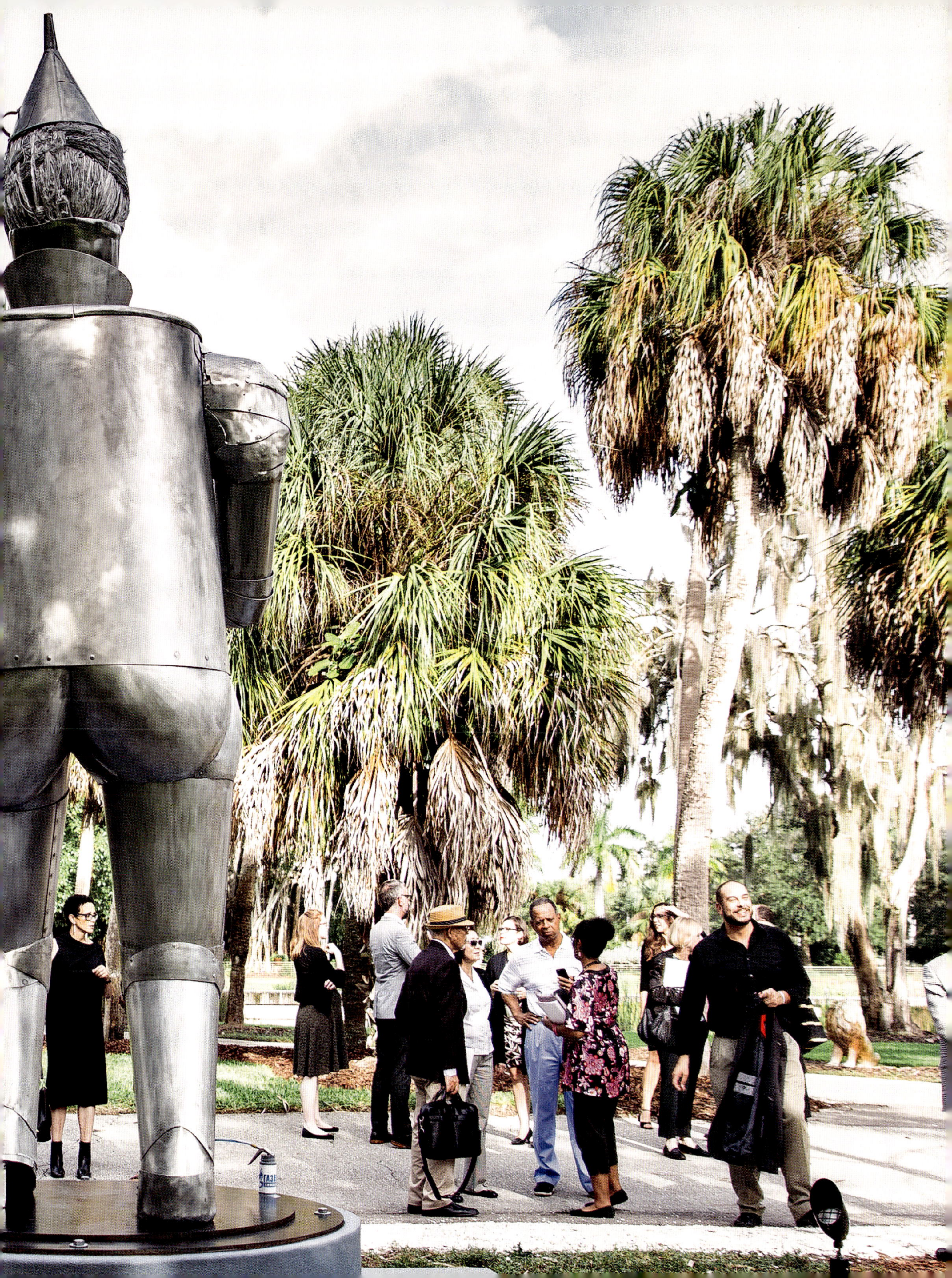

A Censored Prescription

2020

A Censored Prescription marks the early days of the COVID-19 global pandemic through the words of Dr. Li Wenliang, the first to sound the alarm about the escalation of the virus. Before his eventual death, he told the magazine *Caixin*: "I think a healthy society should not only have one kind of voice." Fusco memorializes Wenliang's statement by inviting people from around the world to speak his words in their native tongue. Recorded while in quarantine during the 2020 lockdowns, Fusco constructs a cacophonous murmur of a multilingual crowd from the individual recordings while the aforementioned statement appears on the screen in the various languages being spoken. Participants include Fia Backström, Chang Yuchen, Coco Fusco, Nicolás Dumit Estévez, Chitra Ganesh, Emily Jacir, Paolo Javier, Tammy Nguyen, and Dr. Jane Kim of Brooklyn's Kings County Emergency Room, among many others.

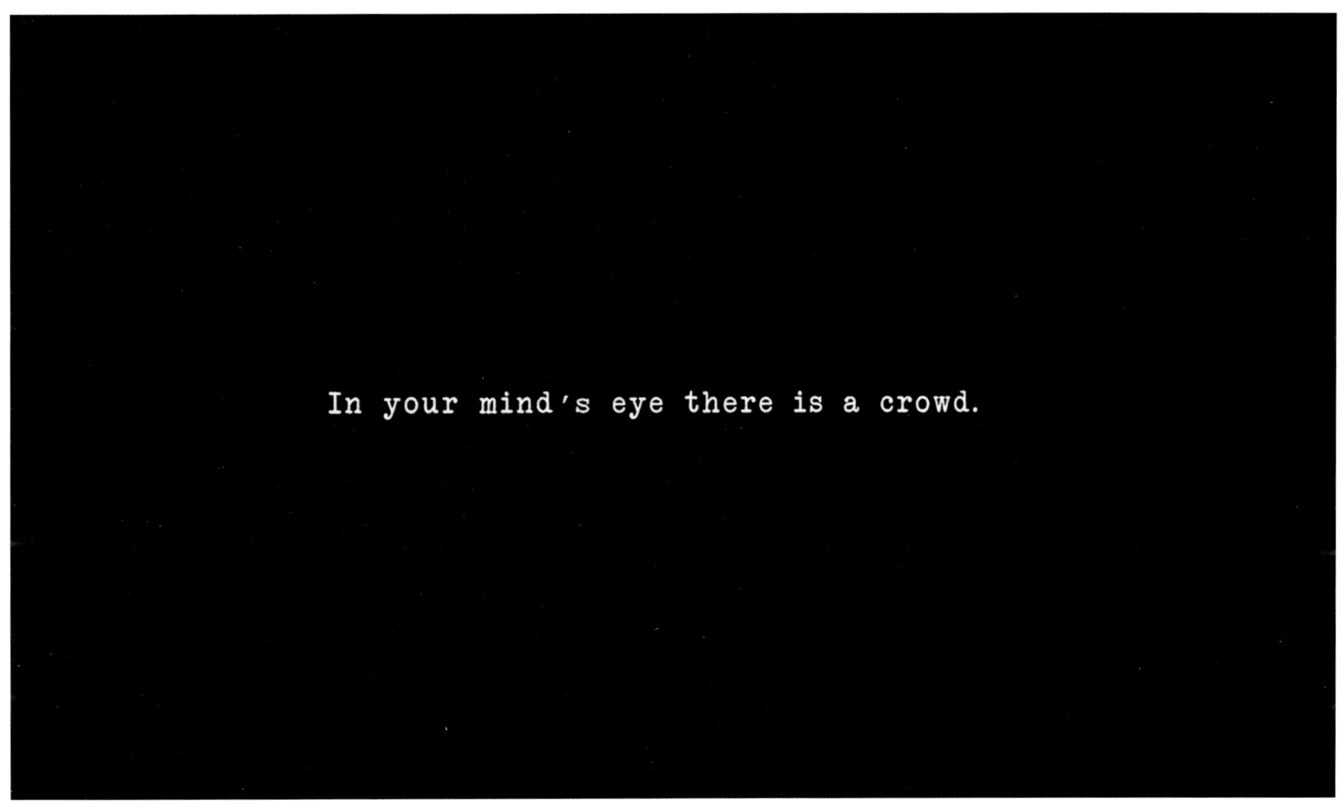

A Censored Prescription, 2020, video

The Woman
by the Window

2020

This video essay focuses on two Cuban writers
who observe the world from their windows: one
is Sergio, the male protagonist from the award-
winning 1968 film *Memories of Underdevelopment*,
the other, award-winning journalist Mónica Baró
Sánchez, who looks out her Havana window in 2020
to observe hundreds of masked people lining up for
food as the island confronts ravaging scarcity and a
pandemic. Seen photographing the food line, Baró
is chastised by a person who screams from below.
She was later visited by a policeman who continued
the intimidation. Fusco brings this situation into
focus by confronting the audience with Cuba's
Decree 370, a law that criminalizes publishing
any information online that is against the state
narrative or interests, thus illustrating how the
Cuban state uses this law to punish people like Baró
to suppress any freedom of speech. This piece was
created for a program produced by *e-flux* and the
International Short Film Festival Oberhausen.

The Woman by the Window, 2020, **video**

     BODY OF WORK 1990–2022

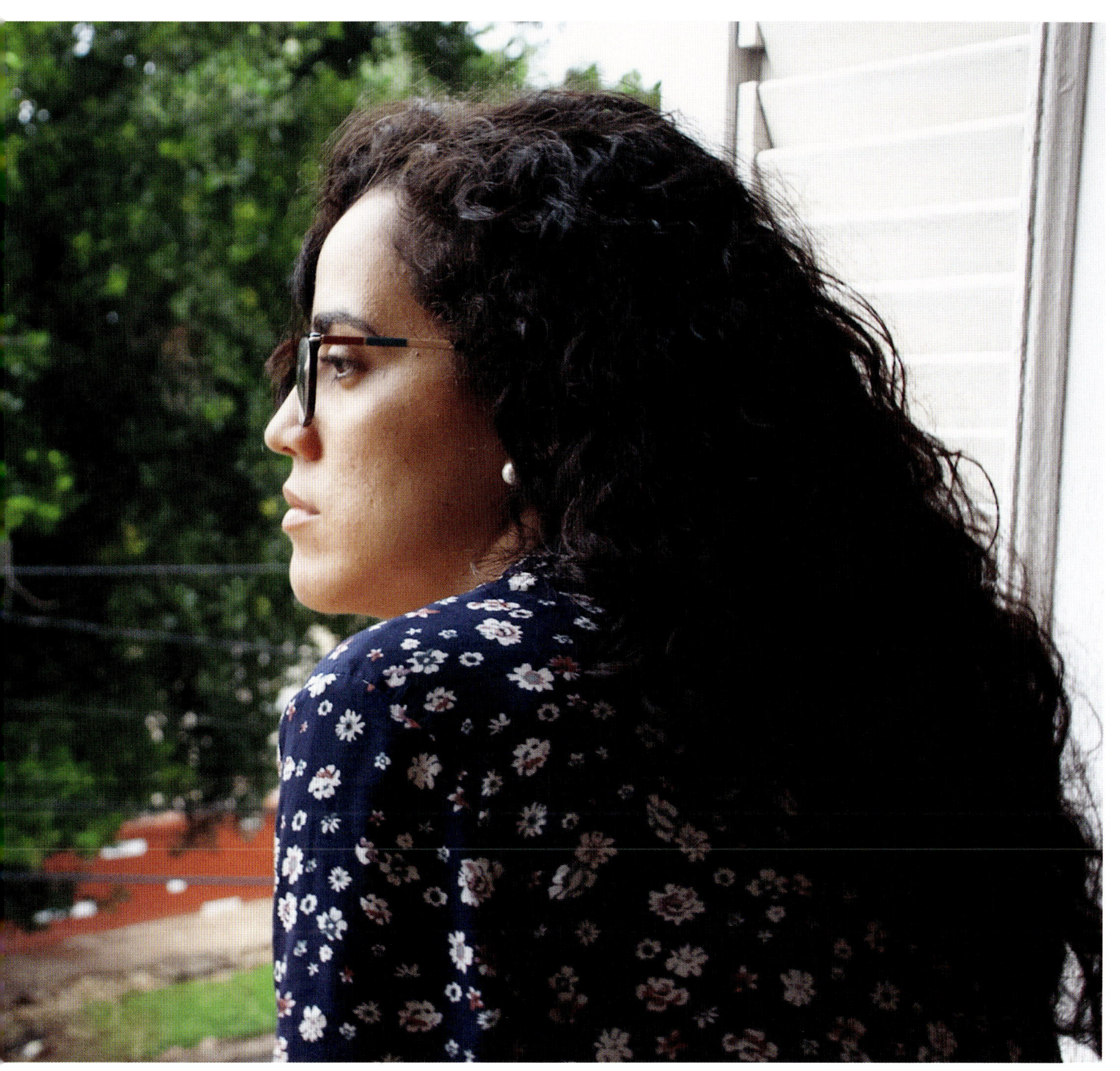

Your Eyes Will Be an Empty Word

2021

This video essay was recorded in the waters surrounding Hart Island, home to the largest mass grave in the United States and the final resting place for New York's unclaimed victims of COVID-19. Fusco created this work just months into a global pandemic that has compelled us to see death and live with the dead in our midst. Lurid tales of corpses hidden in vans, cemeteries without space, families forced to leave their deceased relatives in the streets, and the return of the use of mass graves are reminiscent of earlier centuries when plagues ran rampant. In the video, Fusco circles the island in a small rowboat while a voiceover describes the feeling of survival in the context of the pandemic, as anxieties and protective actions were shared among many across the globe. Commissioned by the Museum of Contemporary Art of Barcelona and the Museum of Modern Art of Medellín, the video includes music by Pauline Kim Harris. Fusco's narration is read by Pamela Sneed.

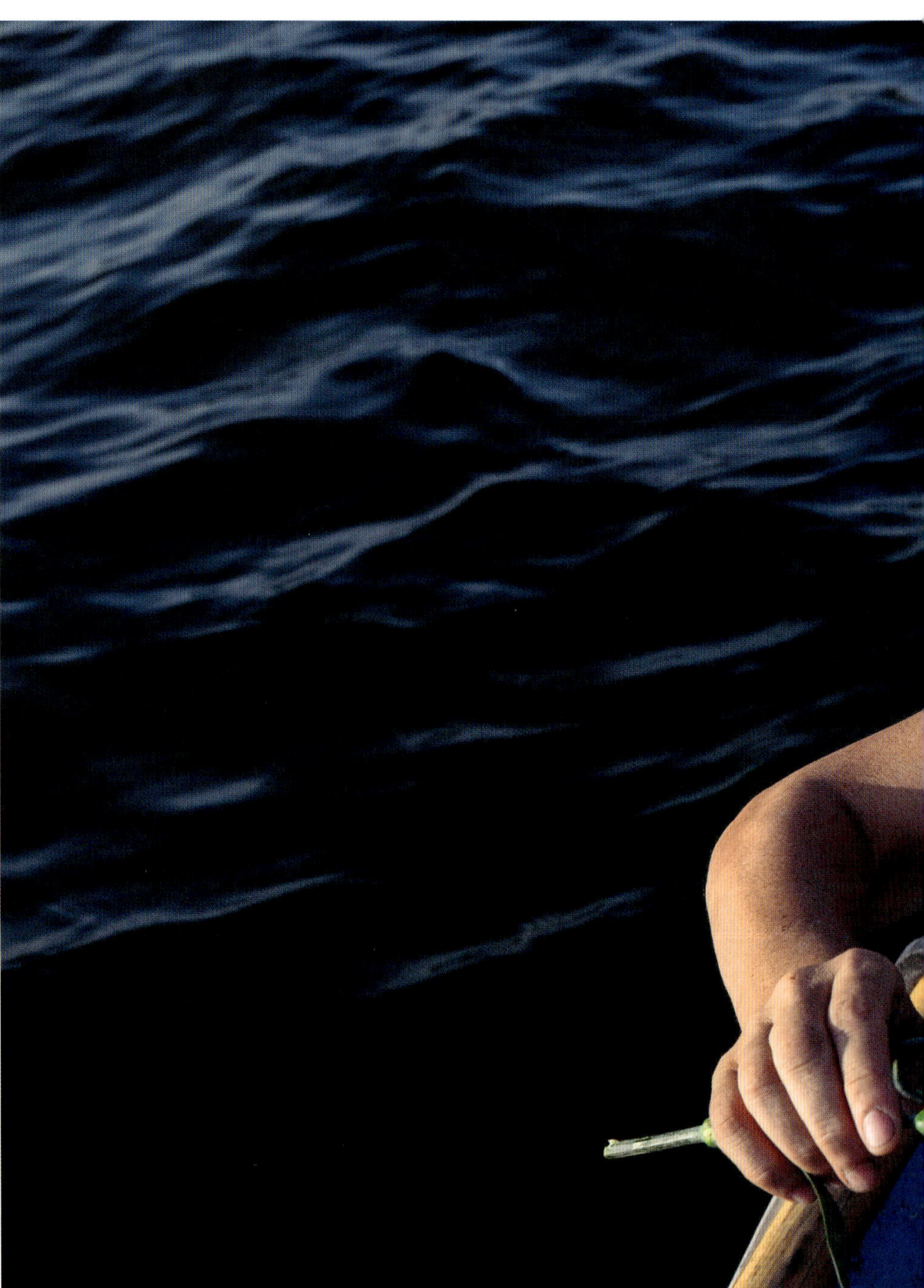

Your Eyes Will Be an Empty Word, 2021, video (also overleaf and pages 192–93)

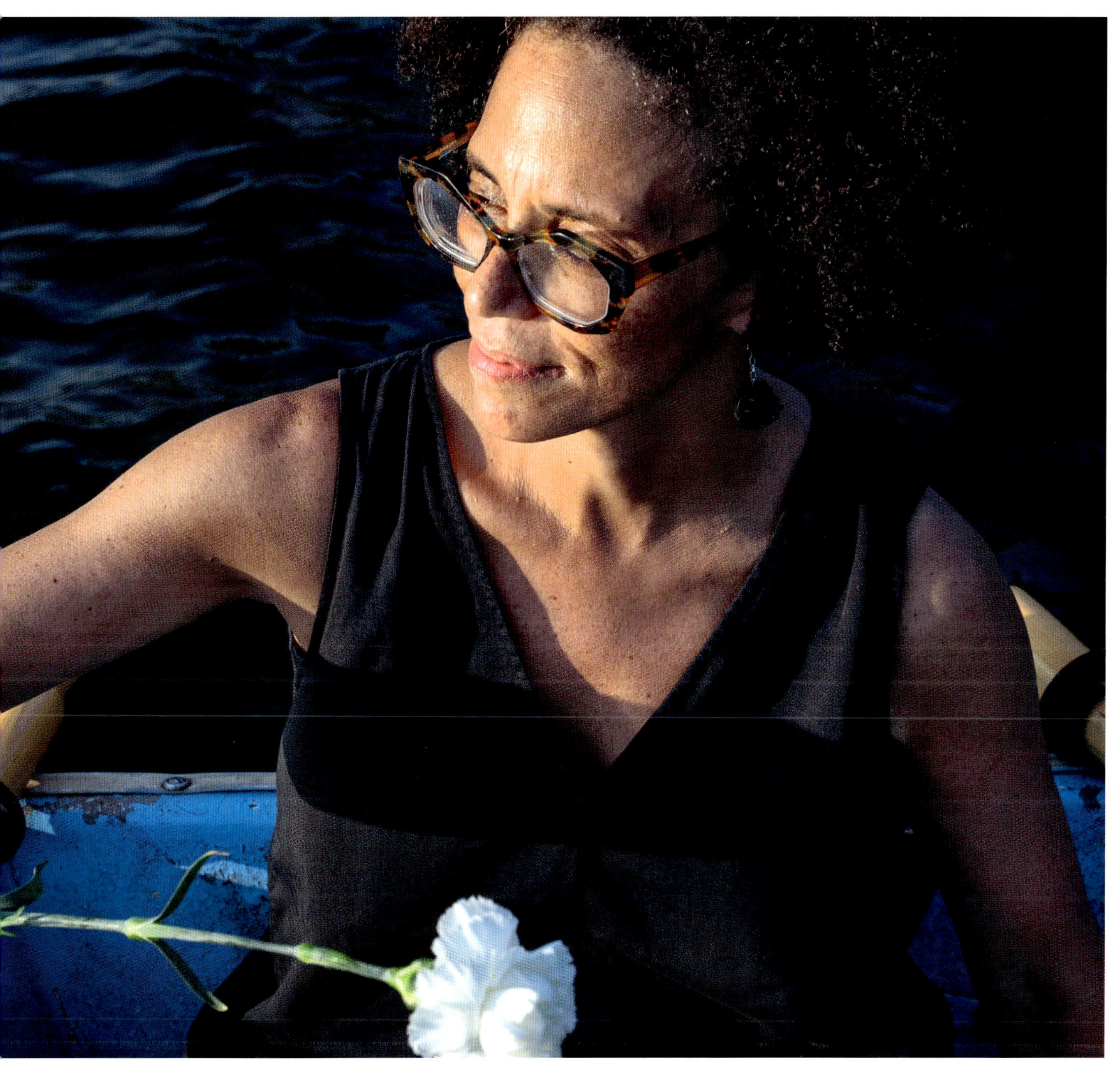

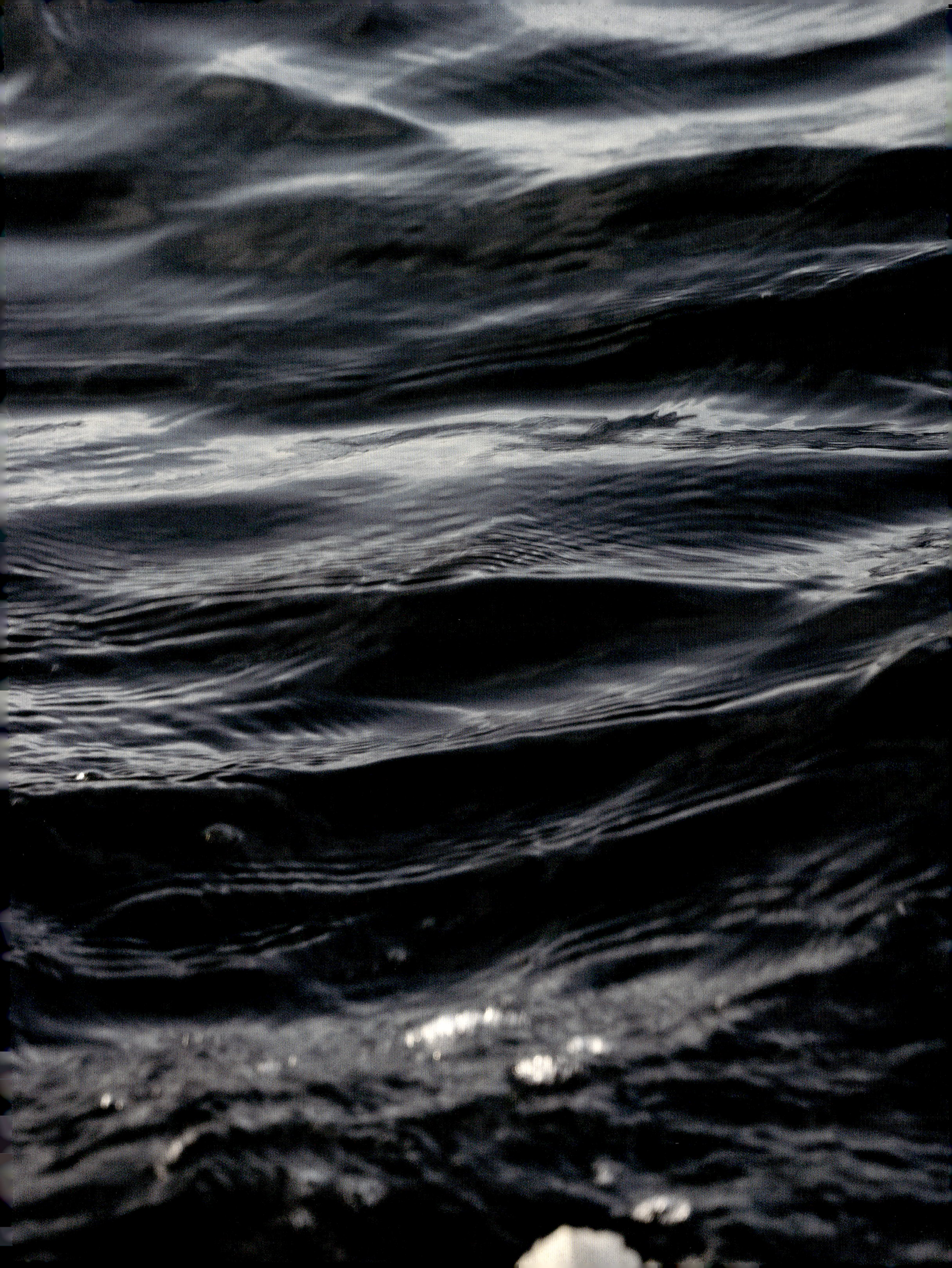

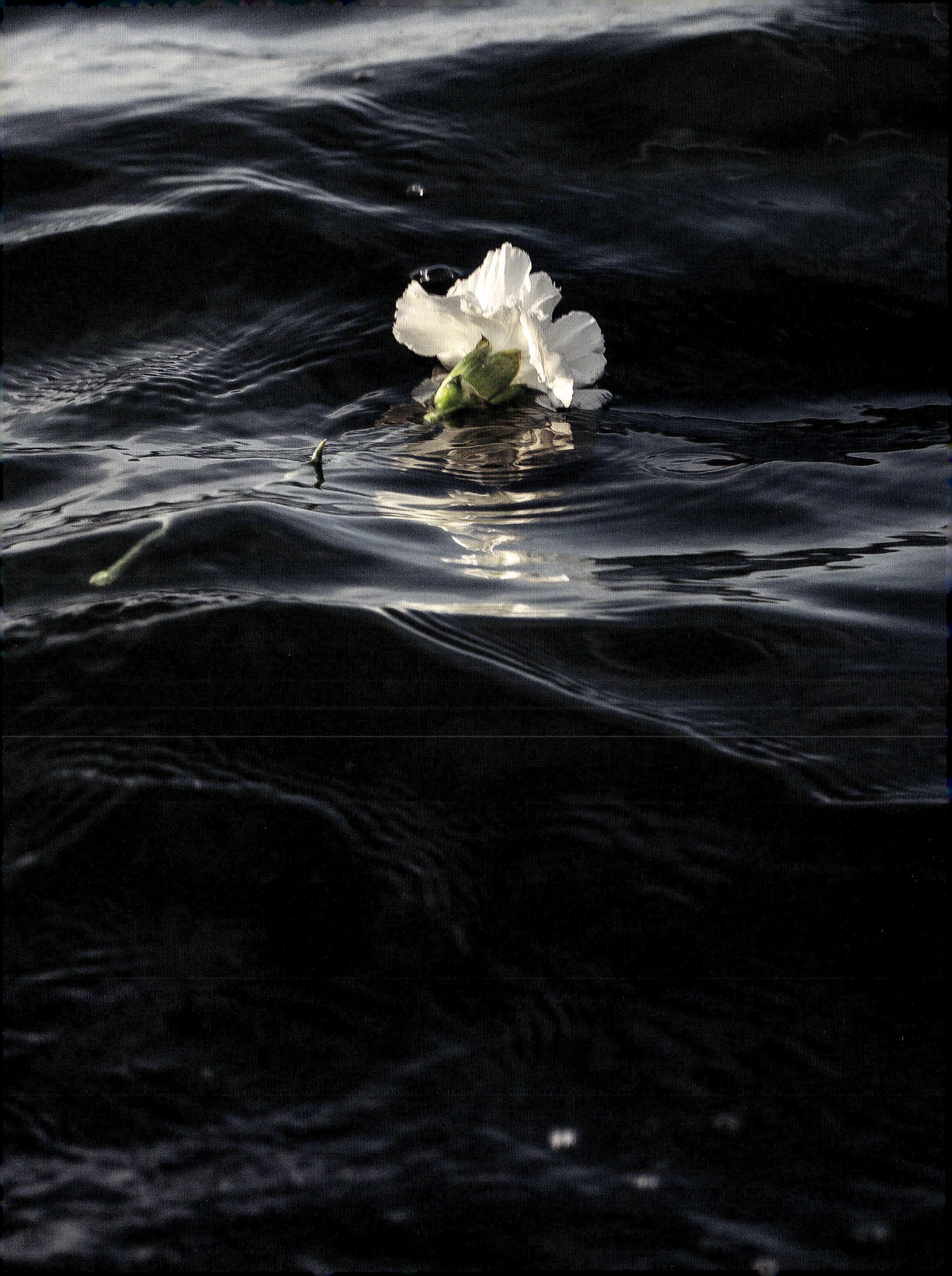

BODY OF WORK 1990–2022

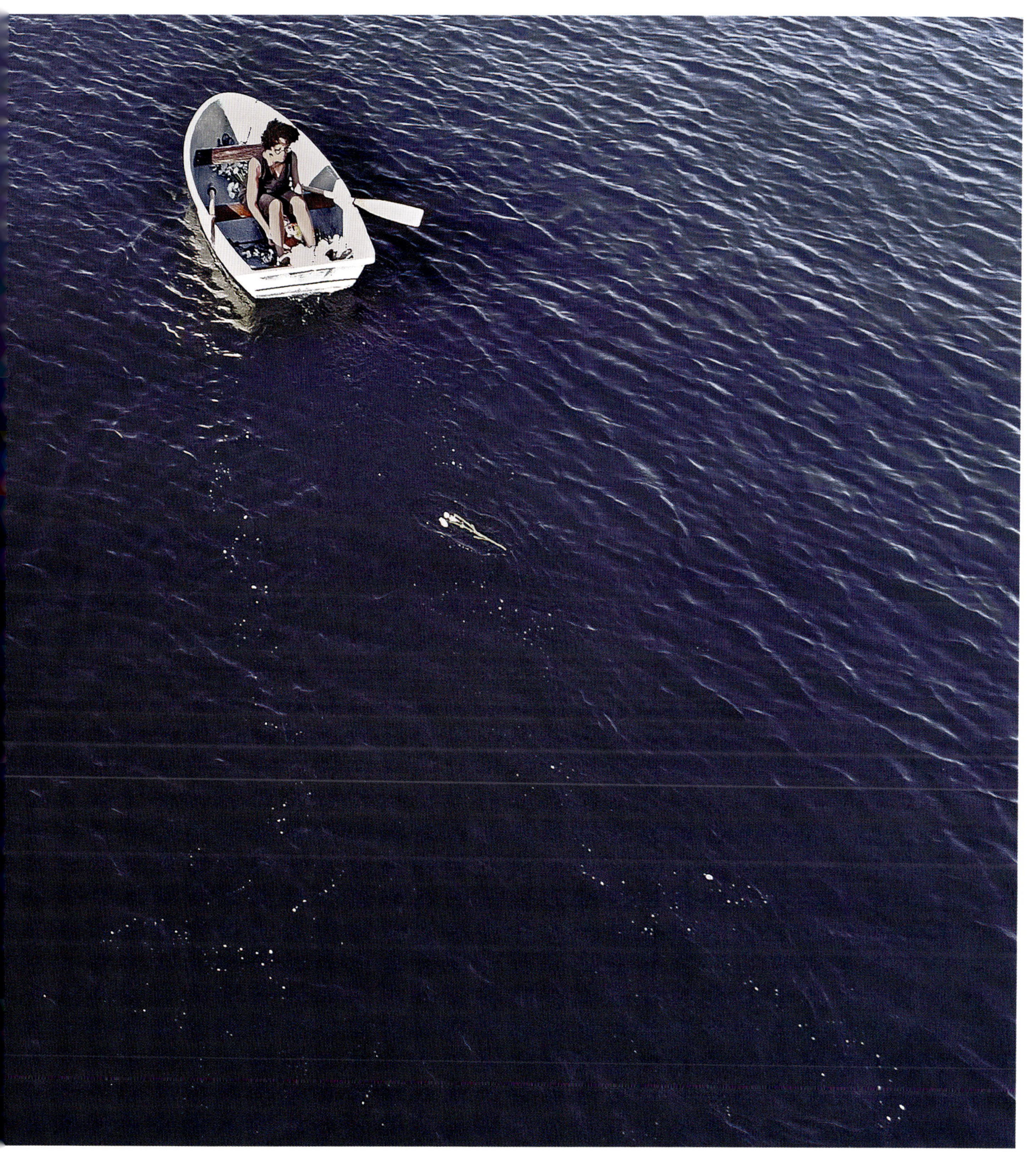

La sombra de Heberto Padilla (Padilla's Shadow)

On April 27, 2021—fifty years after Cuban poet Heberto Padilla's release from prison after thirty-six days—Fusco staged a choral reading of Padilla's legendary confession, streamed via social media throughout the day and night by Pérez Art Museum Miami, Artists at Risk Connection, The Showroom in London, Künstlerhaus Bethanien in Berlin, Franklin Furnace in New York and the Herberger Institute for Design and the Arts in Arizona. To prevent Cuban authorities from attempting to block participation by citizens, Fusco prerecorded all readings, which were transmitted via encrypted messaging. The resulting video commemorates one of the defining moments of the revolution's relationship to freedom of expression The government's treatment of Padilla made its protocol for handling intellectuals and artists visible and has since functioned as a warning to those that seek to challenge the primacy of state authority. While still discussed in the Latin American press, it has been largely forgotten in the United States, even though prominent intellectuals such as Susan Sontag, Jean-Paul Sartre, and Italo Calvino defended Padilla in the 1970s. While many artists know about the event in Cuba today, few have had access to Padilla's words that were uttered on that fateful day. Many of the project's participants told Fusco that they were shocked by the text and reported it had provoked bouts of anxiety, sleeplessness, and nightmares. Padilla's confession is a study in political abjection that is painful to witness and reproduce. But it is necessary, especially now when a new generation of Cuban artists and intellectuals are challenging the state's authority over them. Fifty years after Padilla's *auto-da-fe*, the Cuban government continues to demonize critical voices and characterize intellectuals that challenge the revolution as lackeys of foreign powers.

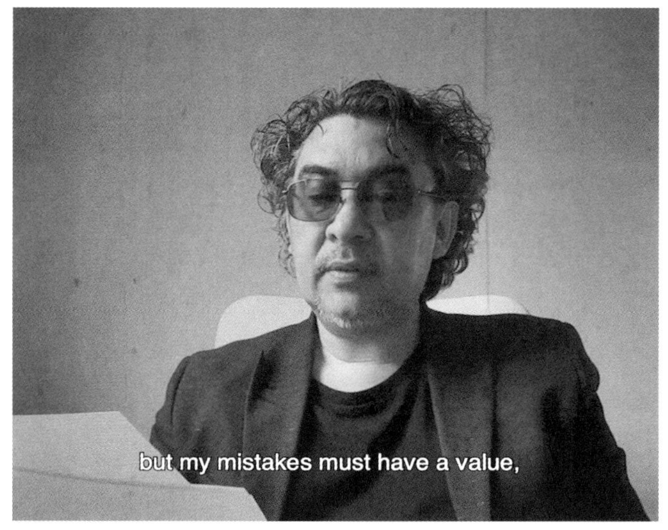

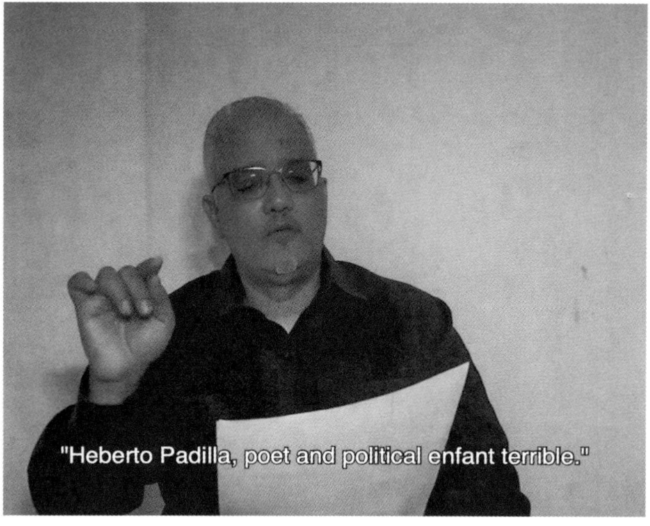

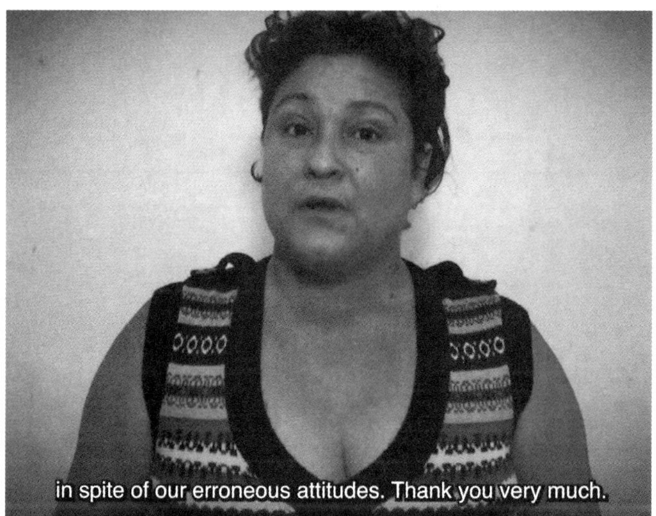

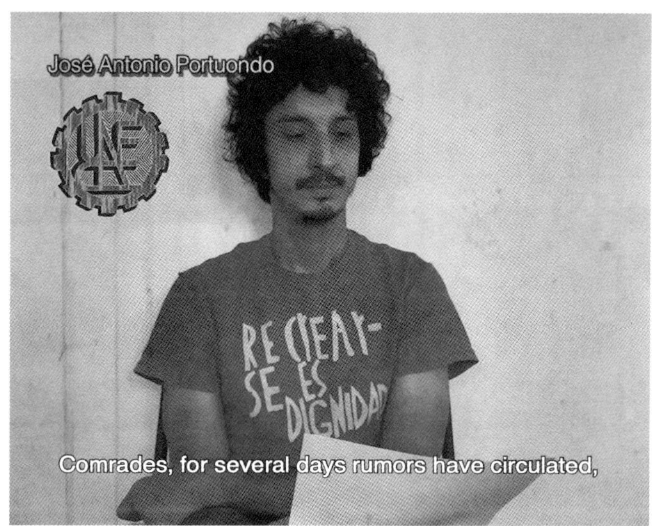

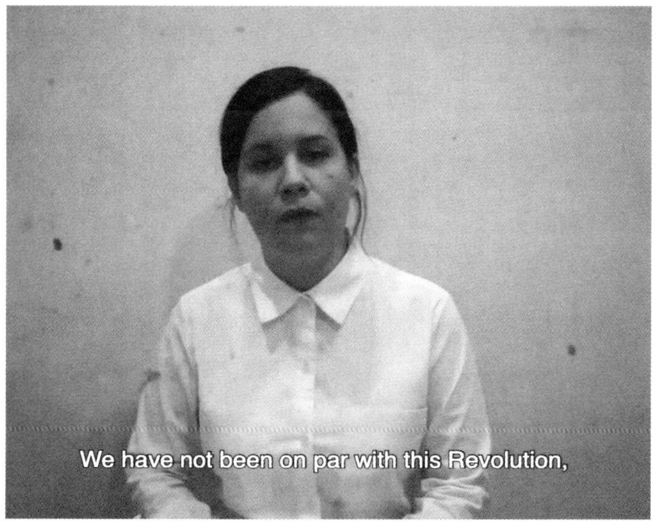

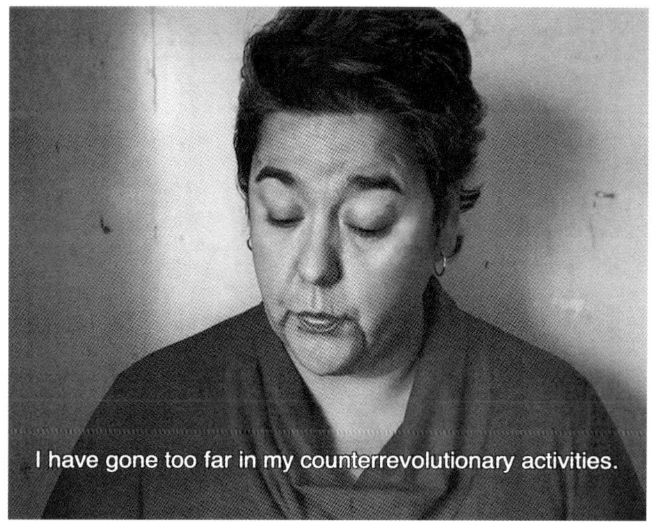

La sombra de Herberto Padilla (Padilla's Shadow), 2021, video

La noche eterna (The Eternal Night)

2022

La noche eterna (*The Eternal Night*) is the story of three young Cuban men who were condemned for their beliefs and their creations. The film is based on the true story of Cuban writer and former political prisoner Néstor Díaz de Villegas, who, in 1974 at age eighteen, was sentenced to five years in prison for writing a poem. Prior to his imprisonment, he had been subjected to systematic censure for his nonconformist attitude, which was deemed "ideologically divergent" by the revolutionary government. The phrase "ideological diversionism" was first introduced as a form of control by Raúl Castro in the early 1970s and aimed to create a legal framework around the criminalization of dissent. It was applied to Cuban citizens who were considered to be overly intellectual, to youths that showed interest in American popular culture and music, to those presumed to be gay or lesbian, and to religious people whose faith prevented them from performing political obedience.

In *La noche eterna*, overlapping stories are shared of a poet who has recently arrived at the prison, a young Evangelical man from the countryside, and an older actor who was accused of trying to assassinate Fidel Castro. The actor introduces the two young men into the social world of the prisoners, showing them how to resist the authorities' attempt to re-educate them, while also convincing the warden to create a cinema inside the prison as a more effective means of teaching inmates about the benefits of socialism.

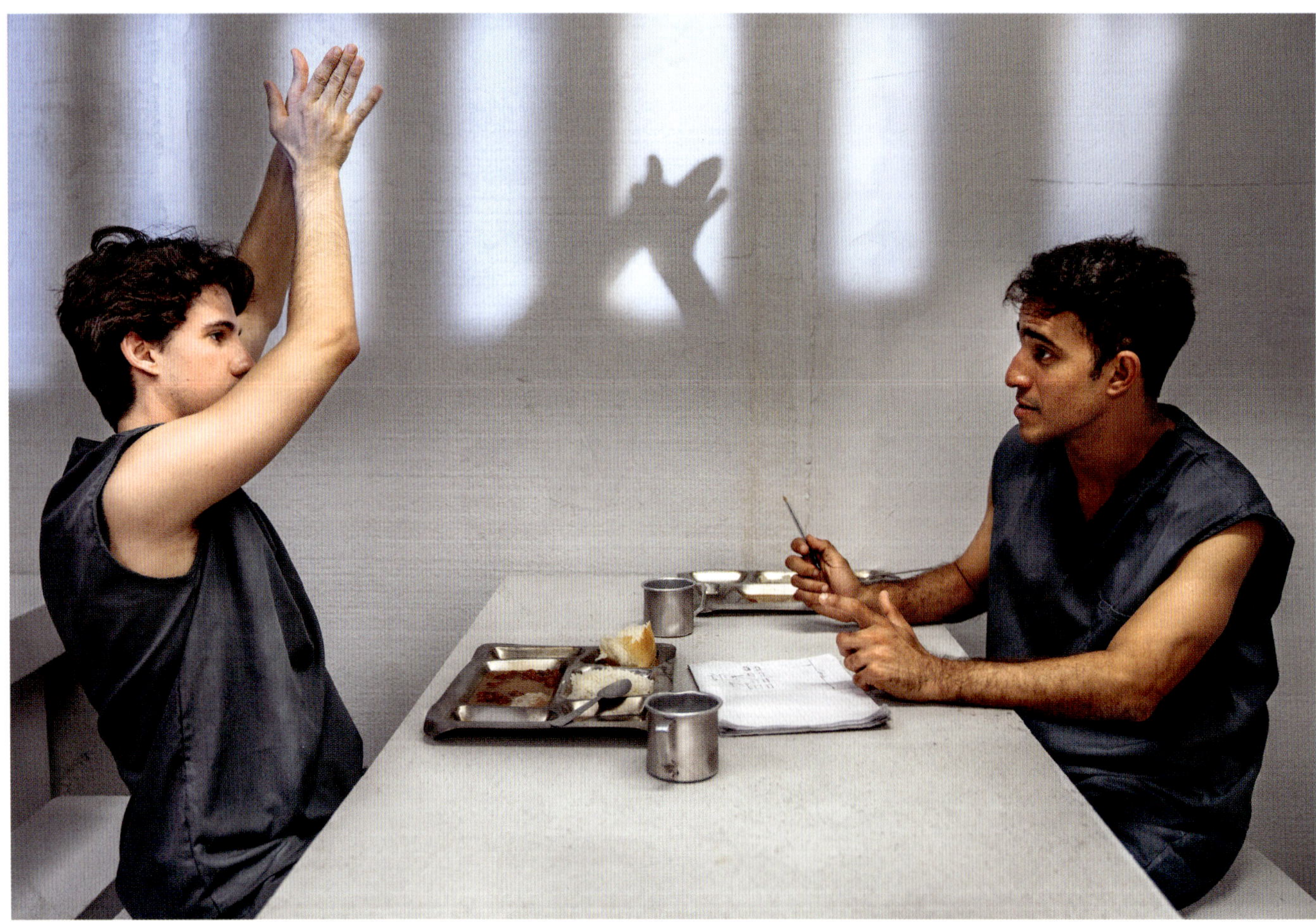

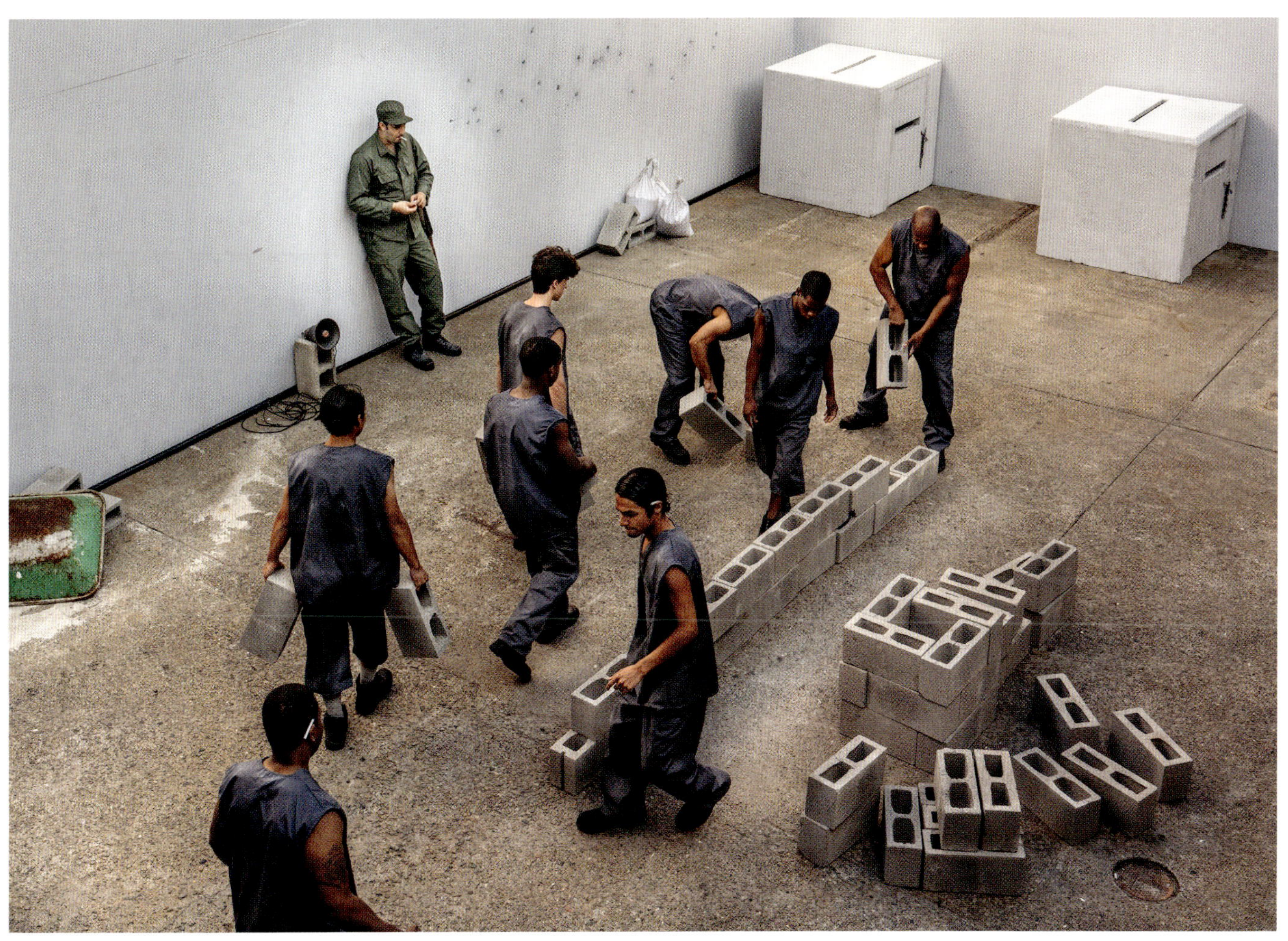

La noche eterna (The Eternal Night), 2022, video (also overleaf and pages 199–201)

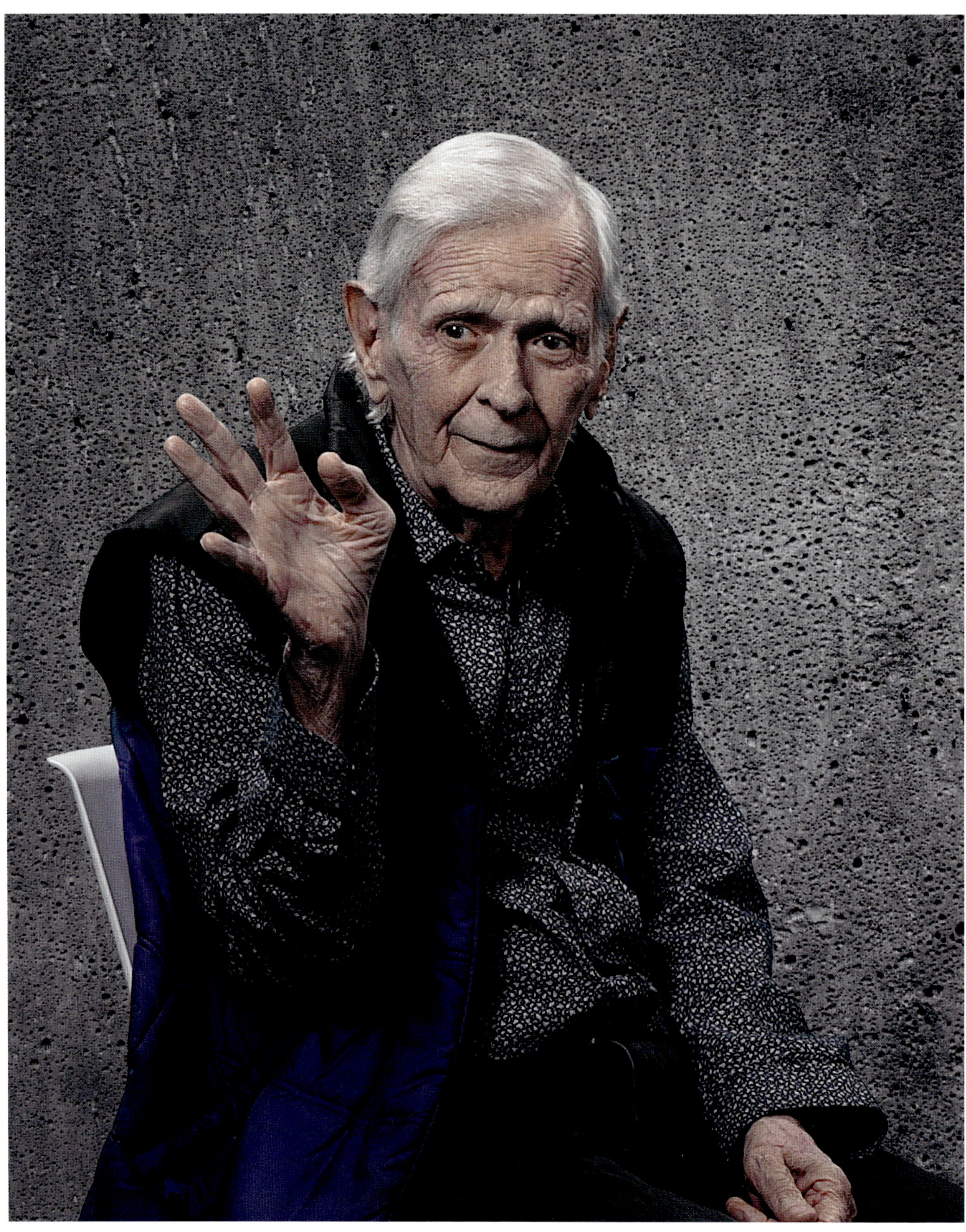

BODY OF WORK 1990–2022

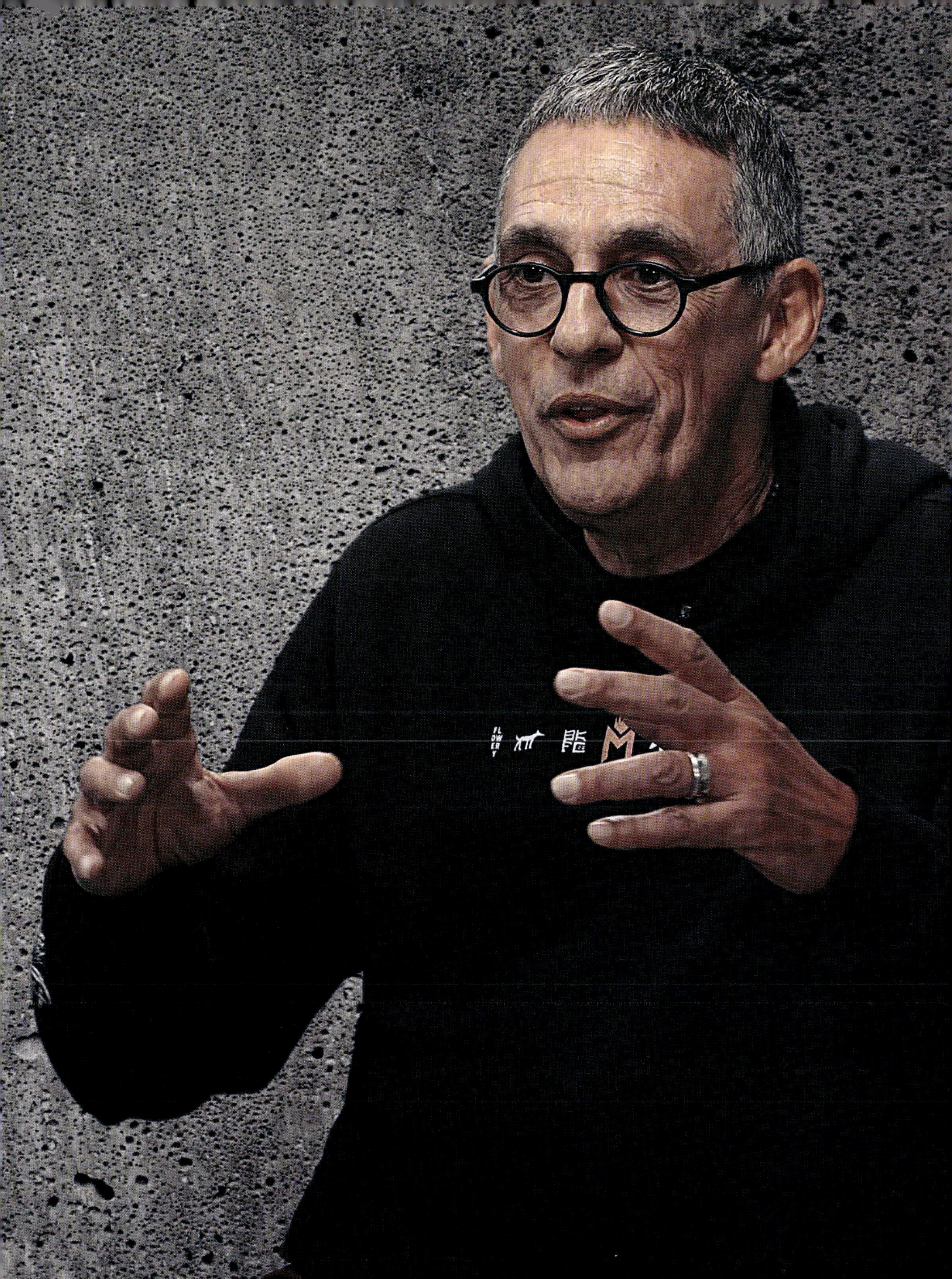

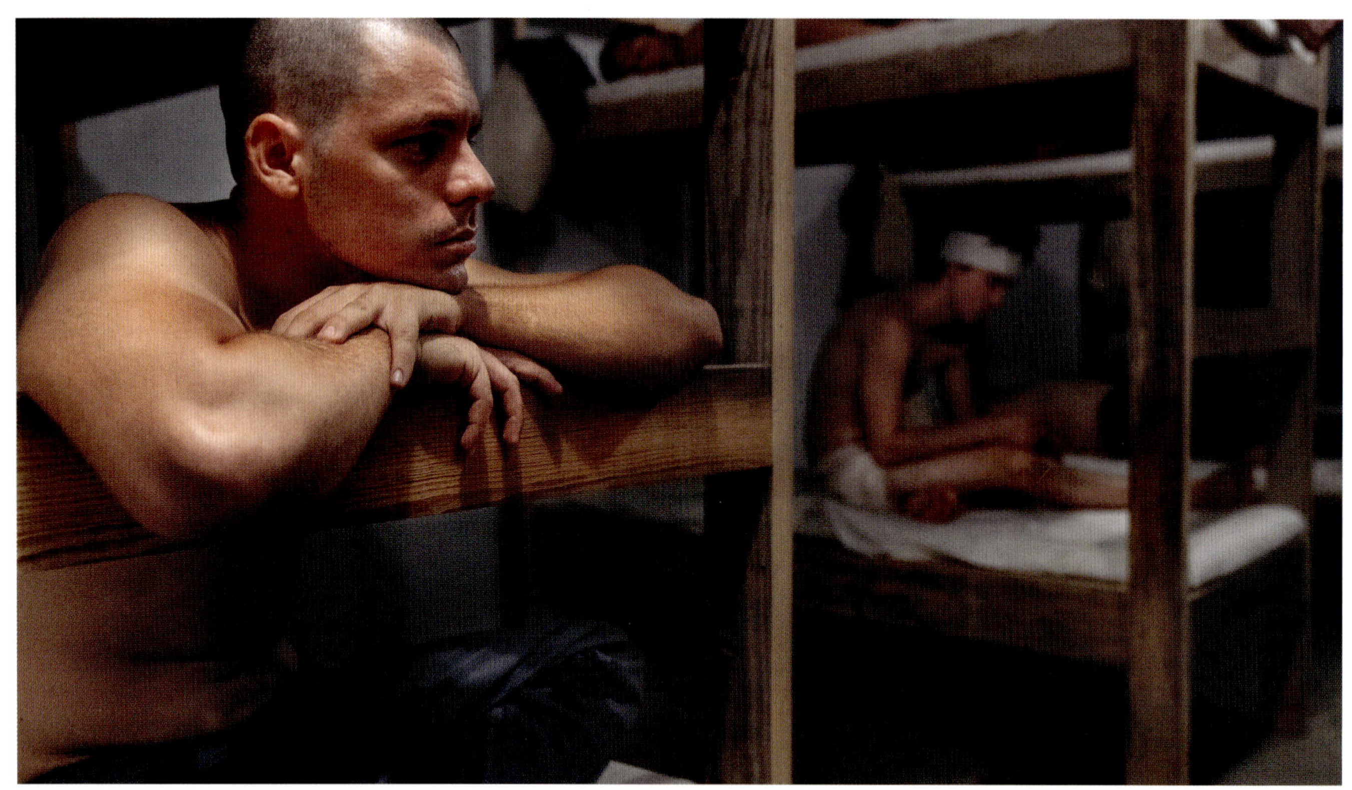

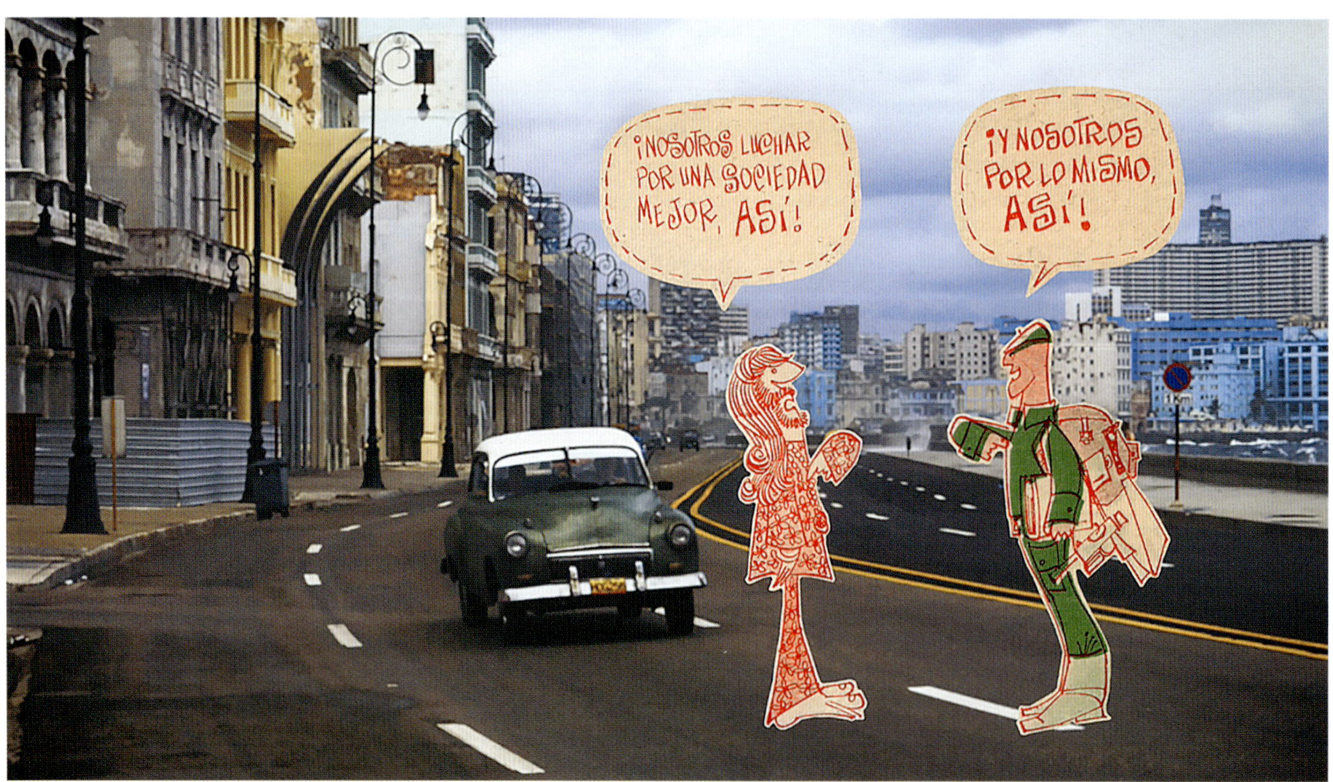

BODY OF WORK 1990–2022

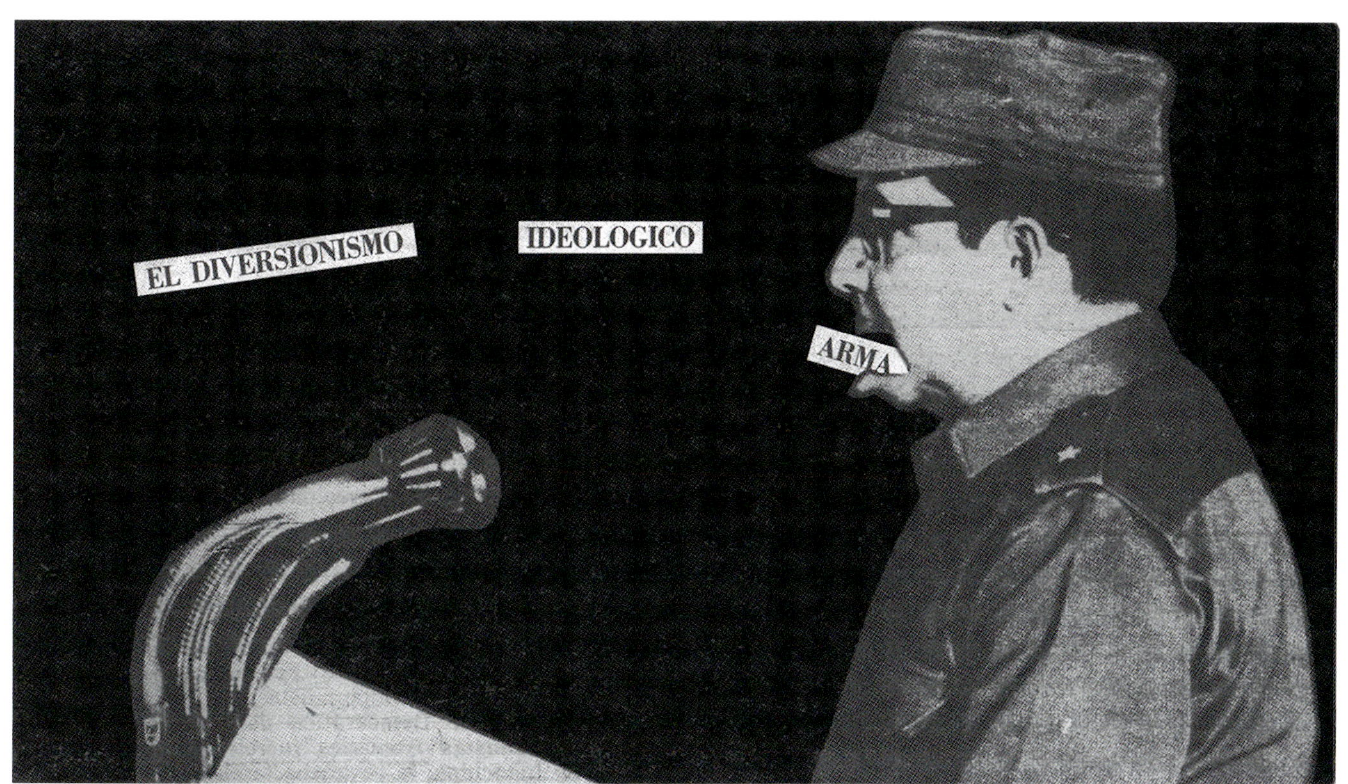

EL DIVERSIONISMO
IDEOLOGICO
ARMA

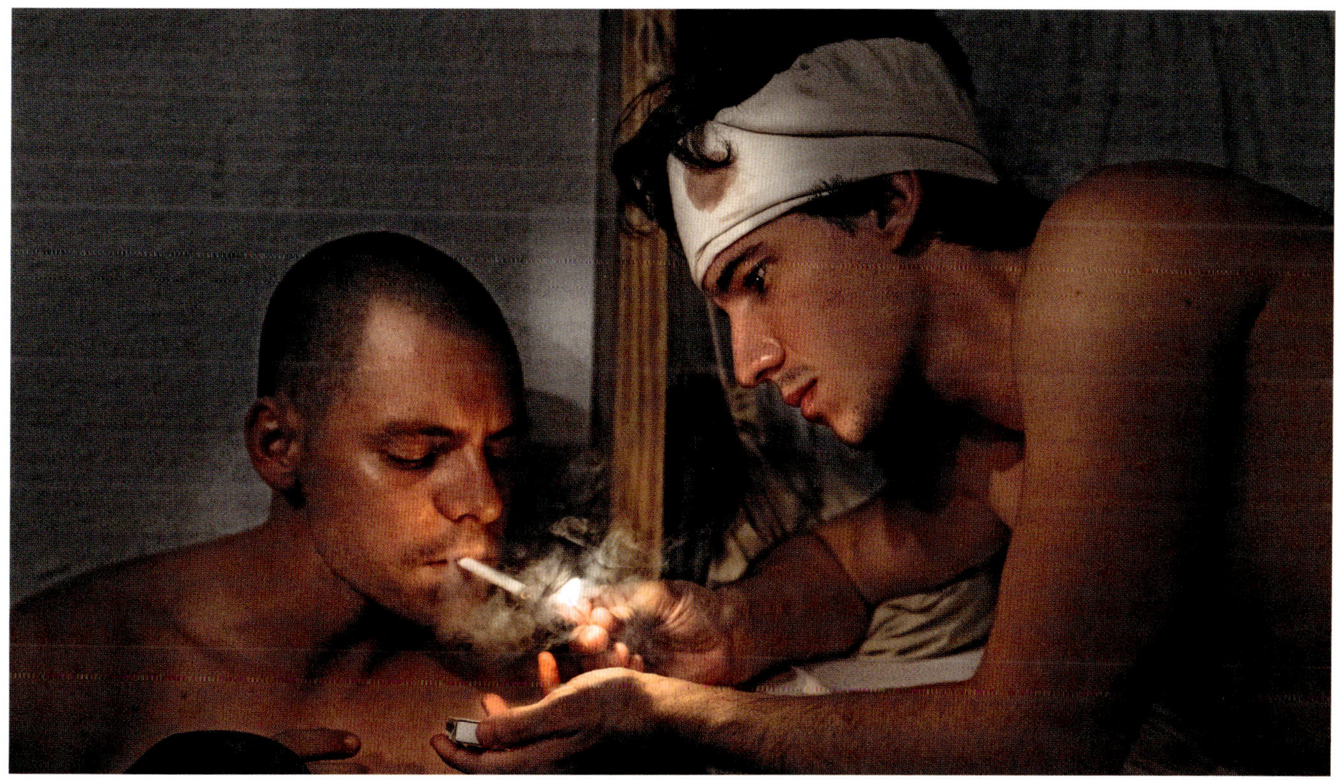

Appendix

CONFIDENCIAL, AUTORES FIRMANTES, 2015
Translations of facsimile documents

DOC 3   CONFIDENTIAL

Comrade Rolando Rodríguez   May 22 1971
General Manager   The Year of Productivity
                                     Dept. of International Relations

Comrade:

Expanding upon our memo from May 19th, we continue with a list of titles of books that we recommend be withdrawn from circulation. We would like to clarify that since there is no complete list of books published by the organization, we cannot be sure yet if our list is exhaustive.

1. Poems for Che
2. New Spanish Poetry
3. The Route of Hernan Cortez – Benítez
4. Limits and Potentialities of the May Movement – ANDRE GORZ
5. The Burning Plain – JUAN RULFO
6. Pedro Páramo
7. Tropisms – N. SARRAUTE
8. A Brief History of the Mexican Revolution – SILVA HERZOG
9. Las Casas and Trujillo – HANS MAGNUS – ENZENBERGER
10. Juan Rulfo – Multiple Evaluations
11. OCTAVIO PAZ
12. CLARIDAD ALEGRIA
13. R. ROSSANDA

Revolutionarily,

Fatherland or Death
We Shall Win!

DOC 4
DGICL – 2901 – (Confidential)

DOCUMENT I

Policy for the CUBAN BOOK INSTITUTE to carry out with regard to those intellectuals (and their works) that have taken a position of open hostility toward the Cuban Revolution due to the Heberto Padilla case

Due to the detention of Heberto Padilla—for frankly counterrevolutionary activities—a group of European and Latin American intellectuals (many of the latter being residents of European capitals), have assumed an attitude of open hostility toward the Cuban Revolution—an attitude that was first shown by the signing of the document that was sent to the Prime Minister of the Revolutionary Government, Commander Fidel Castro; and then by the signing of the second document, also addressed to comrade Fidel, dated after the end of the National Congress of Education and Culture; and the writing of a document sent by Mexican intellectuals, and in various declarations that some of these intellectuals have made to the Mexican press, and other Latin American magazines.

After analyzing the documents we have noted that some of these intellectuals are signatories of the first and second documents sent to our government; signatories as well of the letter from Mexico, and that they have made declarations against our revolution. This is to say, that some of these intellectuals display an open, active and manifest hostility toward our revolution and government. There are others who, after having signed the first documents, did not sign the other two, nor have they made declarations against our revolution. This attitude is to be expected given that they have not publically recognized their having been unjust in their attacks nor have they retracted them.

Confronted with this situation, we are compelled to evaluate the degree of participation of these intellectuals—their degree of involvement is indisputably not the same in all those implicated. For this reason, we think that, if different degrees of participation exist among the said intellectuals, it is necessary to make pertinent distinctions with regard to this case.

There is one person in particular that draws our attention and that is Jesús Silva Herzog, who we think has really been a victim—given his state of decrepitude—of those counterrevolutionary intellectuals who have taken advantage of this situation to obtain a signature of someone like Silva Herzog to appear on their document.

We consider it important to highlight all the counterrevolutionary hate that is hidden in the signatures on the second document sent from Paris to comrade Fidel, in which with incredible virulence, our revolution is attacked, accusing it of using draconian methods to "extract" Heberto Padilla's self-criticism letter. It should be taken into account that already on this date the National Congress of Education and Culture had finished and Fidel spoke at the end; hence the document can be considered as a response to these events.

Looking at the situation in this way we might ask: what should the policy of the Cuban Book Institute be with respect to the attitude of these intellectuals? And what attitude should be taken with regard to their works?

We think that we should outline the actions to be taken in the following terms:
1. There will be no publishing of any works by the signatories of these documents, nor of those who have made declarations against the revolution and the Cuban government.
2. In the case of those authors whose works—of recognized value due to their magnitude and quality—will transcend them and will surely survive them, we should allow history to judge them and determine, on a case by case basis, if they merit being published or not, in the future, based on the criteria that artistic, literary, and scientific creation is part of the patrimony of humanity and not that of its creators.
3. Make an obligatory distinction, give the different levels of engagement, among the many cases and

DOC 7
DGICL – 2901 – (Confidential)

analyze the situation of those who have made declarations in which they recognize how mistaken the positions that they had assumed were or in which they have sent a signal by not signing the aforementioned documents.

4. With regard to export, we should not sell any of the works by these intellectuals outside the country. We should also remove their works from the catalogues we use for export purposes.

5. With regard to national distribution, we should remove titles by these authors from sale if necessary. We consider that this should be done with the works of those who have assumed an openly anti-Cuban attitude. It is possible that <u>many of these titles are already out of stock in bookstores, but if any remain they should be removed</u>.

6. As a means of preserving works that deserve to be saved because of their value, those titles that are withdrawn from sale and reading rooms should be sent to libraries for their conservation and use.

7. With regard to general catalogues from our publishing houses that are in the process of producing books by these intellectuals, that process should be stopped until further notice pending a decision about what other actions to take.

8. Just as we have agreed not to publish, sell abroad or include any works by these intellectuals in our catalogues, we consider that in the future when we are faced with a different situation than the one we currently find ourselves in, we should try to ascertain which authors, and which works of those authors who may have changed their attitude toward our government and our revolution, we might consider publishing, taking into consideration that some of these intellectuals may have been lied to and thereby corralled into signing the documents that attack our revolutionary government and the Cuban Revolution. In short, we should act tomorrow with the same rigor that we employ today to be in tune with reality.

Havana, May 23 1971 – THE YEAR OF PRODUCTIVITY

DOC 8
DGICL – 2901 – (Confidential)

DOCUMENT II

Some considerations with regard to the internal circulation (national distribution) of the titles by the above-mentioned authors

1. Once you are in possession of the list of authors whose book distribution is to be frozen—(paralyzed at this moment). <u>We recommend that they all be concentrated in storage area for their conservation.</u>
2. Once the process now underway of gathering information is complete there should be a meeting of all the <u>Provincial Delegates</u>, in which we can inform them of these problems and we can learn how many copies of these titles exist in different provinces, how many of those are in warehouses and how many have already been distributed. <u>At that meeting we will make clear that we will not start to retrieve materials that have been distributed to reading rooms and libraries</u> and we recommend that each Delegate should <u>slowly remove copies in these venues from circulation.</u>

3. <u>Finally we will propose that a certain quantity of these titles should be sent to certain libraries, in particular the National Library (Havana) and provincial ones, the central libraries of the universities and the schools of the Communist Party, etc.</u>
4. The recently published catalogues from the Art and Literature series that were not distributed before and that are now to be found in the Exhibition Center, the editorial office and the National Warehouse should be concentrated in one single place.

Havana, May 23 1971
THE YEAR OF PRODUCTIVITY

DOC 10
DGICL – 2901 – (Confidential)

DOCUMENT III

Some considerations with regard to the importation of publications by the aforementioned authors

1. We are of the opinion that regardless of whether the positions assumed were of greater or less intensity by a large number of authors, our country should import the titles that have already been published in small amounts. We justify this plan in that:

1.1 We consider all the works of these authors as information; we are not importing large quantities of these works.

1.2 We need to be able to continue to evaluate the works to determine their profundity and which works will survive their authors.

1.3 Commercial intelligence regarding the foreign publishers that issue them. Without a doubt our organization manages international commerce of publications and consequently we need to arrive at opinions regarding our relations with those publishers.

1.4 Maintain an intelligent position with foreign observers who might decide to completely close down.

DOC 11
DGICL – 2901 – (Confidential)

Up to now our country has made key large-scale purchases of technical books, and so even a discreet purchase would not be in contradiction with the position taken up to now.

2. We consider it important that once the above-mentioned aspect is accepted— and before that it is essential that some opinions be fixed.
3. In our opinion, we should make it a rule that none of our country's organizations receive publications by these authors. However, we propose that this measure acquire an internal character, in other words, remaining organizations—those already included, and any that could be added—would not receive any information [about the censorship of the books], but we would proceed to eliminate the imports of these books, and say in the end that the materials not provided (together with all the other titles that we cannot generally provide) have been canceled.

We propose that these organizations be permitted to import discreet quantities of the titles:
Cuban Book Institute (Editorial Series and Leadership that would normally receive the books)
WITH
MINFAR (Ministry of the Armed Forces) – Political Leadership
MININT (Ministry of the Interior) – Political Leadership
MINREX (Ministry of Foreign Relations) – Corresponding Leadership

Universities
Ministry of Education – Political Leadership
National Council of Culture – Leadership and National Library
I.C.R. (Cuban Radio Institute)
I.C.A.I.C. (Cuban Film Institute)
I.C.A.P. (Cuban Institute for Friendship Among Peoples)
Casa de las Américas

Havana, May 23 1971
THE YEAR OF PRODUCTIVITY

DOC 13
DGICL – 2901 – (Confidential)

DOCUMENT IV

Some considerations regarding the Export of publications by the authors referred to

1. We consider that, as a matter of principle, all the titles by the authors who, with greater or lesser intensity, have adopted an anti-Cuban position, SHOULD BE EXCLUDED FROM THE EXPORTABLE COLLECTION. The quantities in existence should be transferred to the National Distribution Group to be stored in same warehouse that houses books in circulation.

2. In our catalogues in progress and the ones we will make in time we should not make any reference to these authors. Cases of rectification should first of all effect our internal circulation, but in the last instance, this is the condition for books to return to being exportable stock from Cuba.

3. In the cases of authors who conversely have maintained a position of revolutionary alignment, their books should be showcased in our flyers and published for export.

Havana, May 23 1971
THE YEAR OF PRODUCTIVITY

DOC 14   June 2 1971
Comrade Miguel Rodríguez   Office of General Management
Comrade René Roca
Comrade Eduardo Neira

DGICL — 2901

CONFIDENTIAL

In agreement with what was proposed in our last note I insist that the matter
involving the signatories to the letters and the authors of declarations made abroad
in relation to the Heberto Padilla case be handled with the utmost discretion.

In the case of those who only signed the first letter and afterward have not made
any other statement we should proceed with great caution in our actions, only
freezing their works or those related to them without assuming an attitude that
could seem definitive with respect to them.

Revolutionarily,

Rolando Rodríguez
General Manager

Havana, June 15, 1971
THE YEAR OF PRODUCTIVITY

TO: Rolando Rodríguez
FROM: Luis García Peraza
SUBJECT: Book by Charles Bettelheim, Socioeconomic Frameworks and the
Organization of Social Planning.

REF: ECS-384

In the Leadership Council meeting of this Publishing House held yesterday,
we analyzed the situation related to the reference book that is among the titles
subject to our plan 71, in response to a request from the Economic Institute at
the University of Havana. This request involves 100 copies for students, 200 for
professors and 50 for libraries, with a total of 350 copies.

After reading an article by Ch. Bettelheim attacking our revolution, that was
published in the French newspaper Le Monde on May 12, we have decided—applying
the agreements that emerged from the Congress on Education and Culture that
were expounded by our Prime Minister Fidel Castro—not to publish that book
and to communicate our decision to the petitioners and the arguments on which
our decision is based.

We believe that the need for the title that the petition described can be sufficiently
covered by the acquisition of 100 copies that should be placed in the library of the
Institute.

 If you are in agreement with this suggestion, please ask that your office make the
necessary request to the comrades in the department of imports in order to carry
out this purchase.

On our part we are conveying to Production to cancel this title and are offering a
political explanation for this decision.

Since we spoke in person about this yesterday, I ask that you please keep me abreast
of any changes or decisions made with respect to this matter.

Without more, revolutionarily yours,
Luis García Peraza

c/C: Archive, Consecutive
LGP/meg.

DOC 16
Havana, June 16 1971
THE YEAR OF PRODUCTIVITY

DGICL: 2995 (CONFIDENTIAL)

Comrade Miguel Rodriguez Varela
Editor in Chief

Comrade René Roca Muchulí
Director Group III

Comrade Eduardo Neira García
International Relations

Due to the situation that has developed in the last few weeks, we have made a final decision with respect to those who have assumed positions relating to the so-called Padilla case, which is to say those who say that the self-criticism was made under pressure or as a result of torture.

In this case there are those signatories of the second letter and those that, in statements and declarations, in cables and publications, have insinuated as much. Among them are Gabriel García Márquez and others who for greater accuracy, I include in an attached list.

The works of these same people, in accordance with the approach set out in the documents produced by this office, should be suppressed in the following manner:

a) All future publication possibilities.
b) The lists that appear in books that have been published in this country.
c) All catalogues
d) Catalogues of titles for export
e) Export
f) The circulation of their works, when they are found to be in reading rooms, or in bookstores.
g) The mention of these people in our publications, bulletins, etc.
h) References to these people, whatever form it might take, other than to make explicit that they are enemies of the revolution and definitely counterrevolutionary.

i) Restriction on import of works by these same writers.
j) Absolute freeze of any and all warehouse stock.

Lastly, these measures should be adequate with respect to our foreign distributors and should be known in our provinces, while we insist on a high level of discretion in their application.

Proceed with communicating the measures taken to fulfill these provisions and the number of pertinent works that are currently in stock.

Revolutionarily,

Rolando Rodríguez
General Manager

DOC 18

To: Comrade René Roca Muchulí   June 22 1971
Director of Group III   Headquarters

DGIVL: 3048
CONFIDENTIAL

Comrade:

To continue, I list the following titles:

1) 6 Poets, Casa, 1970 – A poem by Guillermo Rodríguez Rivera is in it.

2) The Condemned of the County – Norberto Fuentes, 1968 Prize Collection.

3) Eduardo Heras León – Steps on the Grass – Honorable Mention 1970, Casa de las Americas; from the same author, The War Had Six Names, David Prize, 1968, UNEAC.

4) Nicanor Parra – Poems – Latin American Literature Collection, Casa de las Americas.

It is also suggested that the works of José Lorenzo Fuentes should be withdrawn: (both are UNEAC titles)

– After the Seagull
– January Wind

These titles should be removed from our catalogues and also from international circulation; it goes without saying that they should be taken out of national circulation as well. You should use the same measure that we are using for other situations, but those efforts should be separated from these, since they are not related to the same case.

Revolutionarily,

Rolando Rodríguez
General Manager

c.c. Comrade Miguel Rodríguez
Editor in Chief

Comrade Eduardo Neira
International Relations

DOC 19

Havana, July 17 1971
THE YEAR OF PRODUCTIVITY

TO: Comrade Rolando Rodríguez
General Manager

FROM: Comrade Alcibíades Hidalgo
International Relations

C o m r a d e:

I inform you that, while I was reviewing the titles published by the Casa de las Américas, I detected a prologue by Calvert Casey in the edition of "The Whirlwind" by José Eustasio Rivera that is in the Latin American Literature Collection.

Revolutionary greetings F
ATHERLAND OR DEATH
WE SHALL WIN!

a.g.

THIS IS A COPY OF THE ORIGINAL

DOC 20

There are other national authors such as:
Padilla – Arrufat – César López – Yanes – Belkys Cuza – Buzzi – Reinaldo
Arenas – Nogueras – Casaus or Pablo Armando Fernandez.

As examples, whose ideological attitude is known, but we consider that it would
not be tactical to withdraw their books since we do not yet have precise analysis of
those particular cases and the national policies with respect to them.

With regard to the foreign authors listed at the beginning here, although we believe
that they did not deserve to be circulated in Cuba because of the attitude they have
assumed, they should be carefully studied and it is urgent that the decision to
withdraw them and of the method to be used be made, as it is probable that there
will be leaks and this will have serious repercussions because of the quantity and
the reach of the titles in question.

Revolutionarily,

FATHERLAND OR DEATH
WE SHALL WIN!

Exhibition and Performance History

Coco Fusco

Born 1960, New York,
New York, USA

Education

BA, Literature and Society/Semiotics
(double major), Brown University,
Providence, Rhode Island (1982)

MA, Modern Thought and
Literature, Stanford University,
Stanford, California (1985)

PhD, Art and Visual Culture,
Middlesex University, London,
England (2007)

Fusco is Professor of Art at the
Cooper Union School for the
Advancement of Science and Art,
New York, New York

Selected Exhibition and Video Exhibition History

Individual Exhibitions

2023
*Coco Fusco: Tomorrow I Will Become
an Island*, KW Institute for
Contemporary Art, Berlin, Germany

2019
*Coco Fusco: Swimming on Dry Land/
Nadar en seco*, Flaten Art Museum,
St. Olaf College, Northfield,
Minnesota

2018
Coco Fusco: Twilight, John and
Mable Ringling Museum of Art,
Sarasota, Florida

2016
Coco Fusco, Alexander Gray
Associates, New York, New York

2015
*Coco Fusco: And the Sea Will Talk
to You*, Cecilia Brunson Projects,
London, England

2012
Coco Fusco, Alexander Gray
Associates, New York, New York

2008
Coco Fusco: Buried Pig with Moros,
The Project Gallery, New York,
New York

2006
Coco Fusco: Operation Atropos,
MC Projects, Los Angeles, California

2005
*Coco Fusco, Associação Videobrasil
2005, Festival of Electronic Art and
Performance*, São Paulo, Brazil

2004
Coco Fusco: a/k/a Mrs. George Gilbert,
The Project Gallery, New York,
New York

1993
The Year of the White Bear, in
collaboration with Guillermo
Gómez-Peña, Mexican Fine Arts
Center Museum, Chicago, Illinois;
Otis Gallery, Otis College of Art and
Design, Los Angeles, California

1992
The Year of the White Bear, in
collaboration with Guillermo
Gómez-Peña, Walker Art Center,
Minneapolis, Minnesota

Group Exhibitions

2023
*Sharjah Biennial 15: Thinking
Historically in the Present*, Sharjah,
United Arab Emirates

2022
*2022 Whitney Biennial: Quiet as It's
Kept*, Whitney Museum of American
Art, New York, New York

*María Teresa Hincapié. Si este fuera
un principio de infinito*, Museo
de Arte Moderno de Medellín,
Medellín, Colombia; Museu d'Art
Contemporani de Barcelona
(MACBA), Barcelona, Spain

2021
Une exposition mise en scène,
La Ferme du Buisson, France

2020
Global(e) Resistance, Centre
Pompidou, Paris, France

Construção, Mendes Wood DM,
São Paulo, Brazil

From My Window/From Your Window,
online exhibition organized by
e-flux and International Short Film
Festival Oberhausen, Germany

2019
A Confrontation of Ideals,
The 2nd Anren Biennale,
Anren, Sichuan, China

The Tin Man of the Twenty-first Century
presented at Art Basel Unlimited,
Basel, Switzerland

*Building a Feminist Archive: Cuban
Women Photographers in the US*,
Bailey Contemporary Arts,
Pompano Beach, Florida

*Culture and the People: El Museo del
Barrio, 1969–2019*, El Museo del
Barrio, New York, New York

2018
*Walls Turned Sideways: Artists
Confronting the Justice System*,
Contemporary Arts Museum,
Houston, Texas

*Aplicación Murillo: Materialismo,
charitas y populismo*, Centro
de Iniciativas Culturales de la
Universidad de Sevilla, Seville, Spain

Marx@200, SPACE, Pittsburgh,
Pennsylvania

2017
Truth: 24 frames per second, Dallas
Museum of Art, Dallas, Texas

Age of Terror: Art since 9/11, Imperial
War Museum, London, England

*Orlando Museum of Art Florida Prize in
Contemporary Art*, Orlando Museum
of Art, Orlando, Florida

*After the Fact. Propaganda in
the 21st Century*, Lenbachhaus,
Munich, Germany

2016
*Strange Oscillations and Vibrations
of Sympathy*, University Galleries
of Illinois State University,
Normal, Illinois

*Implied Interaction: The Role of
Participant, Artist, and Viewer*,
Miami Dade College, Miami, Florida

The Natural Order of Things, Museo
Jumex, Mexico City, Mexico

*An Island Apart: Cuban Artists
in Exile*, Otterbein University,
Westerville, Ohio

2015
Agitprop!, Elizabeth A. Sackler Center
for Feminist Art, Brooklyn Museum,
New York, New York

Telling Time, 10th Bamako
Encounters, African Biennale of
Photography, Bamako, Mali

Now? NOW!, Biennial of the
Americas, Museum of Contemporary
Art, Denver, Colorado

*A Prologue to the Past and Present
State of Things*, Delfina Foundation,
London, England

*Public Works: Artists' Interventions
1970s–Now*, Mills College Art
Museum, Oakland, California;
Newcomb Art Museum, Tulane
University, New Orleans, Louisiana

*56th Venice Biennial: All the World's
Futures*, Venice, Italy

A Story Within a Story,
Göteborg International
Biennial for Contemporary Art,
Göteborg, Sweden

The Dark Side of the Party, Music
Festival SOS 4.8, Murcia, Spain

Ape Culture, Haus der Kulturen
der Welt, Berlin, Germany

2014
*New Territories: Laboratories for
Design, Craft and Art in Latin America*,
Museum of Arts and Design,
New York, New York; Albuquerque
Museum of Art, Albuquerque,
New Mexico

*Une Histoire, Art, Architecture et Design,
Des Années 80 à Aujourd'hui*, Centre
Pompidou, Paris, France

Unerasable Memories, Serviço Social do
Comércio Pompeia, São Paulo, Brazil

CINTAS Fellowship Finalist Exhibition,
Miami Dade College Museum of Art
and Design, Miami, Florida

Crítica de la razón migrante, La Casa
Encendida, Madrid, Spain

Multitude, Serviço Social do Comércio
Pompeia, São Paulo, Brazil

2013
Foreign & Familiar, Galerie im
Taxispalais, Innsbruck, Austria

Pulp, Beta Pictoris,
Birmingham, Alabama

A Sense of Place, Wellin Museum
of Art, Hamilton College, Clinton,
New York

*NYC 1993: Experimental Jet Set,
Trash and No Star*, New Museum,
New York, New York

2012
*Radical Presence: Black Performance in
Contemporary Art*, Contemporary Arts
Museum Houston, Houston, Texas;
The Studio Museum in Harlem, New
York, and the Grey Art Gallery at
New York University; Walker Art
Center, Minneapolis, Minnesota;
Yerba Buena Center for the Arts,
San Francisco, California

Caribbean Crossroads of the World,
organized by El Museo del Barrio,
Queens Museum of Art, Queens,
New York and The Studio Museum in
Harlem, New York, New York

Indomitable Women, Museo Nacional
Centro de Arte Reina Sofía and
Cineteca Matadero, Madrid, Spain

*Solidarity: A Memory of Art and Social
Change*, A+D Gallery, Columbia
College, Chicago, Illinois

*Surveillance Aesthetics in Latin America:
Work in Progress*, online exhibition

2011
*Ensaios de Geopoética, 8th Bienal do
Mercosul*, Porto Alegre, Brazil

2010
*AFRO MODERN: Journeys Through
the Black Atlantic*, Tate Liverpool,
United Kingdom; Centro Galego de
Arte Contemporanea, Santiago
de Compostela, Spain

*C.O.N.T.R.A.V.I.O.L.E.N.C.I.A.S,
Artistic practices against the aggression
to women*, KM Kulturunea,
San Sebastian, Spain

*Stories in Movement > Video .
Film . Animation . Sound*, Museo
Provincial de Bellas Artes Ramón
Gómez Cornet, Santiago del
Estero, Argentina

Self as Disappearance, Centre d'Art
Contemporain la Synagogue de
Delme, Delme, France

2009
Status Report, BRIC Rotunda Gallery,
New York, New York

Incheon Women Artist's Biennale,
Incheon, South Korea

2008
*KISSS: Kinship International Strategy on
Surveillance and Suppression*, Castlefield
Gallery, Manchester, England

Whitney Biennial 2008, Whitney
Museum of American Art,
New York, New York

*Arte ≠ Vida: Actions by Artists of the
Americas, 1960–2000*, El Museo del
Barrio, New York, New York; Museo
de Arte Contemporáneo Carillo Gil,
Mexico City, Mexico; Museo Amparo,
Puebla, Mexico

Performing Identities, curated by
Jessica Hunter Larsen, Colorado
College Coburn Gallery, Colorado
Springs, Colorado

2007
Killing Time, Exit Art, New York,
New York

2006
Frontera 450+, Station Museum of
Contemporary Art, Houston, Texas

2005
Performa 05, New York, New York

Day Labor, MoMA PS1, Queens,
New York

*DEFENSE: The Body and Nobody in
Self-Protection*, Sweeney Art Gallery,
Riverside, California

Turista Fronterizo (Net.Art),
in collaboration with Ricardo
Dominguez, *InSite 05*

2004
Shanghai Biennale 2004,
Shanghai, China

*Intersections/Intersecciones: An
Exhibition of Cuban Artists*, Holcombe
T. Green Jr. Gallery, Yale University,
New Haven, Connecticut

Nothing if Not Satirical, The Nunnery,
London, England

2003
Transmediale 2003,
Berlin, Germany

*STRANGERS: The First International
Center of Photography Triennial of
Photography and Video*, International
Center of Photography, New York,
New York

Web as Performance Space,
Institute of Contemporary Arts,
London, England

2002
What? a Tale in Free Images,
Memlingmuseum, Bruges, Belgium

Artificial Emotion, Itaú Cultural
Center, São Paulo, Brazil

Proof: The Art of Seeing with One's Eyes,
Australian Center for the Moving
Image, Victoria, Australia

La Costilla Maldita, Centro Atlántico de Arte Modernot, Las Palmas, Canary Islands, Spain

Day Labor, MoMA PS1, Queens, New York

Eco, Xi'ang, Meditations on the African, Andean and Asian Diasporas, Project Rowhouse, Houston, Texas

Context and Conceptualism, Artists Space, New York, New York

2001
Unpacking Europe, Museum Boijmans Van Beuningen, Rotterdam, The Netherlands

2000
Made in California: Art, Image, and Identity 1900–2000, Los Angeles County Museum of Art, Los Angeles, California

Breaking Barriers: Selections from the Museum of Art, For Lauderdale, Contemporary Cuban Collection, Snite Museum of Art, University of Notre Dame, Notre Dame, Indiana

1997
Heaven: Public View, Private View, P.S 1 Contemporary Art Center, Long Island City, New York

Breaking Barriers: Selections from the Museum of Art, For Lauderdale, Contemporary Cuban Collection, Museum of Art, Fort Lauderdale, Florida

1996
Departure Lounge, Clocktower Gallery, New York, New York

1993
1993 Bienniul Exhibition, Whitney Museum of American Art, New York, New York

1992
9th Sydney Biennale, Sydney, Australia

Performances

2019
Words May Not be Found, Click Festival, Elsinore, Denmark

2018
Words May Not be Found, Württembergischer Kunstverein, Stuttgart, Germany

2017
Words May Not be Found, commissioned by the KW Institute for Contemporary Art, Berlin, performed at the Sophiensaele, Berlin, Germany

2016
Observations of Predation in Humans: A Lecture by Dr. Zira, Animal Psychologist, Frieze Projects, Frieze London 2016, England; 9th Liverpool Biennial, Liverpool, England; Museo Jumex, Mexico City, Mexico

2015
Observations of Predation in Humans: A Lecture by Dr. Zira, Animal Psychologist, Performing Franklin Furnace, Independent Curators International and Participant Inc., New York, New York; Brown University, Providence, Rhode Island; Yerba Buena Center for the Arts, San Francisco, California; Haus der Kulturen der Welt, Berlin, Germany

2014
Observations of Predation in Humans: A Lecture by Dr. Zira, Animal Psychologist, Walker Art Center, Minncapolis, Minncsota; Los Angeles County Museum of Art, California

Eu sou um consumidor (I Am a Consumer), Transperformance Festival, Rio de Janeiro, Brazil

2013
Observations of Predation in Humans: A Lecture by Dr. Zira, Animal Psychologist, commissioned by The Studio Museum in Harlem, New York, New York

2012
Y entonces el mar te habla (And the Sea Will Talk to You), Brooklyn Academy of Music, Brooklyn, New York

2008
A Room of One's Own: Women and Power in the New America, Whitney Biennial, Whitney Museum of American Art, New York, New York

2006
A Room of One's Own: Women and Power in the New America, Victoria and Albert Museum, London, England; Kunstnernes Hus, Oslo, Norway; PS 122, New York, New York; The Patricia & Phillip Frost Art Museum, Miami, Florida; Philadelphia Fringe Festival, Philadelphia, Pennsylvania; Maidment Theater, Auckland, New Zealand

2005
A Room of One's Own: Women and Power in the New America, The Kitchen, New York, New York

Bare Life Study #1, VideoBrasil 15th Festival of Electronic Art and Performance, São Paulo, Brazil

2003
The Incredible Disappearing Woman, House of World Cultures, Berlin, Germany; Institute of Contemporary Arts, London, England; Time-Based Arts Festival, Portland Institute for Contemporary Art, Portland,

Oregon; International Performance Festival, Pancevo, Serbia

2001
Dolores from 10 to 10, in collaboration with Ricardo Dominguez, Museum of Contemporary Art, Helsinki, Finland

2000
El evento suspendido, El Espacio Aglutinador, Havana, Cuba

Votos (*Vows*), Nexus Contemporary Art Center, Atlanta, Georgia; The Project Gallery, New York, New York; Open Space, Internationale Frauen Universität, Hannover, Germany; The Hull Time Based Arts Festival, Hull, England

1999
Votos (*Vows*), Third International Performance Art Festival, Odense, Denmark; Washington State University Museum, Pullman, Washington

Stuff, in collaboration with Nao Bustamante, Dixon Place, New York, New York; Rhode Island School of Design, Providence, Rhode Island

1998
Stuff, in collaboration with Nao Bustamante, Western Front, Vancouver, British Columbia; Notre Dame University, Notre Dame, Indiana; Duke University Institute of the Arts, Durham, North Carolina; The Painted Bride, Philadelphia, Pennsylvania; Harn Museum of Art, Gainesville, Florida; Cleveland Performance Art Festival, Cleveland, Ohio; PlanB Evolving Arts, Santa Fe, New Mexico; Urban Institute for Contemporary Art, Grand Rapids, Michigan; MACLA, San Jose, California; Henry Art Gallery, Seattle, Washington; California State University, Chico, California;

Museum of Contemporary Art, Helsinki, Finland

1997
Stuff, in collaboration with Nao Bustamante, Portland Institute for Contemporary Art, Portland, Oregon; Brady Street Theatre, San Francisco, California; Intercult, Stockholm, Sweden; Artspace, Auckland, New Zealand; Otago Polytechnic, Dunedin, New Zealand; Gallery of New South Wales, Sydney, Australia; Waves Festival, Vordingborg, Denmark; Arizona State University, Tempe, Arizona; University of Michigan, Ann Arbor, Michigan; The McKinney Avenue Contemporary, Dallas, Texas

Rights of Passage, 2nd Johannesburg Biennale, Johannesburg, South Africa

El último deseo (*The Last Wish*), Galeria Tejadillo 214, Havana, Cuba

Better Yet When Dead, YYZ Artists Outlet, Toronto, Canada; Festival International de Arte, Medellín, Colombia

1996
Stuff, in collaboration with Nao Bustamante, National Review of Live Art, Glasgow, England, Institute of Contemporary Arts, London, England; Highways, Los Angeles, California

1995
Mexarcane International, in collaboration with Guillermo Gómez-Peña, The London International Theatre Festival, London, England

1994
Mexarcane International, in collaboration with Guillermo Gómez-Peña, The National Review of Live Art, Glasgow, England; Dufferin Mall, Toronto, Canada

Two Undiscovered Amerindians Visit the West, in collaboration with Guillermo Gómez-Peña, Fundación Banco Patricios, Buenos Aires, Argentina

1993
Two Undiscovered Amerindians Visit the West, in collaboration with Guillermo Gómez-Peña, Field Museum of Natural History, Chicago, Illinois; 1993 Whitney Biennial, Whitney Museum of American Art, New York, New York

The Year of the White Bear, in collaboration with Guillermo Gómez-Peña, Mexican Fine Arts Center Museum, Chicago, Illinois; The Otis Gallery, Los Angeles, California

1992
The Year of the White Bear, in collaboration with Guillermo Gómez-Peña, Fine Arts Gallery, University of California, Irvine, California; Walker Art Center, Minneapolis, Minnesota

Two Undiscovered Amerindians Visit the West, in collaboration with Guillermo Gómez-Peña, Edge '92 Biennial, Columbus Plaza, Madrid, Spain; University of California, Irvine, California; Edge Arts Festival, London, England; Edge Arts Festival, Madrid, Spain; Walker Art Center, Minneapolis, Minnesota; The National Museum of Natural History, Washington, DC; 9th Sydney Biennale, Sydney, Australia

1991
La Chavela Realty Company, Brooklyn Academy of Music, Brooklyn, New York

1990
Norte / Sur, in collaboration with Guillermo Gómez-Peña, Festival 2000, Mexican Museum, San Francisco, California

Selected Bibliography

Books by the Artist

2015
Coco Fusco, *Dangerous Moves: Performance and Politics in Cuba* (London: Tate Publishing)

2008
Coco Fusco, *A Field Guide for Female Interrogators* (New York: Seven Stories Press)

2003
Coco Fusco, ed. with Brian Wallis, *Only Skin Deep: Changing Visions of the American Self,* (New York: Harry N. Abrams)

2001
Coco Fusco, *The Bodies That Were Not Ours: And Other Writings* (London and New York: Routledge/Iniva)

1999
Coco Fusco, ed. *Corpus Delecti: Performance Art of the Americas,* (London and New York: Routledge)

1995
Coco Fusco, *English Is Broken Here: Notes on Cultural Fusion in the Americas* (New York: The New Press)

Curatorial Projects

2003
Only Skin Deep: Changing Visions of the American Self, International Center of Photography, New York, New York; Seattle Art Museum, Seattle, Washington; San Diego Museum of Art, San Diego, California

1998
Mexico in Black and White: The Cinematography of Gabriel Figueroa, Brooklyn Museum, Brooklyn, New York

1996
Corpus Delecti, Institute of Contemporary Arts, London, England

1993
Black American Short Films and Videos, Oberhausen International Festival of Short Film, Oberhausen, Germany; Fusco presented related programs in Cologne, Dortmund, and Munster, Germany

1991
The Hybrid State Film Series, Anthology Film Archives, New York, New York

Robert Flaherty Seminar, programmer with Steve Gallagher, Wells College, Aurora, New York

1989
Black in a White World (films), touring program, Gallery Association of New York State, New York, New York

Internal Exile: Films and Videos from Chile, Museum of Modern Art, New York; Exit Art (videos), New York; Pacific Film Archives, Berkeley, California; Los Angeles Festival, Los Angeles, California; Museum of Contemporary Art, La Jolla, California; Neighborhood Film and Video Project, Philadelphia, Pennsylvania

Border Crossings (film), touring program, various cities around New York State

Young, British and Black: The Works of Sankofa and Black Audio Film Collective, touring program

1987
Reviewing Histories: Selections from the New Latin American Cinema, Hallwalls Contemporary Art Center, Buffalo, New York

Performance Scripts by the Artist

"A Room of One's Own: Women and Power in the New America," *The Drama Review*, vol. 51, no. 1 (Spring 2008): 136–59.

"The Incredible Disappearing Woman," *Macalester International*, issue on International Feminisms: Divergent Perspectives, vol. 10 (Spring 2001): 3–44.

"Stuff," *Drama Review*, vol. 41, no. 4 (Winter 1997): 63–82.

Writings by the Artist

"The Other Cuba," *The New York Review*, February 2023.

"For Cuban Artists, Censure is the Norm," NACLA, January 7, 2022, https://nacla.org/cuban-artists-repression-norm.

Coco Fusco and 27N, "Art Communities at Risk: On Cuba," *October*, no. 178 (Fall 2021): 135–43.

"Whose Art Thrives in Cuba?," *The New York Review*, December 16, 2021.

"The Artist as Hostage: Luis Manuel Otero Alcántara," *e-flux Journal,* May 21, 2021.

"Coco Fusco Enlists Cuban Artists to Recite Heberto Padilla's Forced Confessions," *Hyperallergic*, April 27, 2021, https://hyperallergic.com/640914/coco-fusco-enlists-cuban-artists-to-recite-heberto-padilla-forced-confessions.

"Deaccessioning Empire: A few daring curators are confronting the imperial histories of their museums," *The New York Review*, February 25, 2021.

"An open letter to American cultural institutions, arts professionals, journalists, and various Cubaphiles," *e-flux*, December 2, 2020, https://www.e-flux.com/announcements/364681/an-open-letter-to-american-cultural-institutions-arts-professionals-journalists-and-various-cubaphiles/.

"Looking Back on the Year in Art and Protest in Cuba," *Frieze*, December 17, 2018.

"Cuban Artists Rise Up," *North American Congress on Latin America (NACLA)*, September 17, 2018.

"Why Did Cuba Deport Artists Trying to Attend Havana's First Alternative Biennial?," *Hyperallergic*, May 8, 2018, https://hyperallergic.com/441963/cuba-deport-artists-oobienal-de-la-habana.

"Maria Teresa Hincapié," *María Teresa Hincapié: Hacia lo sagrado*, ed. José Roca (Bogotá: Seguros Bolívar, 2017).

"How the Art World, and Art Schools, are Ripe for Sexual Abuse," *Hyperallergic*, November 14, 2017, https://hyperallergic.com/411343/how-the-art-world-and-art-schools-are-ripe-for-sexual-abuse.

"Remembering Linda Nochlin," *Brooklyn Rail*, November 2, 2017.

"Art, Culture, and Appropriation: Some Wrongs Aren't about Rights," *Frieze*, no. 190, October 2017.

"Decades of Identity Politics," *Texte Zur Kunst*, no. 107, September 2017.

"Censorship, Not the Painting, Must Go: On Dana Schutz's Image of Emmett Till," *Hyperallergic*, March 27, 2017, https://hyperallergic.com/368290/censorship-not-the-painting-must-go-on-dana-schutzs-image-of-emmett-till.

"Why an Art Strike? Why Now?," *Hyperallergic*, January 10, 2017, https://hyperallergic.com/350529/why-an-art-strike-why-now.

"How to Fix the Art World, Part 1," *Artnews*, November 18, 2016, https://www.artnews.com/art-news/news/how-to-fix-the-art-world-part-1-7335/.

"Still in the Cage: *Two Undiscovered Amerindians* Twenty Years Later,'" *Social medium: artists writing, 2000–2015*, Jennifer Liese, ed. (New York: Paper Monument, 2016): 190–94.

"Artists and Identity," *Artforum*, Summer 2016.

"Taste as a Political Matter: Coco Fusco on the Guerrilla Girls," *Walker Reader,* Walker Art Center, January 13, 2016, https://walkerart.org/magazine/coco-fusco-guerrilla-girls.

"The Revolution is Dead—But Long Lives the State!, *e-flux journal*, August 1, 2015.

"The State of Detention: Performance, Politics, and the Cuban Public," *e-flux journal*, January 2015.

"The Latest Protests Are Similar to the Occupy Movement," *The New York Times*, December 15, 2014.

"Still in The Cage: Two Undiscovered Amerindians Twenty Years Later," *Modern Painters*, February 2012.

"Regarding History: Harun Farocki," *Frieze*, no. 127, November–December 2009.

"On Line Simulation/Real Life Politics: A Discussion with Ricardo Dominguez on Staging Virtual Theater," *The Drama Review*, vol. 47, no. 2, 2003: 53–57.

"Wide Area Disturbance," a published discussion with Ricardo Dominguez, *Mute Magazine*, vol. 1, no. 23, 2002–03.

"Transformational Acts: An Interview with Michael Elmgreen and Ingar Dragset," *Taking Place: The Works of Michael Elmgreen and Ingar Dragset* (Stuttgart: Hatje Cantz Verlag, 2002).

"All Too Real: The Tale of Black Sale: Coco Fusco Interviews Keith Townsend Obadike," *Thing Reviews*, September 2001.

"Modernity Deferred: The Work of Luis Simon Molina Pantin," *Confort: Luis Molina Pantin: 1996–2000* (Caracas: Museo Alejandro Otero, 2000).

SELECTED BIBLIOGRAPHY

"At Your Service: Latina Performance in Global Culture," *Reverberation: Tactics of Resistance, Forms of Agency in Trans/cultural Practices*, ed. Jean Fisher (Maastricht, Jan Van Eyck Akademie, 2000).

"Una Inmodesta proposición (An Immodest Proposal)," *Zehar Magazine* (Summer 1999).

"Elevator Repair Service," interview, *BOMB Magazine* (Summer 1999).

"En la encrucijada Norte-Sur: Videos de Juan Downey," *With Energy Beyond These Walls* (Valencia, Spain: IVAM, 1998).

"We Wear the Mask," *Talking Visions: Multicultural Feminism in a Transnational Age*, ed. Ella Shohat (New York: New Museum of Contemporary Art/The MIT Press, 1999).

"The Magnificat," *Joyful Noise: The New Testament Revisted*, eds. Rick Moody and Darcy Steinke (New York: Little Brown, 1997).

"Performance and the Power of the Popular," *Let's Get It On: The Politics of Black Performance* (London/Seattle: The ICA and Bay Press, 1995).

"Cuban Art, Foreign Interests," *Cuba: La Isla Posible* (Barcelona, Spain: CCCB—Ediciones Destino, 1995).

"A Letter to South African Artists," *1995 Africus: Johannesburg Biennale* (Johannesburg: Transitional Metropolitan Council, 1995).

"Magdalena Campos-Pons at INTAR," *Art in America*, February 1994.

"Pepón Osorio: En la Barberia No SE Llora," *Pepón Osorio: En la Barberia No SE Llora* (Hartford, Connecticut: real art ways, 1995).

"Cuba's Artworld Comes Undone," *The Los Angeles Times*, December 24, 1993.

"Passionate Irreverence: The Cultural Politics of Identity," *1993 Biennial Exhibition* (New York: Whitney Museum of American Art and Harry N. Abrams, 1993): 74–85.

"Pan-American Post Nationalism: Another World Order," *Black Popular Culture, a project by Michele Wallace*, ed. Gina Dent (Seattle: Bay Press, 1992).

The Hybrid State, exhibition catalogue (New York: Exit Art, 1991).

"Art and National Identity," *Art in America*, September 1991.

"Art and Cuba Now," *The Nation*, June 24, 1991.

"The Latino Boom in American Film," *El Boletin*, Journal of the Center for Puerto Rican Studies, 1990.

"Managing the Other," *Lusitania*, vol. 1, no. 3 (Fall 1990), and *Futur Antérieur*, 1992: 12–13.

Internal Exile: New Films and Videos from Chile (New York: Third World Newsreel, 1990).

"Ethnicity, Politics, and Poetics: Latinos and Media Art," *Illuminating Video: An Essential Guide to Video Art*, eds. Doug Hall and Sally Jo Fifer (San Francisco: Aperture and the Bay Area Video Coalition, 1990).

Black in a White World: Short Films by African-American Independents, The Gallery Association of New York State, 1990.

"About Locating Ourselves and Our Representations," *Framework, Third Scenario: Theory and the Politics of Location*, no. 36, 1989.

"Cuba Libre?," *The Village Voice*, January 10, 1989.

"Fantasies of Oppositionality," *Screen: The Last Special Issue on Race?*, vol. 29, no. 4, Fall 1988, reprinted in *Art, Activism, and Oppositionality: Essays from Afterimage*, ed. Grant H. Kester (Durham, North Carolina: Duke University, 1998).

"Drawing New Lines," *The Nation*, vol. 247, no. 11, October 24, 1988.

Signs of Transition: '80s Art from Cuba (New York: Museum of Contemporary Hispanic Art and The Center for Cuban Studies, 1988).

Reviewing Histories: Selections from The New Latin American Cinema (Buffalo: Hallwalls Contemporary Art Center, 1987).

"Cuba: Cultural Policy, Cultural Politics," *Impulse Magazine*, (Summer 1987).

Scholarly Essays on Fusco's Art

Candice Amich, "Part II: Playing Dead in Cuba, 1997–2000" in "Earth-Body Works: Ana Mendieta and Her Kind," *Precarious Forms: Performing Utopia in the Neoliberal Americas,* (Evanston: Northwestern University Press, 2020): 73–92.

"Transborder Simulations: Coco Fusco, Ricardo Dominguez, and the EZLN Alternative," *Precarious Forms: Performing Utopia in the Neoliberal Americas*, (Evanston: Northwestern University Press, 2020): 93–116.

Małgorzata Dancewicz, "Performatywne misje *simius sapiens*: Coco Fusco na Planecie Małp,*"* *Prace Kulturoznawcze* (Uniwersytet Wrocławski), vol. 23, no. 2–3, 2019: 105–21.

Cecilia De Laurentiis, "Coco Fusco: Arte, Politica, Critica" (master's thesis, Sapienza Università di Roma, 2013).

Juan Carlos Guerrero-Hernandez, "Pensar el interculturalismo: crisis y confesion," *Estetica: Miradas contemporaneas 3*, ed. Carlos Eduardo Sanabria Bohorquez (Bogotá: Fundacion Universidad de Bogotá Jorge Tadeo Lozono, 2010): 45–70.

Karen Beckman, "Gender, Power, and Pedagogy in Coco Fusco's *Bare Life Study #1* (2005), *A Room of One's Own: Women and Power in the New America* (2006–08) and *Operation Atropos* (2006)," *Framework: The Journal of Cinema and Media*, Spring and Fall 2009, vol. 50, nos. 1 & 2: 125–38.

Jonathan Beller, "The Art of War, or Coco Fusco's Occupation," *Nka: Journal of Contemporary African Art*, no. 24, 2009.

Kelly Dennis, "Gendered Ghosts in the Globalized Machine: Coco Fusco and Prema Murthy," *n. paradoxa*, vol. 23, 2009.

José Esteban Muñoz, "A Room of One's Own: Women and Power in the New America," *The Drama Review*, vol. 52, no. 1 (Spring 2008): 136–39.

Federica Timeto, "A Situated Feminist Reading of Turista Fronterizo," *Cultura della differenza. Femminismo, visualita e studi poscolonial* (Turin: Utet Universita, 2008).

Eduardo Mendieta, "The Coloniality of Embodiment: Coco Fusco's postcolonial genealogies and semiotic agonistics," *Unmaking Race, (Re)making Soul: The Transformative Aesthetics of Postcolonial Women Artists*, eds. Angela Cotton and Christa Davis Acompora (Albany: SUNY Press, 2007).

Antonio Prieto-Stambaugh, "La puesta en escena del otro: Teatro, turismo y antropofagia en la obra de Coco Fusco y Nao Bustamante," *Estrategias postmodernas y postcoloniales en el teatro latinoamericano actual. Hibridez-Medialidad-Cuerpo*, ed. Alfonso de Toro (Frankfurt am Main: Editorial K.D. Vervuert Verlag, 2004).

Teresa Marrero, "Scripting Sexual Tourism: Fusco and Bustamante's STUFF, Prostitution and Cuba's Special Period," *Theater Journal*, vol. 55, no. 2, May 2003: 235–49.

Jean Fisher, "Witness for the Prosecution: The Writings of Coco Fusco," *The Bodies That Were Not Ours: And Other Writings* (London: Routledge/Iniva, 2001).

Caroline Vercoe, "Agency and Ambivalence: A Reading of Works by Coco Fusco," *The Bodies That Were Not Ours: And Other Writings* (London: Routledge/Iniva, 2001).

Ana Nuño, "Coco Fusco derrumba fronteras. Parecer o pertenecer, he allí el dilema," *Papel Literario*, Spain, October 31, 1999.

Selected Collections and Awards

Selected Public Collections

Centre Pompidou, Paris, France
Contemporary Arts Museum
    Houston, Texas
Fogg Museum, Harvard Art
    Museums, Cambridge,
    Massachusetts
Forge Project Collection,
    Taghkanic, New York
Imperial War Museum, London,
    England
Musée d'Arts de Nantes, France
El Museo del Barrio, New York,
    New York
Museu d'Art Contemporani de
    Barcelona (MACBA), Spain
Museum of Modern Art,
    New York, New York
Pérez Art Museum Miami, Florida
Smith College Museum of Art,
    Northampton, New York
Smithsonian American Art Museum,
    Washington, DC
Queens Museum, Queens, New York
Walker Art Center, Minneapolis,
    Minnesota
Williams College Museum of Art,
    Williamstown, Massachusetts

Selected Awards, Fellowships, and Grants

2021
Anonymous Was A Woman Award

Latinx Artist Fellowship, The
Andrew W. Mellon Foundation

American Academy of Arts and
Letters Arts Award

2018
The Dorothea & Leo Rabkin
Foundation Award,
Visual Arts Journalism

2016
The Greenfield Prize at the
Hermitage Artist Retreat,
Visual Art

2015
New York Foundation for the Arts
Fellowship, Non-Fiction Literature

2014
CINTAS Foundation Visual
Arts Fellowship

2013
Absolut Art Award for Art Writing
for *Dangerous Moves: Performance and
Political Conduct*

Guggenheim Fellowship Award for
Creative Arts, Film-Video

Fulbright Fellowship

2012
United States Artists Berman Bloch
Fellow, Visual Arts

2009
Shortlist, Index on Censorship
Freedom of Expression Awards

Faculty Development Fund,
The New School

2006
Creative Time Commission,
Who Cares? initiative

2005
InSite Biennial, Commission for
Internet based artwork

2003
Herb Alpert Award in the Arts,
Film/Video category

Honorable Mention,
Transmediale Festival, Berlin,
for *Dolores from 10 to 10*

Arts International Travel Grant

2002
Arts International Commissioning
Grant for performance

2001
Temple University Junior
Research Leave

2000
Tyler School of Art Merit Award
for Outstanding Research

1999
Temple University Summer
Research Fellowship

1998
Multi-Arts Production Fund,
Rockefeller Foundation

Franklin Furnace Fund for
Performance Art

1997
New York Foundation for the Arts,
Non-Fiction Fellowship

Arts International Travel Grant

1995
Los Angeles Department of Cultural
Affairs, Artist's Fellowship

Critics' Choice Award from the
American Educational Studies
Association for *English is Broken Here:
Notes on Cultural Fusion in the Americas*

ATHE Research Award for
Outstanding Journal Article from
the Association of Theatre in
Higher Education. For the essay,
"The Other History of Intercultural
Performance," published in *The
Drama Review*, Spring 1994

Mellon Fellowship, Critical Studies,
California Institute for the Arts,
Valencia, California

1994
Arts International Travel Grant

1991
New York State Council on the Arts,
Media Artist Fellowship

National Endowment for the Arts,
Inter-arts Artist Fellowship

New York Foundation for the Arts,
Non-Fiction Fellowship

1989
New York State Council on the Arts,
Critical Writing on Media

Picture Credits

All works are by Coco Fusco unless otherwise stated. All works Courtesy Alexander Gray Associates, New York © 2023 Coco Fusco/Artists Rights Society (ARS), New York.

2 Photo: Geandy Pavón **4** Photo: Kambui Olujimi **7** Photo: Colección Centro de Estudios Espigas—Fundación Espigas **8 (far left)** Photo: Hamlet Lavastida (Center) Photo: Guiller Chaparro Alternativo Art **10** Photo: Hillevi Lovén, 2004 **11** Photo: courtesy the artist **13** Photo: Alom **14** Photo: Glenn Halvorson for Walker Art Center, Minneapolis **19** Haus der Kulturen der Welt (HKW), Berlin for "In Transit 2003. Customs—Nothing to Declare." Photo: Kambui Olujimi **24** Courtesy Tate Publishing. Book design Loid Der **25** Photo: Peter Barker **27** Photo: Eduardo Aparicio **28** Daniel Turner **29** Photo: Hugo Glendinning **35** Photo: The Studio Museum in Harlem **36** Photo: Courtesy the Leandro Katz Archive **38** Photo: © Acervo Videobrasil—Isabella Matheus **39** Daniel Turner **42** Photo courtesy the artists **45** Harry Gamboa Jr. Spray Paint LACMA, 1972 from the Asco era © 1972, Harry Gamboa Jr. **46** Fales Library and Special Collections, New York University Libraries. © Cathy Weiner **49** Museum of Contemporary Art Kiasma, Helsinki, Finland **50** Photo: FASTWURMS **64–65** Photo: Carolyn Wendt **68 (above)** Photo: Nancey Lytle **(below)** Photo: Peter Barker **69 (above)** Photo: Nancey Lytle **70** Collection of the artist **73** Photo: Glenn Halvorson for Walker Art Center, Minneapolis **74, 75** Photo: FASTWURMS **76, 77, 78 (above, below), 79, 80, 81 (above, center, below)** Photo: Sven Wiederholt **82–83, 84, 85** Photo: Hugo Glendinning **86, 88–89** Photo: courtesy the artists **94–95** Photo: Eduardo Aparicio **97** Photo: Gonzalo Hernandez **98–99** Photo: Alom **104, 105** Museum of Contemporary Art Kiasma, Helsinki, Finland **106, 107, 108 (left, right), 109** Photo: Kambui Olujimi. Haus der Kulturen der Welt (HKW), Berlin for "In Transit 2003. Customs—Nothing to Declare." **114 (above, below), 115, 116 (above, below), 117 (above, below)** Photo: © Acervo Videobrasil—Isabella Matheus **120–21** Photo: Eduardo Aparicio **122 (above, below), 123** Collection of the artist **136–37, 138–39, 140 (above, below), 141** Brooklyn Academy of Music, NY. Photo: Nathan Bett **142** Photo: The Studio Museum in Harlem **143** Photo: Gene Pittman for Walker Art Center, Minneapolis **144–45, 146–47, 148–49** Photo: Janaína Miranda **188–89, 190–91** Photo: Geandy Pavón

Contributors

Julia Bryan-Wilson is Professor of Art History and Archaeology at Columbia University, New York. Studying feminist and queer theory, modern and contemporary art, craft histories, and questions of artistic labor, Bryan-Wilson is the author of *Art Workers: Radical Practice in the Vietnam Era* (2009) and *Fray: Art and Textile Politics* (2017), which won the ASAP Book Prize, the Frank Jewett Mather Award, and the Robert Motherwell Award.

Coco Fusco is an interdisciplinary artist and writer based in New York. Her performances and videos have been presented in the Sharjah Biennial 15, the 56th Venice Biennale, Frieze Special Projects, Basel Unlimited, the Whitney Biennial (2022, 2008, and 1993), and several other international exhibitions. Her works are in the collections of the Museum of Modern Art, the Walker Art Center, the Pérez Art Museum Miami, the Imperial War Museum, the Centre Pompidou, and the Museum of Contemporary Art of Barcelona among others. A professor at the Cooper Union School of Art, she contributes regularly to the *New York Review of Books* and numerous art publications. She is a recipient of a 2021 American Academy of Arts and Letters Art Award, a 2021 Latinx Art Award, a 2021 Anonymous Was a Woman Award, a 2018 Rabkin Prize for Art Criticism, a 2016 Greenfield Prize, a 2014 Cintas Fellowship, a 2013 Guggenheim Fellowship, a 2013 Absolut Art Writing Award, and a 2013 Fulbright Fellowship, among others. Fusco is represented by Alexander Gray Associates in New York.

Anna Gritz is director of Haus am Waldsee in Berlin. Formerly a curator at KW Institute for Contemporary Art in Berlin, she has realized solo exhibitions by Judith Hopf, Lynn Hershman Leeson, Steve Bishop, Amelie von Wulffen, and Michael Stevenson, as well as group exhibitions including "The Making of Husbands: Christina Ramberg in Dialogue" and "Zeros and Ones" (co-curated with Kathrin Bentele and Ghislaine Leung). Previously she held curatorial positions at the South London Gallery (SLG), the Institute of Contemporary Arts (ICA), and the Hayward Gallery, all in London. Gritz writes for catalogues and regularly contributes to art publications. She served as a curatorial attaché for the 20th Biennale of Sydney in 2016, and since 2019, she has been a member of the acquisitions committee at the FRAC Lorraine.

Jill Lane is associate professor in the Department of Spanish and Portuguese at New York University and director of the Center for Latin American and Caribbean Studies. Her areas of interest include Latin American theater and comparative approaches to race and performance in the Americas. She is the author of *Blackface Cuba, 1840–1895* (2005).

Antonio José Ponte is a Madrid-based Cuban author, poet, and essayist known for his incisive critique of the Cuban government. In his literary project *La lengua suelta* (*The Loose Tongue*, 2020), a collection of satirical commentaries about the politics and follies of a range of Cuban intellectuals, Ponte presents himself as the editor of writings by a pseudonymous Cuban based in Hungary. His short story collections, *In the Cold of the Malecón* (2001) and *Tales from the Cuban Empire* (2002), have been published in the United States. He is also the deputy director of the online newspaper *Diario de Cuba*.

Olga Viso is a Cuban-American art historian and curator of contemporary visual art known for her scholarship in contemporary, Cuban, and Latin American art. She is based at Arizona State University's Herberger Institute for Design and the Arts and is the past executive director of the Walker Art Center in Minneapolis and director and curator at the Hirshhorn Museum and Sculpture Garden in Washington, DC. Over thirty years working in museums Viso has organized numerous exhibitions, including "Distemper: Dissonant Themes in the Art of the 1990s", "Regarding Beauty: A View of the Late Twentieth Century", and solo projects with artists Juan Francisco Elso, Robert Gober, the Guerrilla Girls, Jim Hodges, Guillermo Kuitca, Ana Mendieta, and Juan Muñoz.

Index

INDEX

On the cover: *Your Eyes Will Be an Empty Word*, 2021, video (detail)
Half title: *La confesión (The Confession)*, 2015, video
Frontispiece: *Your Eyes Will Be an Empty Word*, 2021, video (detail)
Endpapers: Coco Fusco working in Havana with Sandra Ceballos, 2016. Photo: Alom

First published in the United Kingdom in 2023 by
Thames & Hudson Ltd, 181A High Holborn, London WC1V 7QX

First published in the United States of America in 2023 by
Thames & Hudson Inc., 500 Fifth Avenue, New York, New York 10110

Publication coincides with the exhibition "Coco Fusco, Tomorrow, I Will Become an Island"
at KW Institute for Contemporary Art, Berlin (14 September 2023—7 January 2024).

Exhibition funded by the
German Federal Cultural Foundation

Exhibition funded by the Federal Government
Commissioner for Culture and the Media

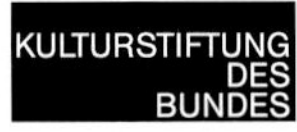

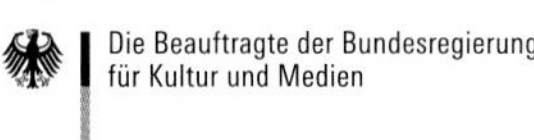

Coco Fusco: Tomorrow, I Will Become an Island © 2023 Thames & Hudson Ltd, London

Foreword © 2023 Krist Gruijthuijsen
Introduction © 2023 Coco Fusco
Essays © 2023 the respective authors
Body of Work, 1990–2022 © 2023 Ursula Davila-Villa and Anna Stothart

All works are by Coco Fusco unless otherwise stated. All works Courtesy Alexander Gray
Associates, New York © 2023 Coco Fusco/Artists Rights Society (ARS), New York

Editor: Olga Viso
Production Editor: Paul Schmelzer
Designer: Studio Mark El-khatib

British Library Cataloguing-in-Publication Data
A catalogue record for this book is available from the British Library

Library of Congress Control Number 2022939715

ISBN 978-0-500-02492-8

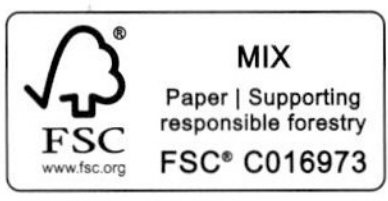

Printed and bound in China by 1010 Printing International Ltd

Be the first to know about our new releases,
exclusive content and author events by visiting
thamesandhudson.com
thamesandhudsonusa.com
thamesandhudson.com.au

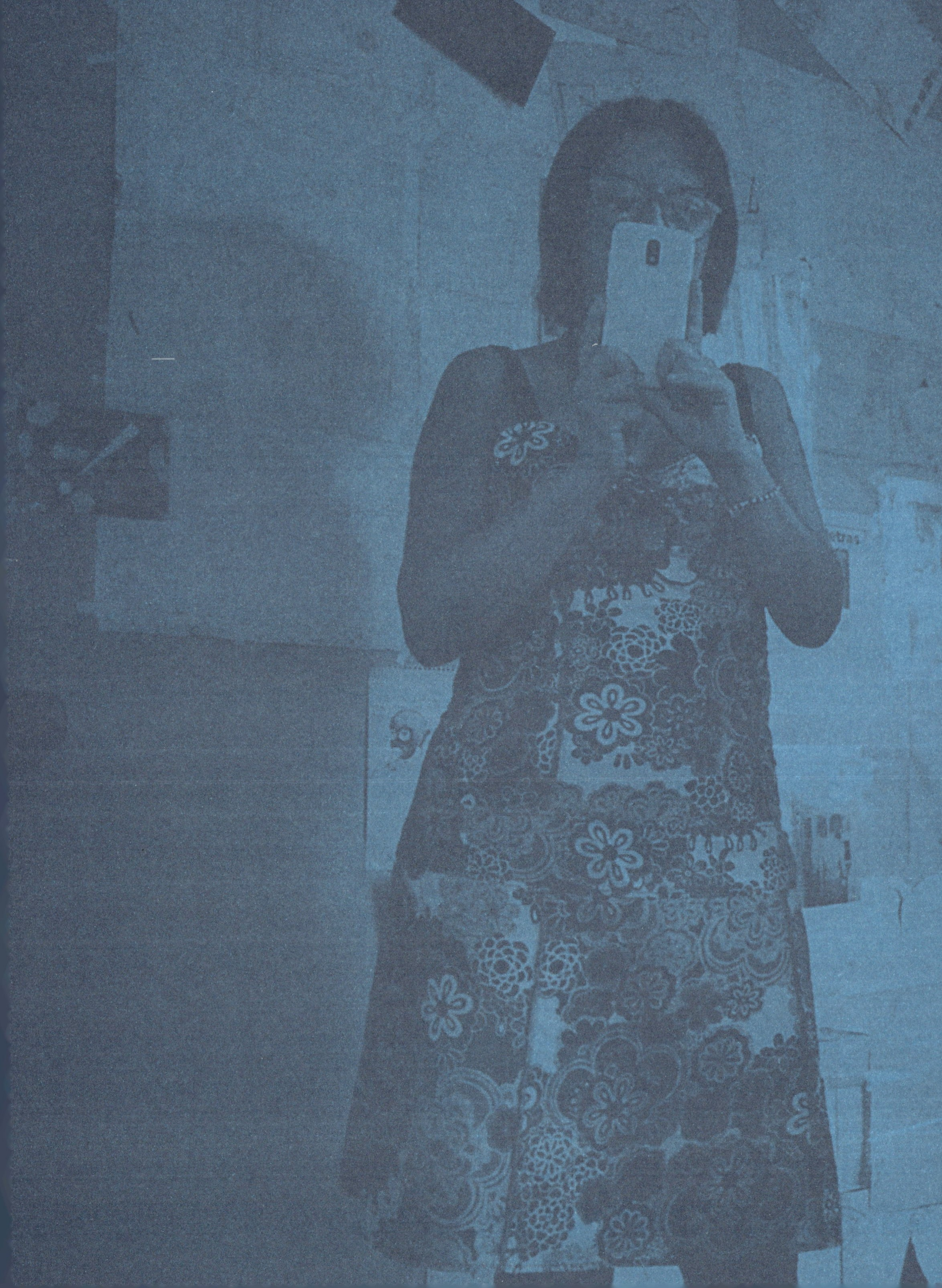